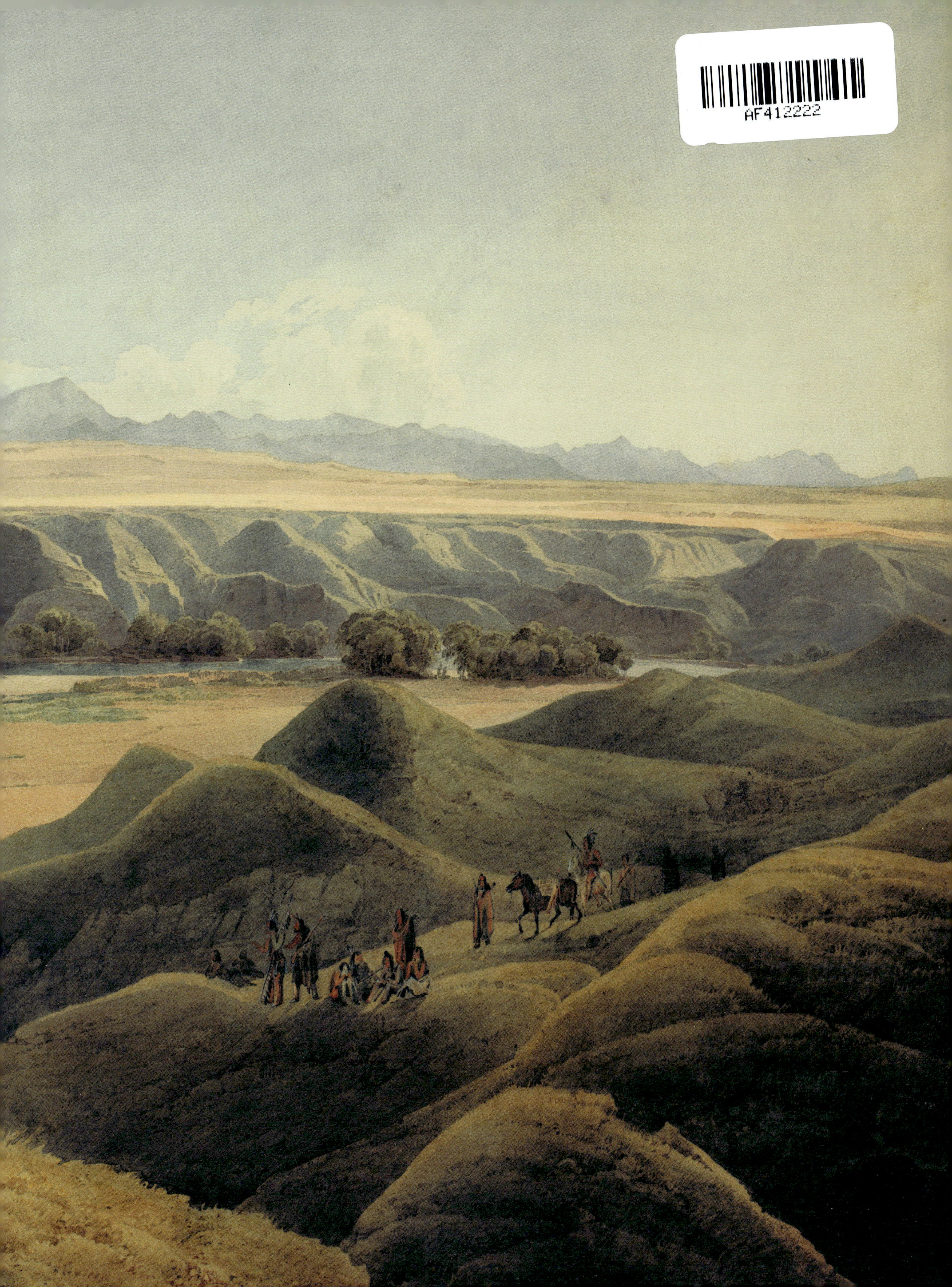

FACES

from the

INTERIOR

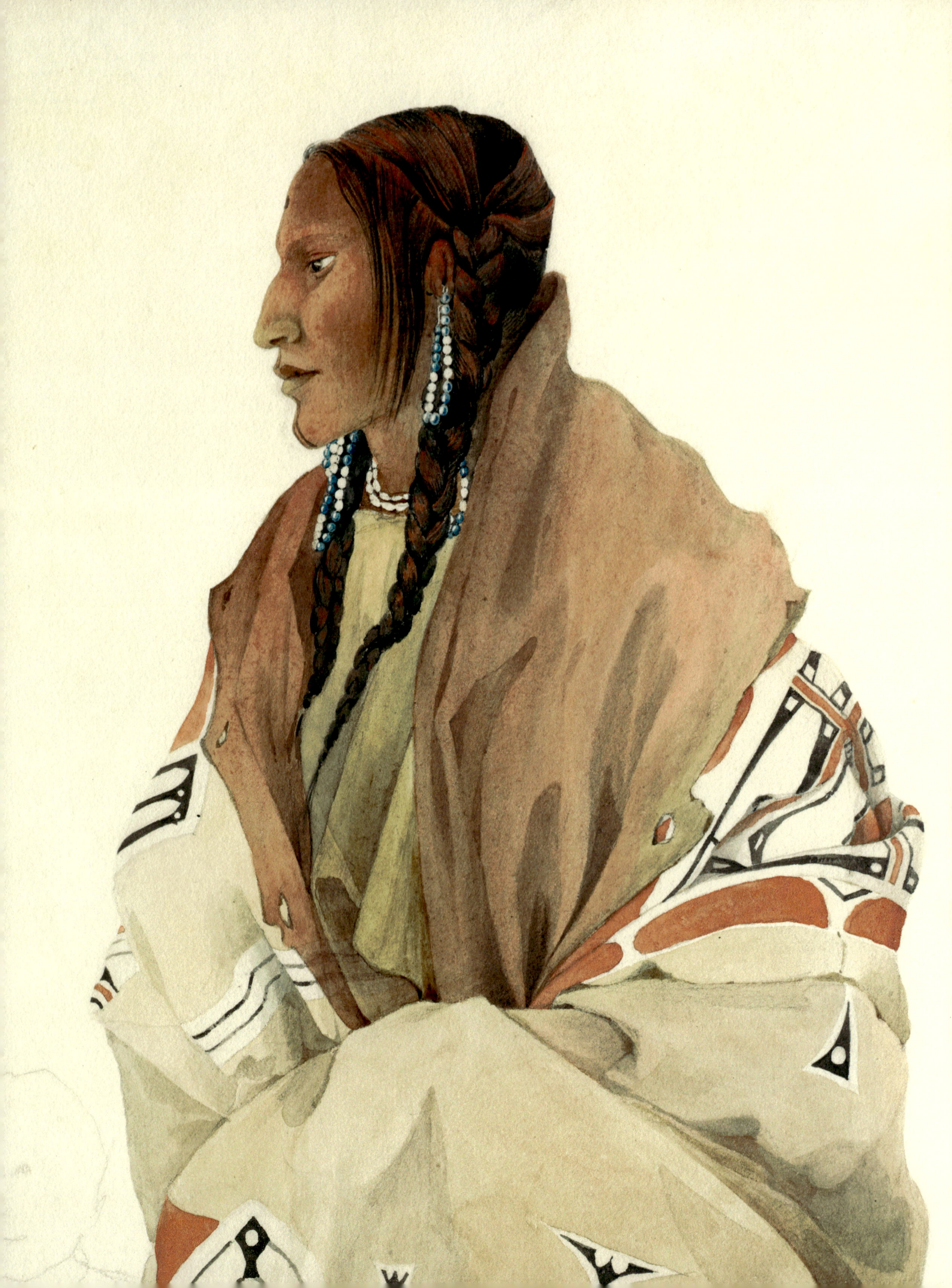

FACES

from the

INTERIOR

———

THE NORTH AMERICAN PORTRAITS OF KARL BODMER

Toby Jurovics, Editor

WITH CONTRIBUTIONS BY

Marsha V. Gallagher

Annika K. Johnson

Kristine K. Ronan

Scott Manning Stevens

Lisa Strong

Margre H. Durham Center for Western Studies

Joslyn Art Museum

OMAHA, NEBRASKA

CONTENTS

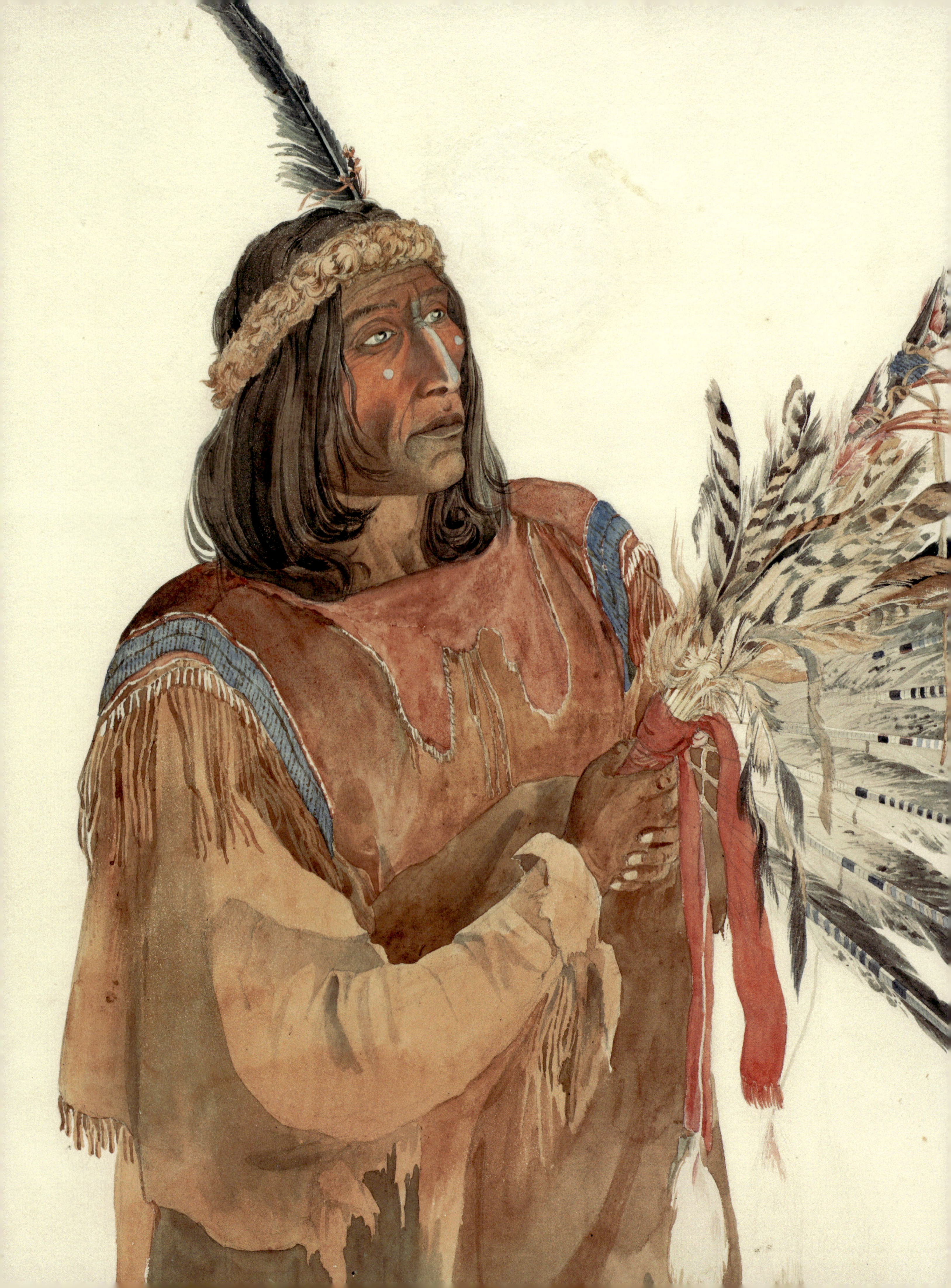

DIRECTOR'S FOREWORD

*Joslyn Art Museum is located on the ancestral homelands of the Umo*ⁿ*ho*ⁿ *people and pays its respects to their elders past, present, and future.*

THE MAXIMILIAN-BODMER COLLECTION HAS BEEN A CORnerstone of Joslyn Art Museum for more than four decades. Housed in the Margre H. Durham Center for Western Studies, the collection is not only a jewel of Omaha but one well known throughout the United States and Europe. Many Omaha residents recount first seeing Karl Bodmer's watercolors on school trips or visits with their families, and the collection has inspired visitors from across the country and overseas, many who come through our doors on an express mission to witness Bodmer's work face to face. A host of scholars and academics has likewise been drawn to Maximilian and Bodmer's singular account of the American interior in the nineteenth century.

Bodmer's watercolors, prints and drawings have always been displayed in Joslyn's galleries of American Western art, yet their presence there is something of an anomaly. Bodmer's work is the reflection of European sensibilities—of the intellectual curiosity of his patron, the German Prince Maximilian of Wied, an accomplished amateur naturalist, and Bodmer's own artistic training as a landscape painter in Switzerland. Together, however, these two visitors produced one of the most important narratives of nineteenth-century America. Overlaying the cultural and scientific principles of Enlightenment Europe on the Missouri River basin, they created an interwoven literary and visual record of the preindustrial West that has arguably never been equaled. Maximilian's account of their voyage, *Reise in das innere Nord-America in den Jahren 1832 bis 1834* (*Travels in the Interior of North America, 1832–34*), accompanied by eighty-one hand-colored prints after Bodmer's original watercolors, defined the appearance of the American landscape and its Indigenous peoples for generations of European and American audiences.

This new volume is the most recent in a series of major publications from Joslyn that focus on the Maximilian-Bodmer Collection, including *Karl Bodmer's America* (1984), *Karl Bodmer's North American Prints* (2004), and the luxurious three-volume translation of Maximilian's journals, *The North American Journals of Prince Maximilian of Wied*

Karl Bodmer, *Hotokáneheh, Piegan Blackfoot Man*, 1833 (detail of pl. 41).

(2008–12). *Faces from the Interior* is notable as the first exhibition and catalogue to examine Bodmer expressly as a portraitist. It also marks the beginning of an endeavor to reconsider these works from an Indigenous perspective.

I would like to thank the scholars who generously contributed to this project, including Scott Manning Stevens, Lisa Strong, and Kristine K. Ronan. Their perception and insight will help to shape a significant new understanding of Bodmer's oeuvre. Marsha V. Gallagher, editor of *The North American Journals of Prince Maximilian of Wied* and former chief curator at the museum, contributed her unparalleled knowledge of the Maximilian-Bodmer collection. Annika K. Johnson, who joined the museum's staff in 2019 as associate curator of Native American art, conducted a meaningful interview with Gerard Baker, of the Mandan, Hidatsa, and Arikara Nation. We are particularly grateful for his willingness to share his personal account with us. Toby Jurovics, former chief curator and Richard and Mary Holland Curator of Western American Art, shepherded this project over many years, contributed the catalogue introduction, and managed its production. He and I had our first conversations about this project more than a decade ago, and it is a satisfying accomplishment for Joslyn to bring this exhibition and catalogue to fruition.

We would also like to thank Eleanor Jones Harvey, Senior Curator of American Art, Smithsonian American Art Museum; Patricia Marroquin Norby, Associate Curator of Native American Art, the Metropolitan Museum of Art; and Erik Holland, Curator of Education, Mark J. Halvorson, Curator of Collections Research, and Paul R. Picha, Chief Archaeologist, State Historical Society of North Dakota. All provided generous commentary and critical advice during the course of this project. At the museum, I would like to acknowledge Kevin Salzman, Candace Berger, and Sarah Haines for their expertise and enthusiasm in helping bring this catalogue to print and their ongoing care of the Maximilian-Bodmer Collection.

Faces from the Interior would not have been possible without the dedication and generosity of the many donors who supported all aspects of this endeavor. Conservation of our complete holdings of Karl Bodmer's watercolors was supported by a significant grant from the Ahmanson Foundation. Additional funding for collection care was generously provided by Terry Hayes.

I want to give a heartfelt thanks to Mary and Joe Daugherty, who made the lead gift for this historic publication. Mary has served on the Joslyn Art Museum Board of Governors for many years and has always been a passionate advocate for the Maximilian-Bodmer Collection. Additional support was provided by Susan and Michael Lebens, the Wyeth Foundation for American Art, and Barbara and Ronald Schaefer.

During the course of this project, longtime supporters of the museum Stacy and Bruce Simon stepped forward to make a major commitment to endow the curator of Native American art. I could not be more delighted that this publication coincides with Stacy's role as Chair of the Joslyn Board of Governors.

It is our great pleasure that this exhibition will debut at the Metropolitan Museum of Art in New York, after which it will return to

Omaha before traveling to its final venue at the Amon Carter Museum of American Art in Fort Worth. At the Metropolitan Museum of Art, I would like to thank Max Hollein, Director; Sylvia Yount, Lawrence A. Fleischman Curator in Charge, the American Wing; and Thayer Tolles, Marica F. Vilcek Curator of American Paintings and Sculpture. At the Amon Carter, our gratitude goes to Andrew J. Walker, Director; and Spencer Wigmore, assistant curator of paintings, sculpture, and works on paper. We could not have had more enthusiastic and agreeable partners.

Karl Bodmer and Maximilian of Wied feel like well-known characters to those of us at Joslyn Art Museum, as do Mató-Tópe (Four Bears) and Péhriska-Rúhpa (Two Ravens), whose profiles are familiar faces in our galleries. It is my sincere hope that *Faces from the Interior* will find new audiences for this remarkable body of work and bring new insights into the lives of the Indigenous peoples with whom Maximilian and Bodmer shared more than a year along the length of the Missouri River. This project is part of an ongoing re-exploration of the collection, as new insights and more generous approaches inform how we understand Maximilian and Bodmer and recognize their voyage as a transformational moment for the peoples who made their home in the Missouri River basin. We hope *Faces from the Interior* will lead to a broader understanding of the past and an acknowledgment of how it shapes the present—and perhaps even informs the ways we move forward in the future.

Jack F. Becker
Executive Director & CEO, Joslyn Art Museum

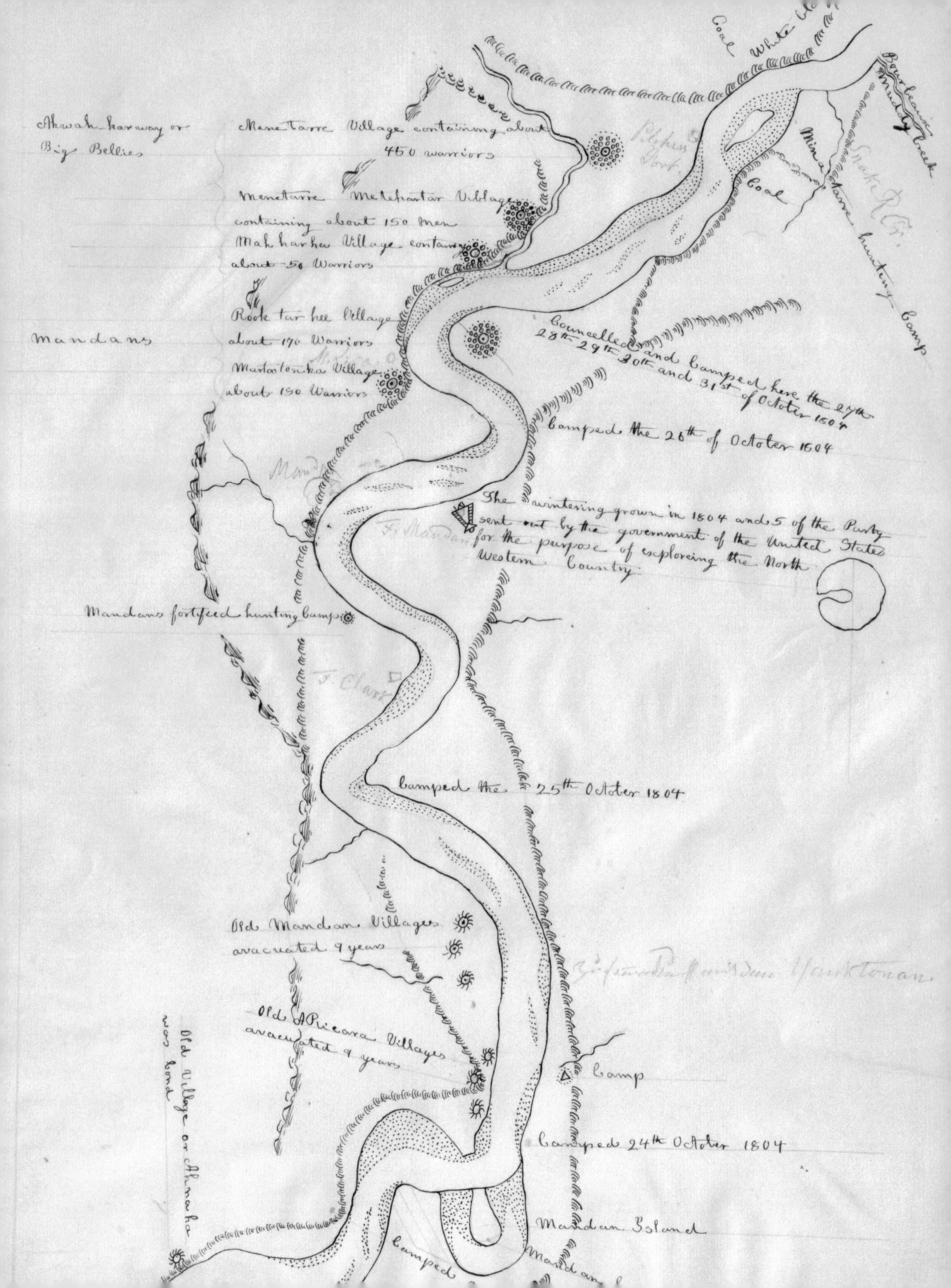

Coal   White Clay R.   Bow beaning Creek   Muddy

Pitchin Fort

Coal

Mina harne   Snake R. Cr.   hunting Camp

Ahwah harway or
Big Bellies

Mene tarre Village containing about
450 warriors

Menetarre   Metehartar Village
containing about 150 men

Mah harha Village containing
about 50 Warriors

Mandans

Rook tar hee Village
about 170 Warriors

Martootonka Village
about 150 Warriors

Councelled and Camped here the 27th
28th 29th 30th and 31st of October 1804

Camped the 26th of October 1804

Coal   Mina   Coal

The wintering ground in 1804 and 5 of the Party
sent out by the government of the United States
for the purpose of exploreing the North
Western Country

F. Mandan

Mandan

Mandans fortfeed hunting camps

F. Clark

Camped the 25th October 1804

Old Mandan Villages
avacuated 9 years

Old A Ricara Villages
avacuated 9 years

Old Village or Ahnaha
was Land

Camp

Camped 24th October 1804

Mandan Island

Camped   Mandan

MISSOURI RIVER NOTES

Toby Jurovics

THE MISSOURI RIVER—THE LONGEST WATERWAY IN THE continental United States—descends from its headwaters in the Rocky Mountains and strikes east across Montana, arcs southward toward Bismarck, North Dakota, crosses through South Dakota, and flows along the Nebraska-Iowa border toward Kansas City before turning eastward again toward its confluence with the Mississippi River at Saint Louis. On a map, it looks like an artery running across the northern Plains, spanning almost half the continent. Sitting on the banks of the Missouri about an hour north of Bismarck in June 2018, it felt permissible to imagine that the river was much as it had been in 1833 when the German Prince Maximilian of Wied (1782–1867) and his companion, the Swiss artist Karl Bodmer (1809–1893), made their way upriver to Fort McKenzie before doubling back to overwinter at Fort Clark, itself only about fifteen or so miles distant by car. The soft earth banks, eight or ten feet above the water, were familiar from Bodmer's watercolors, as was the dapple of late afternoon light filtering through the cottonwoods. By that measure, things felt exactly right. But as Gerard Baker explains later in this volume, if you knew what you were looking at, the world was in fact upside down. It was not simply the need to blur your eyes to obscure the high-tension lines on the opposite bank or to ignore the sluggish flow of the river as it exited the Garrison Dam. "If those guys came back today," Baker says, "they wouldn't even recognize the place."[1] Baker is speaking of not only Maximilian and Bodmer but also of his people, the Mandan and the Hidatsa. And he addresses a more expansive truth: that the landscape is not only river and prairie and trees—it is not simply topography—it is also defined by its people.

At a moment falling almost half way between Lewis and Clark's Corps of Discovery and the meeting of the Union Pacific and Central Pacific Railroads at Promontory Summit, Utah, Maximilian and Bodmer traveled the length of the Missouri River on a self-appointed excursion to uncover what Maximilian called "the natural face of North America"—its landforms, flora and fauna, and especially its Native inhabitants.[2] Born in 1782,

Benjamin O'Fallon, after William Clark, *Clark's Route Map of the Missouri River*, Sheet 18 (Route about October 23–November 1, 1804), 1833, ink, graphite, and watercolor on paper in leather binding. Joslyn Art Museum, Gift of the Enron Art Foundation, NNG.513.

Maximilian was the eighth of ten sons of a nobleman of the principality of Wied-Neuwied on the Rhine River near Koblenz. Displaying an early interest in natural history, he pursued his education at the University of Göttingen under Johann Friedrich Blumenbach, a physician and biologist who explored how geography and environment might explain all the variations in the human race, which he believed shared a common origin. Here, Maximilian would also find himself under the heady influence of Blumenbach's student Alexander von Humboldt, the famed Prussian naturalist who would become both a mentor and inspiration.[3] Guided by Humboldt's tutelage, Maximilian spent two years in Brazil (1815–17) studying natural history and the Botocudo Indians, a trek he chronicled in a well-received two-volume narrative. Although he acted on his own accord when he made his return trip to the Americas almost two decades later, he seemed guided by his desire to fulfill Humboldt's interest in the American interior and in particular its Indigenous peoples.[4] Most interestingly, it may have been Humboldt himself who urged Maximilian to bring a professional artist to document his research, leading the prince to seek out Bodmer.[5] Though we are right to guard against falling under the sway of romantic narratives, Karl Bodmer was indeed the right person at the right place at the right time: had Maximilian not had the good fortune to contract Bodmer to illustrate his North American voyage (the prince paid for Bodmer's passage, provided a monthly salary, and retained ownership of almost all of the artist's watercolors and drawings), it is hard to imagine that the prince's legacy would be as keenly remembered. Born in Zurich, Bodmer received his artistic training in watercolor and engraving at the side of his uncle, the painter Johann Jakob Meier (1787–1858), before moving to Koblenz in 1828. Working with his brother, an engraver, Bodmer gained a reputation for his adept local vistas, but little evidence remains of his early production to hint at his capacity as a natural history illustrator and, most important, as a portraitist.

Departing from Holland in May 1832, Maximilian and Bodmer arrived in Boston on July 4 in the company of David Dreidoppel, the Wied family huntsman. Their itinerary has been ably described in several previous publications from Joslyn Art Museum, including the three-volume *The North American Journals of Prince Maximilian of Wied*, so only a brief summary follows.[6] Traveling first to New York and then to Philadelphia, they met with the painter Titian Ramsay Peale (1799–1885), who had accompanied Stephen H. Long's exploration of the Rocky Mountains in 1819–20. The trio then made their way through Pennsylvania, arriving at the utopian colony of New Harmony, Indiana, that October for an extended stay in the company of naturalists Charles-Alexandre Lesueur and Thomas Say, who had also participated in the Long expedition. Four months later, after Maximilian's recuperation from cholera, they continued their travels by steamship down the Ohio River, reaching Saint Louis on March 24, 1833. There, Maximilian sought the counsel of William Clark, who had completed his own voyage across the continent with Meriwether Lewis less than thirty years prior and was now the superintendent of Indian affairs for the Upper Missouri River. With a passport to the Upper Missouri signed by Clark himself, as well as an atlas of hand-drawn copies of Clark's own maps of the river, Maximilian, Bodmer, and

Dreidoppel booked passaged on the steamer *Yellow Stone*, operated by the American Fur Company. Over the previous winter Bodmer had made a detour from New Harmony to New Orleans, where he made his first renderings of Indigenous North Americans, but it was not until Maximilian was in Saint Louis that the prince interacted with Native peoples. He detailed his meeting with Massica—a Sauk man whose portrait is carefully described in Lisa Strong's essay in this volume (pp. 45–61)—at length in his journal. In Saint Louis, they also had the opportunity to see recent paintings by George Catlin (1796–1872), who had traveled upriver the previous year, and meet the Scottish adventurer Sir William Drummond Stewart, who would travel with painter Alfred Jacob Miller (1810–1874) along the Platte River and into the Rocky Mountains in 1837. Well provisioned, Maximilian's party left Saint Louis on the morning of April 10, 1833. Less than two weeks later, they would reach the Kansas River: "Here, on the point of land between the Kansas and the Missouri, is the boundary of the United States, and one enters the territory of the free Indians."[7]

Although Maximilian and Bodmer were far from the first Euro-Americans to travel this landscape, which had seen centuries of explorers, fur trappers, and voyageurs, this was nevertheless a pivotal moment for the Indigenous people whose homelands flanked the Missouri. Over the coming months, Maximilian's party would make stops at settlements and fur trading posts near present-day Bellevue, Nebraska; Fort Pierre, South Dakota (where they transferred to the American Fur Company steamship *Assiniboine*); and Fort Clark and Fort Union, North Dakota, the latter near the mouth of the Yellowstone River. They made the final push for Fort McKenzie—far into present-day Montana—by keelboat, arriving there in August 1833. Over the course of their voyage, they met Sauk, Meskwaki, Omaha, Ponca, Sioux, Arikara, Mandan, Hidatsa, Assiniboine, Blackfoot, and Cree people. Retracing their route downriver, they made an extended stay at Fort Clark, adjacent to the Mandan earthlodge village Mih-Tutta-Hangkusch, where their party remained from November 1833 to the following spring. There, with the luxury of time to work and establish relationships—brutal cold and desperate conditions notwithstanding—Bodmer made many of what would become his most renowned portraits. Departing Fort Clark on April 18, 1834, Maximilian's party had traveled 5,000 miles and spent just over a year on the Missouri by the time of their return to Saint Louis at the end of that May.

It was Maximilian's intention to publish the findings of his scientific research accompanied by an atlas of prints made after the watercolors and drawings Bodmer created, many of which were completed upon the artist's return to his Paris studio. Although Kristine K. Ronan explains in her essay (pp. 195–209) that Maximilian's *Reise in das innere Nord-America in den Jahren 1832 bis 1834* (*Travels in the Interior of North America, 1832–34*) ultimately took a form more closely resembling a travelogue, Bodmer's prints—especially his portraits—would come to define "the natural face" of the North American interior, particularly for European audiences.[8] As historian William H. Goetzmann noted, "Through scenes handed down to us in Bodmer's work emerges a matchless picture of the American frontier—a collective portrait that was equaled by no other eyewitness artist before the coming of photography."[9]

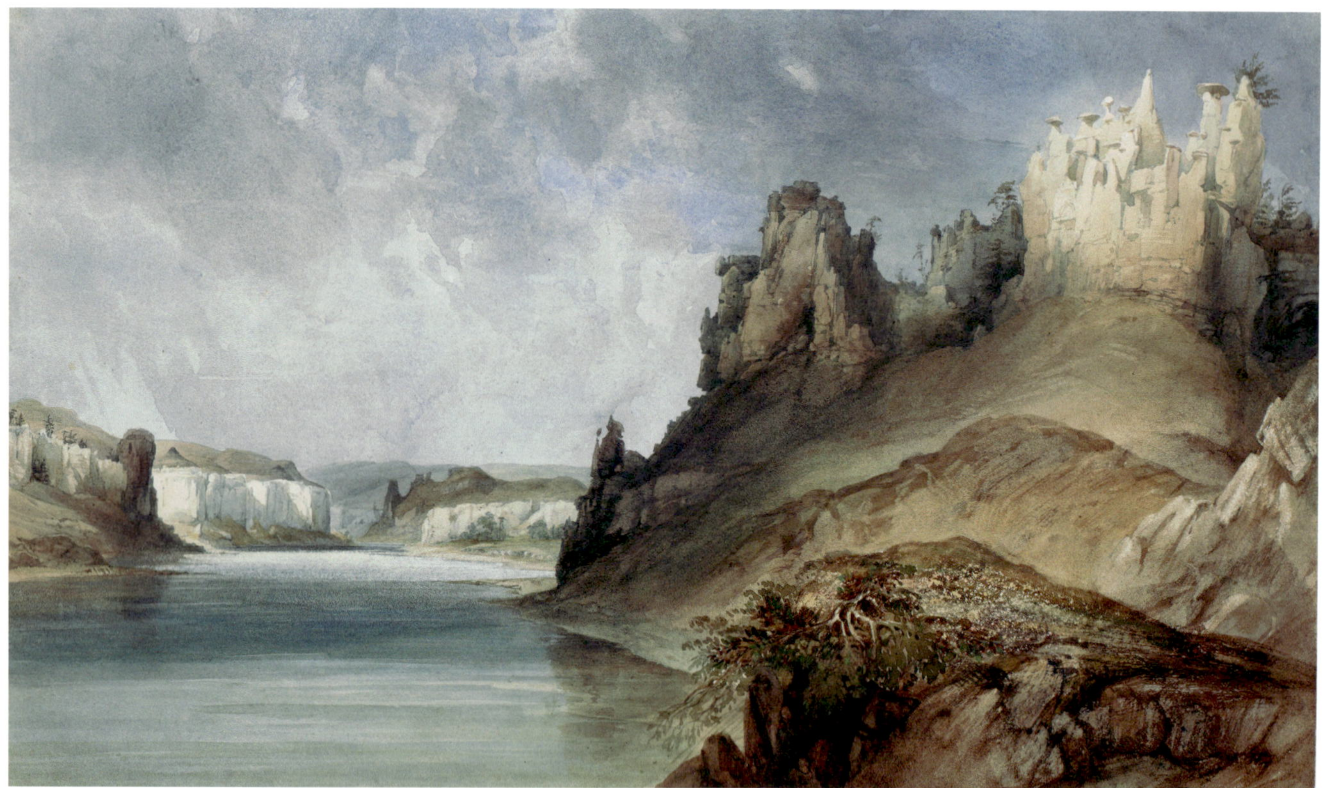

The collection of Bodmer's watercolors and drawings held by Joslyn Art Museum comprises the first comprehensive visual survey of the Missouri River basin. Given the breadth and quality of Bodmer's work, it is fair to say that no artist has equaled him since the invention of photography, either. Bodmer painted and sketched landscapes, portraits, natural history specimens, and anthropological details with a catholic eye and consummate ability. Were he to be judged solely as a landscape painter, Bodmer's watercolors find their only peer in Thomas Moran's account of his first trip to Yellowstone in 1871. *View of the Stone Walls* (fig. 1) completed in Europe after 1834, reveals Bodmer to be every bit the dramatic equal of Albert Bierstadt, limited only by the scale of the materials he carried with him on the river and by his work's having been sequestered from the public for almost a century. Indeed, his views of the confluence of the Missouri and Yellowstone Rivers or the Rocky Mountains beyond Fort McKenzie capture an expansiveness that belies their modest format. No artist since has captured the West with as wide-ranging or capable an eye to document what today we might consider a complete environment or ecosystem.

As Gerard Baker and Scott Manning Stevens (pp. 23–43) attest in this volume, Bodmer's portraits shoulder the many heavily loaded implications of the word *authentic*. The products of a more skilled and refined draftsman than Catlin, Bodmer's portraits assumed a formal authority that remains unrivaled. Although the all-consuming medium of photography would soon snatch away the laurel of accuracy, Bodmer's portraits operate with a unique immediacy and intimacy. While it is a reflection of our contemporary desire to ascribe a sense of personality to

     FACES FROM THE INTERIOR

his portraits—Strong places them within their proper context as ethnographic renderings—Bodmer's precision and attention to detail captured his sitters' likenesses to such a degree that many have been recognized generations later by their descendants. More important, the portraits were made on his subjects' terms—in their territory and in their homelands. Maximilian and Bodmer were guests, and while they were at times welcomed as friends, their presence was always understood as that of temporary observers. The history of Maximilian and Bodmer has most frequently been told as a story of Europeans in America, benign agents with, if not altruistic, then neutral motivations: Enlightenment voyeurs rather than imperialists. The story then shifts to Europe—to Bodmer's labors and the publication of Maximilian's account of his travels, to the movement and distribution of images from their original sources to distant audiences and consumers.

The notion that Maximilian and Bodmer were witness to "the beginning of the end of the unspoiled West" is appealing but overly romantic, suggesting they found a sort of peaceable kingdom that was on the verge of being overturned—it is a common pitfall to assume that a place we are seeing for the first time existed exactly in its present state until the moment of our arrival.[10] Nevertheless, the moment that Bodmer committed to paper was indeed fleeting. As noted, the Upper Missouri had been plied by European fur traders since the previous century, and upon arriving at Fort McKenzie, Maximilian observed, "There were people from all nations: Americans, Englishmen, Frenchmen, Germans, [and] Spaniards."[11] Indigenous peoples were in fact at the center of a vast global trade network for fur and hides that was governed by fashion and desire in New York City and across the Atlantic in the capitals of Europe. In the words of Erik Holland of the State Historical Society of North Dakota, "The Mandan were middlemen in a huge business venture that was coming at

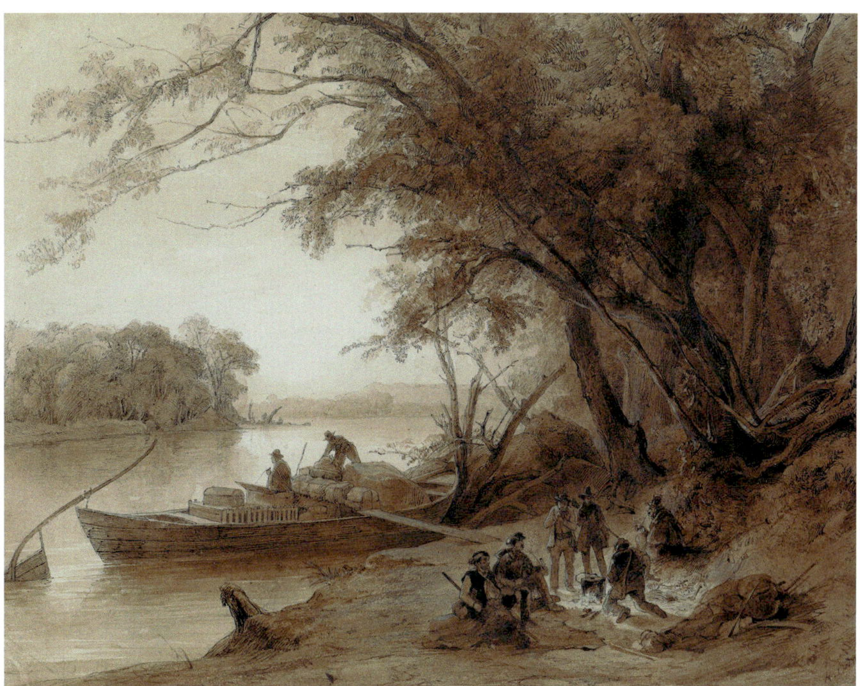

FIGURE 2   Karl Bodmer, *Evening Bivouac on the Missouri*, 1833, watercolor, graphite, and ink on paper. Joslyn Art Museum, Gift of the Enron Art Foundation, 1986.49.380.

them fast."[12] Meanwhile, the American Fur Company was quickly making its way north from Saint Louis, and the landscape itself was being radically altered by the demands of steamships, their boilers' appetite for fuel fed by crews of boatmen prowling the Missouri's banks with axes. The forests flanking the river disappeared, as did the buffalo that wintered in the bottomlands, challenging the tribes that relied on them for survival.[13] Forced to travel further and further from the safety afforded by their well-defended settlements, the Mandans fell victim not only to declining resources but also to nomadic tribes they encountered on the Plains. These intertribal rivalries actively reshaped Indigenous cultural relationships, and alliances were in constant flux up and down the river.

Most critically, the Mandans at the village of Mih-Tutta-Hangkusch would fall to smallpox in 1837, less than three years after Maximilian and Bodmer's departure and two years before *Reise in das innere Nord-America* was published. On June 19 of that year, the steamboat *St. Peter's* arrived at Fork Clark from Council Bluffs loaded with Euro-American and Indigenous passengers and trade goods. Within the space of two weeks it was apparent that the *St. Peter's* had also carried a pathogen, as the symptoms of smallpox appeared in the adjacent Mandan village of Mih-Tutta-Hangkusch as well.[14] Elizabeth Fenn's account in *Encounters at the Heart of the World: A History of the Mandan People* bears repeating: "The firestorm that resulted from the passage of the *St. Peter's* may not have been deliberate, but it represented willful neglect of staggering proportions."[15] Bodmer's triumphant image of the Mandan chief Mató-Tópe (Four Bears) is one of his most renowned portraits—the record of a brave leader and warrior, one who was aware of the value of this particular transaction between sitter and artist. By July 26, 1837, he had fallen ill. Four days later he spoke of his affection for whites, dating back to the passage of Lewis and Clark, but he also acknowledged that they had brought this disease to his people, and he exhorted his kin to "rise all together and Not leave one of them alive."[16] Mató-Tópe died that same day. The Mandans were the hardest hit, and it is estimated that within a year nine in ten perished. But they were not the only tribe that suffered: the steamship carried the virus the length of the river to the Omahas, Otoes, and Pawnees near Council Bluffs; to the Yankton and Santee Sioux at Fort Kiowa; to the Hidatsas and Arikaras at Fort Clark; and, upon its arrival at Fort Union, to the Assiniboines, Plains Crees, Siksika, Piegans, Kainai, and Gros Ventres.[17] Nor was this the first time smallpox had swept the Plains, merely the latest of successive waves of disease that had raced across the Missouri River landscape over the previous century. The Indigenous settlements Maximilian and Bodmer visited had already been gravely altered—entire villages, lost or uprooted, had to reconsolidate and rebuild, sometimes with other tribes—and bore little resemblance to the communities that had existed before Euro-Americans arrived in number. The Mandans near Fort Clark had relocated from their traditional homeland near the Heart River only a decade before Maximilian and Bodmer's arrival, an aftereffect of the smallpox pandemic of 1781. The Indigenous peoples of the Missouri River that Bodmer and Maximilian encountered had endured more than a century of negotiating and accommodating the incursion of Anglo-Europeans pressing into their homelands from the

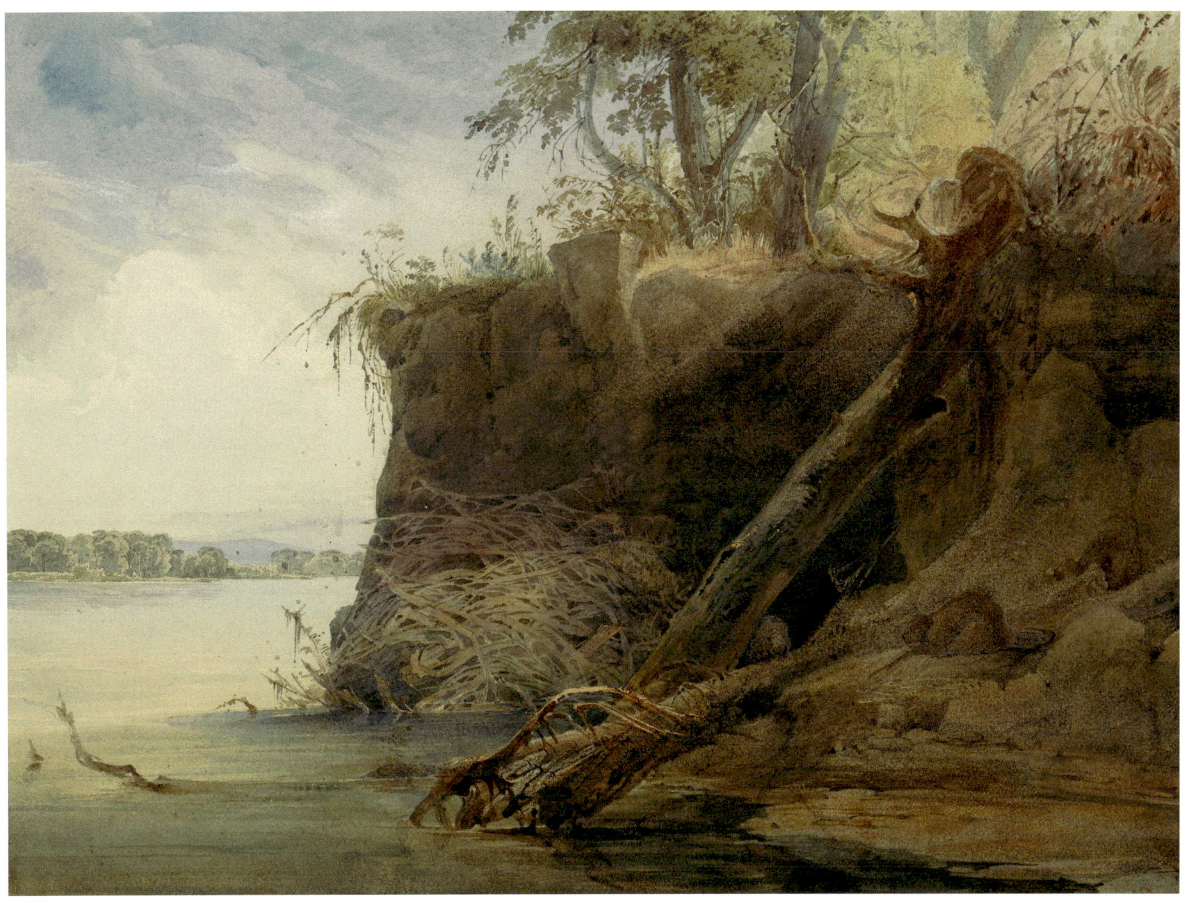

north, south, and east. Maximilian was aware—and critical—of the Indian Removal Act of 1830, and he witnessed the leading edge of US territorial expansion, which would begin in earnest with the burgeoning immigrant trails to California and Oregon and—on an industrial scale—with the transcontinental railroad. Although initially there may have been some trade and profit to be had for tribes in the fur-bearing West, more often than not they were forced to cede what had been theirs. By the end of the century, as the United States raced to the Pacific Ocean, most of what remained would be taken.

As Maximilian's journal makes clear, travel on the river was not always easy or comfortable or even safe. But it could be sublime:

> Toward evening, the wind subsided; it became very pleasant. And, as the sun neared the horizon, [a] magnificent landscape! A series of steep bluffs on the right bank was colored purple. Right and left, green thickets along the bank, [and] before us, beautifully varying hill shapes, including several conical domes, which reveal themselves far distant in the beautiful evening illumination.[18]

But returning to the June afternoon that opened this essay, Gerard Baker's observations remind me of the all-too-easy error we make in assuming that the natural condition of the landscape reflects an absence of people. Beaver, otter, weasel, deer, antelope, elk, fox, coyote, wolf, and

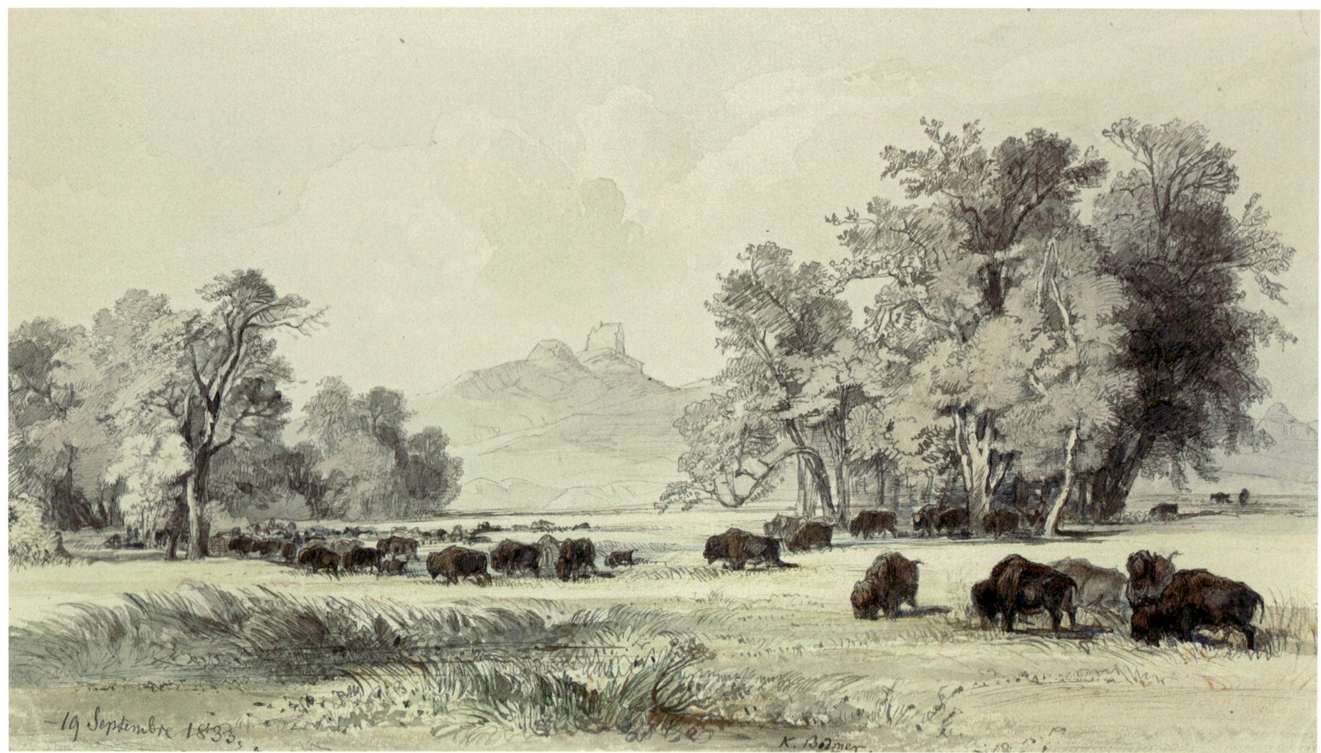

bear were missing. Bison were missing. The skies were nearly silent. But mostly people were missing. The Missouri River as Maximilian and Bodmer knew it was lively and vibrant. Today, at the village sites of Knife River, On-A-Slant, Huff, and Double Ditch, the outlines of abandoned earth lodges are embossed on mown fields, often visible only from an oblique angle or slight rise. Scanning the horizon from the center of Mih-Tutta-Hangkusch, you follow the grade of the Burlington Northern Santa Fe, the power lines running from the Basin Electric Power Cooperative's Leland Olds Station, and the rows of windmills dotting the ridge to the south. You imagine you can almost hear the fracking rigs in the Bakken Formation to the east, where the natural gas orgy of the early twenty-first century has again laid waste to landscape and people. But it is here that one should try to imagine Bodmer: amidst a ruckus of men and women, elders and hunters and warriors, families and children, dogs and horses, and visitors always coming and going. *Faces from the Interior* opens almost two centuries after Maximilian and Bodmer's excursion into the heart of the American interior. Writing this at a transformational moment in our own society, in the opening months of a worldwide pandemic, brings a painful awareness of how rapidly unexpected changes can undermine our most fundamental assumptions. In this light, Bodmer's portraits take on an even greater urgency. Beyond individual likenesses, they are images of peoples, the reflection of tens of thousands of lives lived along the Missouri over hundreds and hundreds of years. We hope that *Faces from the Interior* not only stands as a collection of arresting portraits by an exemplary artist, but also brings a new awareness of the lives that were sustained by the Missouri River in the not-too-distant past and their importance to those who live alongside the river today.

FIGURE 4   Karl Bodmer, *Bison Grazing on the Upper Missouri*, 1833, watercolor on paper. Joslyn Art Museum, Gift of the Enron Art Foundation, 1986.49.393.

NOTES

1. See Annika K. Johnson, "Bringing the Story Back: An Interview with Gerard Baker" in this volume, pp. 91–101 and 140–47.

2. Maximilian of Wied, *Reise in das innere Nord-America in den Jahren 1832 bis 1834* (Koblenz: J. Hölscher, 1839–41), 1:ix.

3. See Eleanor Jones Harvey, *Alexander von Humboldt and the United States* (Washington, DC: Smithsonian American Art Museum; Princeton, NJ, and Oxford: Princeton University Press, 2020) for a comprehensive study of Humboldt and his influence on the natural sciences in the nineteenth century.

4. Harvey, *Humboldt,* 258.

5. Harvey, *Humboldt,* 117.

6. *The North American Journals of Prince Maximilian of Wied*, ed. Marsha V. Gallagher and Steven S. Witte, trans. William J. Orr, Paul Schach, and Dieter Karch, 3 vols. (Norman: University of Oklahoma Press; Omaha: Joslyn Art Museum, Margre H. Durham Center for Western Studies, 2008–12); hereafter *NAJ.* See also the selected bibliography (p. 215) for an overview of Joslyn Art Museum publications on the Maximilian-Bodmer Collection.

7. *NAJ* 2:44.

8. Maximilian of Wied, author's preface to *Travels in the Interior of North America, 1832–34* trans. Hannibal Evans Lloyd (London: Ackermann, 1843), v. Bodmer's original watercolors were publicly exhibited only once in the nineteenth century, but the prints made after them circulated widely via the three editions of Maximilian's publications. See also Kristine K. Ronan's essay (pp. 195–209) and the selected bibliography (p. 215) in this volume.

9. Goetzmann et al., *Karl Bodmer's America,* 3.

10. Goetzmann et al., *Karl Bodmer's America,* 3.

11. *NAJ,* 2:360.

12. Erik Holland, curator of education, Historical Society of North Dakota, in conversation with the author, June 8, 2018.

13. Elizabeth A. Fenn, *Encounters at the Heart of the World: A History of the Mandan People* (New York: Hill & Wang, 2014), 298–99.

14. See Fenn, *Encounters,* 317–25, for a detailed narrative of the infection and outbreak at Mih-Tutta-Hangkusch.

15. Fenn, *Encounters,* 319.

16. Fenn, *Encounters,* 320.

17. Fenn, *Encounters,* 323.

18. *NAJ,* 2:182.

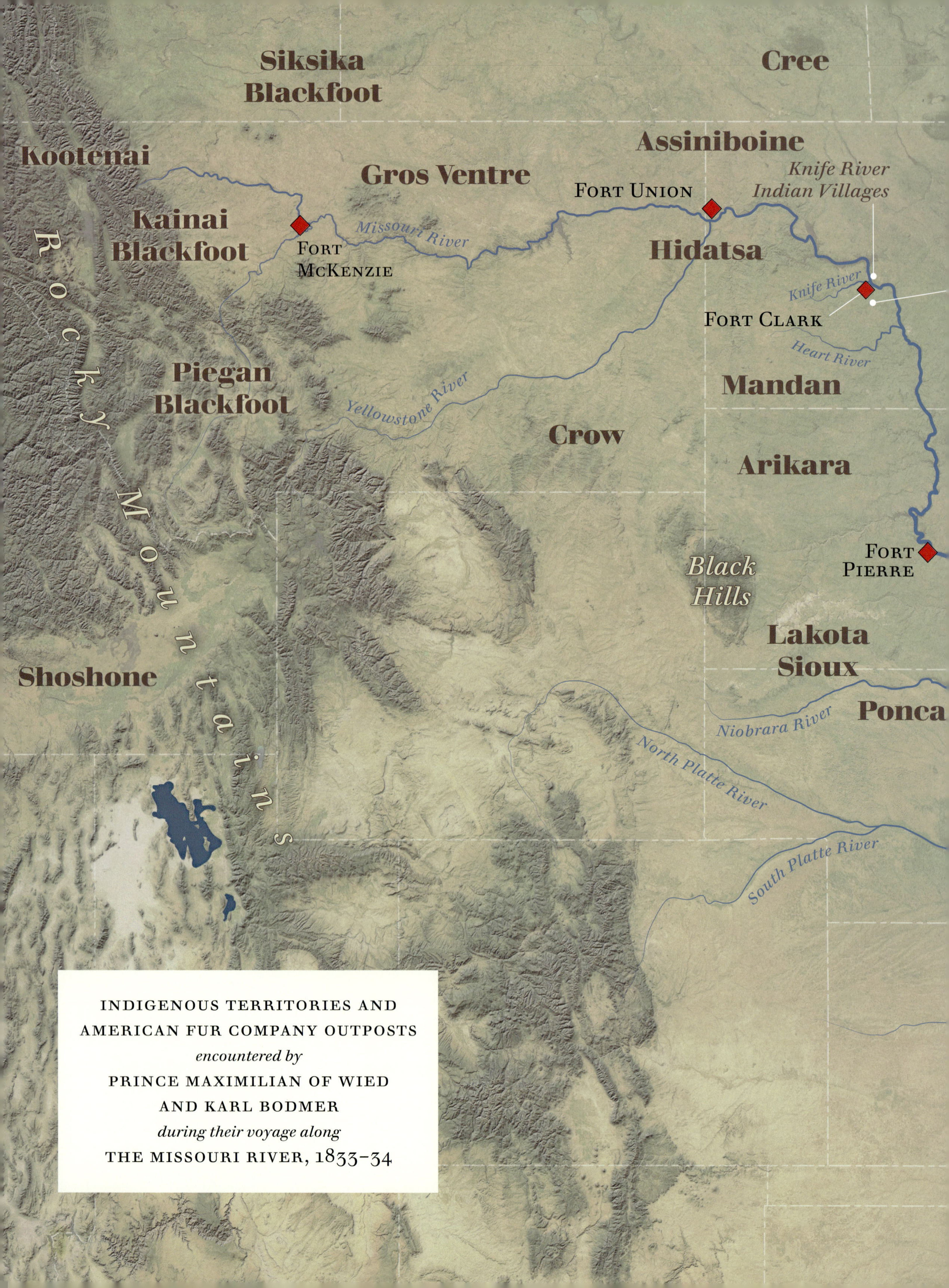

INDIGENOUS TERRITORIES AND
AMERICAN FUR COMPANY OUTPOSTS
encountered by
PRINCE MAXIMILIAN OF WIED
AND KARL BODMER
during their voyage along
THE MISSOURI RIVER, 1833–34

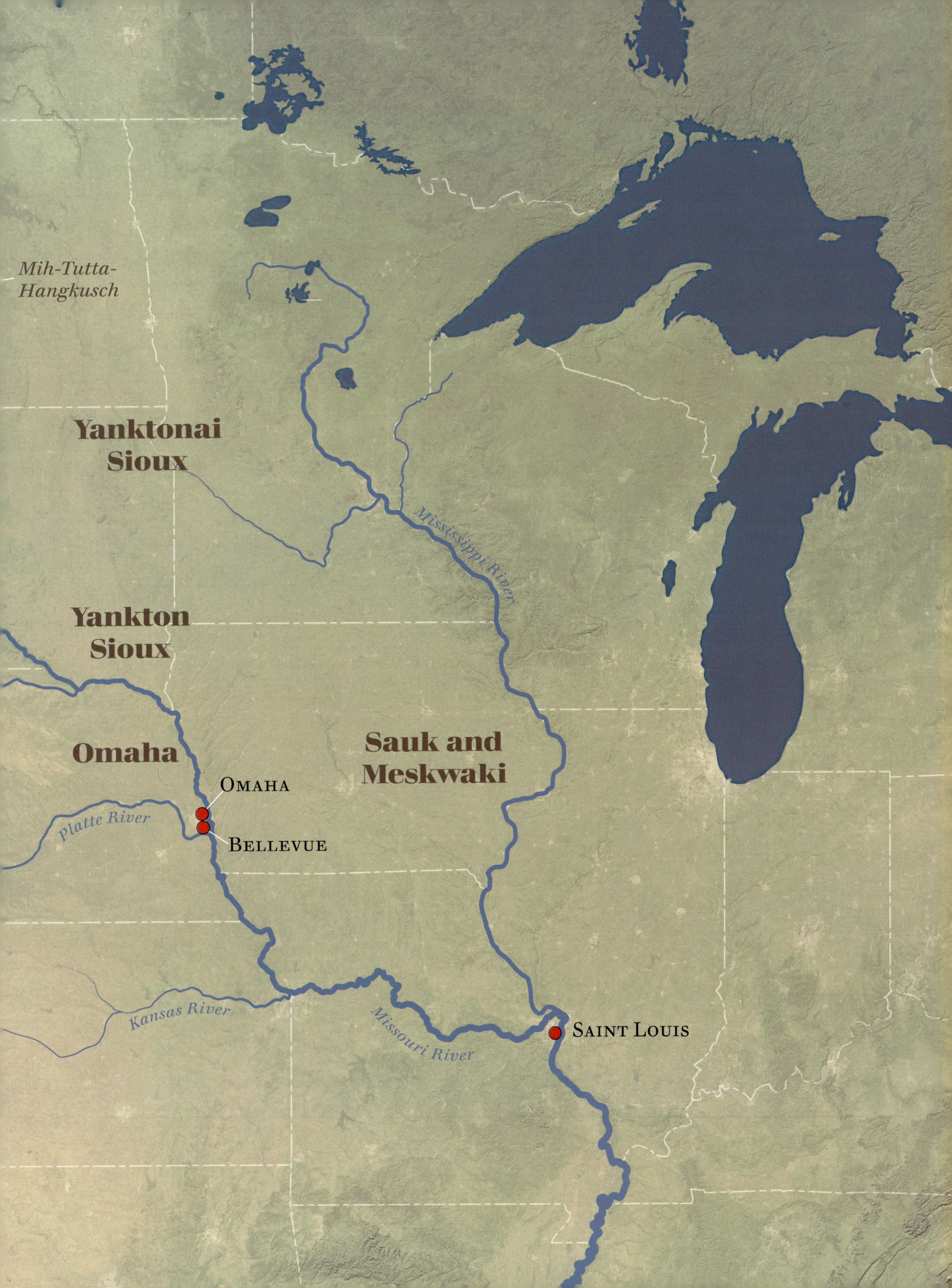

Mih-Tutta-Hangkusch
Yanktonai Sioux
Yankton Sioux
Omaha
Mississippi River
Sauk and Meskwaki
Omaha
Platte River
Bellevue
Kansas River
Missouri River
Saint Louis

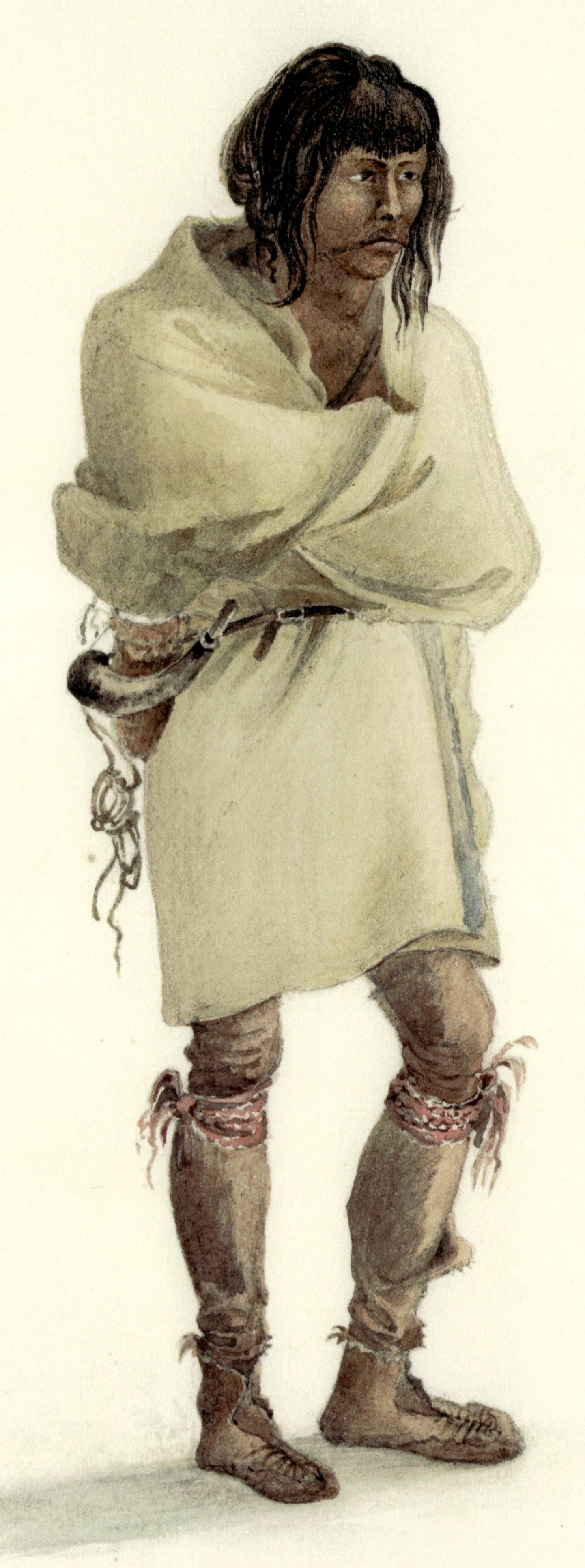

THE ACHIEVEMENT OF KARL BODMER

Scott Manning Stevens

WHILE WE HAVE ALL SEEN COUNTLESS REPRESENTA-tions of the "American Indian" since childhood, that first encounter with Karl Bodmer's watercolor portraits of Native Americans likely sparks a sense of discovery. There is the impression that, like Bodmer, we are seeing these striking representatives of Native nations for the first time. Bodmer's individuals, often seen in profile against a blank or spare sheet, appear somehow unmediated or "unaccommodated." As a result, we are often instantly persuaded that Bodmer has provided us with a porthole into the past. We can be easily seduced by the seeming veracity and, that most problematic of terms, authenticity of his representations. To be sure, he was a skilled draftsman—much more refined than his contemporary George Catlin—and we know from surviving examples of Indigenous material culture that Bodmer was meticulous in his depictions of Native aesthetics and craftsmanship. But the temptation to see his images as "authentic" is just that: a temptation. Bodmer, although only in his early twenties at the time he painted these remarkable watercolors, was not unbound from the artistic inheritance of Western Europe. In some ways, his youth and lack of a cosmopolitan education and artistic training can be counted as benefits in regard to his work. But he was still governed by the picturesque qualities that characterized fashionable landscape paintings at the time, and he could not have escaped the Romantic ethnological opinions of his patron and traveling companion, Prince Maximilian of Wied.

We know relatively little about Karl Bodmer's early life. Born on February 11, 1809, Johann Carl Bodmer was raised in Zurich.[1] Following the military interventions of revolutionary France and Napoleon, new political ideas circulated throughout the Swiss cantons in the early nineteenth century. But Zurich, with a population of just over 10,000 people in 1800, was still provincial in comparison with metropolitan centers such as Paris, London, or Berlin, which boasted populations in the hundreds of thousands, and it remained a largely conservative community, dominated by the mores of the Reformed Church and the business interests of

Karl Bodmer, *Billie, a Choctaw Man*, 1833 (detail of fig. 5).

wealthy elites. Beginning at the age of thirteen, Bodmer studied under his maternal uncle Johann Jakob Meier, a well-known artist and engraver who had himself studied under Gabriel Lory (1763–1840), a celebrated Swiss landscape painter and illustrator. Bodmer was taught primarily in pencil and watercolor, while his older brother, Rudolf (1805–1841), concentrated on etching. Many professional Swiss artists supported themselves through the painting of landscapes and as illustrators of guides along with commissions for family portraiture. With the popularity of the Grand Tour in the seventeenth and eighteenth centuries, Alpine panoramas and river views were especially in vogue. Part of the skill set acquired by studying with an engraver was the exacting ability to reproduce an image from a sketch or watercolor. That precision in draftsmanship is everywhere evident in Karl Bodmer's art.

Though dramatic images of Swiss landscapes were popular commodities, local competition among artists was considerable. By the age of nineteen, Bodmer was ready to seek out new vistas and new venues to practice his art. The appetite for the picturesque was not limited to the Alps, and many a bourgeois household in Biedermeier-era Europe desired images of their local regions or the ones they frequently traveled to. In that spirit Bodmer chose the small German city of Koblenz, located between Cologne and Frankfurt at the juncture of the Rhine and Moselle Rivers. Along those rivers he produced picturesque landscape paintings and engravings known by the Italian painting term *vedute,* or views, some of which his brother Rudolf reproduced as etchings for publication. Bodmer's skill as a painter of natural scenes brought him to the attention of Maximilian of Wied, whose family domain lay in the region. The prince was an avid naturalist and traveler, inspired by the heroic scholarly explorations undertaken by his countryman Alexander von Humboldt. Like Humboldt, Maximilian had studied under the famed natural philosopher Johann Friedrich Blumenbach while a student at the University of Göttingen and was inspired to chart distant realms and expand knowledge of the natural world. Maximilian had already explored portions of the Amazon and the interior of Brazil in 1815–17 and published an important account of the Indigenous peoples and the natural environments he encountered. The prince had supplied his own drawings to illustrate his text but was criticized for their amateurish nature. By the beginning of the 1830s, Maximilian had set his sights on the interior of North America, and this time he was determined to employ a professional illustrator for the account of his explorations he planned to publish when he returned. It is worth noting that it was Bodmer's expertly rendered regional landscapes that brought the artist to Maximilian's attention and not his portraits or depictions of people and animals. These genres were to be learned in the field, as it were.

Maximilian; his huntsman, David Dreidoppel; and Karl Bodmer set out for the United States on May 17, 1832, from Hellevoetsluis in Holland and arrived in Boston on July 4. Bodmer's sketches record his first shipboard views of the New England coast and the landscapes of the antebellum Northeast as they made their way west through Pennsylvania via Bethlehem in the Lehigh Valley. These images are highly valued by historians of the early republic since few other detailed depictions of the

   FACES FROM THE INTERIOR

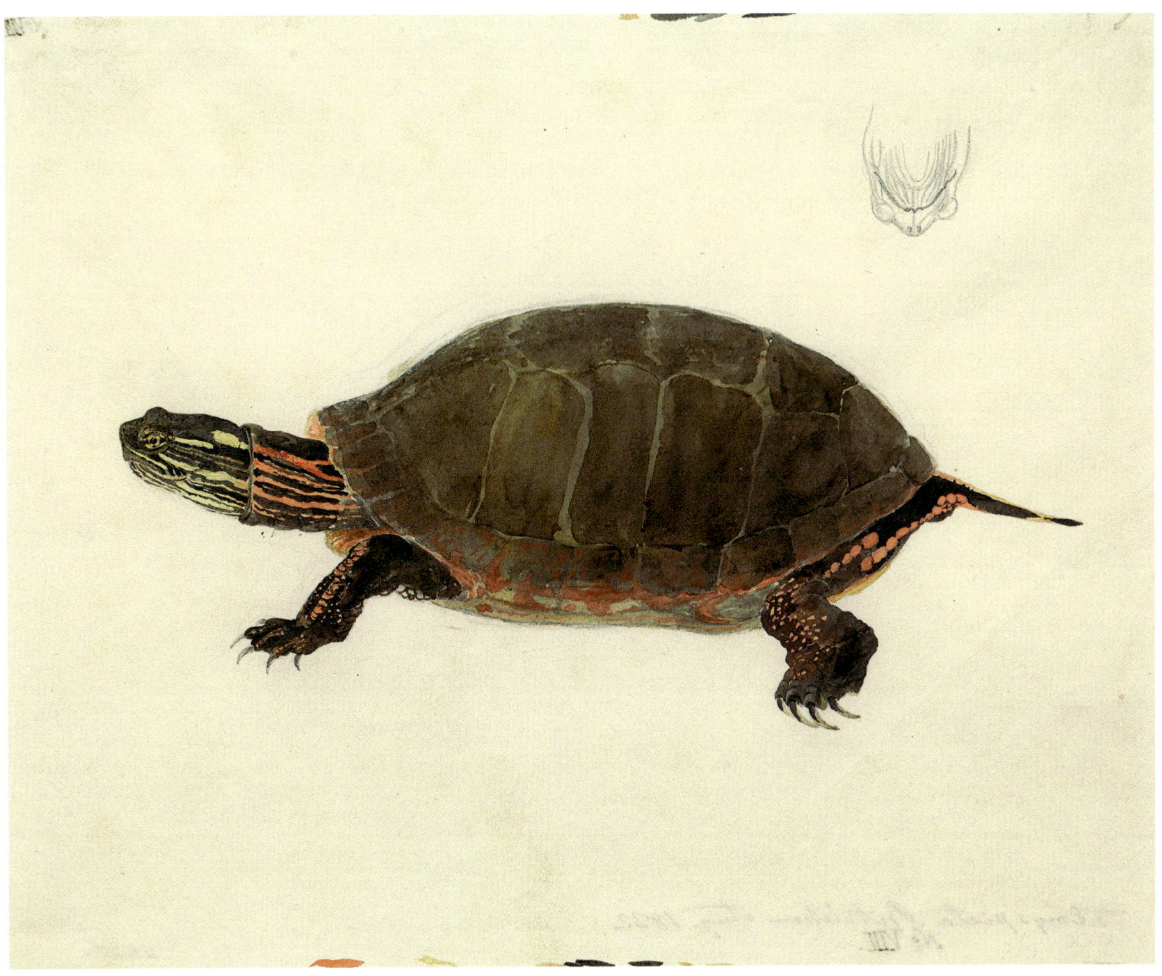

FIGURE 1   Karl Bodmer, *A Turtle*, 1832, watercolor and graphite on paper. Joslyn Art Museum, Gift of the Enron Art Foundation, 1986.49.340.

regions through which they traveled are available. It was also during this portion of the journey that Bodmer began to make detailed illustrations of local fauna that would prove him to be an able naturalist, at least as an observer. His hand-colored sketch of a common painted turtle (fig. 1) is an early indication of his abilities as a draftsman working at a level of detail required by a natural scientist. In part, these skills of reproducing both at the macro- and microscopic perspectives are what give viewers so much confidence in his depictions of Native Americans.

Bodmer's inexperience with Native Americans—or rather, his lack of exposure to the predominant prejudices about them in US society—was fortunate. Most American artists who chose to depict Native Americans either adopted the notion of the savage enemy who was an impediment to American progress or the nostalgic Romanticism that celebrated the so-called "vanishing race." This latter position, known also as a declension narrative, saw the decline and extinction of Indigenous peoples as somehow natural and inevitable with the advent of European civilization in the Americas. It was embraced disturbingly early by European settlers, and by the nineteenth century it was already tinged with Romantic regret. The Noble Savage, a trope created by Europeans, would ultimately be undone by European mores and technological superiority (fig. 2). Such a position also had the benefit of being without fault—after all, who is

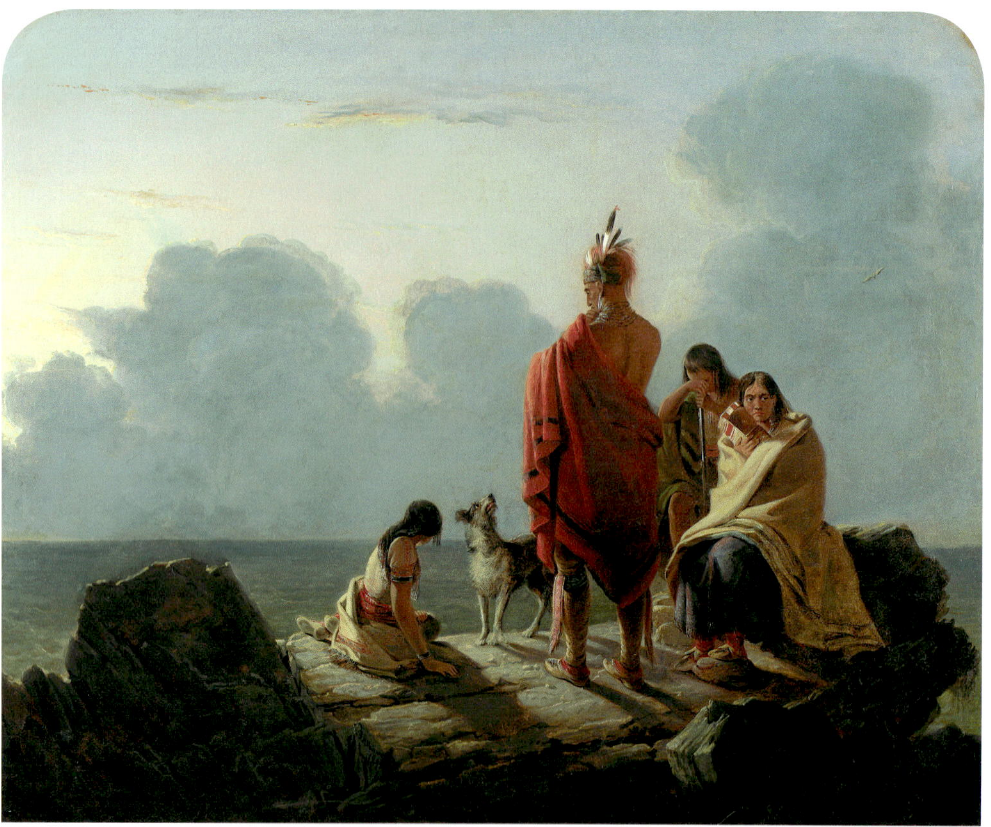

the agent of vanishing? The question that should be asked is *who* "vanished" the Indians? The alternative vision of Native America was simply oppositional: an inhuman enemy, cruel and vengeful. We have seen this representational tradition, with its supposed cannibals and cruel savages bent on violence, since the earliest period of contact. American painters such as Benjamin West (1738–1820) and John Vanderlyn (1776–1852) created well-known images of Indian savagery in the late eighteenth and early nineteenth centuries (fig. 3), and these in turn were frequently reproduced as etchings. Later, in the period of westward expansion during the mid-nineteenth century, plenty more conflict narratives emerged in the paintings of Charles Deas (1818–1867), Arthur Fitzwilliam Tait (1819–1905), and Carl Wimar (1828–1862).

Maximilian—who was more than two decades Bodmer's senior and a notably worldly man of foreign travel, exploration, and elite education—had encountered various Romantic notions of human development and the stages of civilization. His former teacher Blumenbach was himself unsure whether the societies designated as "savage" were so because they stood at an early stage of development or were in a late stage of degeneration. As a man of science, Maximilian would likewise have imbricated such views into his own study of natural history. We know that he sought out examples of a primitive aristocracy or nobility among Indigenous peoples, and this likely explains the prevalence of male leaders depicted by Bodmer. We have relatively few portraits of women and even fewer of children, and many of these figures were later reworked into larger groups in tableaux of social life and ceremonies. It is also likely

    FACES FROM THE INTERIOR

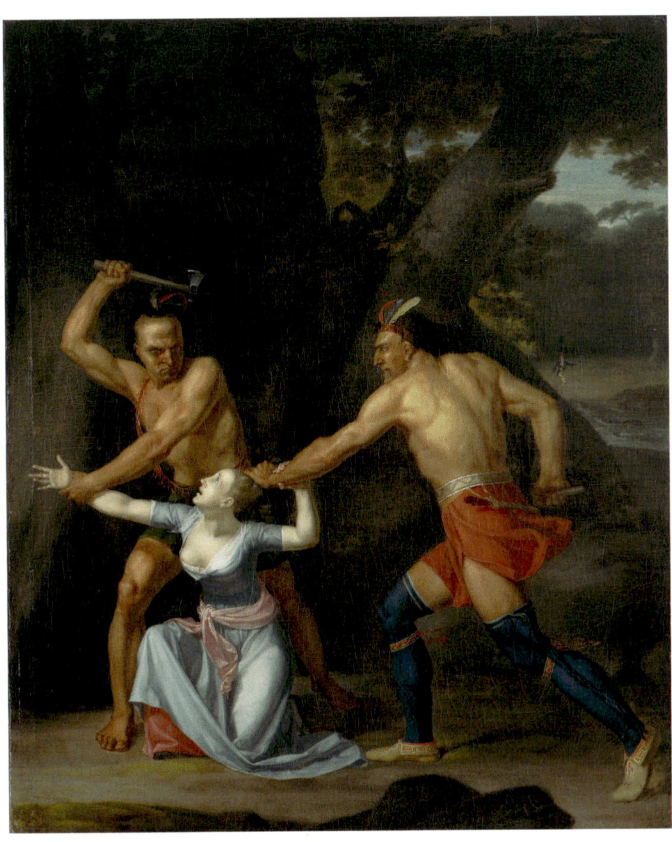

that Native communities had their own strictures regarding interactions between outsiders and the women and children of their communities. How much influence Maximilian had on Bodmer's ideas about Native America we cannot know, but as Bodmer's patron he doubtless selected certain figures to record and also shared his opinions about the inevitable change that was coming to Native American lifeways and his desire to create a record to preserve what he could. Maximilian did not portray the decline of Native American populations as inevitable or fated, the way many Americans did; instead, he made clear who was behind their decline. Describing the present condition of the United States, he wrote, "Instead of its former natural condition, this country now presents a mixture of all nations that continues without pause what it began soon after arriving in the New World: the constant and continuous, irresponsible dispersion and eradication of the original inhabitants."[2] Without being steeped in American beliefs about the "vanishing Indian," Bodmer may well have taken his initial encounters with Indigenous peoples more at face value. We do well to compare him to George Catlin in this respect.

PAINTING IN THE TRANS-MISSISSIPPI WEST

Arriving in Saint Louis in 1830, Catlin embarked on a western journey to visit the Indigenous nations of the Upper Missouri, and he began the work that would make up his famous Indian Gallery, a large portfolio of his works with which he frequently traveled in search of patrons.[3] Self-taught and of uneven artistic accomplishment, Catlin would have encountered keen competition in his quest to become a successful portrait artist in a period when a number of refined painters had established careers in the urban centers of Boston, New York, and Philadelphia. Visiting Philadelphia as a young man, Catlin first encountered Indigenous materials displayed in Charles Willson Peale's museum, many of which had been gathered by Lewis and Clark during their 1804–06 transcontinental expedition. Catlin's imagination and ambition, like those of others to follow, were fired by the unknown frontier and the Indigenous nations living there. But this was also an era of rancorous debate around the proposed US policy of Indian removal, by which all Native nations living east of the Mississippi were to be relocated to regions west of that river. Catlin, who would travel routes similar to those first visited by Lewis and Clark just over two decades earlier, now approached the Indigenous nations of the Trans-Mississippi West with a sense of urgency. Upon his arrival in Saint Louis, Catlin befriended William Clark, governor of the Missouri Territory from 1817 to 1820 and since 1822 the superintendent of Indian affairs for the region. Catlin visited Clark's museum of Indian artifacts before accompanying him on a diplomatic mission up the Mississippi.

Catlin would make four more independent journeys through the Upper Midwest and the Plains between 1832 and 1846, while maintaining a studio in Saint Louis.

Unlike Charles Bird King (1785–1862), an accomplished painter of Native American diplomatic portraits, Catlin wished to encounter the subjects of his paintings in their homelands and at a distance removed from the presumably more civilized East. King, just over a decade older than Catlin, was a formally trained portrait painter who had accepted a commission from Thomas McKenney—superintendent of Indian trade from 1816 to 1822 and, from 1824 to 1830, superintendent of Indian affairs (then part of the War Department) in Washington, DC—to portray Native peoples visiting the capital on diplomatic missions. Dozens of delegations from the West visited the city in the early years of the republic, and between 1822 to 1842 King produced more than 100 portraits of Native leaders and figures of interest at his Washington studio.[4] While providing us with an invaluable record of Native diplomacy and the likenesses of famous Native individuals, King's portraits are not celebrated for their ethnographic qualities as much as for their historic significance. When sitting for King many of his subjects donned European-style clothes that would have been tailored in Washington, while others wore the traditional regalia of leaders in their own communities, and some are shown with a hybrid mixture of styles. King's oeuvre is an early example of salvage ethnology, which sought to chronicle as much accurate ethnographic data as possible before groups underwent a cultural change brought on by contact with settler society; in this case, that contact came during the era of westward expansion and Indian removal. Along with jurist James Hall, McKenney embarked on a project to record the lives of individual Native Americans in the three-volume *History of the Indian Tribes of North America*, published from 1836 to 1844. The great majority of the portraits of contemporary Native leaders that appeared in the project came from copies made from King's portraits or from Henry Inman's copies after King's portraits. *History of the Indian Tribes of North America* was in many ways meant to be a memorial to the passing of one civilization in the face of a new one. Just as antiquarian projects were popular in this era in order to supply the young nation with an ancient history, so a record of the leaders of its first inhabitants was deemed worthy of investigation. In his short prose biographies, Hall saw many of the figures about which he wrote as the "last of their kind."[5]

Catlin was ambitious to make a name for himself as a painter of Indians, but he would do so in their distant western homelands and thus made claims to greater authenticity and exoticism simultaneously. In 1830 he headed west on a mission to create a visual record of the Native nations before they disappeared. As he would later write in an account of his travels, "I have flown to their rescue, not of their lives or their

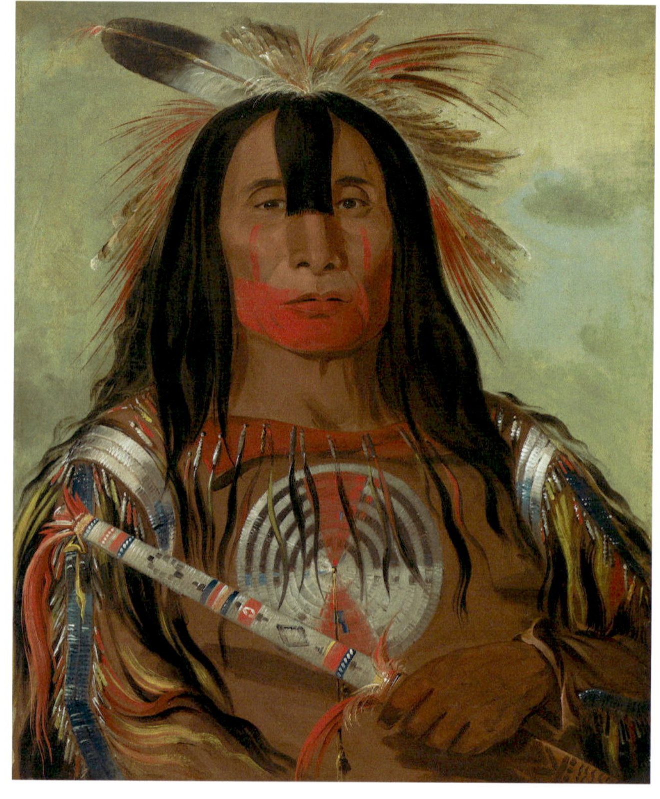

FIGURE 4   George Catlin, *Stu-mick-o-súcks, Buffalo Bull's Back Fat, Head Chief, Blood Tribe*, 1832, oil on canvas. Smithsonian American Art Museum, Gift of Mrs. Joseph Harrison Jr. 1985.66.149.

race (for they are doomed and must perish) but to the rescue of their looks and their modes."[6] Caitlin was a self-taught as a painter of miniature portraits, and his strongest works are his bust-style portraits of Native individuals, such as Stu-mick-o-súcks (Buffalo Bull's Back Fat; fig. 4) or Mauhooskan (White Cloud), and not his paintings depicting landscape or group actions. The artist gave the portraits a heightened level of attention to ethnological minutiae that is often missing or minimalized in his group scenes. This is no doubt in part due to the fact that such particulars were extremely important to the subjects of the portraits since decorative elements signified specific codes of social status and personal achievement. We see a similar attention to detail in Bodmer's works, only with a greater precision that is evident even in large group tableaux.

Though the cultures of the Upper Missouri were as unknown to Catlin as they were to Bodmer, Catlin was not encountering Native Americans for the first time. We know he began his career in the 1820s as a painter of Indians by portraying venerable Haudenosaunee (Iroquois) figures like Sagoyewatha (Red Jacket), who was still living on the Seneca reservation at Buffalo Creek in western New York. These eastern Native communities were considerably more acculturated after 300 years of contact with Europeans than the peoples of the Trans-Mississippi at that time. Catlin could see firsthand the cultural changes that had occurred with the introduction of Christianity and the settlers' socioeconomic structures. This would only contribute to Catlin's embrace of the declension narrative—one that eschewed change, social dynamism, or adaptation. All of those social necessities were seen as markers of inauthenticity. This was so much the case in American settler society that the policy of Indian removal was presented as a means of protecting what was left of Native cultures. Andrew Jackson, the most visible advocate of Indian removal, claimed in an 1829 speech that the policy was the most humane means of dealing with the so-called Indian problem:

> Surrounded by the whites with their arts and civilization, which by destroying the resources of the savage, doom him to weakness and decay, the fate of the Mohegan, the Narragansett, and the Delaware is fast overtaking the Choctaw, the Cherokee, and the Creek. That this fate surely awaits them if they remain within the limits of States does not admit of a doubt. Humanity and national honor demand that every effort should be made to avert so great a calamity.[7]

It is telling that in McKenney and Hall's history, the entry for Sagoyewatha describes him as "the last of the Senecas: there are many left who may boast the aboriginal name and lineage, but with him expired all that had remained of the spirit of the tribe."[8] Catlin approached his projected Indian Gallery with such memorialization in mind. He saw his subjects through the melancholy lens of what scholar Renato Rosaldo has termed "imperialist nostalgia," the mourning of a culture that your society has caused to be destroyed.[9]

Arguably, Bodmer, at age twenty-two, did not approach the Natives he encountered having already internalized this concept of inevitable decline and extinction. To be sure, he may have encountered this opinion from Maximilian or American settlers with whom he interacted

while on his journey, but his engagement with
Native Americans was likely less influenced by
that jaundiced prejudice. Had he thought much
about Native America at all, Bodmer would
probably have had exposure to European ideas
concerning the barbarous Other—a notion
as old as ancient Greece and still active in
European presumptions of cultural superiority to those nations outside its borders. Early
lore surrounding European exploration of the
Americas was filled with wild men, cannibals,
and savages given to human sacrifice and tor-
ture. This monstrous Other was a convenient
trope for those who preferred combat and conquest as a means of gaining a foothold in the
New World; this savage presence justified its
extirpation.

Bodmer may have also heard tales of
the Noble Savage that had developed in
Enlightenment France, where they served primarily as a foil for the social corruption of the
ancien régime then in power. This version of
Native America was about the Natives' inherent or natural nobility and their profound love
of freedom and equality. It had its philosophical
basis in the works of Jean-Jacques Rousseau
and in the fictions of various authors, such as
François-René de Chateaubriand in his novella
Atala (1801). In the period of French political influence in Switzerland after the French

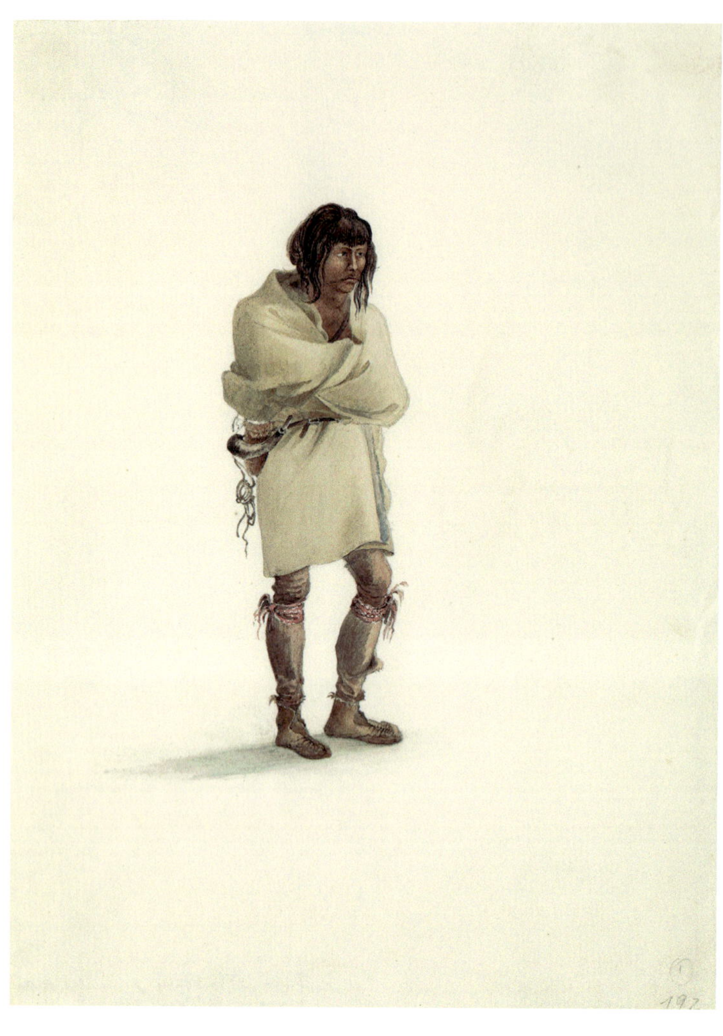

FIGURE 5   Karl Bodmer, *Billie, a Choctaw Man*, 1833, watercolor and graphite on paper. Joslyn Art Museum, Gift of the Enron Art Foundation, 1986.49.332.

Revolution it is possible that such ideas had reached Zurich, but we cannot know the artist's direct relationship to them as he did not leave us a
body writing comparable to that of Maximilian. Such Romantic concep-
tions were more easily maintained in Europe than along the American
frontier. Incursions by fur trappers and squatters into Indigenous territories put added pressure on the environment and brought about inevitable clashes over land and resources. The fact that Maximilian and
Bodmer arrived at the beginning of the Indian removal period could not
have escaped their notice. In fact, Bodmer's first encounter with Native
Americans was not in the northern Plains along the Missouri River but
instead in the Deep South along the Mississippi. On a side trip to New
Orleans and Natchez in January and February 1833 he would record his
first Native Americans, a group of Choctaw refugees being driven west
toward present-day Oklahoma, then Indian Territory.

President Jackson's widely promoted Indian Removal Act had become
law in 1830, and Indigenous nations were being uprooted from their
homelands and sacred places and forced to emigrate to the West. Some
nations, like the Cherokee, would attempt to fight removal through
the US judicial system, but most were coerced into accepting removal
to western territories—territories that were already the homelands of

other Native nations. The Choctaws of Mississippi were among the earliest groups forced out. When Bodmer encountered a group of them in Louisiana (fig. 5), the result was a series of watercolor sketches that demonstrates Bodmer's characteristic attention to detail and a humane interest in the plight of his subjects. If he had been expecting "knights of the Great Plains," these were not them. They were possessed of their own human dignity, even as they were driven from their ancestral homelands. The figure of the refugee might not have been so foreign to Bodmer, born as he was into the tumult of the Napoleonic Europe and then the revolutions of 1830. Europe did not lack for displaced peoples seeking a better life somewhere else.

Awareness of the effects of Indian removal on the Native populations of the Midwest and Southeast likely further persuaded Maximilian of the urgency of his expedition. If he were to play the somewhat belated Humboldt, he would have to get on with the journey in good speed. In the bustling river city of Saint Louis, Maximilian and Bodmer, like Catlin, met William Clark. Clark possessed invaluable knowledge about travel on the Upper Plains and the peoples who lived there. Both Bodmer and his patron would also have benefited from a visit to Clark's famous Indian Museum, the first such institution west of the Mississippi, which contained ethnographic objects gathered by Clark and his associates in their dealings with Native nations throughout the first three decades of the nineteenth century. The collection appealed to a wide range of visitors to Saint Louis, including Catlin, the Marquis de Lafayette, the Sauk chief Keokuk, geographer Henry Schoolcraft, and Scottish adventurer Sir William Drummond Stewart, to name but a few of the more celebrated among them. Though the contents of the museum were dispersed after Clark's death in 1838, an extant inventory provides us with a sense of the type of materials Bodmer would have encountered. Just as Catlin had been inspired to collect artifacts during his travels that would accompany his multimedia exhibits, so too did Maximilian amass an impressive collection of material culture, much of which survives in the Ethnologisches Museum in Berlin and the Linden-Museum in Stuttgart.

Clark also provided the Europeans with practical advice concerning their route and the peoples they would encounter on the river. Maximilian initially considered an overland journey due west from Saint Louis, but Clark seems to have convinced them to take the river route northward, as he did with the Corps of Discovery some three decades before. Maximilian's party set off on the steamboat *Yellow Stone*—the same boat, owned by the American Fur Company, that had carried Catlin upriver a year earlier. It was an arduous journey of more than 2,000 miles of waterway. Maximilian and his companions would meet Native peoples from the Omaha, Sauk and Meskwaki (Fox), Ponca, Yankton Sioux, and other nations that bordered the river. These were the first Indigenous communities Bodmer encountered on that journey up the Missouri, and they provided the subjects for some of his earliest portraits.

PORTRAITS AND THE PEOPLE
We note that Bodmer's images are frequently in the bust portrait tradition and often in profile—as, for instance, in the portraits of Tukán-Hátón,

Psíhdjä-Sáhpa, and Wáh-Menítu (pls. 9–11). Evident early on is Bodmer's
attention to the ethnic phenotypes of skin color and bone structure, along
with his trademark attention to decorative detail. Art historians have frequently noted what has been termed Bodmer's "nobilitation" of his subjects.[10] Whether self-consciously done or not, his habit of portrayal seems
to raise the sitter to a classical ideal. The aquiline noses, high cheekbones, raised chins, and classical postures all seem to reveal Bodmer's
intent to add an air of natural aristocracy to his subjects. But we must
also consider that Bodmer was not trained as a portrait artist; he was
a talented painter of picturesque landscapes and an extremely skilled
draftsman. The young artist was likely drawn to physical features that
he noted as more common among some people—the shapes of noses or
eyes, the prevalence of high cheekbones—and these features he may have
unconsciously exaggerated or made formulaic. And considering the fact
that he was drawing in the field and not a studio, he likely developed
a somewhat systematic style of depicting the features his subjects, who
were numerous and presumably not available for long study. (Though in
some cases, important figures—like the Yankton Sioux chief Wahktăgeli
[Big Soldier; pl. 8]—were said to pose for Bodmer all day and then offer
Maximilian their regalia.) Just as the portraits
produced by Charles Willson Peale for his gallery of Revolutionary War heroes have similar
stylistic features that are more specific to Peale
than his subjects, Bodmer had a particular style
of depicting his Indigenous subjects, such as we
see in his depiction of Kiäsax (pl. 45). It does
not mean they are interchangeable, but arguably his attention was focused on ethnographic
detail. This is clear from his earliest portraits as
well as the works that followed.

Bodmer was just one in a long line of artists who had depicted the Indigenous peoples
of the Americas from the earliest arrivals of
Europeans through the subsequent encounters
throughout the hemisphere. These images vary
wildly in quality and accuracy, but they make
up an archive of the perceptions that Europeans
and settlers had of the original inhabitants.
Many of these interactions marked the first
time these peoples had encountered one
another, while others mark sustained contacts
built over the years. It may be worth revisit-
ing the watercolors of the sixteenth-century
English settler and self-taught illustrator and
mapmaker John White (c. 1540–c. 1593).[11]
White had sailed with Martin Frobisher in 1577
on an Arctic voyage in search of the Northwest
Passage, serving as a mapmaker and illustrator.
During that journey he would produce several
remarkable images of native Inuit people that

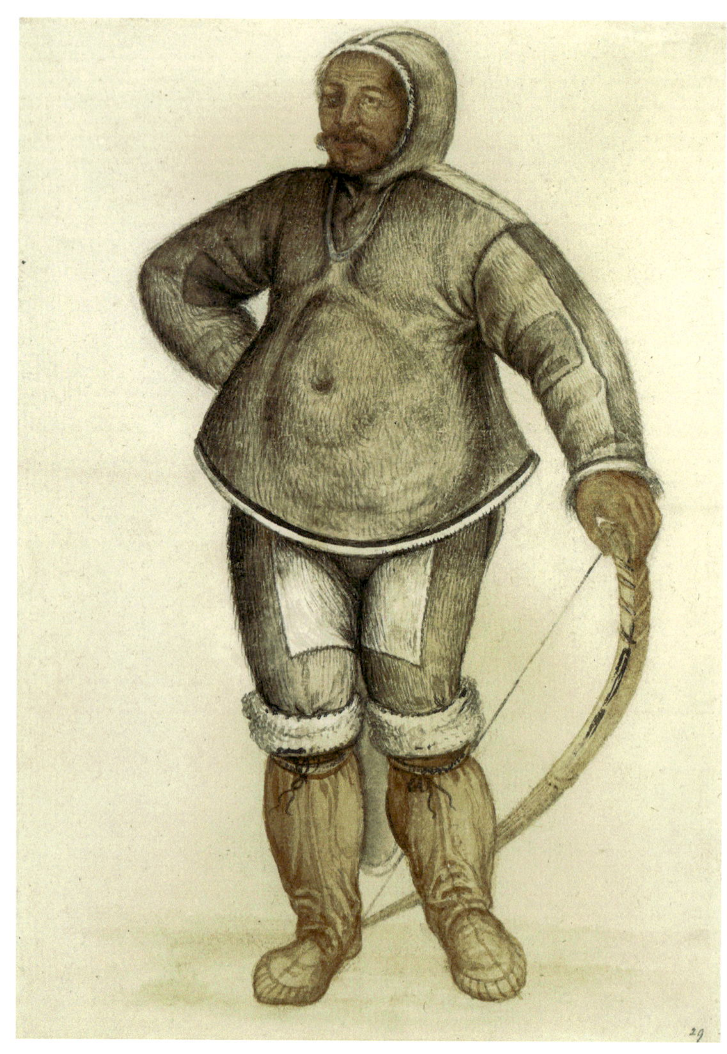

FIGURE 6　John White, *Kalicho, an Inuk
from Frobisher Bay*, 1585–93, pen, ink, and
watercolor over graphite and touched with
white (oxidized). The British Museum,
1906,0509.1.29.

the English explorers had taken hostage. Like Bodmer's, these images are less portraits in the traditional sense than they are records of Inuit culture. White's main figures appear against a blank background, freeing them from narrative elements (fig. 6). It would be anachronistic to call White's rendering Romantic, though well-worn traditions of depicting "wild men" were available to him. Yet White is recording evidence—in this case, evidence of the voyage actually having reached a foreign land inhabited by an unknown people. In the accompanying narrative of Frobisher's voyages, George Best noted the seemingly Asiatic features of the Inuit and surmised that the English expedition must have been close to Tartary, the term used by Europeans to denote areas of Asia unknown to them.[12]

White went on to record the Indigenous peoples inhabiting the lands that England hoped to colonize on what is now the North Carolina coast, at that point still referred to as Virginia in a generalized way, since no colony had yet been established. In 1585 England had installed a small settlement on Roanoke Island but was forced to abandon it temporarily; it was reestablished two years later only to be mysteriously abandoned in 1590, henceforward to be known as the Lost Colony. White's images of Native peoples on Roanoke Island became tremendously well known because twenty-three of the watercolors he produced there served as illustrations to Thomas Hariot's *A Brief and True Report of the New Found Land of Virginia* (1588). The etchings made from White's originals by the renowned Netherlandish de Bry family of engravers—then active in Strasbourg and later Frankfurt, the center of the European book trade—circulated widely throughout Europe. The de Bry versions of White's images took on a life of their own as they were then copied and reprinted without attribution for centuries, which exerted a profound influence on the notion of the Native American even in Bodmer's time. While White's originals appear to possess a degree of naive accuracy, the more polished engravings underwent a classicizing process by which Native bodies were transformed into an almost Greek ideal. This was a common phenomenon with representations of the inhabitants of the Americas, and it has been thoroughly analyzed by scholars such as Bernadette Bucher and Michael Gaudio.[13]

Although Bodmer oversaw the process through which his watercolors and graphite illustrations were recreated as aquatint lithographs, subtle changes still occurred (see Kristine K. Ronan's essay in this volume, pp. 195–209). In some cases, Bodmer placed an individual from a distant Native nation in a composition representing another group entirely, apparently because of his fondness for that particular portrayal, clearly violating Maximilian's desire for accuracy in documentation. In actuality it appears that aesthetics had a greater influence on Bodmer's choices in the printing process than is generally acknowledged. In addition, Bodmer made subtle changes in skin tone and facial contours in the process of copying the original watercolors, giving individual visages in the prints an even more dramatic or stylized aspect.

Still, the legacy of Bodmer's accuracy is restated by scholars as though it were axiomatic. Peter Bolz asserted that "Bodmer's originals today still rank as the epitome in the depiction of 'other' peoples in art and printmaking." Joan Troccoli described Bodmer's work as providing "irreplaceable images of the appearance and activities of the Indians on the Upper Missouri." And William Goetzmann remarked that Bodmer is best known for his "incredibly accurate and haunting pictures of the Indians who lived along the Missouri River."[14] Because they painted at the same time and in some of the same regions, Bodmer is frequently compared to the American artists George Catlin and Alfred Jacob Miller. Maximilian and Bodmer were shown a collection of Catlin's paintings while in Saint Louis, and they also met Miller and his Scottish patron, Sir William Drummond Stewart. Miller was classically trained, first under the American portrait artist Thomas Sully and then as a student at the Académie des Beaux Arts in Paris; Catlin, as noted, was largely self-taught. Whereas Catlin's best portraits of Native Americans have a disarmingly naive presence, Miller's works are far more stylized and show the influence of European Romanticism in both subject matter and technique— qualities that would have appealed to his flamboyant patron. If Bodmer had the draftsman-like qualities of Albrecht Dürer, then Miller's work was reminiscent of Eugène Delacroix, with his loose, undefined contours and dramatic use of light. Miller's portraits of Native individuals are indeed lovely, but they rarely command the praise for ethnographic accuracy that Bodmer and Catlin's images enjoy (fig. 7).

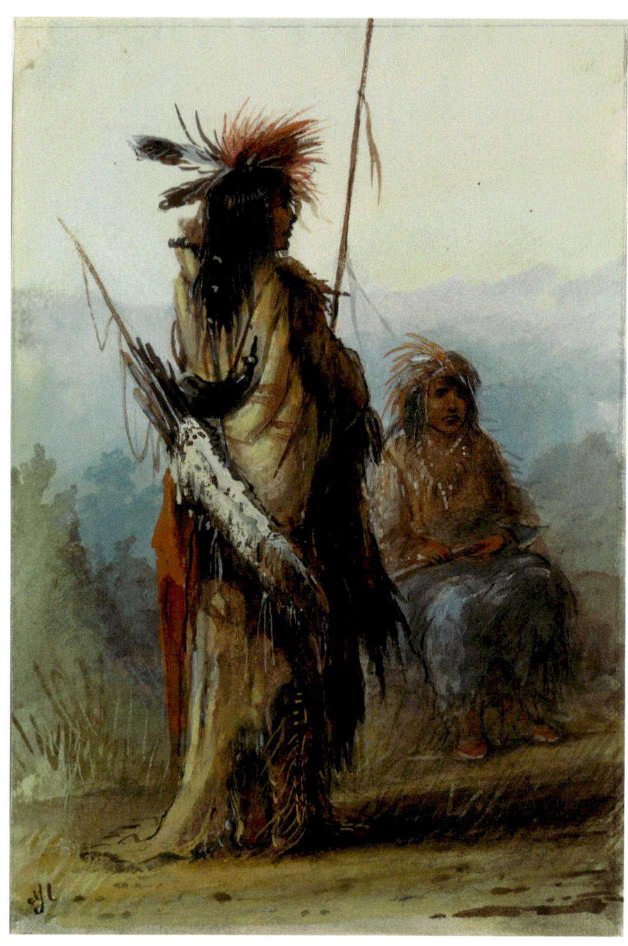

FIGURE 7 Alfred Jacob Miller, *Shoshones, Green River*, 1837 or later, watercolor on paper. Joslyn Art Museum, Museum Purchase, 1988.10.40.

Catlin, Bodmer, and Miller all painted from sketches and watercolors made in the field and based on their interactions with Native Americans. This was not always true of artists who made their names depicting the American frontier, as, for example, Carl Wimar and Arthur Fitzwilliam Tait. Both Wimar's *Attack on the Emigrant Train* (1856) and Tait's *The Prairie Hunter, "One Rubbed Out"* (1852) present settler and Indian conflicts dramatic enough to evoke Hollywood Westerns for modern viewers, though neither artist had direct experience of such conflicts. Wimar lived much of his short life in Saint Louis and painted his scene of an attack on a wagon train while studying at the Düsseldorf Academy; Tait never traveled west of Chicago.[15] Yet such images loom large in the cultural imagination of the United States because they reinscribe and justify the conflict between the settler and Indigenous worlds.

It might be more instructive to consider the depiction of Native Americans in the works of three lesser-known but not insignificant artists who contributed to the visual record of Native America in the early republic: the French amateur painter Baroness Anne-Marguerite Hyde de Neuville (1771–1849); James Otto Lewis (1799–1858), an illustrator for the US Indian Agency; and George Winter (1809–1876), a professional portrait artist in the Midwest. Though Bodmer would not have known their work, they are of interest precisely because they painted their Native subjects from life, and, more important, they recorded the quickly changing

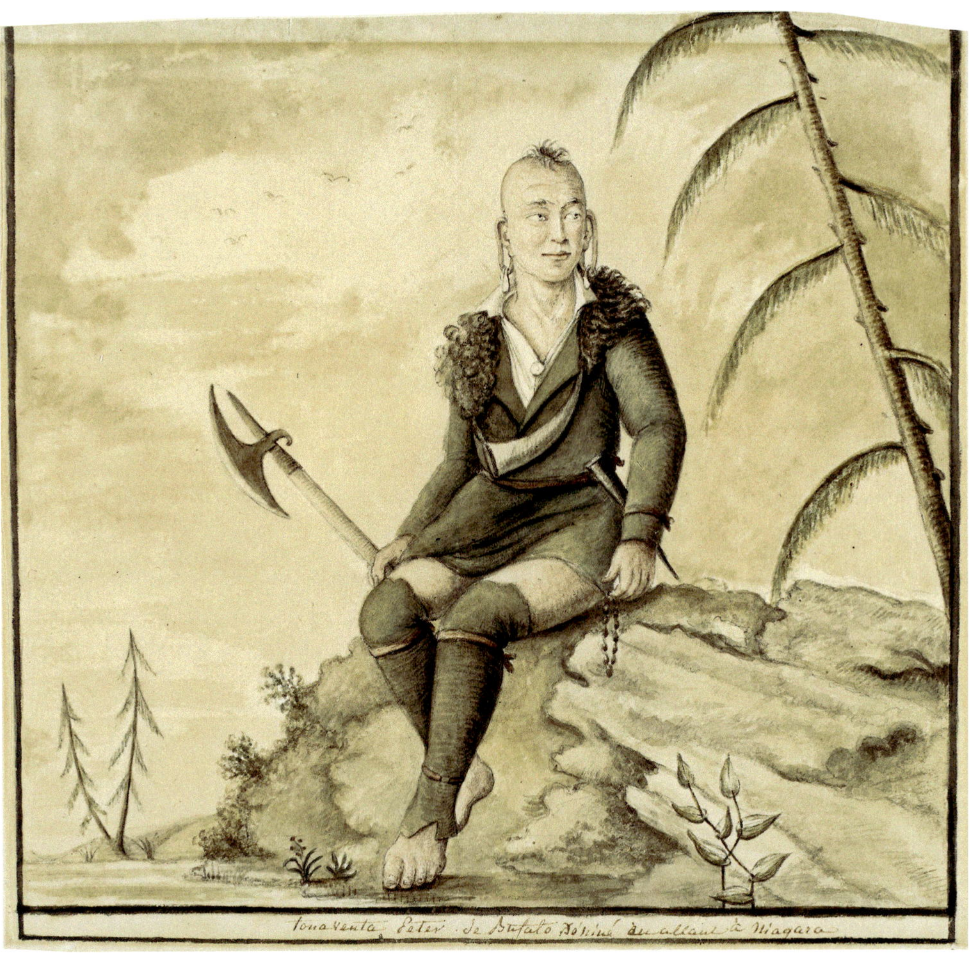

societies and cultures of Indigenous Americans. Like Bodmer, these artists sought to leave a visual record of the Native peoples and societies they knew firsthand. Given this fact, we might do well to consider Bodmer within the context of tradition and change that he had entered when he traveled in the United States. Just as he had witnessed the ongoing displacement and removal of Native peoples when he encountered Choctaw refugees in Louisiana, he would have traveled across regions where Indigenous cultures were in various states of change or upheaval. He and Maximilian did not travel through Haudenosaunee territory on the way west, but they did encounter members of that nation on their return in 1834. The Haudenosaunee had been adapting to European incursions into their lands for more than 200 years. Many had converted to Christianity and lived amidst settler communities on their small reservations.

These are the people that Hyde de Neuville—herself a refugee from Revolutionary France—had encountered and painted at the outset of the nineteenth century. In 1807 she traveled from Albany westward to Niagara Falls and the Buffalo Creek Reservation (dissolved in 1838; the site of the present-day city of Buffalo). Along the way she painted several Haudenosaunee men and women wearing the hybrid-style clothing that would then have been typical of Indigenous people across the traditional Haudenosaunee homelands. Hyde de Neuville's watercolors depict people from every stratum of society in a simple, immediate manner. Her interests stretched across class, race, and gender lines. The image of "Peter of Buffalo" probably portrays a Seneca leader from the nearby Tonawanda Reservation (fig. 8). He wears a hybrid outfit of traditional leggings and garters with a cloth shirt and a fur-trimmed European-style jacket. In his hands are Haudenosaunee symbols of his social position: a contemporary halberd tomahawk, demonstrating prowess in conflicts, and what may be wampum beads, a symbol of diplomacy. The baroness noted his artificially stretched earlobes, typical among men of his generation, and his bare feet. It was precisely this level of hybridity and acculturation that James Fenimore Cooper shied away from when depicting Native nations of the Northeast in his *Leatherstocking Tales* novels (1827–41), which he set as many as 100 years in the past. He liked his savages noble and preferably nonacculturated. The loss of a fixed definition of American Indians— i.e., a prescriptive definition—was threatening to some. Such anxieties brought about by the instability of ethnic categories are usually masked under the guise of nostalgia. In the opening tableau of Cooper's *The Pioneers* (1823), the Euro-American hero Natty Bumpo lamented the decline of the Delaware people even as he dismissed acculturated New England tribes, calling them "Yankee Indians, who, they say, be moving up from the sea-shore; and who belong to none of God's creaters, to my seeming; being, as it were, neither fish nor flesh—neither white-man, nor savage."[16] Luckily, Hyde de Neuville does not seem to have shared Cooper's disdain.

In the decades following the baroness's sojourn in the eastern states there was tremendous activity in the Indiana and Illinois Territories and the western Great Lakes region, as the US government sought to open these areas up to settlement by Easterners hungry for land. Conflict was inevitable, and with the defeat of Indigenous forces at Tippecanoe in 1811 and a series of major treaties—such as the one at Prairie du Chien in 1825—dramatic changes came to the Native nations of these areas. Among the various government agents and fur traders in those territories at the time was a young, self-taught artist named James Otto Lewis. He was born in Philadelphia in 1799 to German immigrant parents who had anglicized their surname from Luedwig to Lewis. At age sixteen he began his training as an engraver and would later travel west with a theater company as an actor and scene painter. Arriving in Saint Louis in 1820, he returned to his vocation of engraving and sold portraits of American figures popular on the frontier, such as Daniel Boone and Henry Clay. He soon left for Detroit to try to earn his living as a miniaturist and engraver, and it was there that Lewis Cass, the territorial governor of Michigan, commissioned him to do a portrait of the

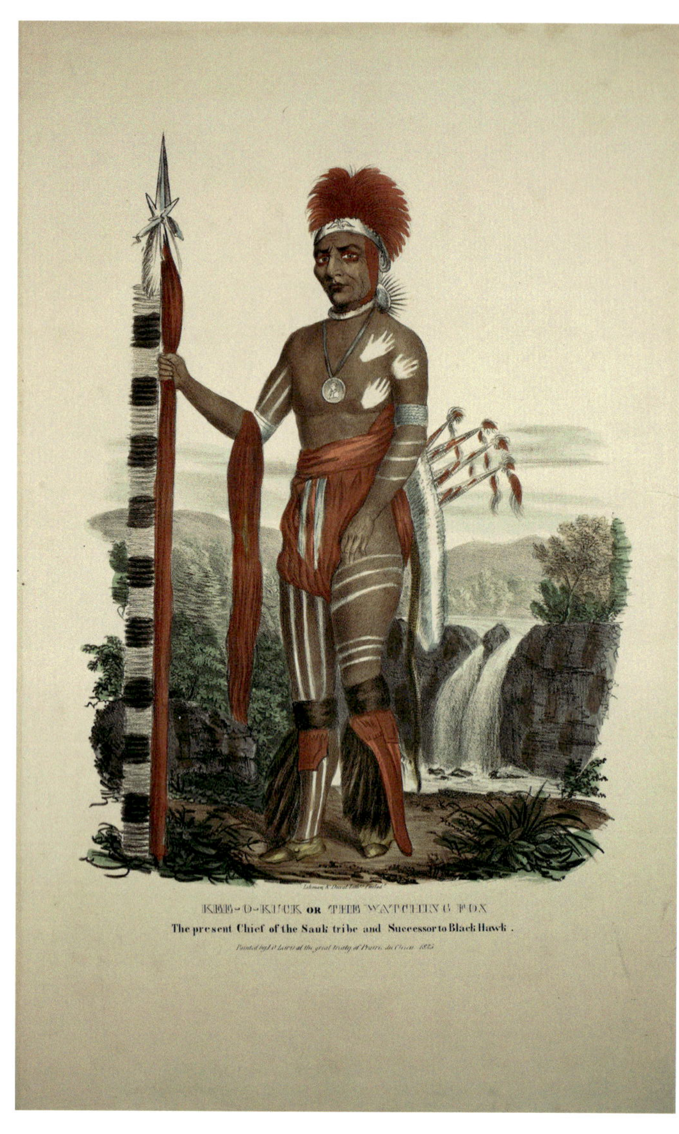

FIGURE 9   After James Otto Lewis, *Kee-o-kuk or the Watching Fox*, hand-colored lithograph from *The Aboriginal Port-Folio* (Philadelphia, 1835). Newberry Library, Edward E. Ayer Collection.

   FACES FROM THE INTERIOR

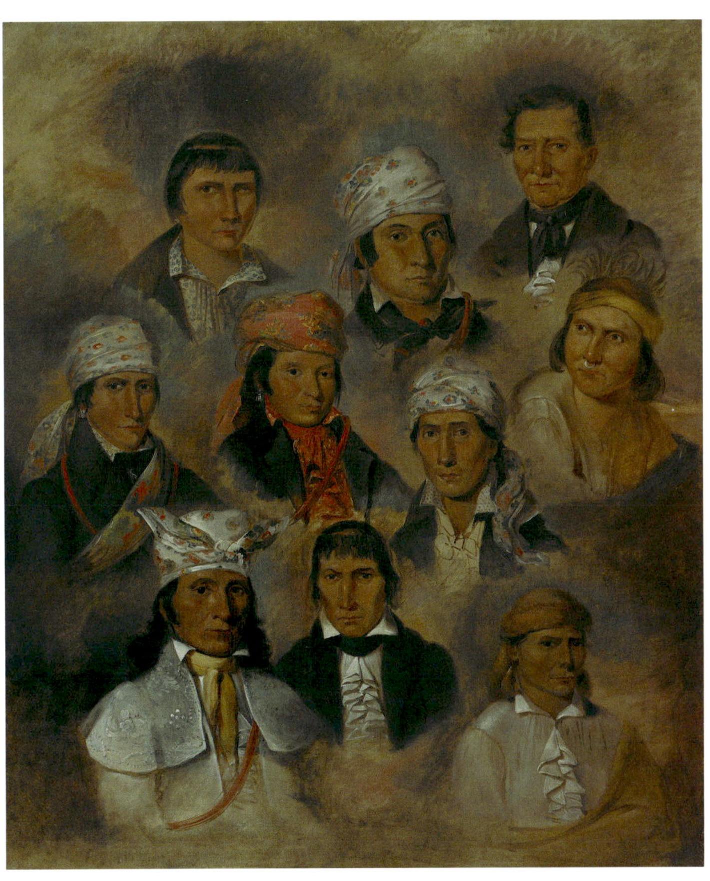

FIGURE 10 George Winter, *Ten Potawatomi Chiefs*, c. 1837, oil on canvas mounted on board. Crystal Bridges Museum of American Art, 2005.22.

Shawnee prophet Tenskwatawa. Thereafter Cass included Lewis in treaty councils as a maker of visual records, including the famous summit at Prairie du Chien.

While attending those negotiations, Lewis produced fifty portraits of Native leaders in the space of five days. His work became known to Thomas McKenney, then beginning his work on *History of the Indian Tribes of North America*, and he purchased some of Lewis's portraits to include in the publication. During the time Bodmer was active on the Upper Missouri, Lewis had returned to Philadelphia in hopes of capitalizing on his portraits of Native leaders. There he soon became aware of the various Indian galleries against which he would be competing. McKenney was already having lithographic copies of Lewis's earlier works made for *History of the Indian Tribes of North America*, but it had yet to appear. Perhaps hoping to scoop McKenney and Hall, Lewis rushed *The Aboriginal Port-Folio* into print in 1835. Containing seventy-two hand-colored prints, the portfolio is considered a rare and valuable work both from the perspective of the history of the book in America and the history of US expansion, but it is rarely praised for its artistic accomplishment. Compared with the work of more renowned painters of Indian galleries, Lewis's figures seem rough and almost cartoonish (fig. 9). Though *The Aboriginal Port-Folio* does contain some invaluable historic and ethnographic information, it pales in comparison with Bodmer's artistic project.

Finally, students of this dynamically shifting period across Native American cultures should not forget the work of George Winter, born in England the same year as Bodmer. Winter in 1830 emigrated to the United States, where he would become one of the first artists of note living in Indiana and chronicling the lives of the Potawatomi and Miami peoples then being forced from their homelands. Winter's sensitive depictions of daily life in these communities are unsurpassed as images chronicling Indigenous life in Indiana during the period of removal. His attention to the details of clothing and other aspects of material culture show him to have been an astute observer of what he surely realized was a world-changing era for thousands of Native peoples throughout the United States. In addition to scenes of quotidian life, Winter portrayed individuals such as Frances Slocum, a white woman who as a child in 1778 was captured by Indians during frontier hostilities and subsequently assimilated into the Miami community. Winter painted several multi-portrait canvases depicting the faces of up to ten community leaders and chiefs, works that are both aesthetically appealing and historically valuable (fig. 10). His works along with those of Hyde de Neuville and Lewis, when combined as a corpus of visual history, help us to appreciate the momentous changes occurring in the lives of Indigenous peoples east of the Mississippi at the very time Bodmer and Catlin were capturing images of a world on the verge of an oncoming invasion.[17]

These artists were all active in the first decades of nineteenth century. In the United States this period was one of cataclysmic change for Native peoples. The Louisiana Purchase had opened millions of square miles of the lands occupied by Native nations. The drive toward Indian removal in the East meant the displacement of thousands of Native peoples and communities that had been resisting the onslaught of settler invasion for centuries. Trade, missionaries, and dislocation all conspired to forever change Native American cultures. Any anthropologist can attest to the fact that social change is an inevitable aspect of human life, and yet Native America was subject to a desire, largely by the majority culture of non-Natives, that Indigenous cultures remain static. That notion informs countless commentaries on the so-called "vanishing race." When James Hall wrote the text for *History of the Indian Tribes of North America,* he was sure that Sagoyewatha was the last of the Seneca—not because he actually was, for Hall noted there were numerous Seneca Indians at the time, but because Sagoyewatha was, in Hall's estimation, the last *authentic* Seneca.

This is a pernicious and ongoing problem for Indigenous peoples. If they adapt to the ever-changing conditions around them, they are seen as losing their cultural identity. No one presumes French or English or German people must live in the past, dress a certain way, avoid certain technologies, etc., in order to be regarded as authentic members of their culture. But for Native Americans, whose *genuine culture* has been defined by others, failure to remain united with that past is akin to failing to be the authentic representatives of themselves. There is a marked difference between assimilation and acculturation, but the majority public pays it little attention. If assimilation is a one-way street by which one culture takes on the traits of another, dominant culture, thus eventually losing its identity, then acculturation is a two-way street by which cultures borrow from each other and share what is desirable. Acculturation usually happens organically, from proximity. The dramatically shifting power structures, religious cultures, and technologies that marked the interaction between Indigenous peoples and settlers in the Americas meant that Native peoples had to adapt in order to survive— something they had always done when environmental and political forces demanded it. Still, some Euro-Americans were more content to define Native people as existing in a sort of original state and wishing them to remain in it, even if it meant their eventual extinction. The persistence of this demand for cultural stasis is reflected in a 1916 poem titled "Changing Is Not Vanishing" by the Yavapai medical doctor Carlos Montezuma, which states: "The feathers, paint and moccasin may vanish, but the Indians,—never!"

It is likely this romantic desire for the *authentic* Indian that explains the continued claim by Bodmer's admirers that we are indeed seeing the real thing when we look at one of his images. But the world Bodmer encountered along the Upper Missouri in 1833 was not pristine. European traders had been in contact with Native communities at least since the mid-eighteenth century. Nor was it ever static before that. Trade had long marked Indigenous lifeways, and adaptation to new resources had already radically changed Plains culture, perhaps nothing more than the introduction and adoption of the horse. Most of us would find it hard to imagine Plains cultures before the horse, but such adaptations are typical of all dynamic societies. Other telltale signs of increased contact with settlers abound: we see warriors depicted with guns, metal-pipe tomahawks produced by settlers or imported from Europe, peace medals from US delegations to the West and, in some cases, Indigenous delegations to Washington, DC. These were not untouched Indigenous societies, but they still lived largely traditional lives in the manner of their ancestors. And they were quite different from the Choctaw refugees Bodmer encountered in New Orleans and Natchez or the much more acculturated Haudenosaunee Maximilian and his party would meet on their return travels through New York. The nations of the Upper Missouri had sporadic contact with fur trappers, US soldiers stationed in forts across the region, and the traders who accompanied them; the traces of those contacts are recorded in the portraits produced by Bodmer. The vestiges of that intercultural contact are subtle in Bodmer's portraits because in many cases they have been thoroughly integrated into Native life and thus may go unnoticed by casual viewers. This in turn contributes to the belief in Bodmer's portraits as representing a level of authenticity, which wrongly presumes minimal influences from foreign cultures.

Bodmer's portraits may betray his habit of ennobling Native phenotypes, but the images as a whole depict so much more than presumably accurate images of individual facial features. As an illustrator and reporter, Bodmer showed us who these figures were within their respective societies. In some cases, the warriors' regalia is likely every bit as specifically meaningful as a modern military uniform with its stripes and medals and oak-leaf clusters or stars. Similarly, facial paint and hairstyles and headdresses are no less important to a subject's identity than their nose. One imagines Bodmer's subjects admiring his skills as a draftsman. Knowing how much labor and attention went into their material arts, the Native sitters must have been extremely satisfied to see them rendered so exactly and carefully.

Maximilian's prose contains a wealth of information that can help us understand the circumstances around many of Bodmer's images, and the artist's attention to minutiae has made it possible for later ethnologists and anthropologists to elucidate some details for contemporary viewers. For example, if we look at the picture of the Omaha boy with the shaved head (pl. 4), we might assume that curious tonsorial choice was a whim of his parents or that its significance is now lost. But scholars have explained that the Omahas were organized into ten bands, or *gentes*, each with specific social duties. Boys between the ages of three and eight had their head shaved in particular patterns distinguishing which *gente* they belonged to. Boys were expected to identify the unique obligations of each kinship group at a young age and to carry this knowledge into adulthood.[18] Such details in Bodmer's portraits frequently make researching their meanings remarkably satisfying.

Bodmer's remarkable attention to the details of Indigenous material culture suggests a genuine appreciation for the skill and artistry that went into the elaborate quillwork and accoutrements associated with Native leaders and ritual performances. While this admiration is clearest in images of great warriors and chiefs, it extends as well to women—though, admittedly, examples of these are many fewer in number. As mentioned above, we cannot know if that imbalance is a result of Maximilian's directions or a reflection of gender mores within a given Indigenous society. In one watercolor we see a woman identified as a "Lakota Sioux," or more properly an Oglala Lakota, wearing a buffalo robe that has been beautifully decorated in a traditional style (pl. 12). This highly abstract geometric form of decoration, one associated with female artists, has come to be known as a box-and-border design.[19] In many Plains cultures a division in the visual arts exists between figurative designs produced by men and abstract geometrical designs created by women. In the case of this particular buffalo robe, possibly decorated by the woman depicted wearing it, we have the actual material artifact in Maximilian's collection, now housed in the Linden-Museum Stuttgart (fig. 11). We must take many depictions of Native clothing on faith; we may find other garments of the same type from the same ethnic group, but rarely do we have access to the same piece represented by an artist. In this case, we are allowed to compare the actual artifact with its representation and assess the accuracy of

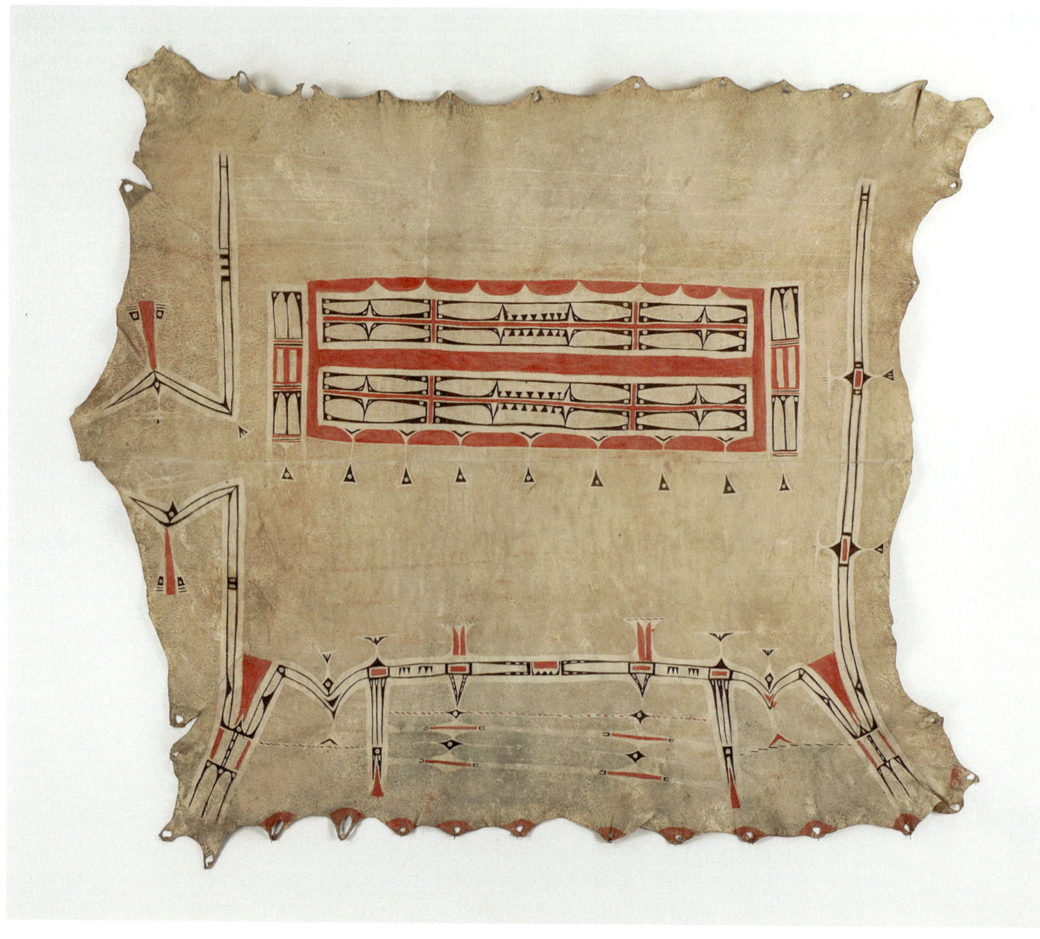

FIGURE 11 Lakota artist, Buffalo Robe, c. 1830, native-tanned leather, pigment. Linden-Museum, State Museum of Ethnology, Collection Prince Maximilian zu Wied, 36102.

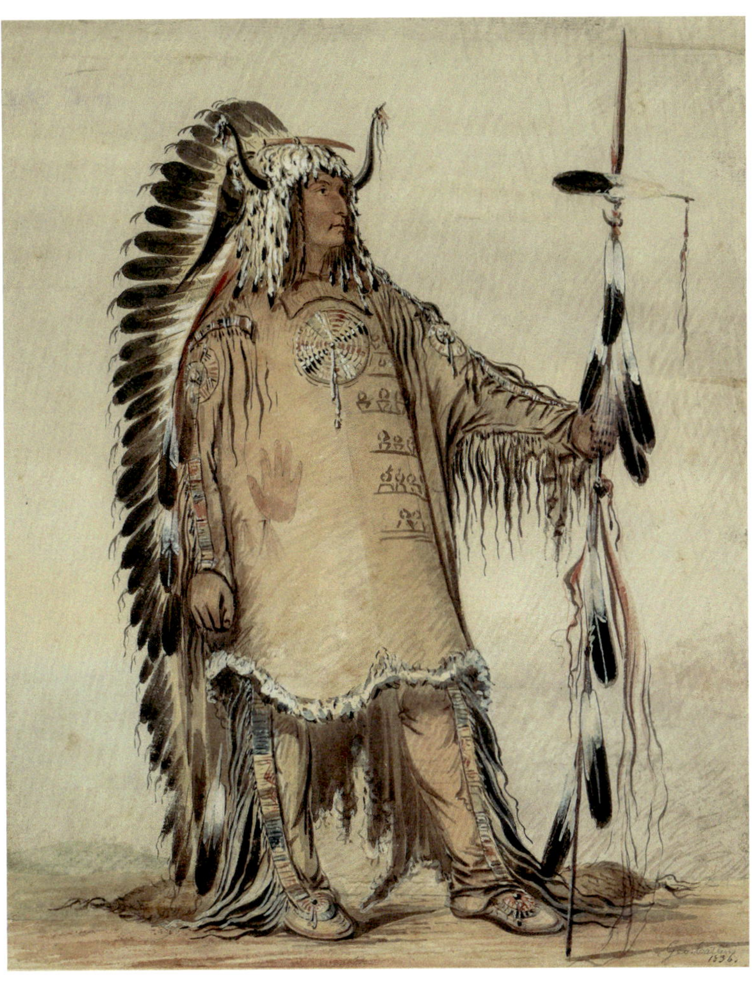

FIGURE 12   George Catlin, *Mah-to-toh-pah, the Four Bears*, 1856, watercolor. Gilcrease Museum, Gift of the Thomas Gilcrease Foundation, 1955, 02.1543.

Bodmer's depiction, and from this we get a sense of how invaluable Bodmer's legacy is.

Other comparisons are also possible. Because both Catlin and Bodmer visited some of the same communities within a year of one another, they each painted some of the same individuals. One of these was the Mandan chief Mató-Tópe (Four Bears), a man greatly admired by his own people and the white officers of nearby Fort Clark (fig. 12; pls. 22 and 23). One imagines he was a commanding figure, not only from the "Apollo of the Belvedere"–type pose both artists had him assume, but also from the vivid descriptions both Catlin and Maximilian left of their interactions with him and his position as well as Mató-Tópe's own accounts of his deeds as a warrior. Bodmer created two very different images of the Mandan chief, and he also reproduced Mató-Tópe's own visual representation in pictographic form as painted on a Buffalo hide (fig. 13). Here again Bodmer's attention to visual and material culture provides us with another facet of Mandan culture. This is especially poignant given that fact that in 1837 small-pox pathogens would be passed from white traders in the region to the Mandan and would kill approximately ninety percent of that nation, including Mató-Tópe. Both Catlin and Bodmer were devastated to learn of this news.

We need not see Bodmer's paintings merely through the lens of nostalgia, as images of a world now changed forever. All pasts are lost to us at some level, but these images make up part of the visual legacy of those Native nations, just as their oral traditions provide their history. There are numerous ways of valuing Bodmer's images: historically, ethnographically, aesthetically, and, for some Native peoples, on a deeply personal and cultural level. Bodmer's exacting eye for detail and his skills as a draftsman were not compromised by his aesthetic sensibilities. His landscapes engage the picturesque even as they provide the viewer with consistently accurate depictions of specific topographical features and environments. There can be no question that Bodmer sometimes exaggerated topographical elements in favor of a picturesque presentation—a nobilitation of the landscape, as it were, to convey the drama of this exotic environment to Maximilian's readers. Still the overall accuracy of Bodmer's depictions is compelling enough that the photographer Robert Lindholm and the anthropologist W. Raymond Wood embarked on a journey using rephotography as a tool to understand aspects of Bodmer's journey and his landscape art.[20] Their study was published by the University of Oklahoma Press in 2013, not as a means of confirming

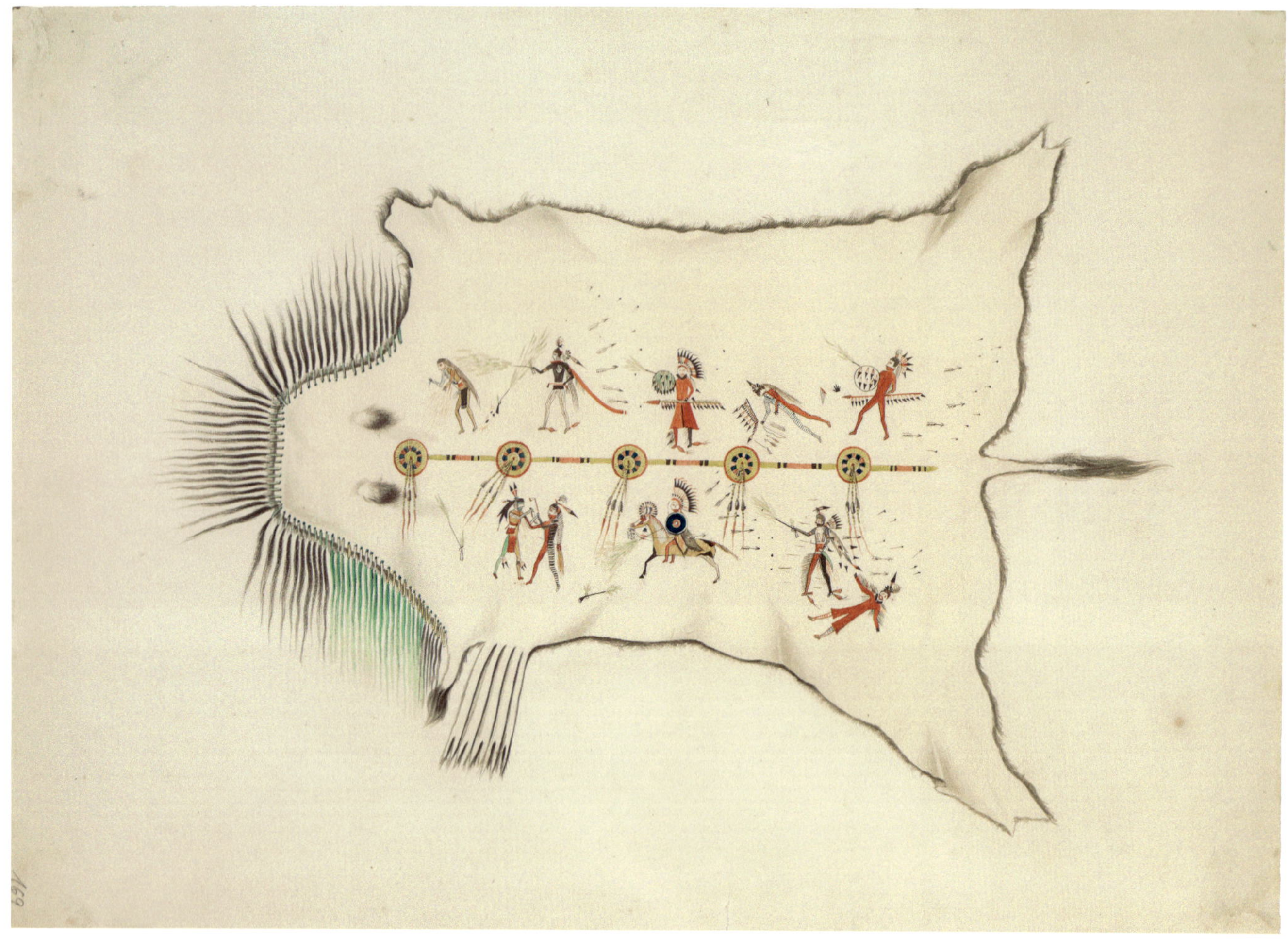

or critiquing Bodmer's depictions, but in an attempt to discover changes in the landscape as well as areas that remained seemingly untouched. Readers would likely note places where Bodmer chose to emphasize certain features of the landscape and possibly exaggerate their dimensions, but part of the point of this exercise is to encourage us to consider Bodmer's artistic sensibilities and not merely his draftsmanship. We should do the same with his portraits. Whereas some have erroneously held them up as though they represented a lost world preserved in amber, we know that they offer instead a view of a world already on the cusp of calamitous change. Subtle details in the depiction of material culture show the dynamic cultural interactions that had been occurring between Indigenous and settler societies in those regions since the eighteenth century. The communities visited by Bodmer were for the most part living according to their traditional lifeways and were still largely autonomous. This would change soon and drastically with the advent of crippling epidemics, US military incursions, and the wholesale influx of the settler world into the Upper Midwest. Bodmer presented us with compelling portraits that continue to engage members of the descendant communities, students of the art of the American West, and those seeing Bodmer's images for the first time.

NOTES

1. For biographical details of Bodmer's life, see William Orr, "Karl Bodmer: The Artist's Life," in *Karl Bodmer's America* by William H. Goetzmann, David C. Hunt, Marsha V. Gallagher, and William J. Orr (Omaha: Joslyn Art Museum; Lincoln: University of Nebraska Press, 1984), 449–76. See also William H. Goetzmann and William N. Goetzmann, *The West of the Imagination* (New York: Norton, 1986), 44–57; and Joseph C. Porter, "The Eyes of Strangers: 'Fact' and Art on the Ethnographic Frontier, 1832–1834," in *Karl Bodmer's Studio Art: The Newberry Library Bodmer Collection* by W. Raymond Wood, Joseph C. Porter, and David C. Hunt (Urbana: University of Illinois Press, 2002), 25–98.

2. Maximilian of Wied, *Reise in das innere Nord-America in den Jahren 1832 bis 1834* (Koblenz: J. Hölscher, 1839–41), 1:10.

3. See Brain W. Dippie, *Catlin and His Contemporaries: The Politics of Patronage* (Lincoln: University of Nebraska Press, 1990).

4. Herman J. Viola, *The Indian Legacy of Charles Bird King* (Washington, DC: Smithsonian Institution Press, 1976), 15.

5. Inman was commissioned by McKenney to copy the original portraits by King after 1830, when McKenney was dismissed by President Jackson from his position as superintendent of Indian affairs. See Viola, *The Indian Legacy of Charles Bird King*.

6. George Catlin, *Illustrations of the Manners, Customs, and Condition of the North American Indians* (London: Chatto and Windus, 1876), 1:16.

7. Andrew Jackson, "First Annual Message" (December 8, 1829), in *A Compilation of Messages and Papers of the Presidents, 1789–1902*, ed. James D. Richardson (New York: Bureau of National Literature and Art, 1904), 2:458.

8. Thomas McKenney and James Hall, *The History of the Indian Tribes of North America* (Philadelphia: Greenough, 1838), 1:1.

9. See Renato Rosaldo, "Imperialist Nostalgia," in "Memory and Counter-Memory," special issue, *Representations* 26 (Spring 1989): 107–22.

10. Hartwig Isernhagen, "Bodmer—Wied—America: A Journey of Exploration," in *Karl Bodmer: A Swiss Artist in America, 1809–1893*, ed. Hartwig Isernhagen (Zurich: Scheidegger & Spiess; Nordamerika Native Museum, 2009), 18–63.

11. Kim Sloan, *A New World: England's First View of America* (Chapel Hill: University of North Carolina Press, 2007).

12. William C. Sturtevant, "The Sources for European Imagery of Native Americans," in *New World of Wonders: European Images of the Americas, 1492–1700*, ed. Rachel Doggett (Washington, DC: Folger Shakespeare Library), 25–33; and George Best, *The Three Voyages of Martin Frobisher* (London: Hakluyt Society, 1867), 281.

13. See Bernadette Bucher, *Icon and Conquest: A Structural Analysis of the Illustrations of de Bry's "Great Voyages"* (Chicago: University of Chicago Press, 1981); and Michael Gaudio, *Engraving the Savage: The New World and Techniques of Civilization* (Minneapolis and London: University of Minnesota Press, 2008).

14. Peter Bolz, "Karl Bodmer, Heinrich Rudolf Schinz and the Changing Image of the American Indian in Europe," in Isernhagen, *Bodmer: Swiss Artist in America*, 66; Joan Carpenter Troccoli, *Painters and the American West: The Anschutz Collection* (New Haven, CT: Yale University Press, 2000), 1:41; Goetzmann and Goetzmann, *The West of the Imagination*, 47.

15. See Julie Schimmel, "Inventing 'The Indian,'" *The West as America: Reinterpreting Images of the Frontier*, ed. William H. Truettner (Washington, DC: Smithsonian Institution Press, 1991), 165–67.

16. James Fenimore Cooper, *The Pioneers*, (1823; New York: Putnam, 1853), 500.

17. See James Otto Lewis, *The Aboriginal Port-Folio: A Collection of Portraits of the Most Celebrated Chiefs of the North American Indians* (Philadelphia: J. O. Lewis, 1835); Roberta J. M. Olson, *Artist in Exile: The Visual Diary of Baroness Hyde de Neuville* (New York: New-York Historical Society, 2019); and Sarah E. Cooke and Rachel B. Ramadhyani, *Indians and the Changing Frontier: The Art of George Winter* (Lafayette, IN: Tippecanoe County Historical Society, 1993).

18. See David C. Hunt and Marsha V. Gallagher, "Annotations," in Goetzmann et al., *Karl Bodmer's America*, 162.

19. On the role of gender in Plains art, see Janet Catherine Berlo and Ruth B. Phillips, *Native North American Art*, 2nd ed. (Oxford: Oxford University Press, 2014), 113–24. On the "box-and-border" design, see Richard Conn, *Circles of the World: The Traditional Art of the Plains Indians* (Denver: Denver Art Museum, 1982), 137.

20. See Robert Lindholm and W. Raymond Wood, *Karl Bodmer's America Revisited: Landscape Views across Time* (Norman: University of Oklahoma Press, 2013).

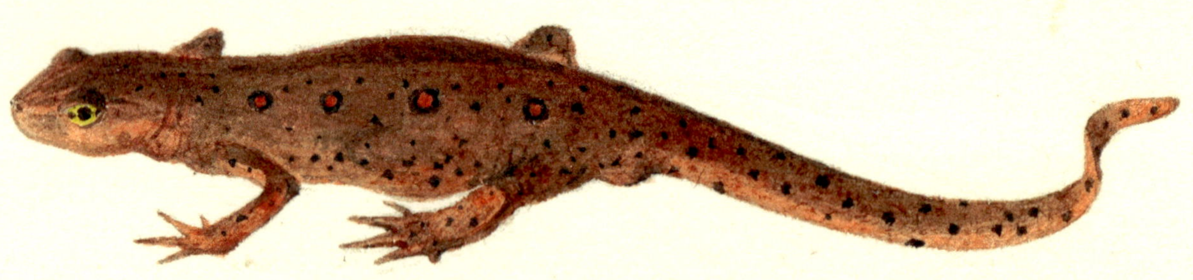

NO DETAIL TOO SMALL

KARL BODMER'S PORTRAITS AND ANTHROPOLOGICAL ILLUSTRATION

Lisa Strong

IN HIS JOURNAL, PRINCE MAXIMILIAN OF WIED DESCRIBED A cool June morning in 1834 outside Fort Clark in present-day North Dakota during which he and Karl Bodmer packed natural history specimens for shipment to Europe. They were interrupted in their work by a party of Sioux people, which they followed to a nearby encampment. There Bodmer found an intriguing subject for a portrait, a young woman named Chan-Chä-Uiá-Te-Üinn (pl. 12).[1] As with almost all of his North American portraits, the artist painted her standing, with her face in full profile, and, notably, in minute detail. We can easily see her clothing and accoutrements, but more significantly, we can count the round blue and white beads that compose her earrings and even discern their metal clasp. Strands of hair painted with vermilion are worked into her braids, and individuated silver conical tinkler bells line the hem of her dress. Bodmer's portraits are exceptional for their description of different textures: Chan-Chä-Uiá-Te-Üinn's hair is smooth; her beads, shiny; and her summer-weight robe, soft and supple. The crisp rendering of the blocks of red, white, and black decorating her robe were clear enough for anthropologist John Ewers to identify a border-and-box pattern more than 100 years later.[2]

Bodmer's careful rendering of her robe, however admirable, raises an interesting question about his project as a whole. Maximilian's expedition was primarily scientific in aim. In addition to taking notes, collecting and preserving plant and animal specimens, and commissioning Bodmer's watercolors and drawings as part of his scientific research, Maximilian also amassed a collection of Native American material culture, including clothing, paraphernalia, household goods, tools, and weapons to support his findings.[3] His collection contained at least two other painted hide robes with a border-and-box pattern from the Sioux people, and he succeeded in purchasing Chan-Chä-Uiá-Te-Üinn's robe the following day.[4] Bodmer, who had been assisting Maximilian in packing his collections, was surely aware of this fact. If this robe or similar ones were making the return journey to Europe with them, why then did he make

Karl Bodmer, *Salamander*, 1852 (detail of fig. 6).

the considerable effort in the difficult medium of watercolor to render Chan-Chä-Uiá-Te-Üinn's robe with such precision?[5] Certainly, there was the danger of losing materials: seven crates of animal specimens and ethnographic material were lost when the steamship *Assiniboine* sank in July 1835, an event Maximilian lamented in his published account of his journey, *Reise in das innere Nord-America in den Jahren 1832 bis 1834* (*Travels in the Interior of North America, 1832–34*).[6] The conventions of botanical and zoological research also called for drawing each specimen in the field as well as collecting it. Yet, as we will see, the scientific illustrations of Bodmer's peers are not characterized by a comparable level of precision.

Almost without exception, historians of Bodmer's work praise its careful detail. "So skillful and detailed is Bodmer's style, and so ethnographically accurate," wrote William Truettner, "that each ingredient . . . comes alive even under casual scrutiny."[7] Ron Tyler called Bodmer's portraits of the Sauk man Massica and the Meskwaki man Wakussáse "stunningly detailed," and William Goetzmann noted that details such as individual beads were so finely rendered as to be lost in poor-quality reproductions.[8] However, after praising his detail, historians tend to see past it, focusing instead on the people depicted. Bodmer's high level of detail should not be taken for granted, however, because it reveals much about the purpose and meaning of his portraits. Although these same historians invariably allude to the scientific aims of Maximilian's trip, they have not focused on how Bodmer's artworks actually advanced the prince's scientific research.

On its surface, detail is a necessary tool of scientific illustration, allowing artists and scientists to record what they see as critical botanical, zoological, or anthropological data, such as physical features or coloring. The sharply rendered bodies and clothing in Bodmer's paintings of Native Americans permitted careful examination and yielded clues to intercultural contact and genealogical relationships between his subjects. Yet detail is only one means and measure of accuracy in painting.

Other European and American expeditionary artists and scientists who painted Indigenous people around the same time—such as George Catlin, Louis Auguste de Sainson (1800–1848), and even Maximilian himself, who sketched the Botocudo people he encountered in Brazil in 1815–17 for an earlier publication (fig. 1)— did not employ the level of detail that Bodmer did, nor is it clear from the evidence discussed below that they felt it necessary. Bodmer himself later conceded that a lack of experience had led him to "copy with unusual eagerness and attention every aspect realistically and this is also why all my portraits and sketches have been made in an almost ridiculously fussy manner, but also with as much authenticity and truth."[9] His retrospective characterization of his work as "almost ridiculously

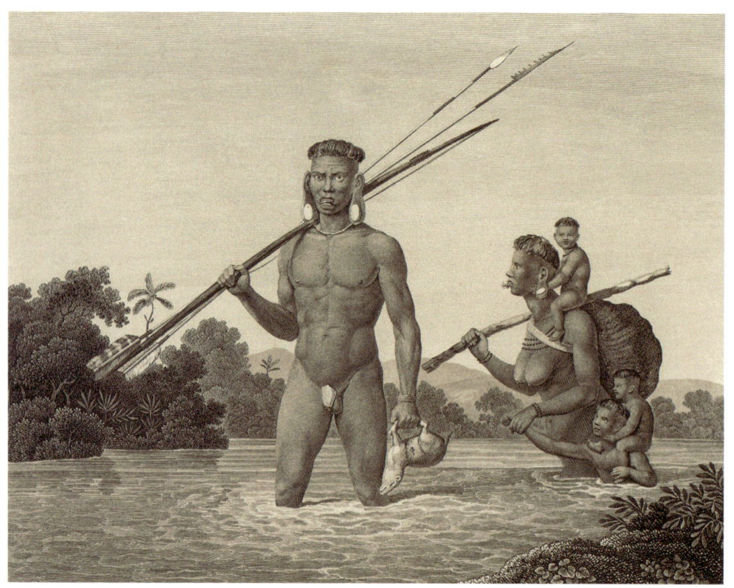

FIGURE 1 After Maximilian of Wied, *Eine Familie der Botocudos auf der Reise*, engraving from *Reise nach Brasilien in den Jahren 1815 bis 1817* (Frankfurt, H. L. Brönner, 1820–21). DeGolyer Library, Southern Methodist University.

     FACES FROM THE INTERIOR

fussy" suggests that he himself later viewed his detail to be in excess of what was required either artistically or scientifically.

While Bodmer's relative inexperience with scientific illustration may have been a factor in his representational choices, subtle shifts in what constituted truth and objectivity in scientific illustrations profoundly shaped Bodmer's approach. To the extent that the artist appeared to (and claimed to) have "copied" the visual information before him, he participated in an important historical shift within the sciences from an ideal of individual interpretation to that of disinterested objectivity. While Bodmer—who was comfortable swapping the names ascribed to his portraits or pairing unrelated sitters in a single image (the watercolor of Chan-Chä-Uiá-Te-Üinn includes an unrelated sketch of a Blackfoot girl he made later that year)—may not have claimed complete accuracy, he did argue that his scrupulous attention to detail gave his images visual "authenticity and truth."[10] Credibility was a particularly important issue in light of the work of his chief rival, George Catlin, whose depictions of Plains people were widely mistrusted and against whose work Bodmer's would be judged. Bodmer's stance as a passive and disinterested copyist was thus key to his claims of "authenticity and truth." Likewise, the stillness of Bodmer's sitters, which was required to render such exacting detail, foreclosed any narrative elements in the paintings. This absence of narrative implied both personal and cultural stasis among Bodmer's sitters, a feature reinforced by other aspects of the portraits. For example, Euro-American garb, commodities, and implements appear in Bodmer's sketches, but they are otherwise devoid of references to broader changes in culture, etiquette, foodways, or other behaviors as a result of contact with Europeans and Americans.[11] Likewise the specter of smallpox—which Maximilian mentioned in several places in his text and which would, in fact, kill most of Bodmer's sitters before his atlas of engravings went to print—is not directly alluded to in any of the paintings.[12] Instead, Bodmer's sketches of Indigenous people are detailed, legible, and static, presenting an image of timelessness that reinforced their credibility and value as anthropological evidence.

DOCUMENTING NORTH AMERICA

Bodmer's images of Native Americans are generally discussed as portraits. However, they are first and foremost scientific—more specifically, anthropological—illustrations. In the fullest sense, portraits are images "in which the artist is engaged with the personality of his sitter and is preoccupied with his or her characterization *as an individual* [emphasis mine]."[13] Until the late eighteenth century, scientific illustrations of plants or animals were by definition aimed at depicting that which was generally true or characteristic across multiple specimens, either by showing an ideal composite of physical traits or an individual item with features representative of the whole species. However, anthropology and anthropological illustration were relatively new disciplines in the nineteenth century, and their visual idioms had yet to be codified. Bodmer's work can thus be seen as an attempt to formulate a model of anthropological illustration that drew on earlier conventions for compiling visual data about plants and animals. This is not to say that Bodmer or his patron regarded Indigenous people as akin to plants or animals; rather, it is to suggest that one aspect of Maximilian's research, which was founded in a belief in an orderly system of Linnaean classification, relied on the same kind of visual evidence that botanical or zoological research did. The extent to which Maximilian's scientific interests shaped Bodmer's practice is reflected in Bodmer's portraits. Before discussing how the portraits reflected the scientific aims of the expedition, it is important to lay out what those aims were and how Bodmer's artistry intersected with them.

Maximilian's stated goal in undertaking his expedition to North America was to fill a void in the literature on the natural history of the continent. Rather than focusing on the populous and relatively well-documented area east of the Mississippi, however, Maximilian focused on its northwestern regions: "the rude primitive character of the natural face of North America, and its aboriginal population."[14] Maximilian's research encompassed the totality of the environment, including flora and fauna, but the emphasis on Indigenous peoples in his journal and published text suggest it was the latter that interested him the most.[15] Likewise, for Bodmer, roughly a third of the more than 380 extant sketches from their journey are Native American subjects, as are more than half of the eighty-one prints in the atlas.

Maximilian's study of the Indigenous people of North America was part of a larger project by early German anthropologists to document the physical and cultural variations among humans worldwide. His ideas about humankind were formed at the University of Göttingen under Johann Friedrich Blumenbach. Historians of anthropology consider Blumenbach to be the progenitor of what we today call physical anthropology, but he was also keenly interested in the still more recent field of ethnography, the study of customs or cultures.[16] As the keeper of the Göttingen museum's collection of ethnographic materials, which included objects collected from Captain James Cook's voyages to the Pacific (1768–71; 1772–75; 1776–80), Blumenbach had ample opportunity to compare cultural adaptations to different environments through material culture.[17] These studies resulted in important contributions to the central debate for early anthropologists—namely, whether humans were all one species (the monogenist view) or multiple ones (the polygenist view). On the basis of comparative physiognomy and anatomy of crania, together with an understanding of varying cultural practices, Blumenbach concluded that humans were one species, divided into "varieties" or "races." Different varieties were, in turn, the product of different environments and cultural responses to them.[18] Blumenbach's theory, which was widely accepted by the scientific community at the time, distinguished five varieties of humans: Asian, Native American, European, Austral Asian, and African. The European was the "primeval" form of human kind, whereas Native American, Austral Asian, Asian, and African were variations. For Maximilian, who followed his professor's theories, the goal was to find evidence to support Blumenbach's claim that Indigenous people in North and South America shared physical characteristics that united them as Native Americans and distinguished them from Europeans. He also sought to understand the entirety of their environment and their cultural adaptions to it in order to understand better how environmental conditions shaped their cultural traits.[19] As mongenists, both Blumenbach and Maximilian agreed that all humans had the same base intelligence and physical attributes. Any differences in physical appearance were strictly the result of circumstances of climate and cultural adaptations rather than inherent inequality.[20]

As the one responsible for documenting (or collecting) essential data about the physical appearance of people, material culture, animals, and places, Bodmer played a central role in the expedition's research. Blumenbach himself had relied heavily on artists' representations of non-Western people when formulating his theories about the history of humankind. He wrote that his picture collection was "one of the first, principal, and authentic sources of anthropological studies; and so for the last twenty years I have taken an immense deal of trouble to collect a quantity of such drawings, taken from life, and what is very important, by good artists."[21] In order to support or refute Blumenbach's theories, Maximilian required Bodmer to document the physical characteristics and material culture of Native Americans. We must assume that Bodmer consulted with Maximilian about what he painted, but Maximilian also mentioned instances when Bodmer himself chose the subjects—such as Chan-Chä-Uiá-Te-Üinn.[22] The ultimate nature of the patronage relationship was reflected in the contractual terms of Bodmer's employment: all the sketches save twelve belonged to Maximilian following their trip.[23] Bodmer also continued in Maximilian's employ once they returned, playing a crucial role in transferring his sketches into the prints that would illustrate Maximilian's *Reise in das innere Nord-America in den Jahren 1832 bis 1834* (see Kristine K. Ronan's essay in this volume, pp. 195–209).

Given the scientific goals of the journey, Bodmer's learning curve must have been steep. He had begun his artistic training at the age of thirteen with his uncle, landscape painter Johann Jakob Meier, who taught Bodmer to draw, paint in watercolors, and reproduce his work in engraving. Bodmer first met Maximilian in January 1832, but they did not settle on their final contract until April, just a month before their departure.[24] If, as it appears from the extant records of their meeting, Bodmer did not have much time to prepare for their trip, he would not have been able to learn much about scientific or anthropological illustration in Germany. Rather, it is likely that Bodmer learned how to apply his skills of draftsmanship to scientific illustration *during* the trip—first in Philadelphia, where he visited the Peale Museum. There, he could have seen examples of topographical and zoological sketches by Titian Ramsay Peale and Samuel Seymour (ca. 1775–after 1823) made on the 1817–23 expedition of Stephen H. Long.[25] Maximilian mentioned seeing Mark Catesby's *Natural History of Carolina, Florida and the Bahama Islands* (1731–43), Alexander Wilson's *American Ornithology* (1807–14), and the first volumes of John James Audubon's *Birds of America* (1827–38) in the library of the American Philosophical Society in Philadelphia.[26] It is hard to imagine that Bodmer did not accompany him there. Bodmer almost certainly received informal training when he and his party resided in the utopian community of New Harmony, Indiana, alongside experienced expeditionary artists Thomas Say—who, with Peale and Seymour, had accompanied the Long expedition as chief zoologist to the Rocky

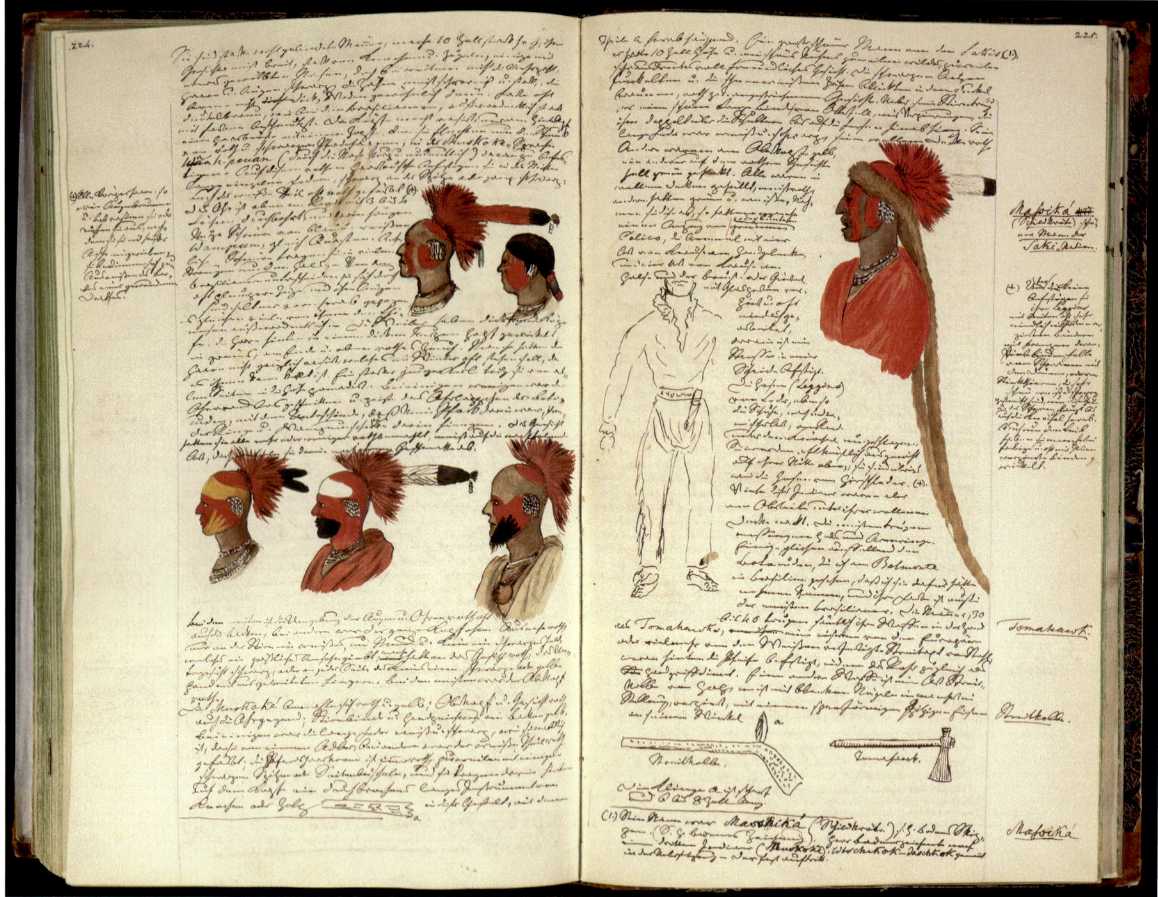

Mountains and up the Mississippi River—and Charles-Alexandre Lesueur, who served as artist-naturalist on Nicolas Baudin's voyage of exploration to Australia in 1801. Not including the six weeks the artist spent on a journey to New Orleans, Bodmer was in New Harmony for nearly four months. During his time there, he made numerous sketches of animals that he likely shared with Lesueur and Say. In Louisiana, he also made a number of paintings of the Choctaws and Cherokees, which would have provided him an opportunity to receive feedback from Maximilian and the naturalists. Given these circumstances, it follows that Bodmer's artistic vision was shaped by prevailing scientific conventions as well as the specific aims of Maximilian's expedition. This is not to say that Bodmer did not express his own vision in his North American work, only that his vision was ostensibly circumscribed by the stated goals of his employment.

Following their departure from New Harmony, Maximilian and Bodmer made their way to Saint Louis. There, in March 1833, they met a Sauk and Meskwaki party that had journeyed to the city to petition for the release of some of their compatriots captured during the Black Hawk War of 1832 from the prison at Jefferson Barracks in Missouri. The Sauks and Meskwakis were the first North American Native American people Maximilian encountered. He described his excitement at seeing them and then immediately integrated his observations into Blumenbach's anthropological theory:

FIGURE 2 Maximilian of Wied, Journal (*Tagebuch*), vol. 1, pp. 224–25, entry for March 25, 1833, ink and watercolor on paper in bound journal. Joslyn Art Museum, Gift of the Enron Art Foundation, 509.NNG.

In the morning a steamboat arrived with many Indians from the two tribes of Sauk . . . and Meskwaki. . . . We hurried into the building near the water that had been assigned to them as temporary quarters. On the riverbank we saw a crowd of people, and among the Europeans, strange-looking figures wrapped in red, white, and green blankets. When we reached them, they were already in the building. My first view of them, which, to be sure, astonished me greatly, nevertheless revealed to me their great similarity with the Brazilians and that they are absolutely of the same race.[27]

Maximilian went on in his journal to describe the physical characteristics of the Sauk and Meskwaki, including their height (six feet), hair color, stature (strong and well built, arms not thick, calves extraordinarily thin), and teeth (mostly very white and strong), and then he observed their mode of dress. The party was "heavily smeared with paints" and had most of their hair removed by cutting or plucking, leaving only a long, thin lock, which they braided and used to attach decorative horsehair ornaments called *wâwiyêpenwâni* (roaches).[28] Maximilian described the designs painted on their faces in red, white, black, and yellow, and he drew his own sketches in his journal to illustrate. He singled out one man for mention: Massica was about six feet tall and had a "nice bold face, sometimes wild, sometimes very expressively friendly." Maximilian included in his journal a bust-length sketch of him wearing a fine otterskin head ornament and a red roach (fig. 2, right). "His black eyes sparkled," Maximilian wrote, "and his snow-white teeth gleamed in the dark brown face, which was partly painted red."[29]

Over the next few days, Maximilian and Bodmer had multiple encounters with Massica and the larger party. On the afternoon of March 25, the Europeans attended an audience at William Clark's Saint Louis home that included the territorial governor and about thirty of the Sauk and Meskwaki party. The following day, they accompanied the Sauks and Meskwakis by steamboat downriver to Jefferson Barracks, where the party visited their imprisoned leaders, Black Hawk and Wabokieshiek (White Cloud; the Prophet). Massica was among the group and again elicited special notice from Maximilian: "The tall, handsome young man . . . was the most interesting of all the Indians. His revealing, wild, and at times extremely friendly, expressive eyes immediately engaged us, and with the help of the interpreter, I was able to record several words of the two very closely related Indian languages."[30] The following day, some of the Sauks and Meskwakis visited Maximilian and Bodmer at their lodgings. The Europeans offered gifts of apples, almonds, and cigars, as well as payment in exchange for a painting of Wakussáse and at least one other man. The next morning, before Massica and his party boarded a steamship headed for home, Bodmer painted him.

Unlike Maximilian, Bodmer had previously seen and sketched Native Americans—including Choctaw, Cherokee, and Creek men, women, and children—while on his excursion to Louisiana during the winter of 1832.[31] Nevertheless, his sketches from New Orleans are closer in spirit to genre scenes than scientific illustrations. They show Native Americans engaged in such activities as selling their wares or sitting in their encampments.

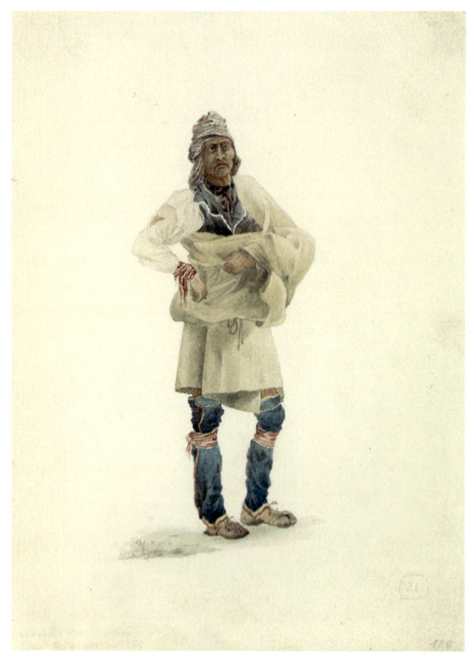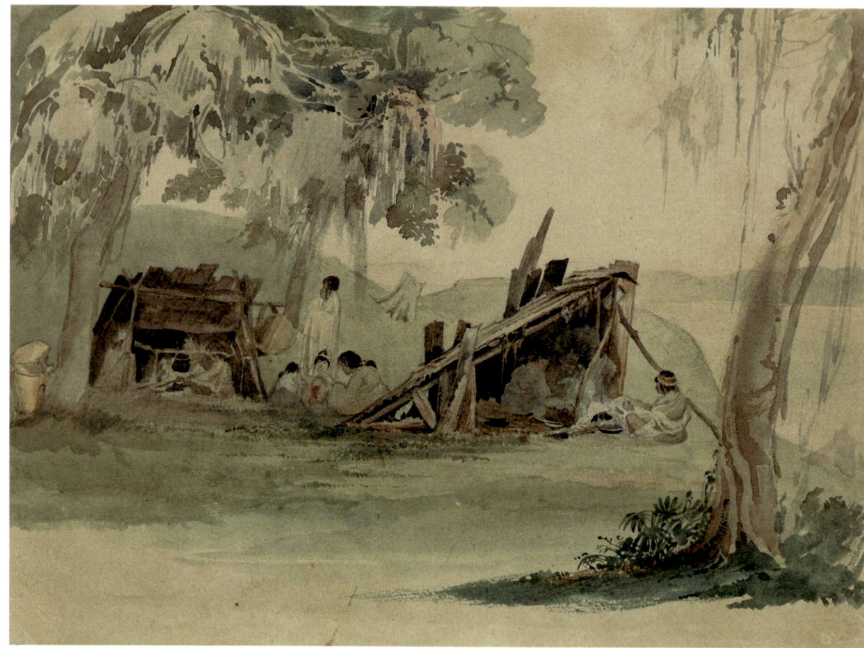

They usually pose wearing colorful garters, belts, or head wraps popular among Native peoples in the south, but these works lack the level of detail present in Bodmer's paintings of Upper Missouri people (figs. 3 and 4). In contrast, Bodmer's detailed rendering of Massica (pl. 1) addresses the research interests of his patron. Bodmer pictured Massica close up, in profile, looking upward and off the page. His face is uniformly bright red, almost certainly from vermilion, a European trade item made of ground cinnabar (mercury sulfide) and mixed with fat or another binder to ease application. Across his cheek is black paint in a striated pattern, perhaps from a stamp or a design abraded by wear. (Maximilian noted that the Sauks reapplied their face paint several times a day.)[32] Massica's hair is closely cropped, leaving a short row, probably stiffened with clay, that ends in a thin braid. His eyebrows, eyelashes, and all but a small tuft of hair under his lower lip have been plucked clean, as was the habit of the Sauks.[33] Massica's mouth is opened slightly, showing the row of small white teeth that Maximilian mentioned twice in his text. His earlobes fold over under the weight of multiple strands of blue and white tubular beads. Bodmer included a wealth of detail, including the fine strands of hair on his chin and the twisted loops of beads in his ears, each bead individually rendered.

When artist-naturalists such as William Bartram (1739–1823), Titian Ramsay Peale, or Charles-Alexandre Lesueur (fig. 5) carefully recorded the visual evidence by which individual plants, animals, insects, or marine life could be classified into different species, they worked within the theoretical framework of eighteenth-century Swedish botanist Carl Linnaeus, whose taxonomic system organized the natural world into kingdoms, classes, orders, and genera. Under such a system, small details, such as the number of toes or the presence of webbing between them, were essential information for the process of classification.[34] Bodmer followed these conventions in his sketch of a red-spotted newt he observed near

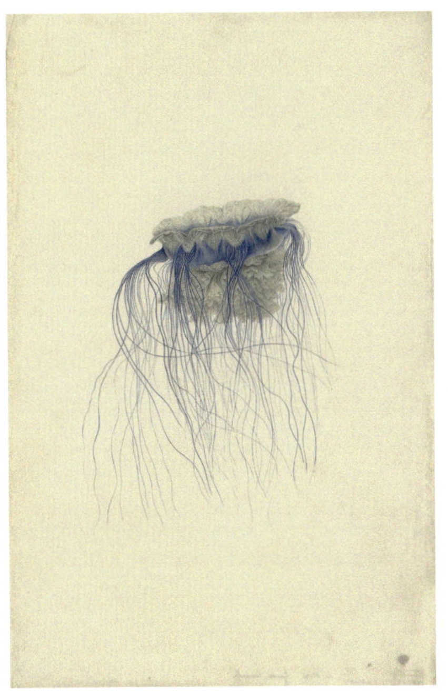

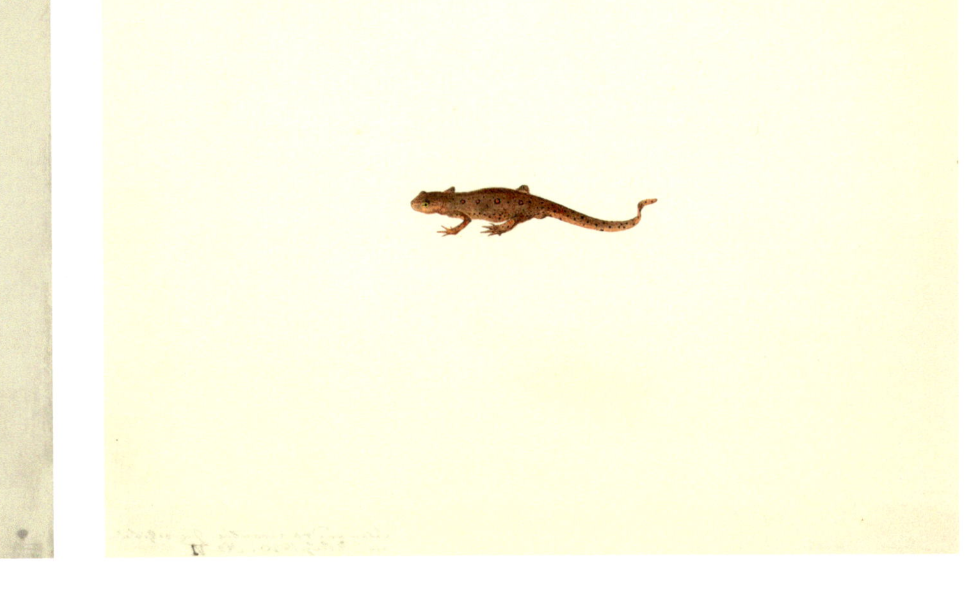

Bethlehem, Pennsylvania (fig. 6). The artist rendered the defining features of the salamander family, including a blunt snout, short limbs, and
round, protruding eyes. Other traits specific to the red-spotted newt (a
subspecies of *Notophthalmus viridescens*, eastern newt) in its adolescent
("red eft"), terrestrial phase include its bright red color, black spots, and
matte skin texture. Bodmer's choice to isolate the amphibian against the
white page, a convention of scientific illustration, helps to highlight the
newt's distinctive coloration, as well as its toe count (four toes on the front
legs, five on the back—traits that distinguish salamanders from lizards).
Its small size relative to the sheet is a reflection of its being scaled to life:
the painted red eft is 2⅞ inches long (although its tail is curved), while its
living peers are between 1½ and 3½ inches long.

Just as the salamander is isolated on the sheet in profile so that the
viewer may observe the salient traits of its head, body, and markings,
Bodmer posed Massica in profile and positioned him intimately enough
to reveal the overall contours of his face as well as finer details of his
appearance. According to Maximilian's journal, "Most of the [Sauks] have
broad faces and sturdy bones and features. Some of them, though by far
not the majority, have somewhat aquiline noses."[35] In his published text,
Maximilian contextualized this observation within Blumenbach's theory that Indigenous people from North and South America were of one
"variety": "The nose is large and prominent, often much arched, but not
always, a trait which occurs much more rarely among the Brazilians."[36]

Ordinarily, detail helps to particularize—or, in the case of portraits,
individualize—a painting. In eighteenth- and early nineteenth-century
scientific illustration, however, details of form, color, and texture were
the means by which the artist-naturalist conveyed the defining features
of a genus and species. The pattern of spots on the red eft is not there to
help us recognize this *particular* red eft (which presumably died in the
process of being collected and painted) but to recognize *any* red eft one

encountered in the future. Aspects of Bodmer's painting of Massica similarly help the viewer understand him as a "type" of Sauk man. We see many of the physical features that Maximilian described: Bodmer articulated his hairstyle, his bone structure, and his skin color. Notably, however, the painting gives us scant indication of his outgoing personality, the boldness and friendliness that Maximilian repeatedly mentioned in his text. We are given nothing to show that he was the most interesting of the Sauks, nor that he was the one who assisted Maximilian in recording a basic Sauk vocabulary.[37] Isolated on the page and void of any setting or context, without any movement or activity on Massica's part to create an individualized narrative, Bodmer failed to convey his gregarious personality. When his image was reproduced in print, Massica was similarly posed in profile, this time wearing his roach but still lacking any indication of the personal traits that Maximilian highlighted in his journal. This is because Bodmer's point (and Maximilian's) was not ultimately to help a viewer recognize Massica, although certainly one could.[38] Rather it was to describe those things that are included, namely the particularities of Sauk hairstyles and the culturally specific use of plucking and roaches.

While it may seem problematic at the very least to portray a human being within a set of artistic conventions usually used to depict plants and animals, it was not unusual given the set of questions nineteenth-century anthropologists sought to answer. Blumenbach's theories about the history of the human race were a refinement of Linnaeus's classification of homo sapiens as part of the animal kingdom. Just as naturalists turned to art to help them classify plant or animal specimens, so Blumenbach turned to artwork to help him research and then illustrate his theories about varieties of humans. Describing the work of artist-naturalists who accompanied Cook to the Pacific, Bernard Smith noted that the Indigenous people of Polynesia—such as those drawn by English painter William Hodges (1744–1797), the artist on Cook's 1772–75 voyage—"could

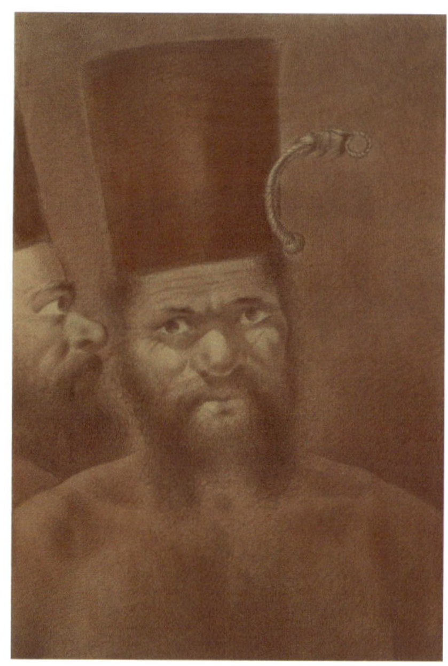

FIGURE 7 William Hodges, *Man of New Caledonia*, 1773, crayon on paper. National Library of Australia, PIC Drawer 12 #R754.

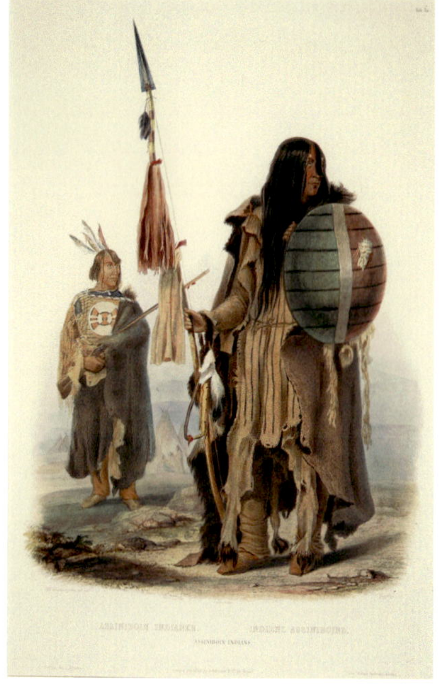

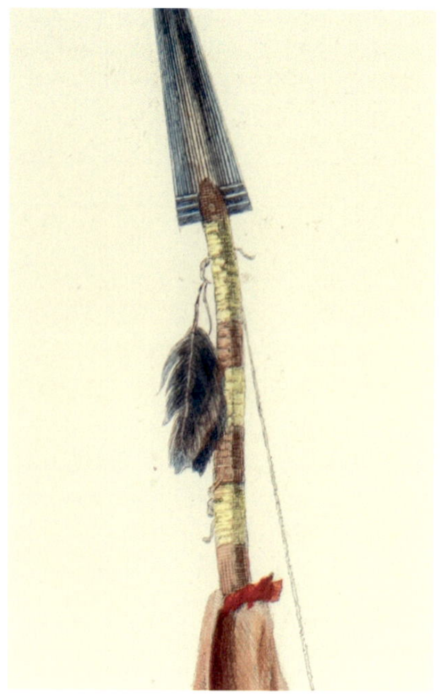

FIGURE 8 Charles Michel Geoffroy, after Karl Bodmer, *Assiniboine Indians*, 1837–43, hand-colored aquatint. Joslyn Art Museum, Gift of the Enron Art Foundation, 1986.49.517.32.

FIGURE 9 Charles Michel Geoffroy, after Karl Bodmer, *Assiniboine Indians* (detail).

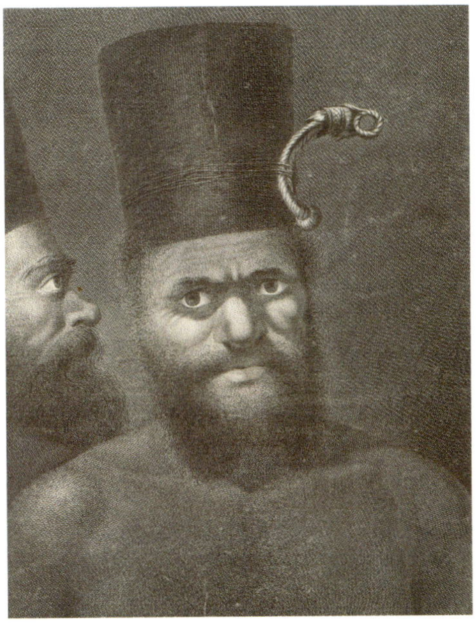

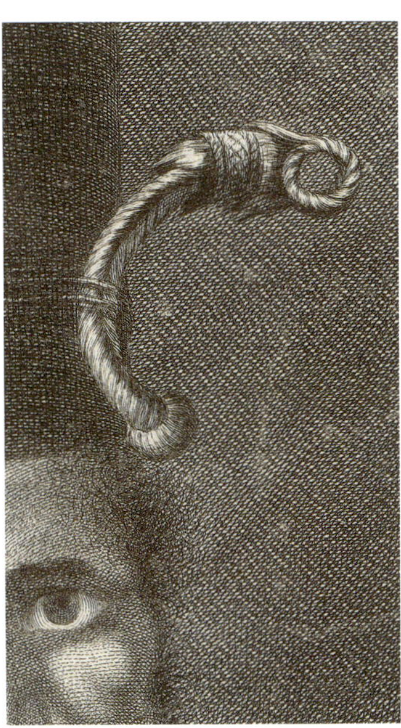

FIGURE 10   After William Hodges, *Man of New Caledonia*, 1777, engraving and etching from *Atlas to Cook's Voyages, vol. 2, 1777–1784*. National Maritime Museum, London (PAI4077).

FIGURE 11   After William Hodges, *Man of New Caledonia* (detail).

be portrayed as though they were objects of natural history, seen as plants or animals to be classified."[39] Hodges's drawing *Man of New Caledonia* (1773; fig. 7) includes visual information that would have been significant to Blumenbach, such as facial form, nose shape, and hair. The addition of a profile view behind the frontal one more fully captures the shape of the man's forehead, nose, and chin. Significantly, Blumenbach named Hodges's images of the South Pacific as an important and reliable source for anthropologists in contrast to the work of other artists, which, "when we examine them closely and compare them with genuine representations, or with nature, are scarcely of any use for the natural history of mankind."[40]

Comparing Hodge's *Man of New Caledonia* with Bodmer's *Pitätapiú, Assiniboine Man* (pl. 32) in both painted and printed form, we see that the latter depiction appears significantly more detailed. Hodges's chalk drawing is monochrome, but the chalk media does not allow him the kind of crisp contours needed to clearly render individual strands of hair or other textural details that Bodmer highlighted, such as the fur lining of Pitätapiú's robe or the tiny braid strung with a bead in his hair. Even in the print version of Bodmer's image (figs. 8 and 9), the precisely etched lines contrast the tonal effects of aquatint to convey the differences in texture between the hard blade of Pitätapiú's lance; the thin, taut sinew thread that runs the length of its shaft; and the soft feathers that trim it. In contrast, the crosshatching employed in the engraving after Hodges's drawing does not distinguish between material textures (figs. 10 and 11). What is significant here, however, is not just that Bodmer's painting is more detailed than Hodges's, but that Hodges's sketch was detailed enough for Blumenbach's purposes.

THE INDIVIDUAL AND THE CHARACTERISTIC

Why, then, did Bodmer provide more detail than was necessary to address Maximilian's interest in humankind? On the face of it, Bodmer clearly

valued a wealth of detail, dispar-
aging sketches such as those from
Jules Sébastien César Dumont
d'Urville's 1837–40 expedition to
Antarctica as "only half blurred
outlines."[41] Maximilian likewise
referred disapprovingly to Catlin's
illustrations as "outline sketches"
and linked his criticism to Catlin's
supposed inaccuracy, particularly
in comparison with Bodmer: "Mr.
Bodmer perceived the likeness by
far more faithfully [*treuer*] and
with a more correct characterization [*richtigerer Characteristik*] of
his Indian portraits."[42] Embedded
in the apology to his patron cited
at the outset of this chapter,
however, is Bodmer's claim that
he needed to "*copy* with unusual eagerness and attention
every aspect realistically."[43] His

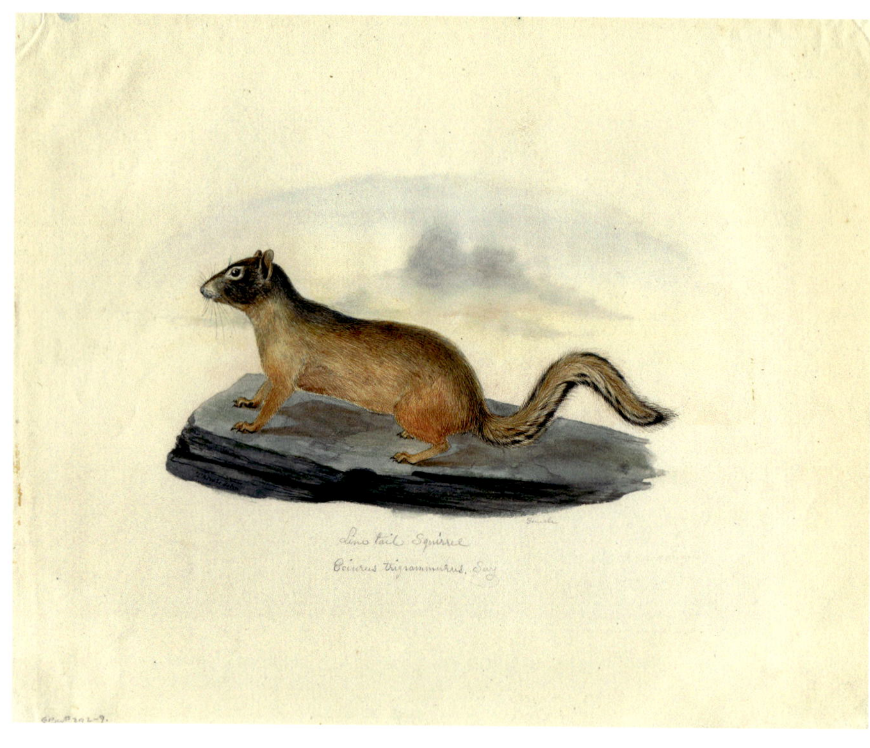

FIGURE 12   Titian Ramsay Peale, *Line-Tail Squirrel. Female (Sciurus trigrammurus Say)*, 1820, watercolor on paper. American Philosophical Society, Mss.B.P31.15d.

use of the word "copy" introduces the idea that he reproduced what he saw without the imposition of personal attitudes or feelings. Today, we think of objectivity as both fixed in its meaning and central to scientific inquiry, but objectivity in the modern sense of the word—loosely defined as "knowledge that bears no trace of the knower"—only gradually came to be applied to the sciences in the nineteenth century.[44] In the eighteenth century, artist-scientists following Linnaean theory sought "truth to nature" in their representations of the natural world. Their depictions aimed to be accurate insofar as they captured the essential, shared traits of a specimen.[45] Thus artist-naturalist Titian Ramsay Peale, whose work was familiar to Bodmer from his time in Philadelphia, did not attempt to capture an individual line-tail squirrel in his watercolor from the Long expedition (fig. 12). Rather, he used knowledge he attained from observing many such squirrels to create an image bearing the general and universal qualities of the animal. Scientific illustrations in the Linnaean tradition aimed to portray the specimen as a "type" or composite of the species' general attributes. Such work required that scientists exercise considerable expertise and judgment in determining how to abstract from the individual specimen to arrive at the type.[46] With the proliferation of knowledge about new species gathered from expeditions in the Americas and the South Pacific in the first third of the nineteenth century, however, scientists began to recognize the limitations of the Linnaean theory of fixed and unchanging nature and sought to study and record deviations in individual specimens.[47] Likewise, medical texts devoted to pathologies required more specificity to depict not the type but the deviation from it.[48] At the same time, there was the growth of an international community of scientists who began to form professional organizations (the first anthropological society was formed in 1839) and to publish more widely in scientific journals. These scientists required standardization in process and presentation in order to communicate results effectively. Mechanical measurements of size, weight, or climatic conditions became increasingly important when collecting specimens and eventually replaced the personal judgments of scientists, regardless of their experience and expertise.[49] By the late nineteenth century, individual specimens collected with impartiality and illustrated in atlases exactly as found became the accepted practice.

In the 1820s and 1830s, however, the process was still unfolding. Bodmer's sketches nevertheless do offer a bridge between the subjective judgment of scientists such as Peale or Bartram, who is admired today for his deeply personal observations of the flora and fauna of the American South, and the modern objectivity of the mid-nineteenth century. In almost every one of his portrait sketches, Bodmer represented his sitters in full or three-quarter profile. Although Maximilian's text refers multiple times to his and Bodmer's warm interactions with their "Indian friends," the profile pose that Bodmer selected did not allow him to portray such relations with his subjects. Bodmer's eye scanned the topography of Chan-Chä-Uiá-Te-Üinn or Pitätapiú's skin, hair, and clothing as an artist's eye might scan the landscape. His close transcription of color and texture, like his use of the word "copy," suggests an egoless process of visual "collection." Likewise, Bodmer's profile renderings of his Indian subjects suppress any hint of interaction between artist and sitter that might come from the eye contact and facial expression visible in a frontal pose. Rather, Bodmer positioned himself as a disinterested observer who, by virtue of his disinterestedness, disavowed the kind of personal judgments that defined expertise in the eighteenth century. Bodmer's portraits are thus all the more significant because they occupy a midpoint in the transition from the search for a composite type (as with Peale's squirrel) to an individual subject, objectively rendered and able to stand for the larger population.

Most of Bodmer's portraits and their resulting prints hover between the individual and the characteristic. They are titled with the sitter's name, followed by a general descriptor, such as *Mató-Tópe, Mandan Chief* (pl. 22). In Bodmer's full-length portrait of Mató-Tópe (Four Bears), his subject stands in three-quarter profile, staring forward, hand on hip, holding a lance. While almost all of Bodmer's male sitters wore facial paint, quilled hunting shirts, and head ornaments, Mató-Tópe's eagle-feather-and-bison-horn headdress, red-and-blue-quilled hunting shirt, distinctive profile, and striated facial paint all serve to individualize him. Yet even more than Bodmer's other sitters, Mató-Tópe is specifically identified by the biographical references depicted on and embodied in what he wears. Maximilian's text describes how the miniature wooden knife that Mató-Tópe wears in his hair (a duplicate of the one portrayed in his half-length portrait [pl. 23] was collected by Maximilian and is now in the collection of the Linden-Museum Stuttgart) refers to the knife he wrested from and used to kill a Cheyenne man.[50] His lance, decorated with an eagle feather across the blade, is the one he used to kill the Arikara man who killed his brother. His hunting shirt has a cut and droplets of blood to represent an earlier wound from battle.[51] Likewise, in Bodmer's full-length portrait of *Péhriska-Rúhpa, Hidatsa Man* (pl. 29) we see a highly finished watercolor depicting the sitter in his finest dress. Péhriska-Rúhpa (Two Ravens) wears a Crow-made hunting shirt, an expensive item that connoted the wearer's high status. It is embellished with dyed horsehair in red, white, and blue with yellow quillwork on the sleeves. He holds a long-stem pipe trimmed with blue and white quillwork and brass tacks and fitted with a lead or silver inlay bowl. On the one hand, each element speaks to Péhriska-Rúhpa's individuality, and Maximilian's text likewise includes particularized characterizations of him. We learn, for instance, that he had a falling out with Mató-Tópe. When Mató-Tópe arrived in Maximilian's quarters for a visit while Péhriska-Rúhpa was there, Péhriska-Rúhpa immediately departed.[52] Yet Maximilian's text is also careful to point out that Péhriska-Rúhpa's hairstyle is typical of the Mandans, and Bodmer used his portrait and the full-length image of Mató-Tópe to illustrate general descriptions of Mandan dress.[53]

By creating detailed images of specific individuals who could stand as characteristic of their group, Bodmer advanced the current trends of anthropological illustration. His objectivity also served another professional end: it stood as a bulwark against critics who might question his and Maximilian's research. Maximilian's party and the trappers and traders they traveled with were among the few to meet and interact with the Assiniboines and Blackfeet, who lived a considerable distance from white settlements. It would be a full two decades before the Blackfeet made their first treaty with European Americans. Maximilian and Bodmer's correspondence following their trip expresses both concerns that audiences might doubt their depictions and a keen awareness that the success of their publication rested in part on the novelty of their subject matter among Europeans.[54] At the same time, both were also skeptical of their competitor, George Catlin, whose paintings they saw in the Saint Louis collection of Indian agent and fur trader Benjamin O'Fallon and probably that of O'Fallon's uncle, William Clark, as well.[55] Catlin, like Bodmer and Maximilian, had traveled up the Missouri River with the in-kind sponsorship of the American Fur Company, which transported him on their steamships and housed him at their forts. Following his return, Catlin— whether ungrateful, honest, or just impolitic—fiercely criticized the American Fur Company's treatment of Native Americans. The company responded with an all-out attack on the accuracy of Catlin's paintings and later his written account, *Letters and Notes on the Manners, Customs, and Condition of the North American Indians* (1841). Historian Brian Dippie said that Catlin "was defamed from post to post." "Almost everyone who went up the Missouri after Catlin branded him a humbug," Dippie wrote, "some, for variation, settled on charlatan. Complaints that he had embellished the stories of veteran fur traders, repaid company generosity with ingratitude and misunderstood what he saw darkened into an attack on his honesty."[56] Maximilian's journal notes some of Catlin's minor errors and repeats a story he heard about how Catlin insulted Mató-Tópe by giving him cheap gifts in exchange for two painted bison robes.[57] He later wrote a multipage review of *Letters and Notes* that went through Catlin's text point by point, refuting his translations of Native American languages, his accounts of customs, and his illustrations.[58] Bodmer's detailed and objective renderings of Native Americans helped to establish their credibility against the kind of doubts Catlin experienced.

Along the same lines, within post-Linnaean natural science, the circulation of ideas and the shared, global project of classifying the whole of the natural world meant that scientific ideas were increasingly in competition with one another. Indeed, scholars have argued that the impulse to standardize scientific data and illustrations was a response to increasing competition. Scientists sought to create even clearer information to compete with alternate scientific theories.[59] Bodmer's objective renderings of people, as well as animals and landscapes, offered an obvious advantage over the work of Catlin not only because Bodmer's wealth of detail made him seem disinterested in contrast to the purported exaggerations of Catlin, but also because they provided a scientific audience with more readily consumable visual data.

Bodmer's detail served the scientific aims of his images, projecting an objectivity that allowed his artworks to compete successfully for a dominant position within scientific discourse on the Indigenous people of the Upper Missouri River region. For the artist himself, however, scientific objectivity came at a price. While the scientific community, as exemplified by Alexander von Humboldt, approved of his illustrations, the artistic community gave them little notice.[60] When Bodmer exhibited his paintings at the Salon in Paris in 1836, a reviewer for *L'Artiste* noted only their sensational subject matter and their "artlessness."[61] Bodmer and Maximilian's publication sold few copies and left them both in debt, and the development of the daguerreotype threatened the end of the illustrated travelogue.[62] But perhaps most telling was Bodmer's own attitude toward his project. Late in Bodmer's life, a reporter for *Les Annales Politiques et Littéraires* visited the "once famous, but now forgotten" artist in his apartment on the top floor of an ancient house on a lonely street in Paris. During his interview, Bodmer reminisced "with a smile on his wrinkled face" about his North American travels, recounting his travails in persuading his subjects to sit for him. In the article, the artist claimed King Louis Philippe I of France had offered him the Grand Cross of the Legion of Honor for his North American paintings, but Bodmer refused it. He was too proud to accept it for such work, he said. "He wanted to win the red ribbon [the Legion of Honor], to conquer it [but] with higher and more personal works."[63]

NOTES

1. *The North American Journals of Prince Maximilian of Wied*, ed. Marsha V. Gallagher and Steven S. Witte, trans. William J. Orr, Paul Schach, and Dieter Karch (Norman: University of Oklahoma Press; Omaha: Joslyn Art Museum, Margre H. Durham Center for Western Studies, 2008–12), 2:157–58 (hereafter *NAJ*).

2. John C. Ewers, "An Appreciation of Karl Bodmer's Pictures of Indians," in *Views of a Vanishing Frontier*, ed. John C. Ewers (Omaha: Joslyn Art Museum, 1984), 80.

3. Marsha V. Gallagher, "A Brief Description and History of the Maximilian-Bodmer Collection and the Maximilian Journals Project" in *NAJ*, 1:xxviii. For more information on Maximilian's collection of Native American artifacts, see Sonja Schierle, "Prince Maximilian of Wied's North American Collection at the Linden-Museum Stuttgart: Far More than a Testimony of Early Native American History," and Peter Bolz, "Prince Maximilian's North American Collections in Berlin," in *Karl Bodmer: A Swiss Artist in America 1809–1893*, ed.

Hartwig Isernhagen (Zurich: Scheidegger & Spiess; Nordamerika Native Museum, 2009), 18–43 and 66–87.

4. *NAJ*, 2:159.

5. Maximilian noted in this passage that Chan-Chä-Uiá-Te-Üinn valued her possessions very highly, suggesting he may have been negotiating for the robe's purchase as Bodmer painted her. *NAJ* 2:157.

6. *NAJ*, 3:282M25; Maximilian of Wied, *Travels in the Interior of North America, 1832–34*, trans. Hannibal Evans Lloyd (London: Ackermann, 1843), 292, 328 (hereafter *TINA*).

7. William Truettner, *Painting Indians and Building Empires in North America, 1710–1840* (Berkeley: University of California Press, 2010), 85.

8. Ron Tyler, "Karl Bodmer and the American West," in *Karl Bodmer's North American Prints*, ed. Brandon K. Ruud (Omaha: Joslyn Museum of Art; Lincoln: University of Nebraska Press, 2004), 10; William H. Goetzmann, "Introduction: The Man Who Stopped to Paint America," in *Karl Bodmer's America*, by William H. Goetzmann, David C. Hunt, Marsha V. Gallagher, and William J. Orr (Omaha: Joslyn Art Museum; Lincoln: University of Nebraska Press, 1984), 15–16.

9. Karl Bodmer to Maximilian of Wied, Paris, July 18, 1840, Michael Harrison Collection, University of California, Davis; a copy of this letter in English translation is held in the Joslyn Art Museum Archives.

10. David C. Hunt and Marsha V. Gallagher, "Annotations," in Goetzmann et al., *Karl Bodmer's America*, 190; Brandon K. Ruud, Tableau 3, in *Karl Bodmer's North American Prints*, 94; Bodmer to Maximilian, July 18, 1840.

11. In Goetzmann et al., *Karl Bodmer's America*, see, for instance, *Assiniboine Man* (pl. 202), who holds a gun; *Kiäsax, Piegan Blackfeet Man* (pl. 257), who wears Navajo jewelry and blanket; and *Addíh-Hiddísch, Hidatsa Chief* (pl. 326), who wears a European hat and a peace medal.

12. Joseph C. Porter, "The Eyes of Strangers: 'Fact' and Art on the Ethnographic Frontier, 1832–32," in *Karl Bodmer's Studio Art: The Newberry Library Bodmer Collection* by W. Raymond Wood, Joseph C. Porter, and David C. Hunt (Urbana: University of Illinois Press, 2002), 49, 81; *NAJ*, 2:79, 82, 91, 104, 106M52; *TINA*, vii.

13. John Gere, ed., *Portrait Drawings, XV–XX Centuries* (London: British Museum, 1974), as quoted in L. Campbell, "Portraiture," Grove Art Online, January 1, 2003.

14. Maximilian of Wied, author's preface to *TINA*, as quoted in Porter, "Eyes of Strangers," 24.

15. Porter, "Eyes of Strangers," 23–24.

16. Here I am following nineteenth-century German terminology to distinguish anthropology (the study of human history or races) from ethnology (the study of cultures). See Hans F. Vermeulen, *Before Boas: The Genesis of Ethnography and Ethnology in the German Enlightenment* (Omaha: University of Nebraska Press, 2015), 6–10, 357–59.

17. Vermeulen, *Before Boas*, 381.

18. Vermeulen, *Before Boas*, 376.

19. George W. Stocking, *Victorian Anthropology* (New York: Simon and Schuster, 1991), 26; Porter, "Eyes of Strangers," 27, 83n14.

20. *TINA*, 351.

21. *The Anthropological Treatises of Johann Friedrich Blumenbach*, ed. Thomas Bendyshe (London: Longman, Green, Longman, Roberts, and Green, 1865), 159.

22. *NAJ*, 2:158.

23. William J. Orr, "Karl Bodmer: The Artist's Life," in Goetzmann et al., *Karl Bodmer's America*, 352–53; "Points for a Contract," signed by Maximilian of Wied and Karl Bodmer, April 20, 1832, Joslyn Art Museum Archives.

24. Maximilian and Bodmer departed May 17, 1852: Goetzmann, "The Man Who Stopped to Paint America," 5–6; "Points for a Contract."

25. Goetzmann, "The Man Who Stopped to Paint America," 5; Kenneth Haltman, *Looking Close and Seeing Far: Samuel Seymour, Titian Ramsay Peale, and the Art of the Long Expedition, 1818–1823* (University Park: Pennsylvania State University Press, 2007), 175.

26. *NAJ*, 1:86.

27. *NAJ*, 1:372–73.

28. *NAJ*, 1:373 and n122.

29. *NAJ*, 1:374nM13.

30. *NAJ*, 1:381.

31. Goetzmann, "The Man Who Stopped to Paint America," 8.

32. *NAJ*, 1:383

33. *NAJ*, 1:373.

34. Roger B. Stein, "Charles Willson Peale's Expressive Design: The Artist in his Museum," in *Reading American Art*, ed. Marianne Doezema and Elizabeth Milroy (New Haven, CT: Yale University Press, 1998), 57; see also Thomas Hallock, "Vivification and the Early Art of William Bartram," in *A Keener Perception: Ecocritical Studies in American Art History*, ed. Alan Braddock and Christoph Irmscher (Tuscaloosa: University of Alabama Press, 2009), 48.

35. *NAJ*, 1:373.

36. *TINA*, 103.

37. *NAJ*, 1:381.

38. John Ewers gives an account of a conversation he had in the 1940s with a Kainai (Blood) man who was able to recognize Bodmer's portrait of Stomíck-Sosáck (pl. 51) by its resemblance to Stomíck-Sosáck's son, whom he knew. See Ewers, "An Appreciation of Karl Bodmer's Pictures of Indians," in Ewers, *Views of a Vanishing Frontier*, 96.

39. Bernard Smith, *Imaging the Pacific in the Wake of the Cook Voyages* (New Haven, CT: Yale University Press, 1992), 33.

40. Johann Friedrich Blumenbach, *On the Natural Variety of Mankind* (3rd ed., 1795), in *The Anthropological Treatises of Johann Friedrich Blumenbach*, ed. Thomas Bendyshe (London: Longman, Green, Longman, Roberts, and Green, 1865), 161, https://www.biodiversity library.org/item/107931#page/177/mode /1up.

41. Karl Bodmer to Maximilian of Wied, February 13, 1841, Joslyn Art Museum Archives.

42. Maximilian of Wied, "A Few Remarks about Catlin's Book, 'Letters and Notes on the Manners, Customs, and Condition of the North American Indians,'" English translation of "Einige Bemerkungen über Catlin's Werk, *Letters and Notes on the Manner, Customs, and Conditions of the North American Indians*," typescript, Joslyn Art Museum Archives.

43. Bodmer to Maximilian, July 18, 1840.

44. Lorraine Daston and Peter Galison, *Objectivity* (New York: Zone Books, 2007), 17.

45. Daston and Galison, *Objectivity*, 55–59.

46. Lorraine Daston and Peter Galison, "The Image of Objectivity," *Representations*, no. 40 (1992): 94, accessed April 10, 2020, doi:10.2307/2928741.

47. Hallock, "Vivification," 55–56.

48. Daston and Galison, "The Image of Objectivity," 86.

49. Lorraine Daston, "Objectivity and the Escape from Perspective," *Social Studies of Science* 22, no. 4 (November 1992): 6–9; Bruno Latour, "Drawing Things Together," in *Representations in Scientific Practice*, ed. Michael Lynch and Steven Woolgar (Cambridge, MA: MIT Press, 1990), 24–25.

50. *NAJ*, 3:148nM8; *TINA*, 450.

51. Hunt and Gallagher, "Annotations," 308. Catlin read Mató-Tópe's dress with even more specificity in *Letters and Notes on the Manners, Customs, and Condition of the North American Indian*, (New York: Dover, 1973), 1:145–48.

52. *TINA*, 431.

53. *TINA*, 338–39.

54. Karl Bodmer to Maximilian of Wied, March 25, 1841, Joslyn Art Museum Archives.

55. Between 1816 and 1838 Clark displayed an array of Indian portraits and material culture as well as animal and mineral specimens in a 100-foot wing on the back of his house. Ewers speculated that some of the portraits may have been by Catlin. John C. Ewers, "William Clark's Indian Museum in St. Louis, 1816–38," in *A Cabinet of Curiosities: Five Episodes in the Evolution of American Museums* (Charlottesville: University of Virginia Press, 1967), 49–72, esp. 54 and 65. Maximilian visited Clark's collection (see *TINA*, 107) and Benjamin O'Fallon's collection of Catlin's paintings (*NAJ* 1:384). Bodmer made a sketch after one by Catlin in O'Fallon's collection: see *Unidentified Man* in Joslyn Art Museum, 1986.49.222, compared to George Catlin, *The Black Rock, a Two Kettle Chief, Teton Dakota* (Western Sioux) in *The O'Fallon Collection of American Indian Portraits by George Catlin*, auction catalogue, December 2, 2004 (New York: Sotheby's), cat. 9.

56. Brian Dippie, *Catlin and His Contemporaries* (Omaha: University of Nebraska Press, 1990), 59.

57. *NAJ*, 2:311 and 459, 3:185. For the incident with Mató-Tópe, see 3:55.

58. Orr, "Karl Bodmer: The Artist's Life," 360–63.

59. Latour, "Drawing Things Together," 23–26.

60. Ron Tyler notes that Bodmer spoke to the Société Ethnologique in Paris in 1839 and received great praise: Tyler, "Karl Bodmer and the American West," 20. Alexander von Humboldt also wrote approvingly of his images: Alexander von Humboldt to Maximillian of Wied, Berlin, September 18, 1843, typescript, Joslyn Art Museum Archives.

61. Tyler, "Karl Bodmer and the American West," 16.

62. Brandon K. Ruud, "'A Faithful and Vivid Picture': Karl Bodmer's North American Prints," in *Karl Bodmer's North American Prints*, 72.

63. Adolphe Brisson, "Portraits Contemporains: Un Oublié: Karl Bodmer," *Les Annales Politiques et Littéraires*, November 20, 1892, 323–25. I would like to thank Sylvie Durmelat for finding this article and pointing me to it.

PLATES

INTRODUCTION AND NOTE ON
TRIBAL NOMENCLATURE

FIFTY-TWO OF KARL BODMER'S REMARKABLE LIKENESSES of Indigenous people are reproduced in the following three portfolios, organized geographically to reflect the relative location of their homelands as Maximilian and Bodmer traveled north up the Missouri River. The commentary accompanying each plate, which was written by Marsha V. Gallagher, is primarily derived from Prince Maximilian of Wied's personal journals and publications. A two-volume account of his expedition, *Reise in das innere Nord-America in den Jahren 1832 bis 1834*, was published in Koblenz in 1839–41, accompanied by a portfolio of eighty-one prints created after Bodmer's watercolors. This was followed by a French translation in 1840–43 and an abridged, one-volume English edition in 1843: *Travels in the Interior of North America, 1832–34*, the source for several of the quotations in the captions (cited as *TINA*). Most of the quotations and specific details are drawn from Maximilian's handwritten journals, which were the basis for his publications and contain substantial additional information. These three manuscript volumes—along with archival documents and Maximilian's collection of Bodmer's watercolors, drawings, and prints— were retained by the Wied family for more than a century before being purchased by M. Knoedler and Company in New York in 1959. Three years later, the collection was acquired by Northern Natural Gas Company of Omaha. After being placed on long-term loan to Joslyn Art Museum, it was donated to the museum's permanent collection in 1986. The journals were later translated, annotated, and published as *The North American Journals of Prince Maximilian of Wied* (cited in the plate texts as *NAJ*).[1]

Because Bodmer continued to work on many of his watercolors after his return to Europe, the exact dates of their production can be difficult to ascertain. For consistency, the date of each portrait in this catalog reflects when Bodmer encountered the sitter. The portrait titles are descriptive and reflect the Indigenous-language personal names recorded in Maximilian's journals and published texts. The identities of some individuals were not recorded or have been lost. The personal names, orthographies, and English translations were taken from Maximilian's *Journals*, the editors of which drew largely on his *Reise in das innere Nord-America*. English translations imperfectly approximate the meaning of Indigenous-language names and their personal significance.

With some exceptions (*), the sitters' tribal affiliations referenced in the portrait titles are also taken from the *Journals*, which standardized

Maximilian's variant spellings—most often in accordance with the *Handbook of North American Indians*[2] and the Smithsonian Institution's National Museum of the American Indian. They do not entirely reflect an Indigenous nation's chosen name (autonyms) or federally recognized name. Listed below are the chosen names of the nations represented in the *Journals*, and, thus, the plates. In many cases spellings and translations of personal and tribe names vary or the original meaning of a name is no longer known. Joslyn Art Museum continues to work with Native American communities to research and interpret the Maximilian-Bodmer collection.

MAXIMILIAN'S *JOURNALS*	CHOSEN NAMES AND TRANSLATIONS
Arikara	Sahnish, Original People from Whom All Other Tribes Sprang
Assiniboine	Nakoda, Friend or Allies
Blood Blackfoot*	Kainai, Many Chiefs People
Cree	Nehiyawak, People of the Plains
Gros Ventres des Prairies*	A'aninin, White Clay People
Hidatsa	People of the Willows
Kootenai	Ktunaxa, untranslated
Mandan	Nueta, the People
Meskwaki	Red Earth People
Omaha	Umonhon, Against the Current or Upstream People
Piegan Blackfoot	Piikani, Scabby Robes People
Ponca	Disputed origin and translation
Sauk	Oθaakiiwaki, Yellow Earth People
Shoshone	Newe, the People
Siksika Blackfoot	Black Foot People
Sioux	Ocheti Sakowin, Seven Council Fires
Teton Sioux*	Lakota, Friends or Allies
Yankton Sioux	Ihanktunwan, People of the End Village
Yanktonai Sioux	Ihanktunwanna, People of the Little End Village

NOTES

1. See the selected bibliography (p. 215) for an overview of Joslyn Art Museum publications on the Maximilian-Bodmer Collection.

2. William C Sturtevant, ed., *Handbook of North American Indians*, 15 vols. (Washington, DC: Smithsonian Institution, 1978–2008).

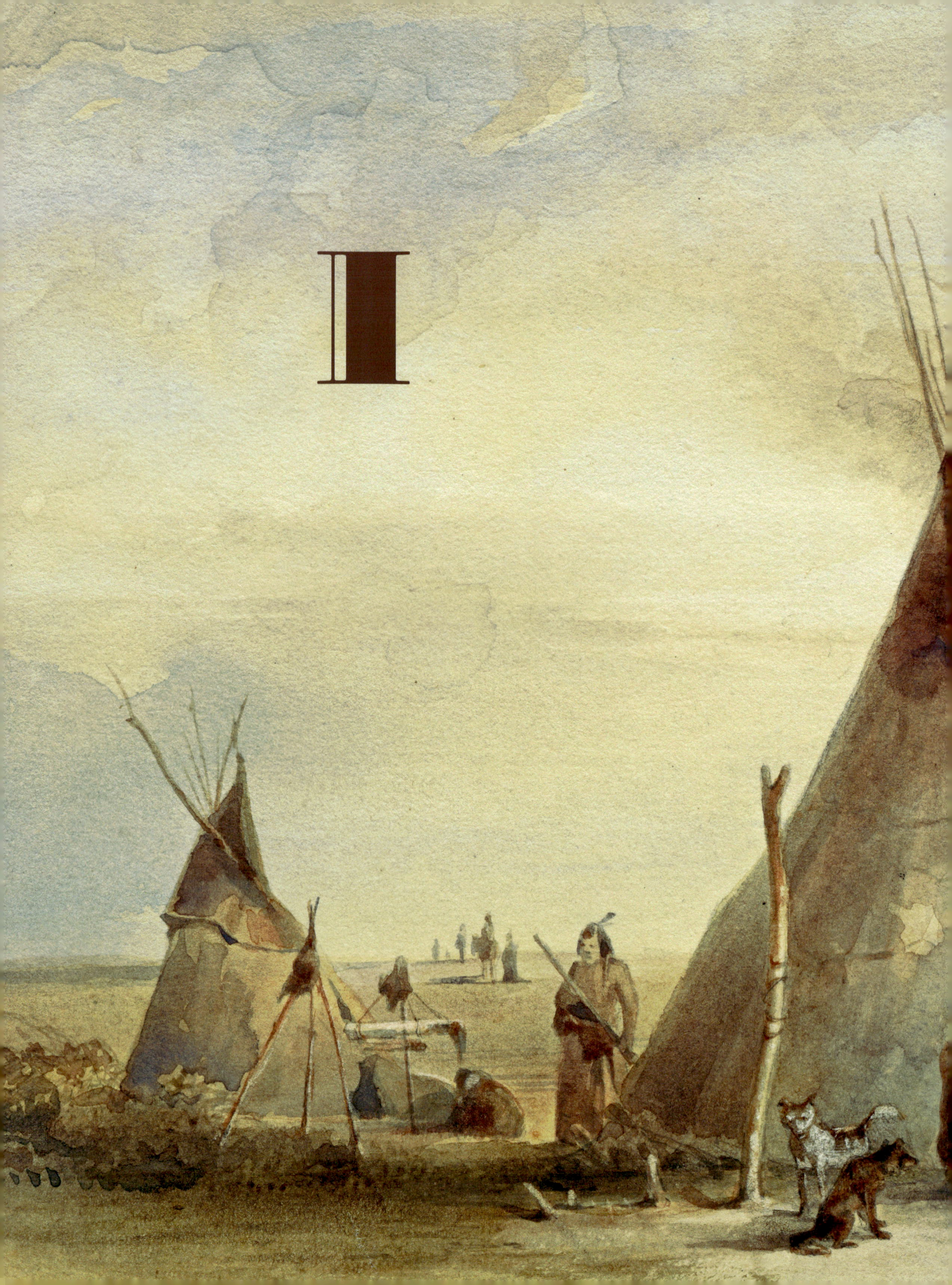

II

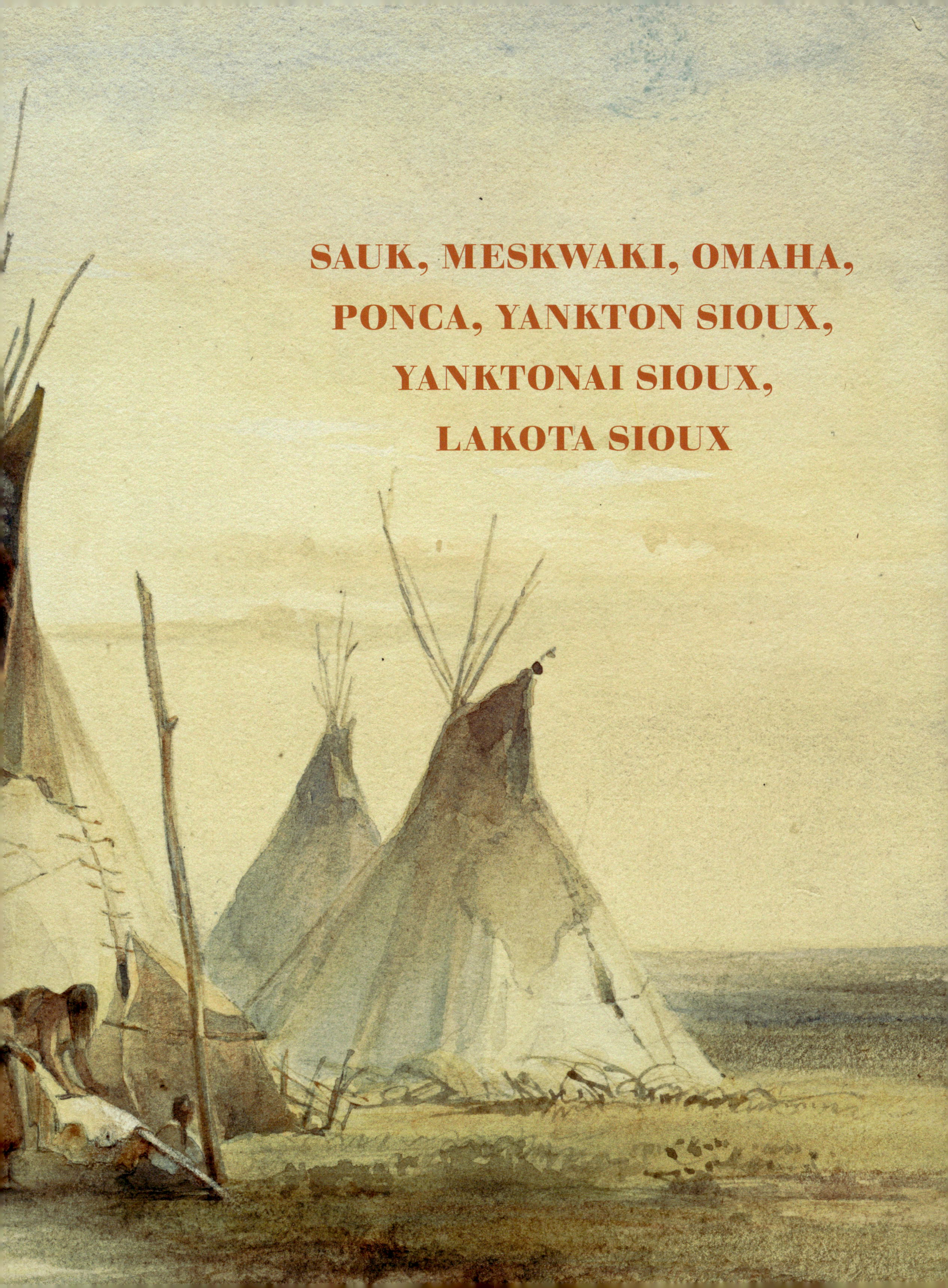
SAUK, MESKWAKI, OMAHA,
PONCA, YANKTON SIOUX,
YANKTONAI SIOUX,
LAKOTA SIOUX

1. Massica, Sauk Man

1833

On March 24, 1833, after eight months of travel across the United States from Boston through Pennsylvania and down the Ohio River Valley, Prince Maximilian of Wied, Karl Bodmer, and David Dreidoppel, the Wied family huntsman, arrived in Saint Louis. The following morning, a sizeable party of Sauk and Meskwaki Indians came to town to plead for the release of Black Hawk, one of their leaders who was imprisoned after attempting to reclaim tribal land in Illinois. This was Maximilian's first view of Indigenous North Americans. Among the visiting warriors was Massica (Turtle/Snapping Turtle). Bodmer showed Massica's cleanly shaven head with a braided hair tuft, which served as an anchor for a crest-like roach—an ornament popular among eastern tribes and later on the Plains. (*NAJ* 1:374–75nm13)

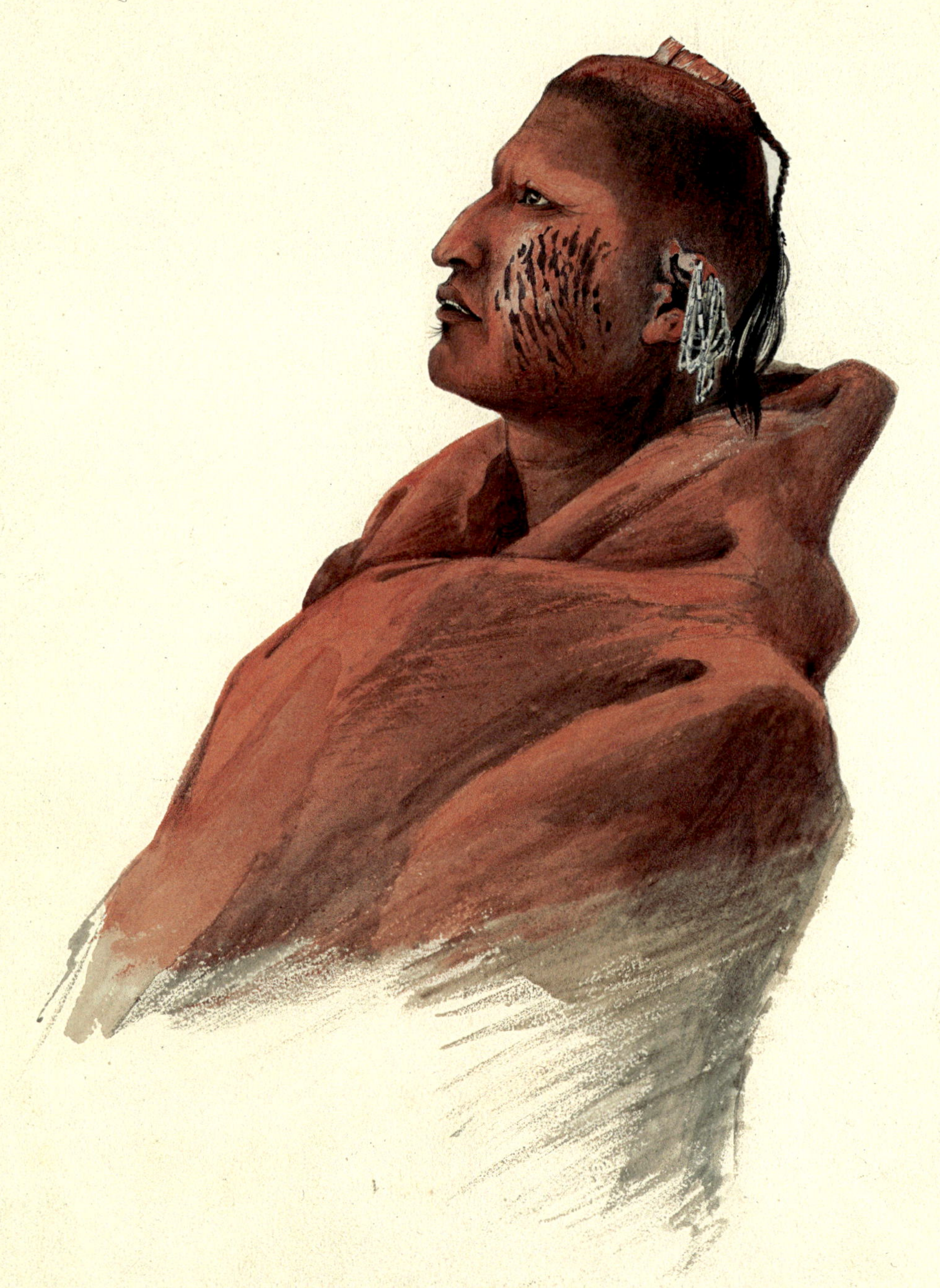

Massika (Pfielmödn). Saki.
Am 28 ten März 1833. St. Louis.

2. Wakussáse, Meskwaki Man

1833

Neither Maximilian nor Bodmer provided details about this sitter, who may have been among the crowds of Sauks and Meskwakis they observed in Saint Louis in March 1833. Wakussáse appears with Massica in a combined portrait in the print portfolio accompanying Maximilian's *Reise in das innere Nord-America.* Roaches like the one Wakussáse wears were typically made from turkey "beards" and deer, horse, badger, and/or porcupine guard hairs twisted together like a cockscomb and attached to the top of the head; feathers were common additions. Wakussáse also wears numerous shell or metal earrings. Maximilian observed that several Sauks and Meskwakis pierced their ears with multiple holes and "from them hang short strings of blue and white [shell] wampum [beads], like tassels." (*NAJ* 1:373)

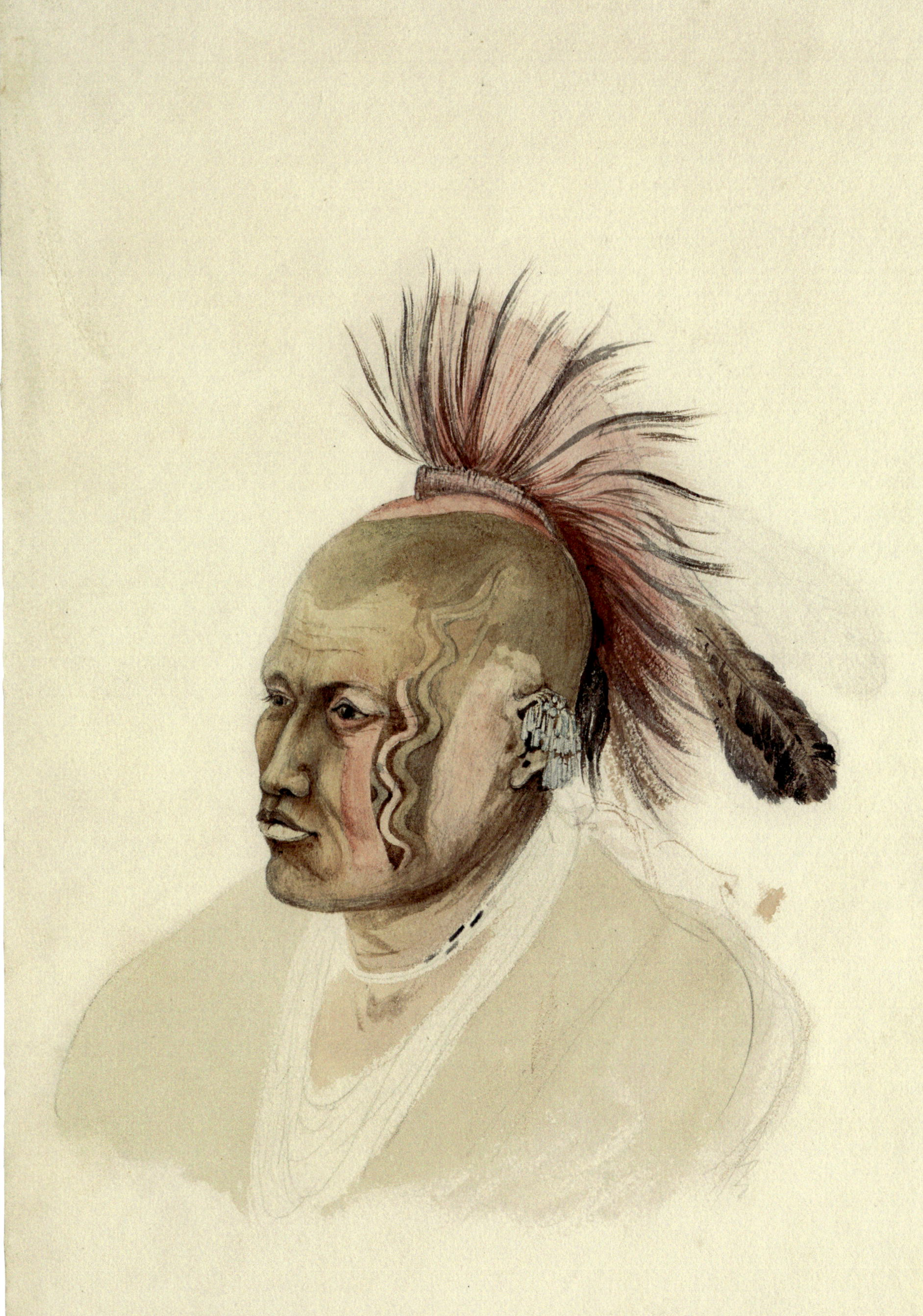

III.
Wakusásse (Muskoke).
Am 27 ten Merz (e eulgischgemalen).
1833

3. Omaha Man

1833

In Saint Louis, Maximilian explored his opportunities for
traveling further into Indigenous territories. Following
the recommendation of William Clark, who was then the
federal superintendent of Indian affairs at Saint Louis, he
sought passage up the Missouri River under the aegis of
the American Fur Company. Maximilian's interactions
with Indigenous peoples seeking to trade hides and furs
at American Fur Company posts were likely to be more
numerous than chance encounters, and his party's extensive cargo (scientific equipment, art materials, hunting
gear, and other supplies) could be readily accommodated
on the company's vessels. On April 10, 1833, Maximilian,
Bodmer, and Dreidoppel boarded the *Yellow Stone,* the first
steam-powered vessel to ascend the Upper Missouri River.
They passed through Missouri and, on April 21, beyond
the mouth of the Kansas River, into Indigenous territories. Upon reaching the American Fur Company trading
post near what is now Omaha on May 4, they encountered
a group of Otoes and Omahas. This man's long hair hangs
loose, and he grips his closed robe beneath his chin. A bow
and quiver are faintly outlined in pencil. His son is pictured
in plate 4.

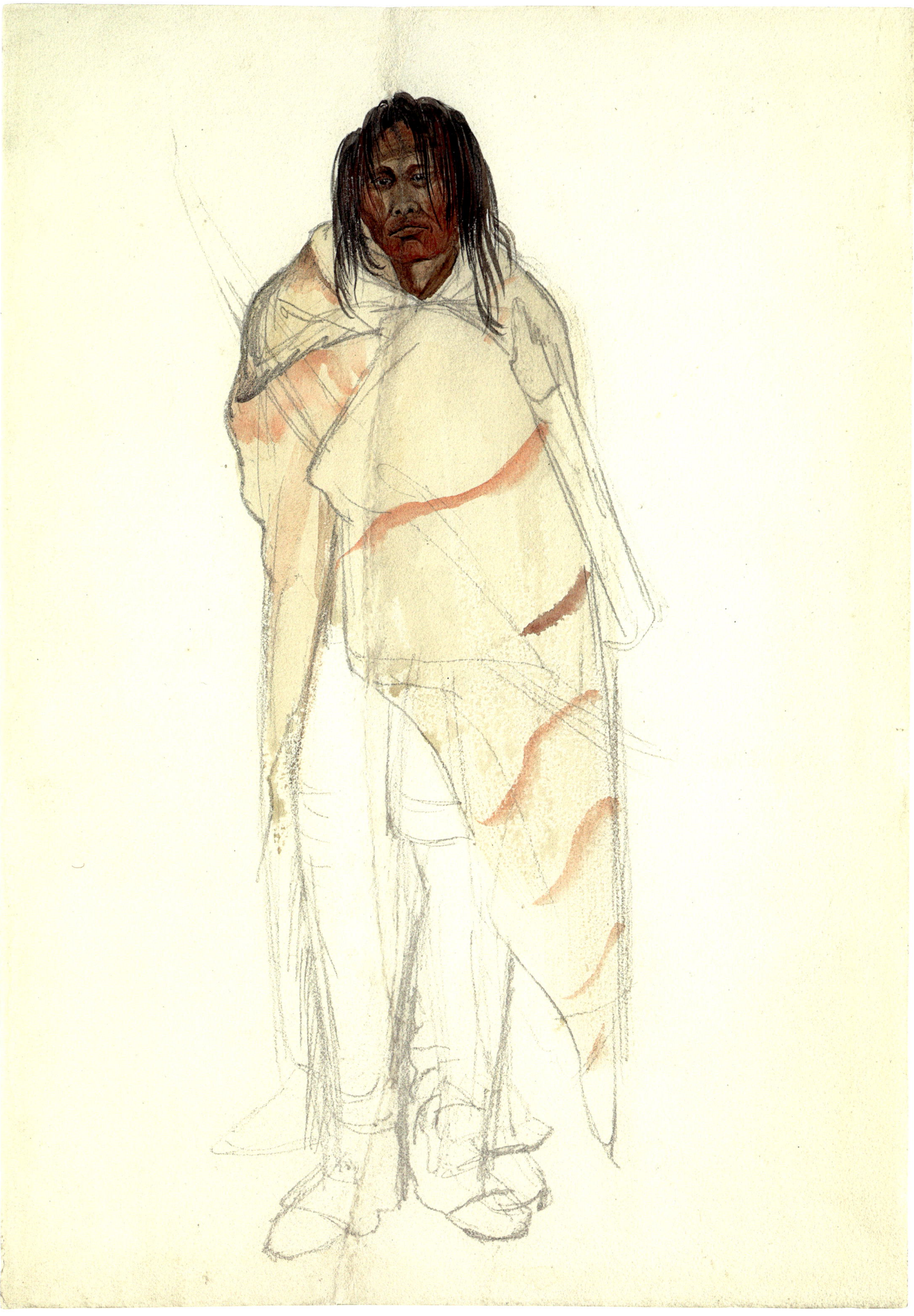

4. Omaha Boy

1833

Before posing for Bodmer on May 4, 1833, this child's face
was painted by his father (pl. 3) with bright vermilion, a
popular pigment obtained from traders. Like all Omaha
boys, he had his hair cut in a distinctive style or pattern
to identify his clan and to help instruct him and his peers
about important kinship affiliations. His ornaments
include a feather tied to a hair tuft, earrings, bangles,
and a cleanly dressed buffalo robe.

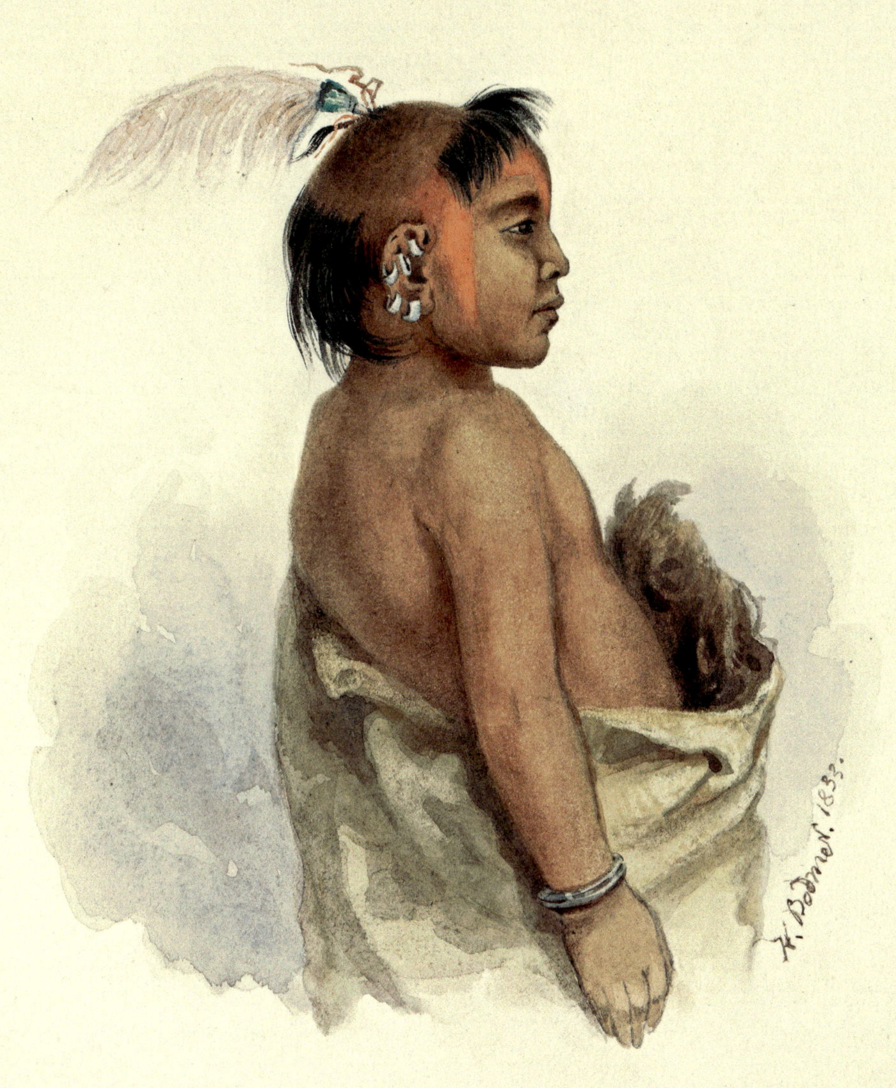

5. Schudegácheh, Ponca Chief

1833

Shifting watercourses, shallow channels, and submerged snags made steamboat travel a challenge, necessitating frequent stops to clear the passage, make repairs, or wait for higher water. Taking advantage of these delays, Maximilian's party often left the *Yellow Stone* to search for plant and animal specimens to collect and topographic landmarks to record. On May 11, 1833, they returned from an excursion near present-day Yankton, South Dakota, to find three Ponca men on their ship, including the chief named Schudegácheh (He Who Smokes/Makes Smoke). Here, he wears around his neck a silver peace medal bearing the likeness of President James Madison. Ostensibly symbols of friendship and allegiance, these medallions were distributed by federal officials and emissaries and were often prized by their recipients. On their return journey down the Missouri nearly a year later, Maximilian and Bodmer met Schudegácheh again, this time more elaborately dressed in a shirt and cap made of otter skin. (*NAJ* 2:104nM43)

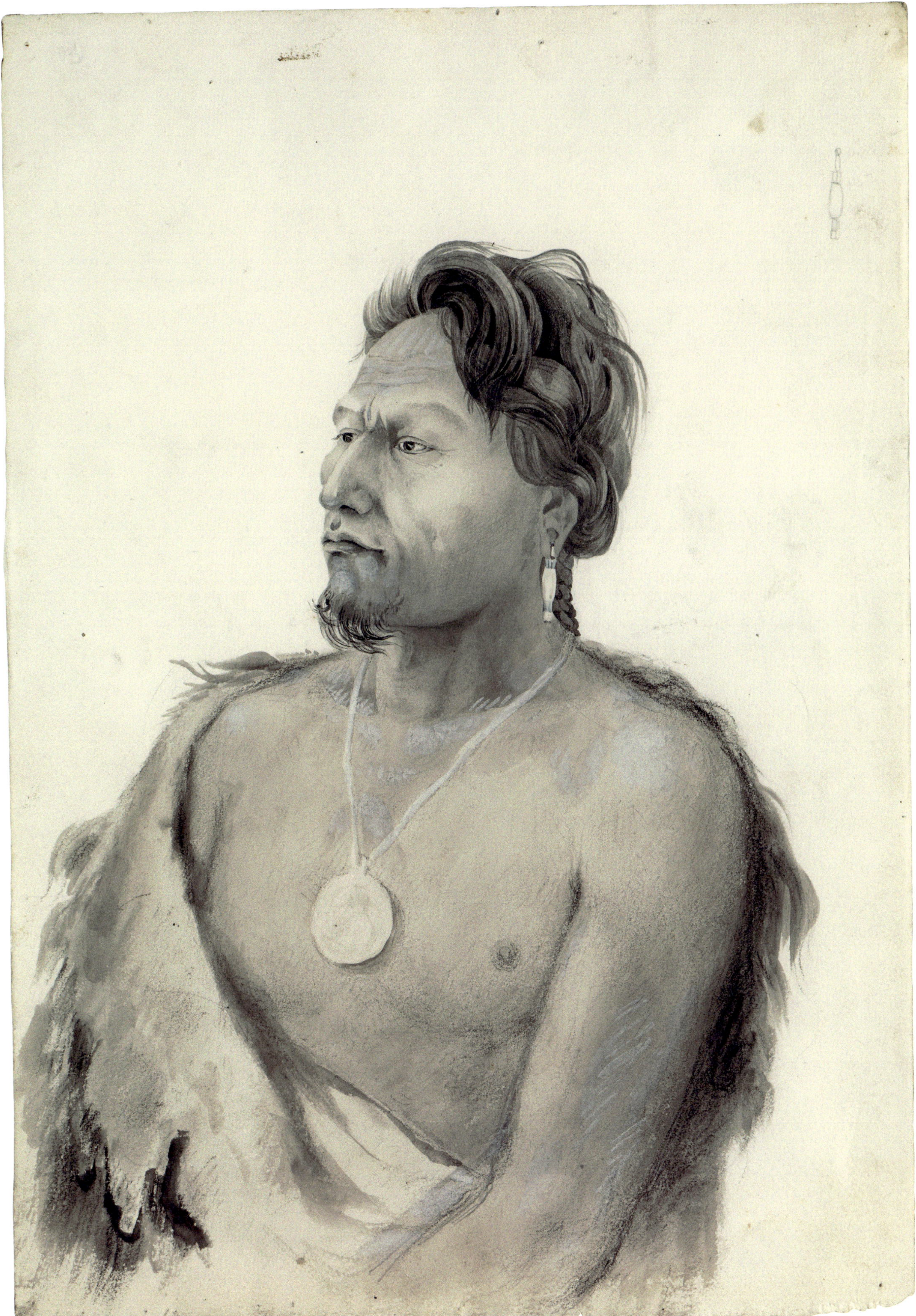

6. Passítopa, Ponca Man

1833

Passítopa (Four Tips) was with his brother Schudegácheh (pl. 5) on the day in May 1833 when their small party of Poncas met Maximilian and Bodmer. Here, Passítopa wears his buffalo robe draped over one shoulder with the fur side out and a bright neckband of beads or ribbon. (*NAJ* 2:104nM44)

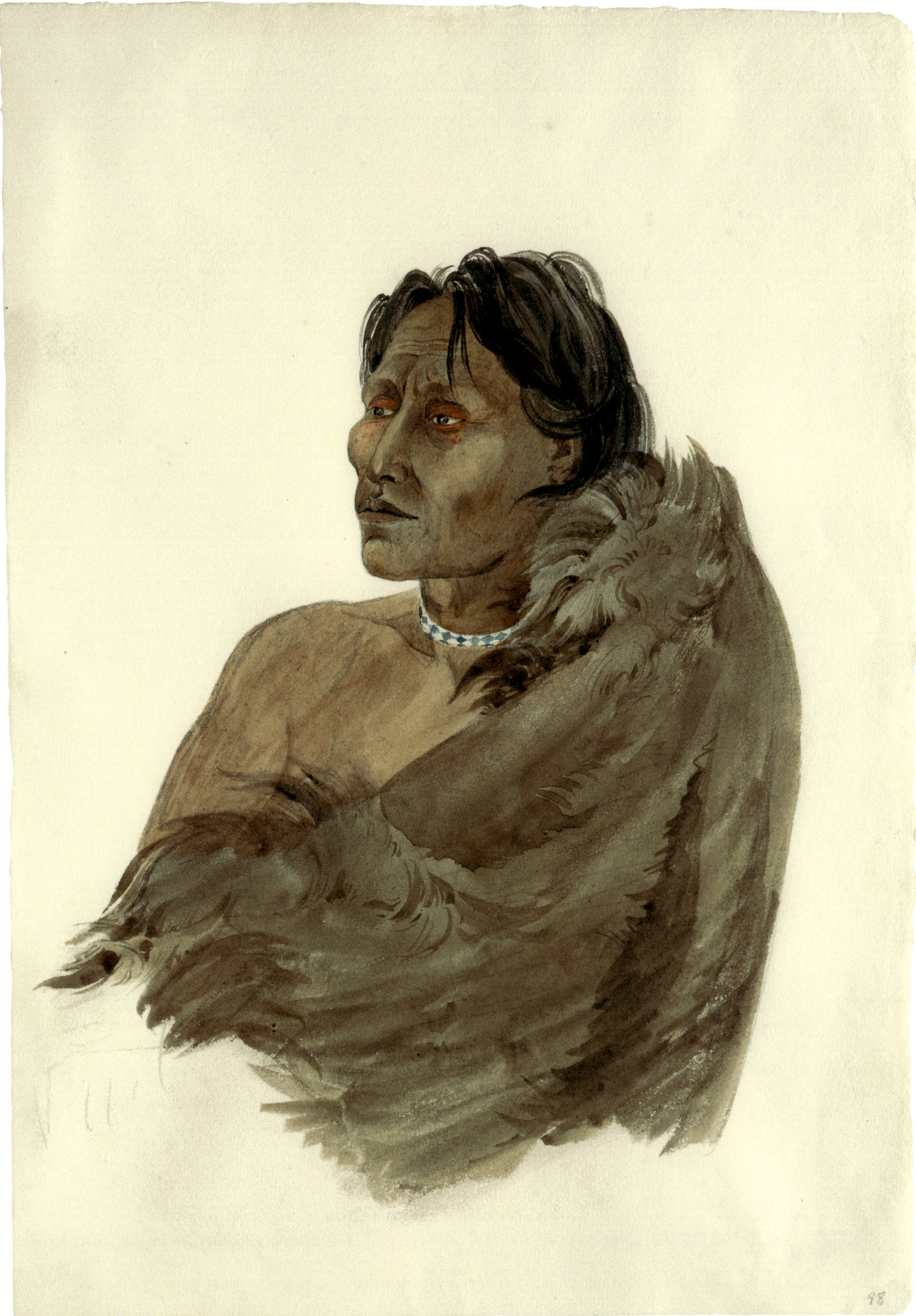

98

7. Hó-Ta-Mä,
Ponca Man

1833

On May 30, 1833, the *Yellow Stone* arrived at Fort Pierre, in modern-day South Dakota, a major American Fur Company post. There, the ship was loaded with bartered hides for its return to Saint Louis. After several days at the fort, Maximilian's party boarded the *Assiniboine,* another American Fur Company steamer, to continue the journey up the Missouri. Early on in their short sojourn at Fort Pierre, Bodmer painted a portrait of Hó-Ta-Mä, described by Maximilian as a handsome young Ponca man. Hó-Ta-Mä was either visiting or living among the numerous Sioux camped near the fort. A modern translation of his name is Goes about Bellowing, perhaps a reference to the power and roaring of male bison during breeding season. (*NAJ* 2:158 and n8; *TINA* 160)

 FACES FROM THE INTERIOR

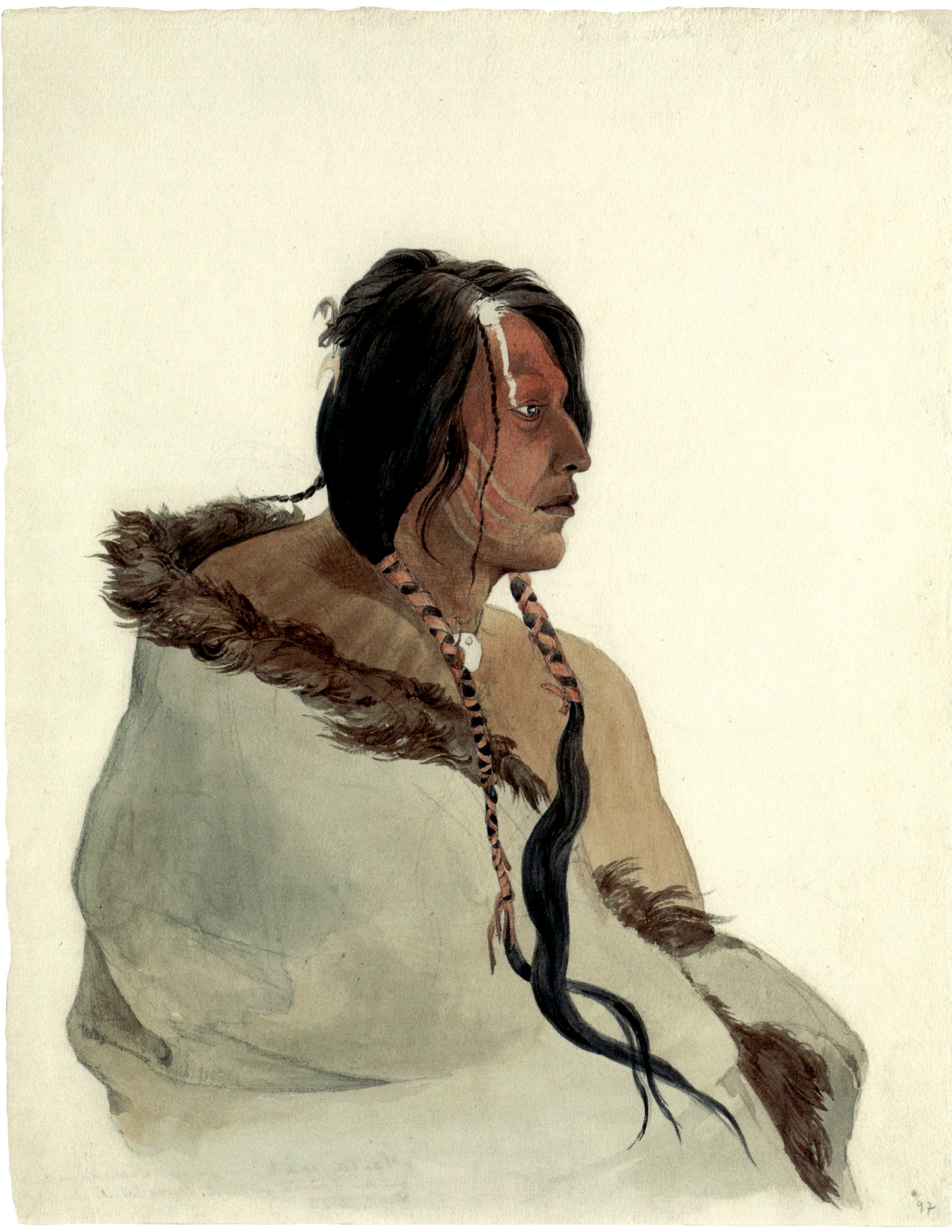

8. Wahktǎgeli, Yankton Sioux Chief

1833

At a federal Indian agency located somewhere near the modern city of Chamberlain, South Dakota, Maximilian and Bodmer met a chief described by Maximilian as "the foremost . . . Yankton Indian at the Sioux Agency." The name Wahktǎgeli was translated by the prince as Valiant Warrior; Americans called him Big Soldier. Bodmer began his likeness on May 25, 1833, and continued the following day. "The chief appeared in full regalia, his face painted completely red with cinnabar. . . . On his head he wore long feathers from birds of prey . . . fastened with a red ribbon; . . . hanging on his chest the medal he had received from the president of the United States. . . . His leather leggins, painted with dark transverse lines and crosses and very nicely adorned at the outer seam with a wide [strip] embroidered in porcupine quills with yellow, red, and sky-blue figures. . . . He wore a large buffalo hide, tanned white on the outside and wrapped around his body; in his hand was the pipe-tomahawk, which he smoked." (*NAJ* 2:139–40)

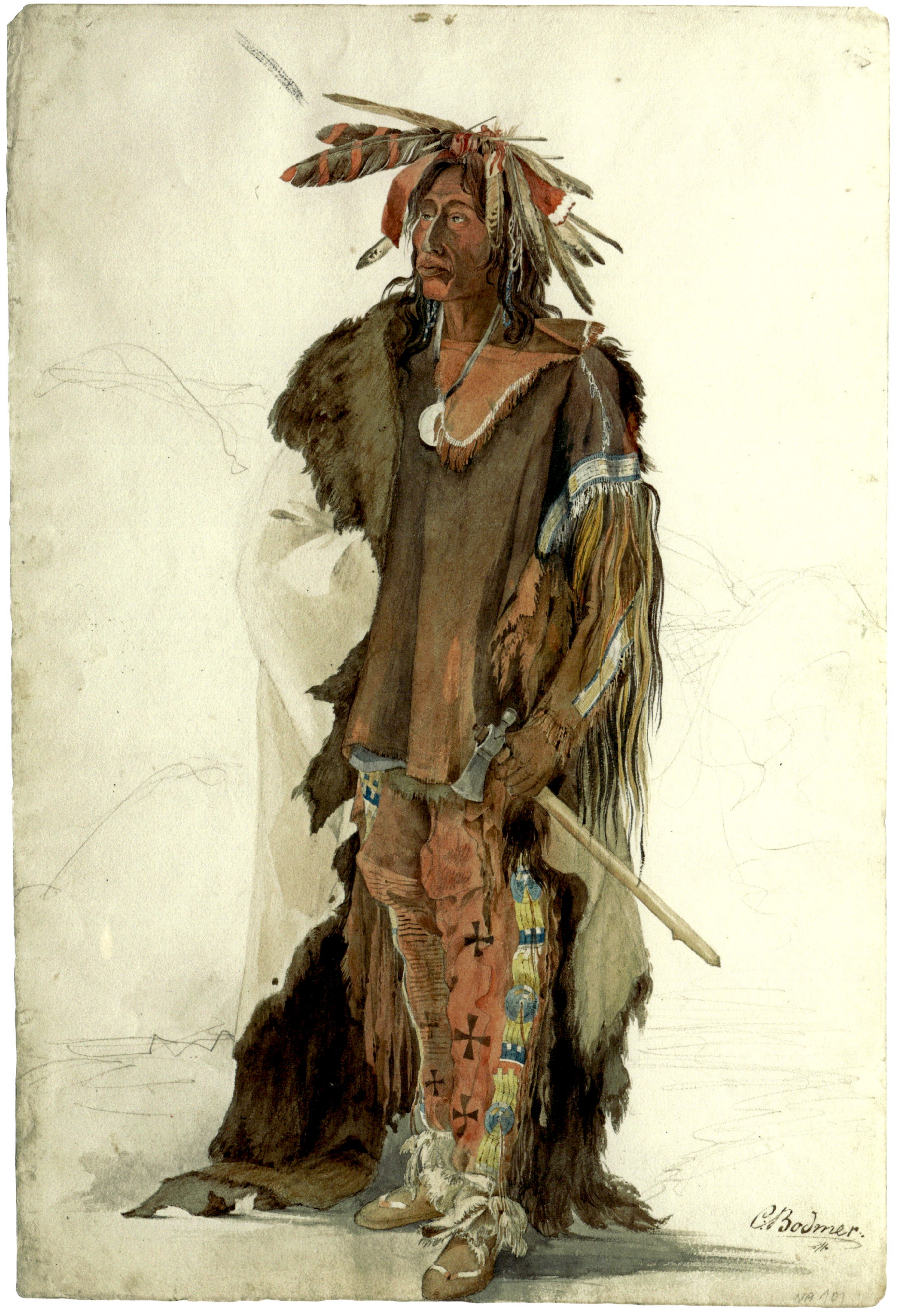

9. Tukán-Hätón,
Yankton Sioux Chief
1833

At the time his portrait was made in May 1833, Tukán-Hätón and his family were in mourning for some of their children who had recently died. Maximilian observed that they were "poorly and plainly dressed" to show their grief. Tukán-Hätón's hair, bound in what appears to be patterned cloth, looks roughly cut or shorn, likely another expression of sorrow. Tukán-Hätón (Horned Rock) seems to have been called Little Soldier by the Americans. (*NAJ* 2:146 and NM80)

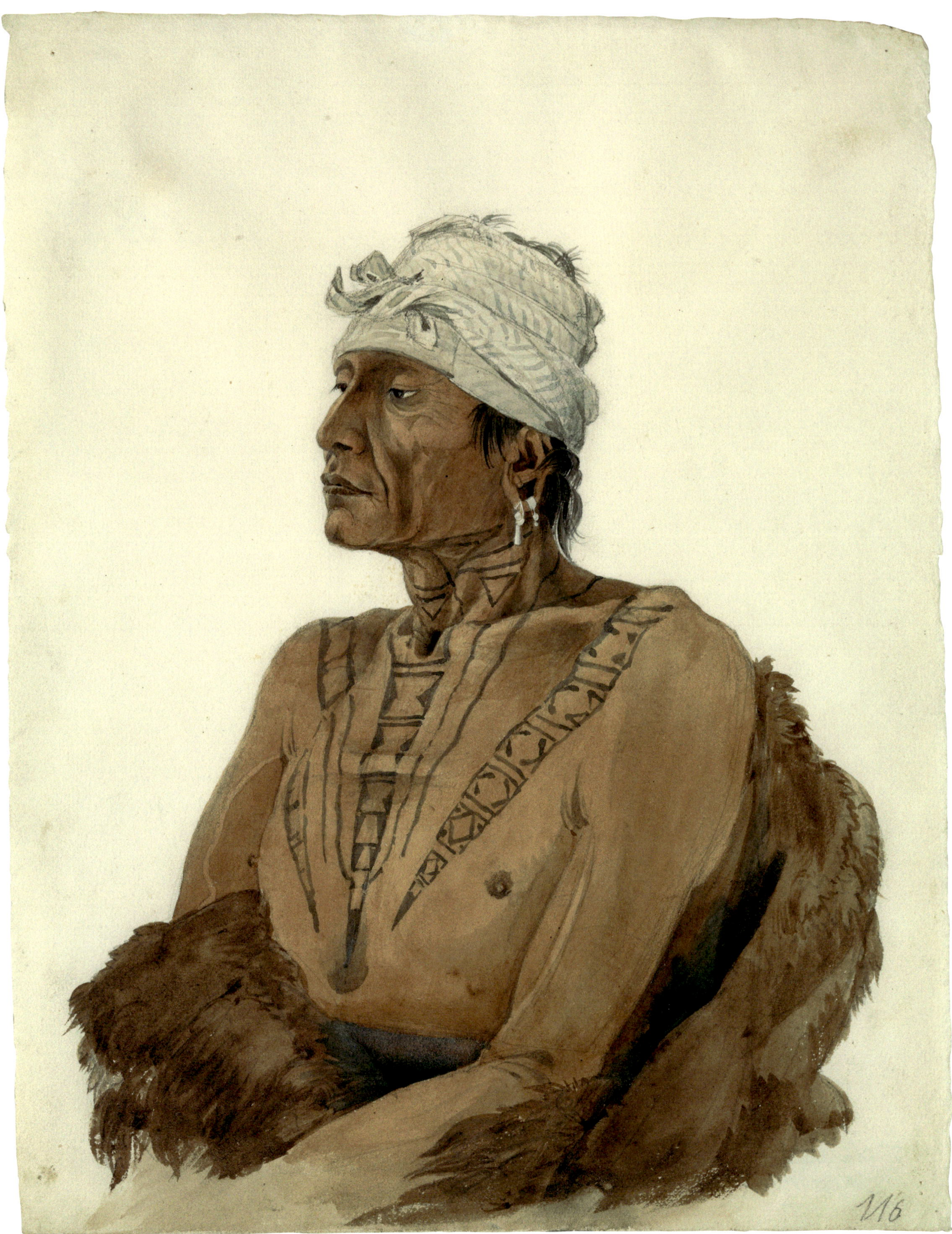

116

10. Psíhdjä-Sáhpa, Yanktonai Sioux Man

1834

This Yanktonai Sioux man visited Fort Clark—near what is now Bismarck, North Dakota—in January 1834. Initially reluctant to have his portrait made by Bodmer, he was persuaded by a Mandan comrade, Síh-Chidä (pl. 21). His ornaments include beaded hair bows, strings of beads and dentalium shells in his ears, and brass bangles. A modern rendering of the name Psíhdjä-Sáhpa is Black Swallow. (*NAJ* 3:238 and NM1)

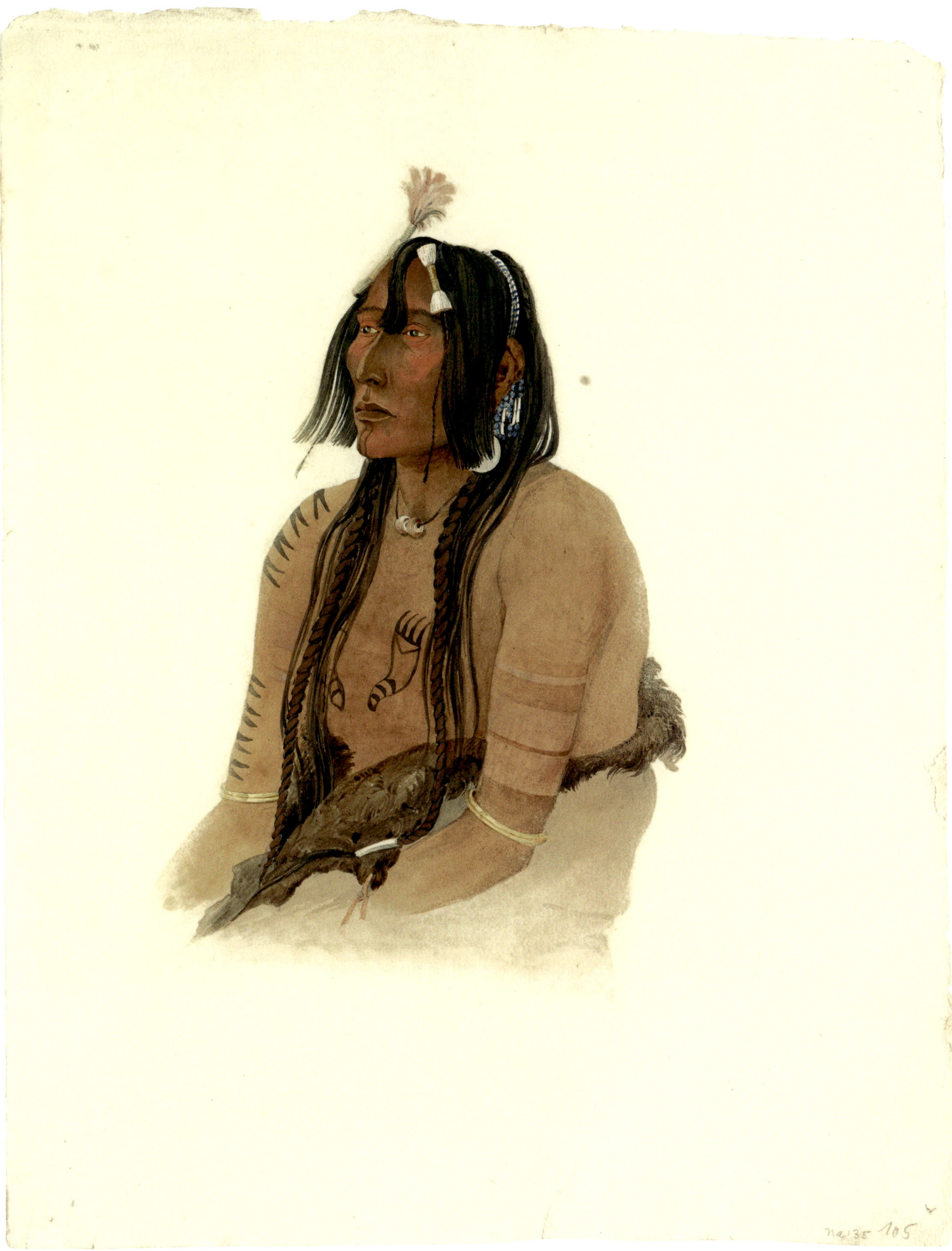

na 135 105

11. Wáh-Menítu, Lakota Sioux Man

1833

Wáh-Menítu (Spirit/God in the Water) was among a small party of Lakotas that visited the *Assiniboine* while it was docked at Fort Pierre on June 4, 1833. He had a "strikingly prominent upper lip and gently bent nose. . . . His hair hung around his head in disarray and in a queue over his left eye; on top . . . [he wore] a feather from a bird of prey in a horizontal position. . . . Mr. Bodmer gave him cinnabar so that he might freshly paint himself and make himself more handsome; this he did, whereupon he was sketched." Maximilian recorded that any warrior who touched a slain enemy under hostile fire was entitled to fasten a horizontal feather in his hair; Wáh-Menítu wears three. Maximilian and Bodmer met him again at Fort Pierre on their return journey downriver in April 1834. He was from the Sicangu (Brule) band of Lakotas. (*NAJ* 2:161)

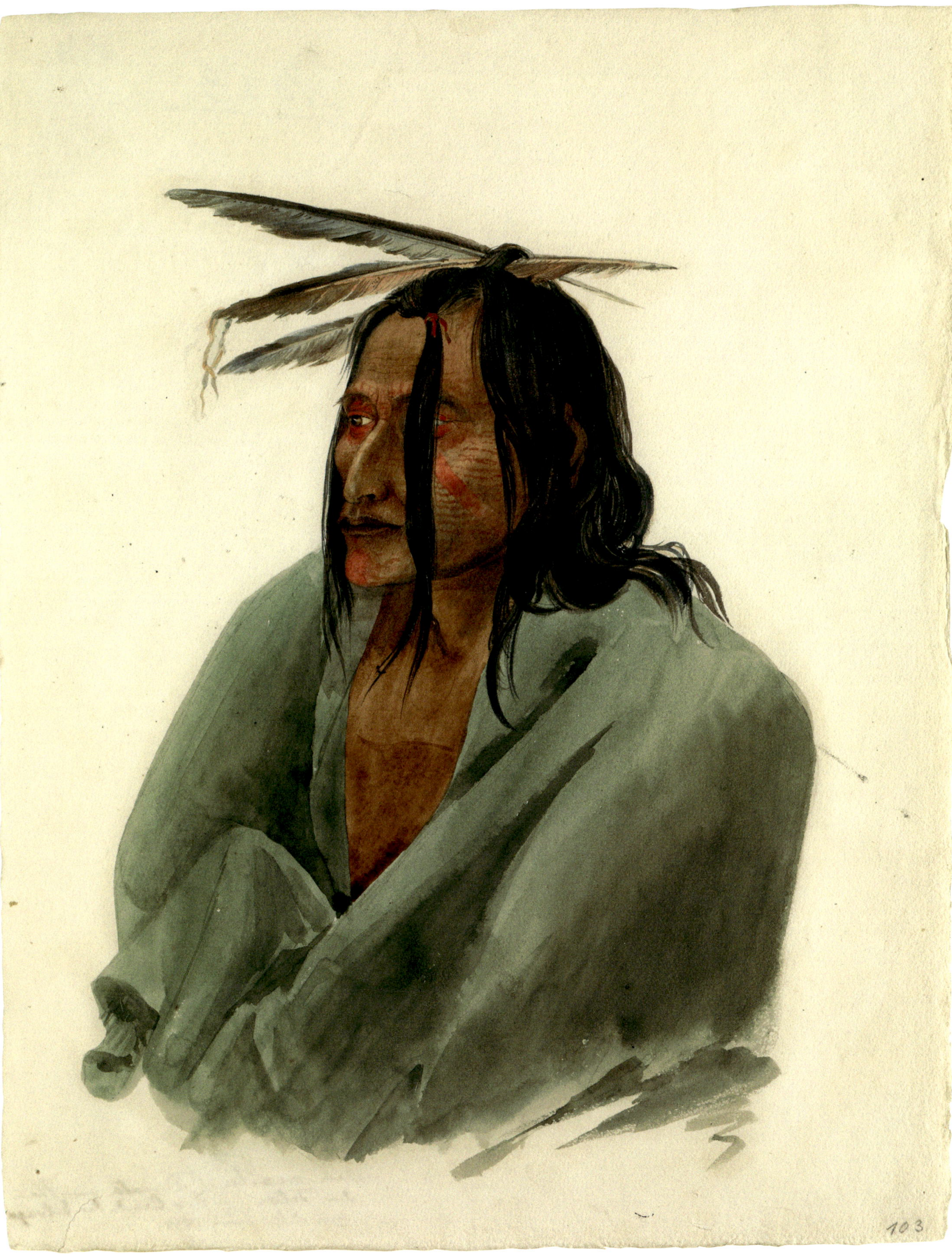

103

12. Chan-Chä-Uiá-Te-Üinn, Lakota Sioux Woman

1833

Maximilian and Bodmer met many of the Lakota and
Yankton people who were camped around Fort Pierre in
early June 1833. Among them was this well-dressed woman
whose name was translated by Maximilian as Woman of
the Crow Nation. She wears a buffalo robe in the box-and-
border style, characterized by geometric patterns painted
along the robe's edges; these designs were painted exclu-
sively by women. The small metal cones that line the hem
of her dress would have tinkled musically as she walked.
Maximilian purchased the robe, which may be one of two
similar robes now in the collection of the Linden-Museum
Stuttgart. A faint pencil outline of a girl on the left side of
the sheet appears to be an Assiniboine and Blackfoot child
Bodmer met four months later at Fort Union (see pl. 35),
a major American Fur Company trading post located on
the Missouri River near the present-day North Dakota–
Montana border. After the expedition, Bodmer combined
the two unrelated portraits into a single image as one of
the many prints that illustrated Maximilian's publication
about their travels. (*NAJ* 2:159nM11)

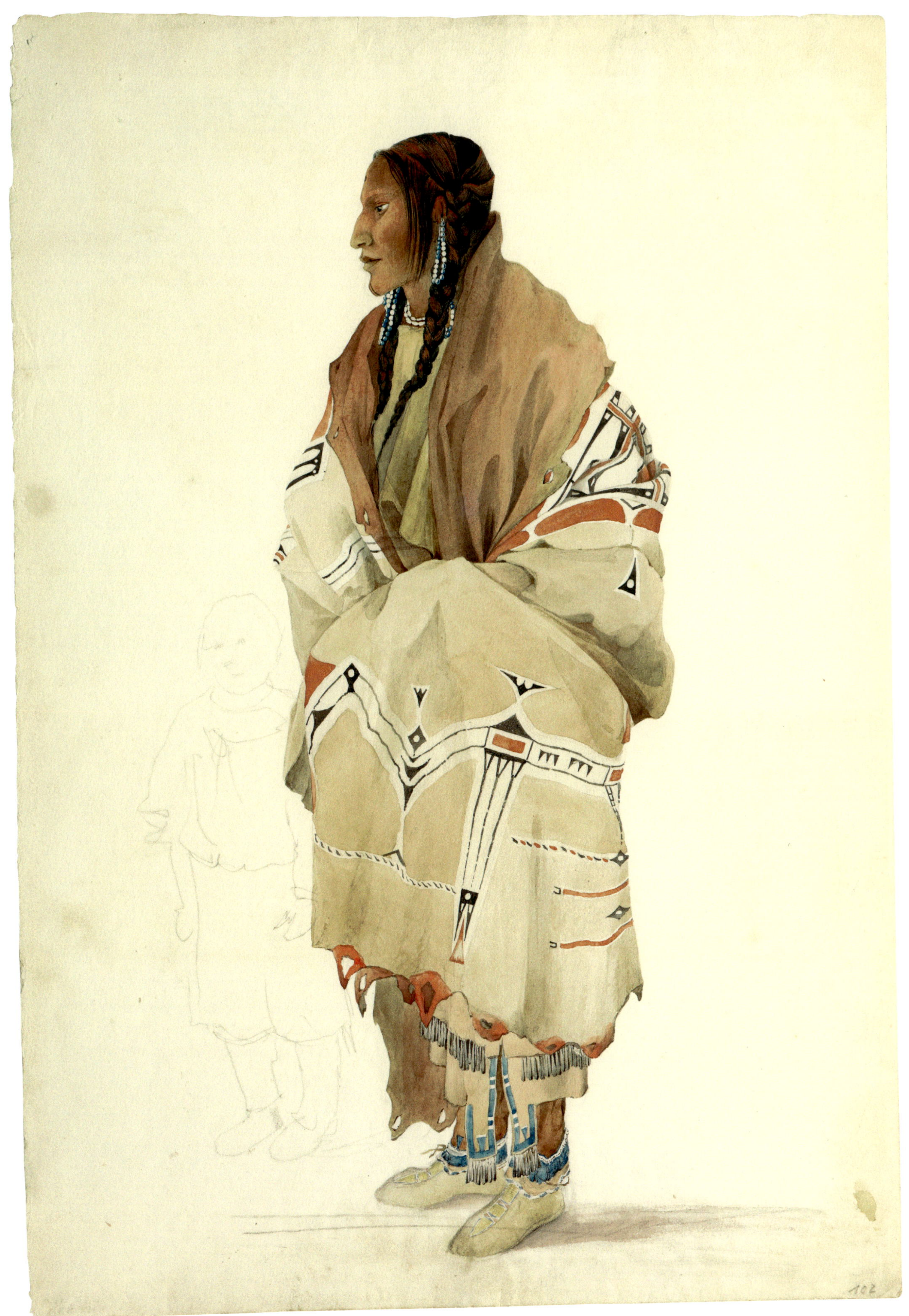

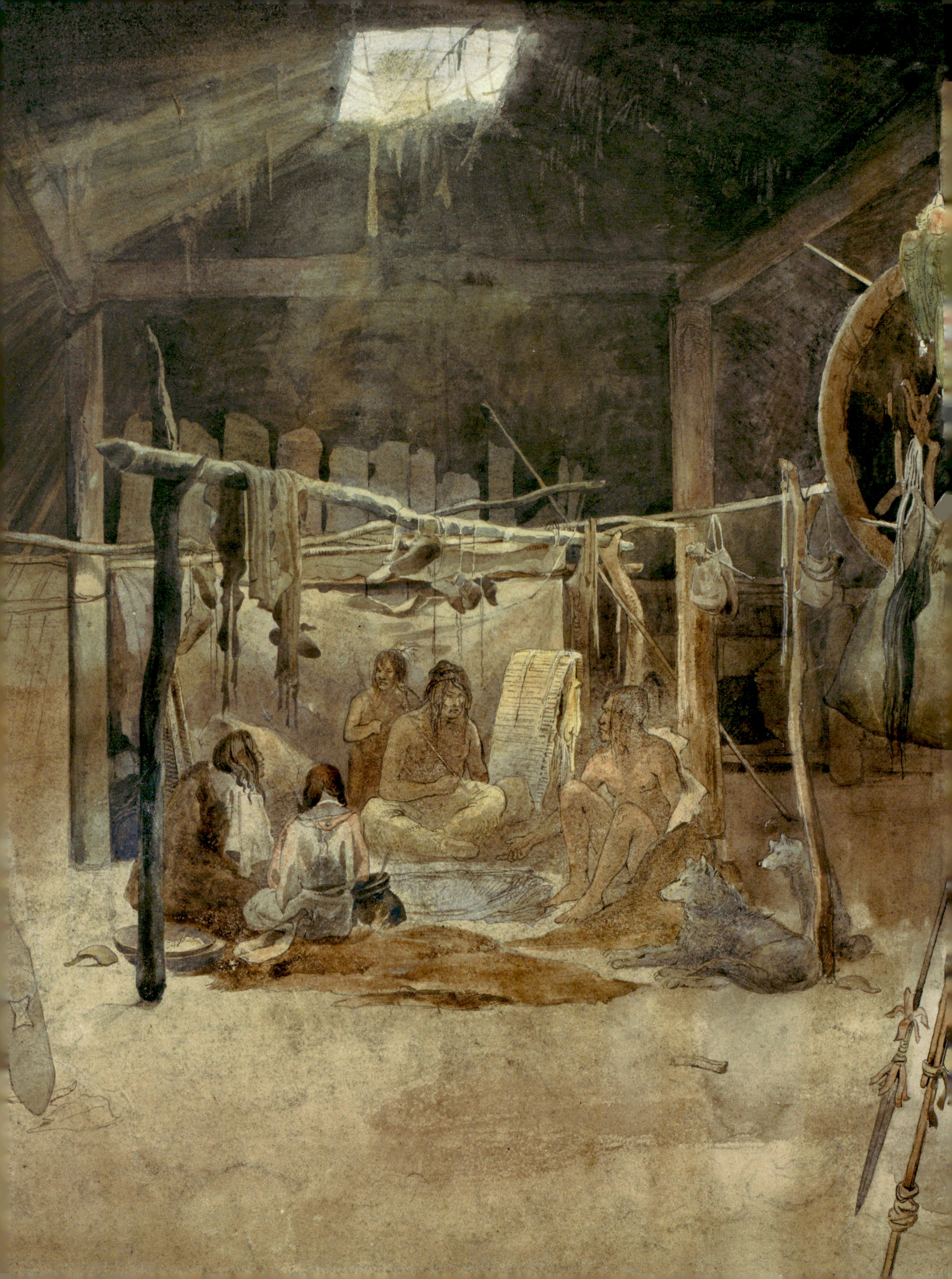

BRINGING THE STORY BACK

AN INTERVIEW WITH GERARD BAKER

PART 1: THE EARTH LODGE

Annika K. Johnson

KARL BODMER AND PRINCE MAXIMILIAN OF WIED SPENT more time with Mandan and Hidatsa people than any other community during their travels along the Missouri River. Between November 1833 and April 1834, they stayed at Fort Clark and visited Hidatsa and Mandan villages along the Knife River, which is now a National Historical Site managed by the National Park Service. Maximilian and Bodmer's robust textual and visual record of this time have introduced subsequent generations to individuals such as Mató-Tópe (Four Bears) and Péhriska-Rúhpa (Two Ravens) as well as aspects of village life in the wintertime, the season of storytelling and ceremony.

Maximilian's journals and Bodmer's watercolors have been invaluable resources for Gerard Baker in his research on his Mandan and Hidatsa ancestors. Baker grew up on the Fort Berthold Indian Reservation in North Dakota, home to the Mandan, Hidatsa, and Arikara Nation (the Three Affiliated Tribes). His career working for the National Park Service began close to home in 1979, at the Knife River Indian Villages National Historic Site. Baker has advocated for Native American voices in the interpretation of numerous historic sites, notably as superintendent of the Little Bighorn Battlefield National Monument, the Mount Rushmore National Memorial, and the Lewis and Clark National Historic Trail. Baker retired from his position as assistant director of American Indian relations at the National Park Service in 2010.

In the following interview, Baker attests to the importance of balancing non-Native historical documents with oral history, traditional knowledge, and the experiences of Indigenous people. Baker's extensive knowledge of life along the Upper Missouri River and his commitment to cultural revitalization are indispensable to the interpretation of Bodmer's watercolors and their continued importance. He sees these works as scientific illustrations that convey as much about the technique required to make a bull boat or a headdress as they do about dynamic cultural relationships of the time. In Baker's community, Bodmer's watercolors have

Karl Bodmer, *Interior of a Mandan Earth Lodge,* 1833–34 (detail of fig. 1).

retained their relevance not only as ethnographic documents but as pictures of relatives—familiar persons and lands with stories to tell.

Over the course of three days at his home in Montana, Baker shared his impressions of the Mandan and Hidatsa people encountered by Bodmer and Maximilian. Our conversation began with a discussion of Bodmer's watercolor of the interior of an earth lodge.[1] For the agricultural communities living along the Upper Missouri River, life was centered around seasonal villages composed of earth lodges, large, semipermanent, circular dwellings made of earth and grasses that covered an internal frame of cottonwood posts and beams. Women typically owned and managed these majestic lodges that could house extended families. Earth lodges were considered sacred structures imbued with cosmological symbolism. Lodges had spaces set aside for a shrine, regalia, and bundles of sacred objects—often called medicines—that embodied an individual's visionary power, often associated with animals. An individual can obtain medicine power through a dream or belong to a medicine society charged with spiritual responsibilities to the community. Medicine was a recurring theme in our discussions.

ANNIKA JOHNSON: Bodmer's *Interior of a Mandan Earth Lodge* (fig. 1) is one of your favorite watercolors. What does this tell us about Bodmer's painting practice in the field and about earth lodges?

GERARD BAKER: Bodmer obviously had a very good rapport with Maximilian, and vice versa. In reading the journals, I think they had to have been talking all the time in the field.[2] Of course, they had interpreters with them, but as far as I'm concerned the problem with the interpreters, especially at that time, is you're going through different languages. If it's Mandan, you've got the Nuptare and Nuetare dialects; if it's Hidatsa, Awadixa, or Awaxawi, each one of those has a different dialect. There's a lot of communication that I think was not complete because of who they were talking to, who was in the room at that time, and who felt safe talking.

Interior of a Mandan Earth Lodge tells a story. There are three women; the men are smoking trade pipes; the kids are missing, so maybe they are in bed already along the back wall. Atutish, or Lodge Boy [a mythical figure], would reside inside the outer ring where the families put their belongings.[3] What I like about this painting is that it shows the household: it shows the household bags—it's like us hanging up our frying pans; they're drying off moccasins above the fire so they won't burn; and they must be drying out a shirt, too. These details show that the painting was actually done there.

I was first introduced to Bodmer not on the reservation or in my home but at the Knife River Indian Villages [National Historic Site]. I always knew about Knife River, and I always knew what was inside an earth lodge, but not in detail like in this watercolor. I didn't realize the men sat around so much, but it's wintertime, I guess. When you look at it in detail, you can see what the old guys were talking about. When they built the earth lodges, for example, it was a woman's job, it was their house. The women who had the medicine to build a lodge would get paid in buffalo

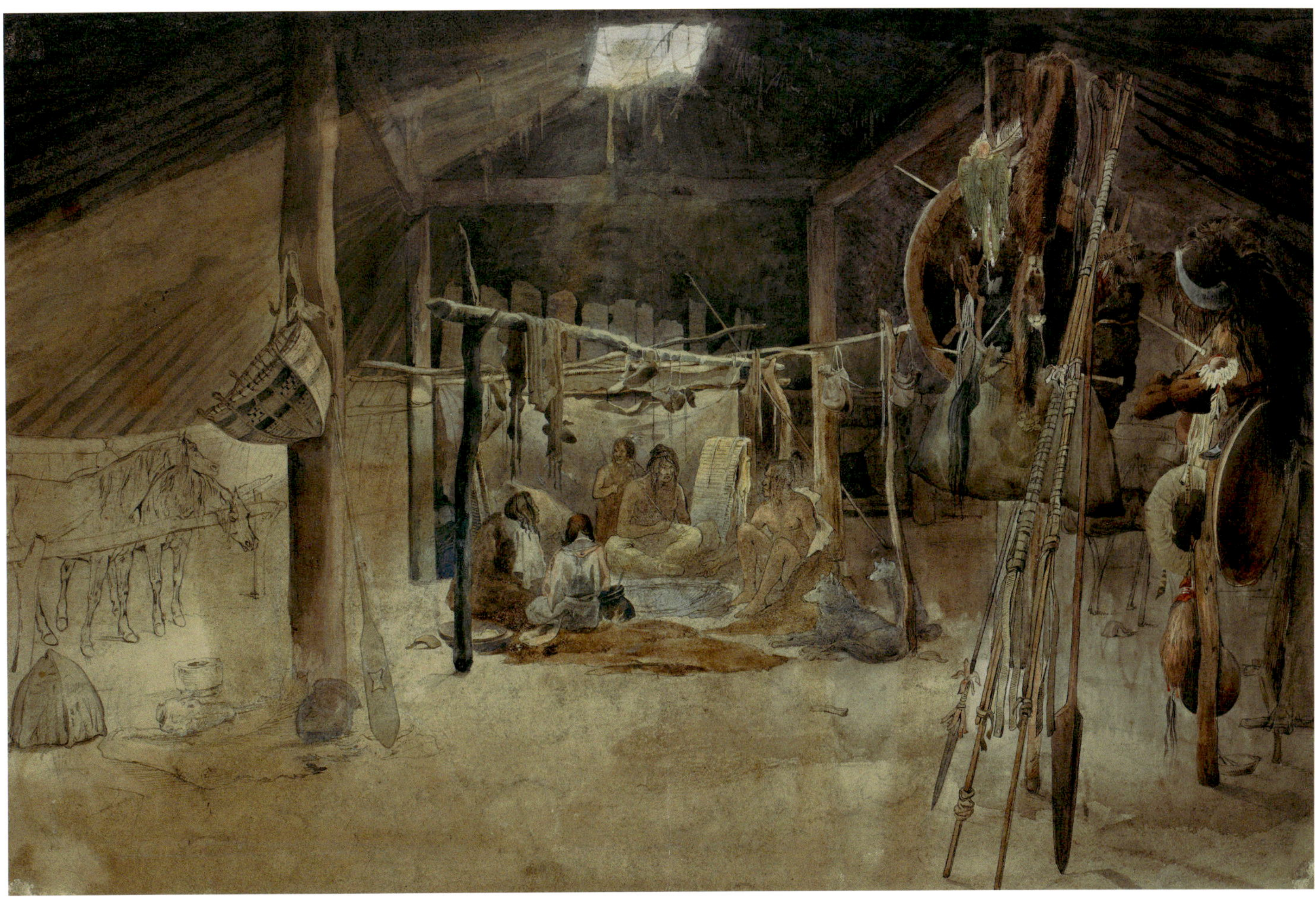

robes and food—*xuba,* dried meat and that type of thing. She'd get paid more for a creating a round smoke hole versus a square hole above the lodge's hearth.[4] The square hole was considered a little bit weaker from a physics standpoint, whereas a round hole would hopefully have the same amount of weight around it. I often think of the bark that's coming down from the rafters [in the painting]. This detail really personalized it. At the same time, I wonder what is not supposed to be in Bodmer's paintings [for culturally sensitive reasons], and I don't know that. And maybe the family put some of the sacred medicines away [before Bodmer could see and paint them].

AJ: For viewers who don't have cultural knowledge to draw from and only have Bodmer's images and Maximilian's journals, is there a danger in regarding Bodmer's paintings of Mandan and Hidatsa culture as "accurate"?

GB: I look at it the opposite way. Bodmer wanted to do his best to portray the earth lodge scientifically, which means he painted everything as precisely as he saw it. Bodmer, like George Catlin, made mistakes—not from an accuracy standpoint, but in the process of creating composite images.[5] This is because he didn't know too much about us, and that's also evident in Maximilian's writings. But I think the paintings show what he actually saw. What I like about this is that I don't see anything that's not supposed to be in the lodge. I see things misplaced, but that was a practical matter.[6] Do those guys sitting around the fire know he's there? I think so.

AJ: You mentioned that you first encountered *Interior of Mandan Earth Lodge* when you worked at the Knife River Indian Villages National Historic Site.

GB: Growing up on the reservation, we used to talk a lot about the historical activities of Mandan families, but not necessarily about where they lived, like earth lodges. I knew about their gardens, but I didn't know specifics about how they planted. I knew a lot about the men things, not about women things. My mom wouldn't tell me about women things, even when she got really old. I was getting desperate because I knew she was going to be going, and I wanted to visit with her. And I would say, "You can tell me mom. I won't tell anybody." And she would say, "I can't tell you. You're not supposed to hear that, and we're not supposed to discuss it."

I didn't know who Bodmer was. I didn't know who Maximilian was. I barely knew who Lewis and Clark were until when I got that in Indian school at Mandaree, on the Fort Berthold reservation. Before Indian school, I never heard about Lewis and Clark. I heard about York [a person enslaved by the Clark family who accompanied William Clark on the expedition]; I didn't know his name, but he was known as the Black guy back in those days. And I knew about the woman, Sakakawea—who we call by a different name now: Ma-esu-weash [Hidatsa for "Eagle Woman"].[7] I knew a lot of people were coming up the river to deal with us, trading and that kind of stuff. But because of what they went through and because of what their folks went through and because of what their grandparents went through, the elders of today weren't really in tune with these villages. They weren't in tune to the way of life back in those days because of all the crap they went through: the boarding schools, forced education, losing of land, breaking of the treaties, and that went on for generations.

The way I see it is that if we pay attention to him, Bodmer is bringing that story back to a certain extent through pictures. I'll read Maximilian's stuff, but I'll read it with a grain of salt. I really think Bodmer and Maximilian tried to be the camera of the day. When I read recently that Bodmer was working from a scientific standpoint rather than from an artistic standpoint, that made a big difference to me.[8] That means Bodmer really tried to be accurate. What I do with Maximilian's writings—and [anthropologist Robert] Lowie's, Catlin's, and whoever else's I can find— you read everything and then put a picture together.[9] You have bits and pieces, and it turns into a supposedly full story.

When we grew up I think most people on the reservation learned about social customs and primarily the bad things—smallpox, the flu epidemics, the tribes after we got sick and died, and the government officials who were killing the rest of us. All of this changed, all the things

Bodmer painted changed. And the time that he painted was a completely different time. We lost a lot of the specifics about our history for a long time because of everything [the colonization of this region]. So now there's a lot of us on the reservation that are becoming aware of Bodmer because of places like Knife River, because of places like maybe Joslyn—although we're not going down there very much; we will, but people don't know about the paintings down there. I think that we're starting to get an eye into that, and we need to because we're losing it.

AJ: When you look at these images, do you think Bodmer had a sense of the great changes that were underway during this time due to the incursion of Europeans and the territorial expansion of the United States?

GB: Not yet, no. These are relatively pure. Later on, you see those changes. This goes back to what Bodmer with Maximilian were trying to accomplish: an accurate scientific study. I'm sure the influence of other tribes can be seen in these paintings, because they show the European-introduced steel implements that came from other tribes or the American Fur Company.[10] I think what Bodmer did—and he was probably the last to do it—was create an accurate, or almost accurate, account of some of the sitters. For example, the Mandan and Hidatsa lodges were supposed to always be clean, and this one here is really clean. I don't know what that object is [beneath the two dogs]. I was thinking that it was associated with those dogs; maybe a bone. Would he do that? If he did, then it'd be fantastic, because then he's doing detail. Then he's doing the scientific stuff.

AJ: How do you think Bodmer's images relate to Maximilian's journals? Do you feel that it's helpful to go back and forth between the journals and Bodmer's paintings?

GB: They match up really well because they both needed each other to process what they were doing. Maximilian, being the interpreter, if you will, talked with them. Bodmer, being the scientific painter, really needed the information that Maximilian was getting about the culture so he could draw it accurately. The more you know about what you're drawing, the more accurate you're going to be. Especially with the Indians, because, remember, you have to go through translators. That was always the difficult part. The time-consuming part was to sit there and have somebody talk to you about this [scene]. I would imagine that if you were drawing this kind of stuff, a person would say, You drew that wrong. It should be this way. I bet that happened, too; it wasn't a cut-and-dried thing. So I think Bodmer and Maximilian needed each other, and they worked hand in hand. When they went back to Paris, that's when they really had to depend on Maximilian's journals. When you're away from that village, you start losing detail.

AJ: What do you think of his unfinished drawings, like *Hidatsa Scalp Dance* (fig. 2)?

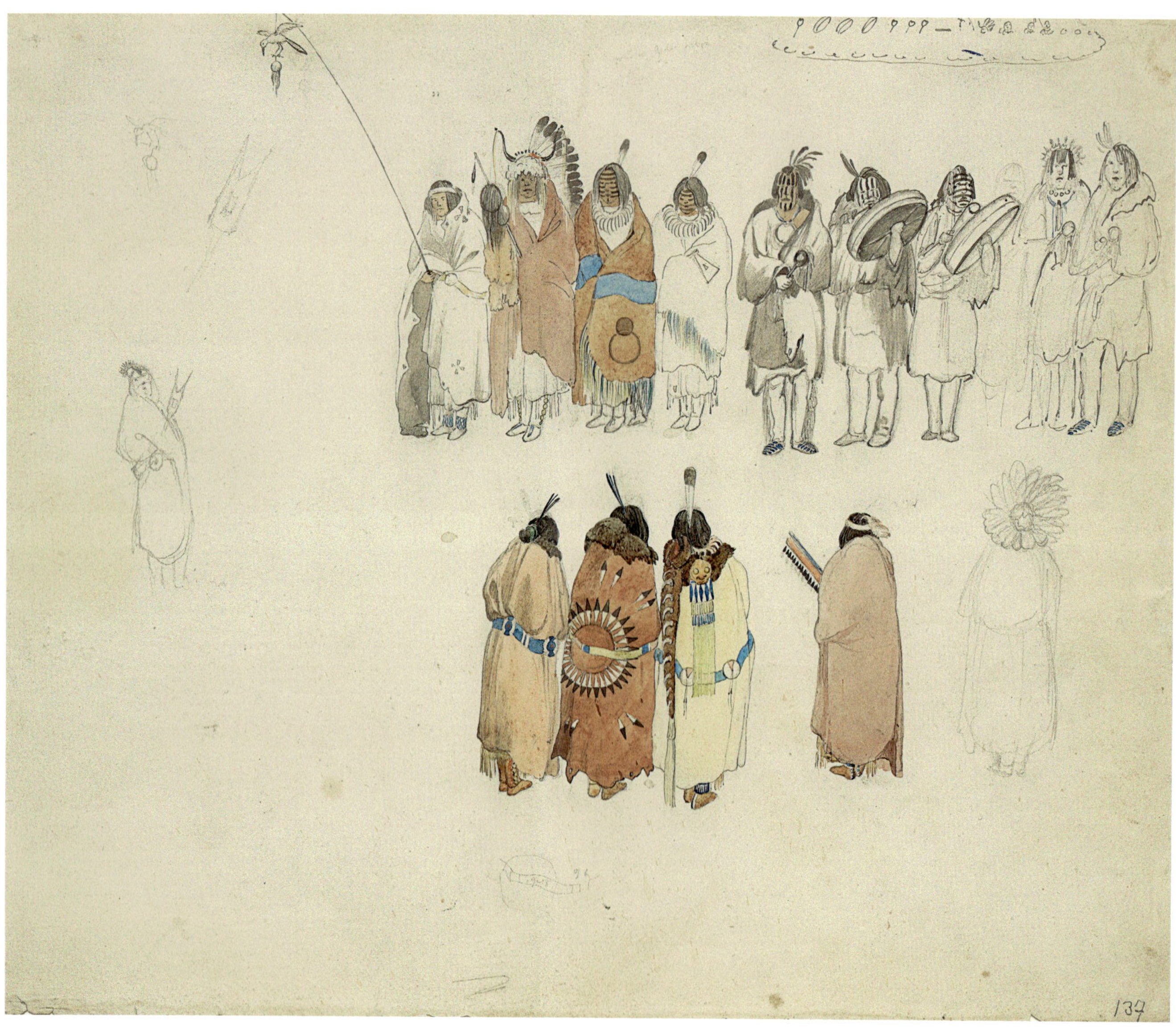

FIGURE 2   Karl Bodmer, *Hidatsa Scalp Dance*, 1833, watercolor and graphite on paper. Joslyn Art Museum, Gift of the Enron Art Foundation, 1986.49.279.

GB: He's trying to make them extremely accurate but not complete; he'd finish it in Paris and pair it with Maximilian's narration. There are certain aspects that are really well done. Why is one robe all red and painted with a blue strip [where other figures aren't as complete]? There's a bird attached to a willow rod—they must have dried it with its wings out, and it's holding onto a scalp; there has to be meaning for that. Each woman has different moccasin designs and leggings. Scalp dances are supposed to be done by women: When guys came back from war, they gave their scalps to the women, the women would put them on poles, and these guys would sing, and the women would dance. Musicians had big hand drums back in those days.

AJ: Did they have the square or circular drums that sat on the ground in those days?

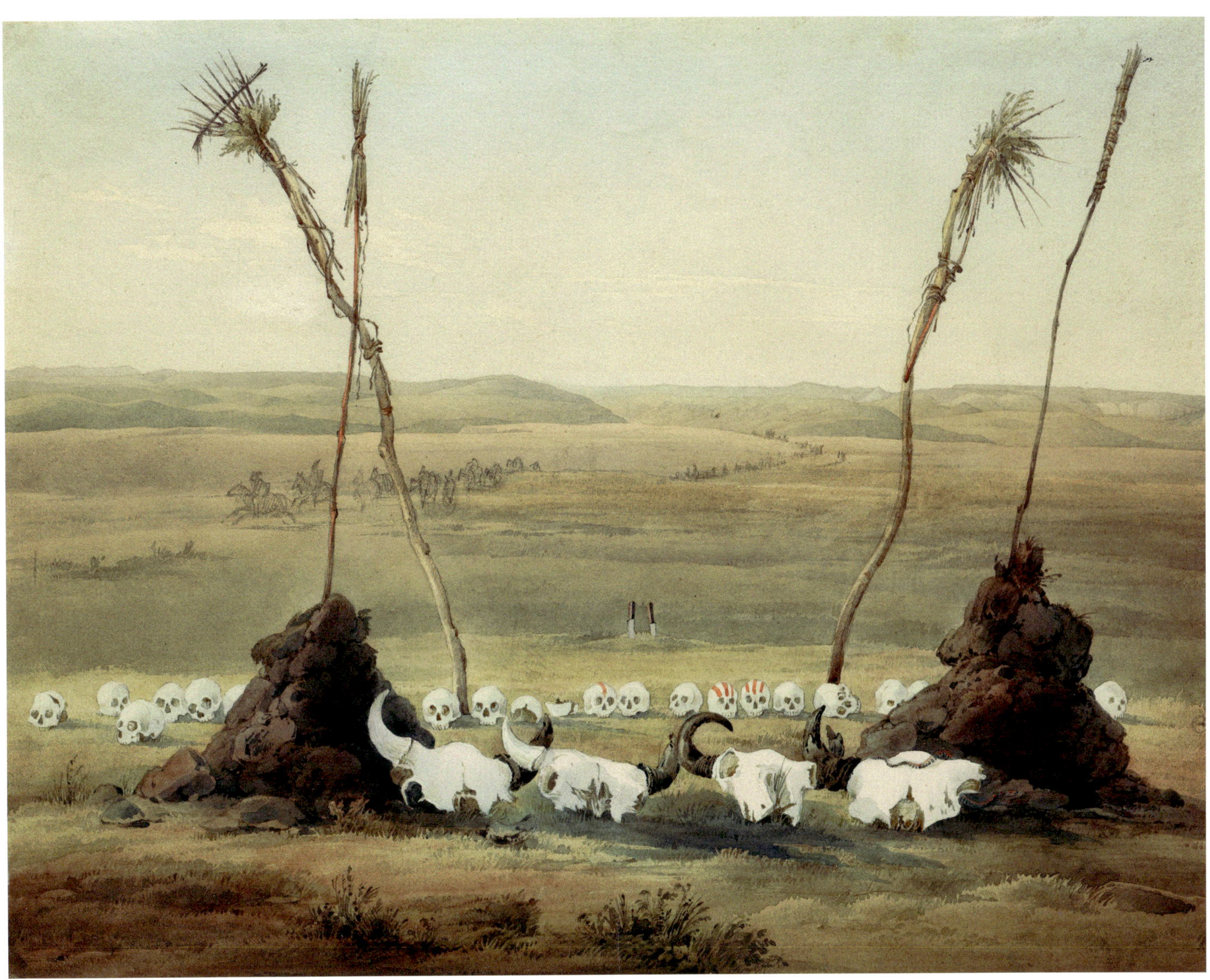

GB: We didn't get those until the 1920s or 1930s when the government said, Okay, you guys can start singing again, you can start celebrating again.[11] Before that we couldn't do [the scalp dance] because the government disallowed it—or it died out because of smallpox in 1837. When the government said we could get together again, it came with stipulations. That's when they created grass dance songs. Our grass-dance songs—those come from the Santee. My understanding is that they bought them from the Santee at Sisseton in southeastern North Dakota. When scalping was outlawed, they'd use grass instead of scalps and put it on their belts. If you did a grass dance and scalp dance at the same time, they wouldn't match up; they look completely different. But philosophically they would match if you understand the meaning behind the grass dances.

AJ: Now we are looking at Bodmer's *Mandan Shrine* (fig. 3). Does the term "shrine" convey the meaning behind this arrangement of human and buffalo skulls?

GB: No, that's a non-Indian term. The stories about these is that the skulls come from the scaffold burials, when you bury a person on top of a scaffold and wait until the body decays enough for the bones to fall down. The [family would] take those skulls and put them in a ring, like in this image. The buffalo is always the protector, so that's why you have the four buffalo skulls representing the four directions of the earth, the four sacred areas. They would be in a prominent place so that when you came by, you could bring rocks and leave them there. That's a village moving in the background; maybe they're going back to summer lodges from the river. I've always liked this image because it shows the symbolism and the protection and how we depend on our spirits to help us.

When we look at Bodmer, George Catlin, Alfred Jacob Miller, and everybody who painted in the region, that's where the misconception of us being extremely holy all the time comes in. Because they always print the good stuff. There's no humanism in [their pictures] when it comes to the actual living and the actual thinking. What Bodmer does is select certain ceremonial events and sometimes pull them together [in composite images], and it enforces that idea that we're always doing holy things. No, we weren't! These paintings only represent certain times of the year. When I worked for Park Service, I'd get sick of tourists who were coming down and saying, You guys are so holy and prayed all the time. Baloney! We were human beings. We had jealously and hatred just like everyone else.

AJ: Are there still remnants of similar burials and memorials in present-day North Dakota?

GB: If we looked really hard, I'm willing to bet we could find some of these burials. At Knife River, I used to know where a lot of the turtle effigies were around the villages. I went there lately to try to find them again to show my cousin. I was so mad because the farmers had cleared out all their fields, and they put rocks on top of those things—they didn't know what they were. From a scientific standpoint, that's good because they're now protected. It's destroyed from a visual standpoint, but it's still there, so that's a good thing. A lot of the landscapes have been changed by modern ranching, farming, and transportation.

AJ: When you look at Bodmer's landscapes, what are some of the major ecological changes you see since Bodmer's time?

GB: There are big-time changes that tie into stories. For example, at Knife River, there's a huge change because we now we have coal-fired power plants there. They had to knock down big cottonwood trees in order to get the fields and put the crops there. Slash and burn, right?

That was all predicted by the Creator when they made the earth. One of the stories I've always heard is that after everything [the earth] was made, the creators were going to leave, and they told the people, "We're going to go now. Everything is all done. We taught you how to live and gave you everything you can get from the animals that taught you as well." On and on like that. "But there's going to be a time when you're going need us again. There's going be a time when your tongues are going to fall out. There's going to be a time when you're going sit in the same bed as your sister." They started saying all these different things that were going to happen and that came true.

Our tongues are falling out today. You know what that means, right? We are losing our language. We've lost respect for the female, and we're supposed to respect her. Anyway, they said, "We're not just going to pop in and say 'We're here.' We're going to give you signs to watch for, and when those four signs happen, we'll be back. And then we'll have to gather everybody and have a big meal and basically start over again." They said to watch for the first sign when the grandfather [the Missouri River] goes north. The second sign is when the trees grow in straight lines. The third sign is when the grass turns upside down, and the fourth sign is when the trees lie with their roots in the air. They said when all those happen, watch for us, and they left.

Those things have all happened. The river is going north. If you look at the Missouri, you realize that we have three big dams on it: the Oahe, the Garrison, and the Fort Peck. That essentially has stopped that river, and it is going north. Even in times of drought, the banks are falling in, and it is still coming back north. If you go to Knife River and over in that direction and even toward Minnesota, we have trees unnaturally growing in straight lines now that are planted by farmers: windbreaks. When the grass turns upside down is easy: that's plowing. And the last one is when the big trees lie upside down. The people couldn't believe that would happen; they thought that you could never do that. Well, when they first started the open-pit mining, what did they do? They pulled all those cottonwood trees down to get them out of there, and they're lying upside down. So all that's happened: the landscape has changed to fit the prediction. At least at Knife River. I'm sure other tribes have those same things. Up and down the river, all those landscapes have changed.

When I was giving my talks about Lewis and Clark, I used to always say that I put things into four different categories of natural and cultural resources: before Lewis and Clark, during Lewis and Clark, the last two hundred years and what's happening now, and the future. You can picture that it would be the same thing with Bodmer. Let's say he goes around Knife River, standing on those buttes, looking down at the big flares, the big open mine pits, and all of the traffic. Line them all up: put Catlin there, put Bodmer there, put the Mandan chief Mató-Tópe there—put whoever else you got there, some of the women, obviously, too—and ask them, What do you think? Because you guys helped do this, you guys helped settle this country. You have to ask them, Are you happy, or does it make you cry? And when it comes to landscapes, that's what we have to ask ourselves to this day. To me it's really sad, our so-called progress, because they changed everything.

AJ: The universe is essentially upside down in that prophecy.

GB: Yup, everything has changed. The landscape changes, and it's going to keep changing. We're killing our landscapes. We've essentially killed the big cottonwood trees below the dam, because by putting those dams up and stopping the flooding, we've killed those trees. We needed that flooding for those trees to survive. And so we're continuing to kill this land, we're continuing to kill the landscape as it was during Bodmer and Catlin's time and before. If those guys came back today, they wouldn't even recognize the place. And we're moving so fast in our lives now that we don't even recognize it anymore, and we don't even try to recognize it anymore. We just look at it as progress. And it doesn't make sense to me.

If you read the journals or listen to the old stories—our stories—and if the stories are said good enough or if the journals are read good enough, you can actually feel what people may interpret to be the emptiness of the land. But we Indians interpret it to be the fullness of the land. It's full of birds, it's full of grasshoppers, it's full of wind. It's not only the visual aspects of the landscapes; it's the taste, it's the smell, it's the feeling. It's your spirit that is damaged now, and we don't know how to heal it. So that's where the landscapes are at—according to Baker.

1. This interview is condensed from several hours of recorded conversations between Annika K. Johnson, the Stacy & Bruce Simon Curator of Native American Art at Joslyn Art Museum, and Gerard Baker. These conversations took place in February 2020 at Baker's ranch near Miles City, Montana. They have been edited for length and clarity. Original audio and transcripts of these interviews are held in the Margre H. Durham Center for Western Studies, Joslyn Art Museum. The author would like to thank Gerard and Mary Kay Baker for their enthusiasm and generosity during the recording and editing of this interview.

2. Maximilian organized his field notes (present location unknown) into three volumes of handwritten manuscript journals now located at Joslyn Art Museum. Baker refers to the translated version published as *The North American Journals of Prince Maximilian of Wied*, ed. Marsha V. Gallagher and Steven S. Witte, trans. William J. Orr, Paul Schach, and Dieter Karch (Norman: University of Oklahoma Press; Omaha: Joslyn Art Museum, Margre H. Durham Center for Western Studies, 2008–12), 2:157–58 (hereafter *NAJ*). See also the selected bibliography (p. 215).

3. Traditional Hidatsa stories tell of the hero twins Lodge Boy and Spring Boy, who were ripped from their mother's womb by a monster. Lodge Boy was cast to the outer ring of an earth lodge interior, and Spring Boy was given away to a spring outside the village. These cultural figures are associated with various sacred rites. See Alfred Bowers, *Hidatsa Social and Ceremonial Organization*, Smithsonian Institution Bureau of American Ethnology Bulletin 194 (Washington DC: Smithsonian Institution Bureau of Ethnology, 1965), 304–08.

4. The smoke holes were constructed in the center of the earthen roof directly above the lodge's hearth.

5. Bodmer's lithographic tableaux are often composites of several watercolor portraits and landscapes. For more on this, see Kristine K. Ronan's essay in this volume, pp. 195–209.

6. According to Baker, the buffalo headdress and other regalia seen in the right foreground must have been moved aside to make room for Bodmer to sketch. This view faces the doorway and provides the most comprehensive view of the lodge interior while also shielding the medicine area, to which only certain individuals were admitted.

7. A group of elders from the Three Affiliated Tribes are in the final stages of publishing an account of the true story of Ma-esu-weash, better known to the world as Sakakawea. It traces her family connections from the time before Lewis and Clark to the present.

8. On the topic of Bodmer and scientific illustration, see Lisa Strong's essay in this catalogue, pp. 45–61.

9. See Robert Harry Lowie, *Societies of the Crow, Hidatsa, and Mandan Indians*, Anthropological Papers of the American Museum of Natural History 11, part 3 (New York: American Museum of Natural History, 1913); and George Catlin, *O-Kee-Pa: A Religious Ceremony; and Other Customs of the Mandans* (Philadelphia: Lippincott, 1867).

10. Other items prominently featured in Bodmer's watercolors include European trade beads known as "Crow" or "pony" beads and Chinese vermilion pigment obtained through the fur trade. Buffalo robes, moccasins, and other items were frequently traded or gifted between tribes.

11. Native American religious practices were banned by the US government on reservations between 1884 and 1935.

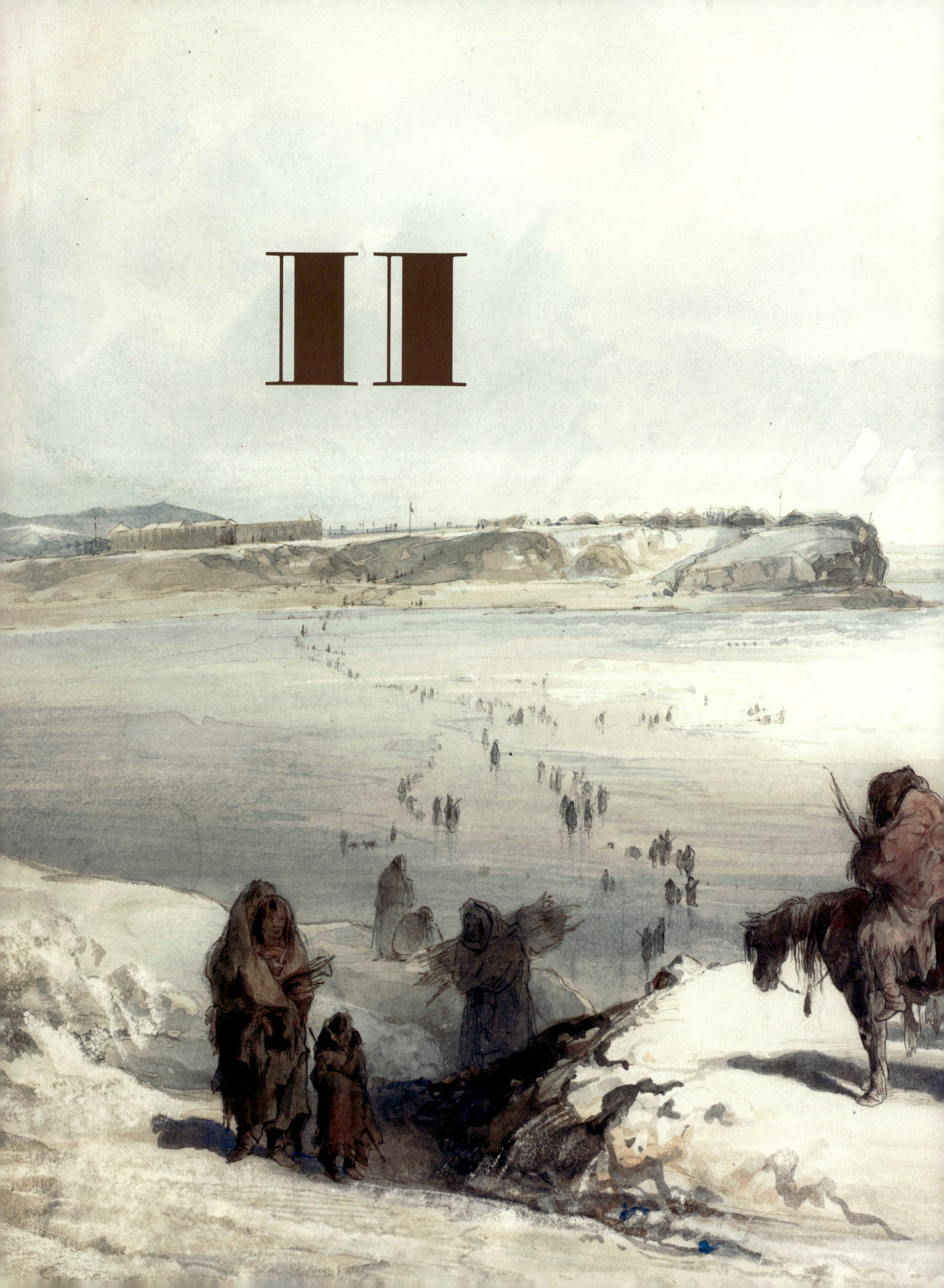

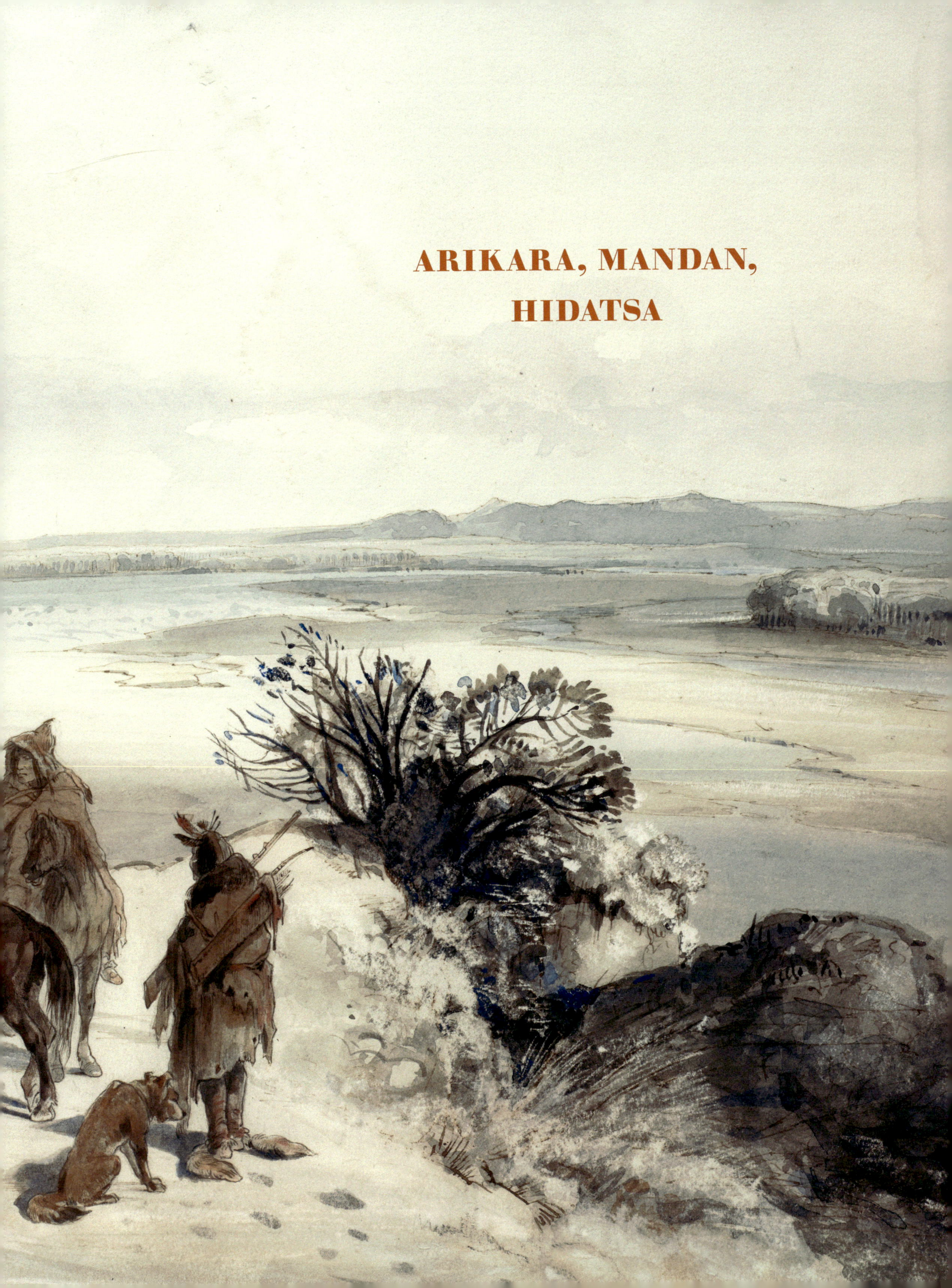
ARIKARA, MANDAN,
HIDATSA

13. Pachtüwa-Chtä, Arikara Man

1834

Bodmer painted Pachtüwa-Chtä's portrait in March 1834 at Fort Clark, near present-day Bismarck, North Dakota. Pachtüwa-Chtä was a comrade of Mató-Tópe (pls. 22 and 23), who introduced him to Bodmer. Pachtüwa-Chtä had recently participated in a war party that killed three traders near the Heart River in present-day North Dakota and presents a warrior-like appearance in this depiction. In the crook of his arm he carries a warclub with a painted blade; his chest has painted black circles resembling gunshot wounds, and the feathers and red sticks in his hair likely also commemorate battle encounters. Pachtüwa-Chtä asked Maximilian to draw a bear for him; then he also "wanted something like a forest on his picture, which I assured him I was not able to do . . . [and] Bodmer took over." (*NAJ* 3:269)

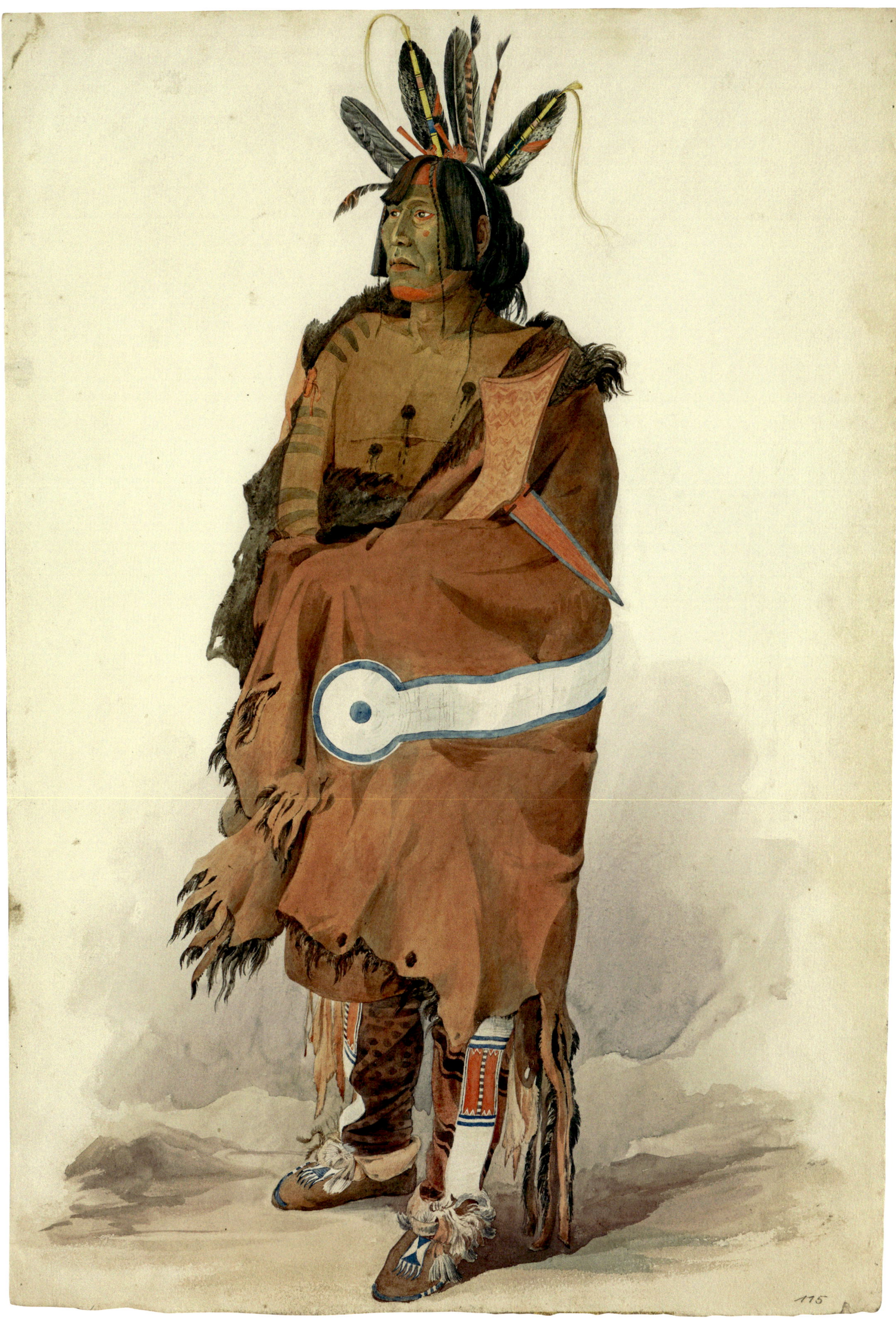

115

14. Leader of the Mandan Beróck-Óchatä

1834

Men's societies in Plains cultures were defined by age or warrior status. These carefully defined groups offered social benefits to their members, who in turn fulfilled responsibilities to the community at large. Maximilian observed six men's societies among the Mandans, including the prestigious Beróck-Óchatä, or Buffalo Bull Society. Its members were accomplished warriors, and their distinctive regalia included a mane-like headdress of buffalo hide with horns. Among these men, chosen by colleagues as the bravest of them, were two who wore a full mask: "a perfect facsimile of [an entire] buffalo head with its horns, set on their heads. They look out [through] its artificial eyes, [each] surrounded by a ring of iron or tin." One of these honorees posed for Bodmer at Fort Clark in April 1834. In addition to specific regalia, each society had a number of distinctive songs, which they sang when they danced as a group. Not long after this image was made, Maximilian and Bodmer witnessed a Beróck-Óchatä performance, which Bodmer recreated in a tableau in Maximilian's *Reise in das innere Nord-America* (right). (*NAJ* 3:166)

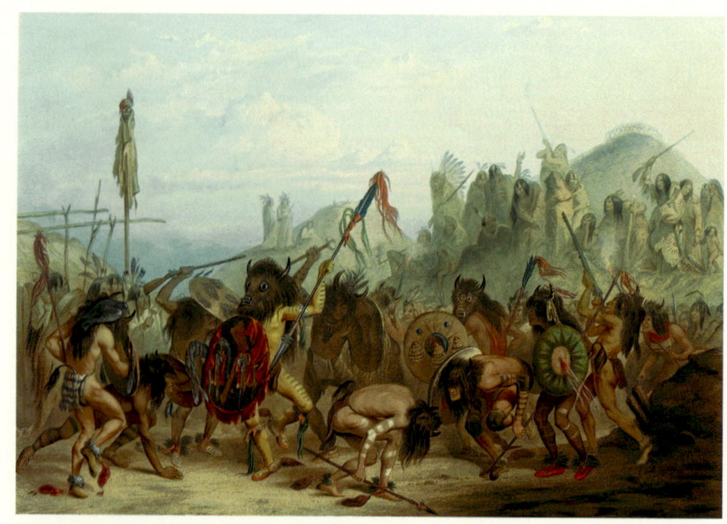

Alexandre Damien Manceau, after Karl Bodmer, *Bison-Dance of the Mandan Indians in front of their Medicine Lodge in Mih-Tutta-Hangkusch*, 1842, hand-colored engraving and aquatint. Joslyn Art Museum, Gift of the Enron Art Foundation, 1986.49.517.18.

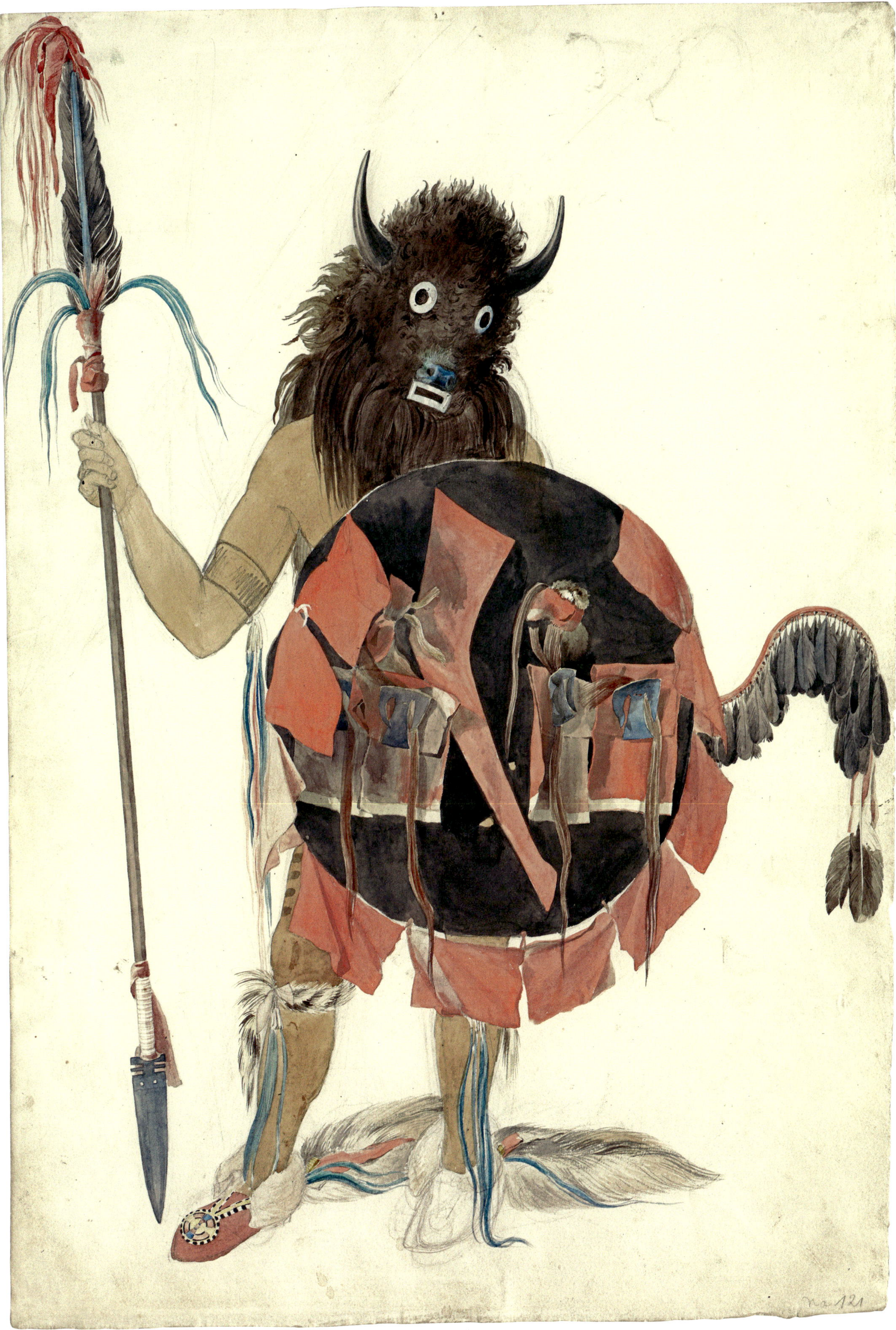

No 121

15. Máhchsi-Karéhde, Mandan Man

1833–34

Máhchsi-Karéhde (Flying War Eagle) frequently visited the cabin Maximilian, Bodmer, and Dreidoppel occupied at Fort Clark during the winter of 1833–34, sometimes staying the night. In this portrait, which Bodmer worked on over several days, Máhchsi-Karéhde wears a "beautiful bear claw necklace and a reddish-brown robe well decorated with [blue and white] glass beads." He also has a painted eagle feather in his hair and carries a ceremonial fan made of an eagle wing. Máhchsi-Karéhde's brother is depicted in plate 16. (*NAJ* 3:94 and n97)

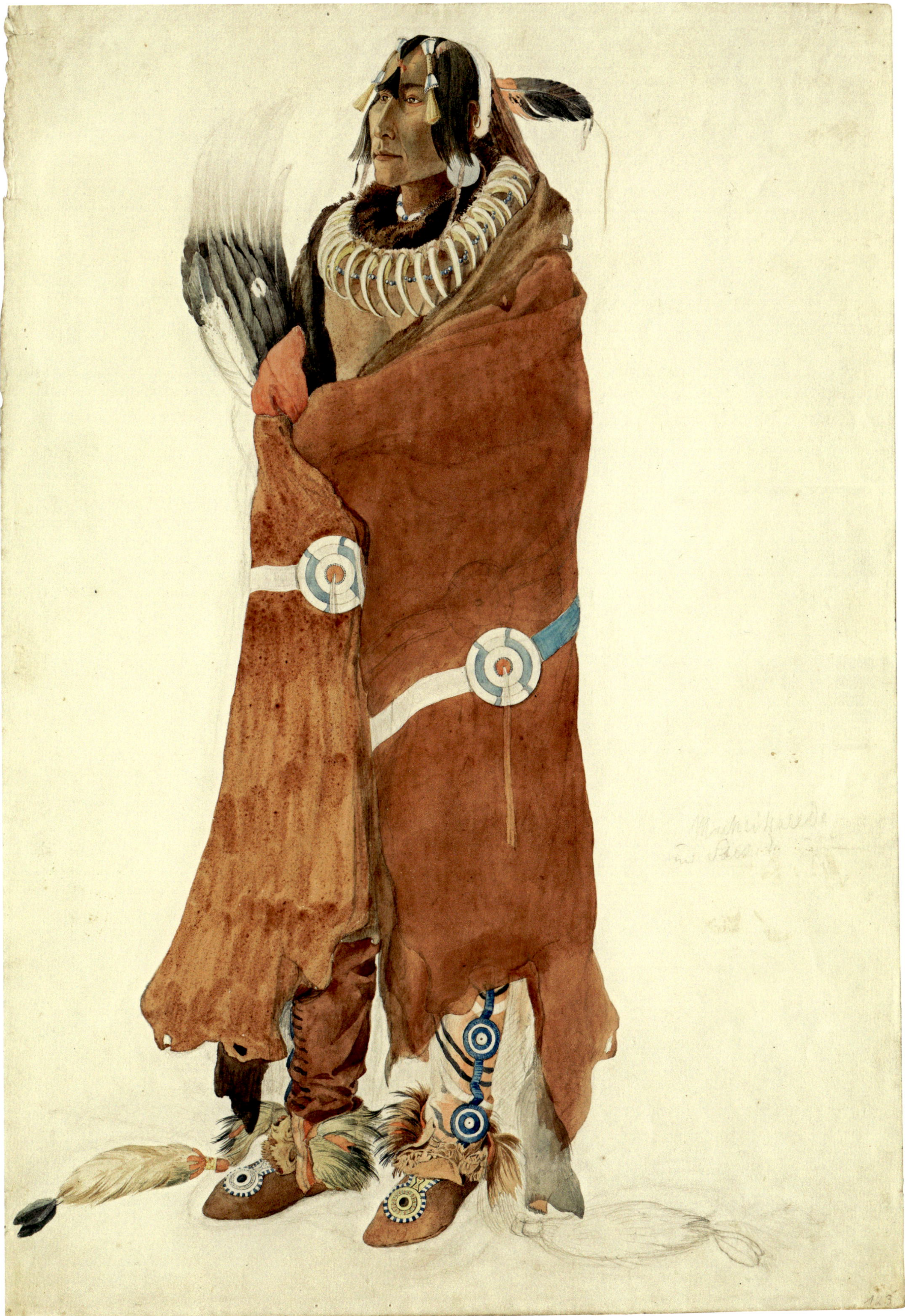

16. Mándeh-Páhchu, Mandan Man

1834

Bodmer began Mándeh-Páhchu's portrait at Fort Clark on
March 11, 1834, but the following day he was turned away
in favor of the "far better dressed" Péhriska-Rúhpa (pl. 29),
so the younger man's image was finished later that month.
Here, Mándeh-Páhchu's hair is richly adorned with bands
of brown and white fur, and at least one lock is extrava-
gantly bound and tasseled with blue and white trade beads.
His hairbows trail long strings of alternating blue beads
and white dentalium shells, ending in strips of what might
be ermine. His earrings include rectangular shell pendants,
possibly abalone traded from the Pacific coast, and his neck
is encircled with an unusual choker-style necklace, likely
made of soft rolls of buckskin covered in white and blue
beadwork. Maximilian took particular interest in Mándeh-
Páhchu's flute, describing it as wooden and about twenty
inches long, from which Mándeh-Páhchu could produce "a
soft sound similar to that of our flute; however, he blew it
buzzing with a tremolo when not holding the pipe horizon-
tally." Mándeh-Páhchu, whose name may be translated as
Eagle's Beak, had a brother, Máhchsi-Karéhde, also painted
by Bodmer (pl. 15). (*NAJ* 3:169nM41, 273)

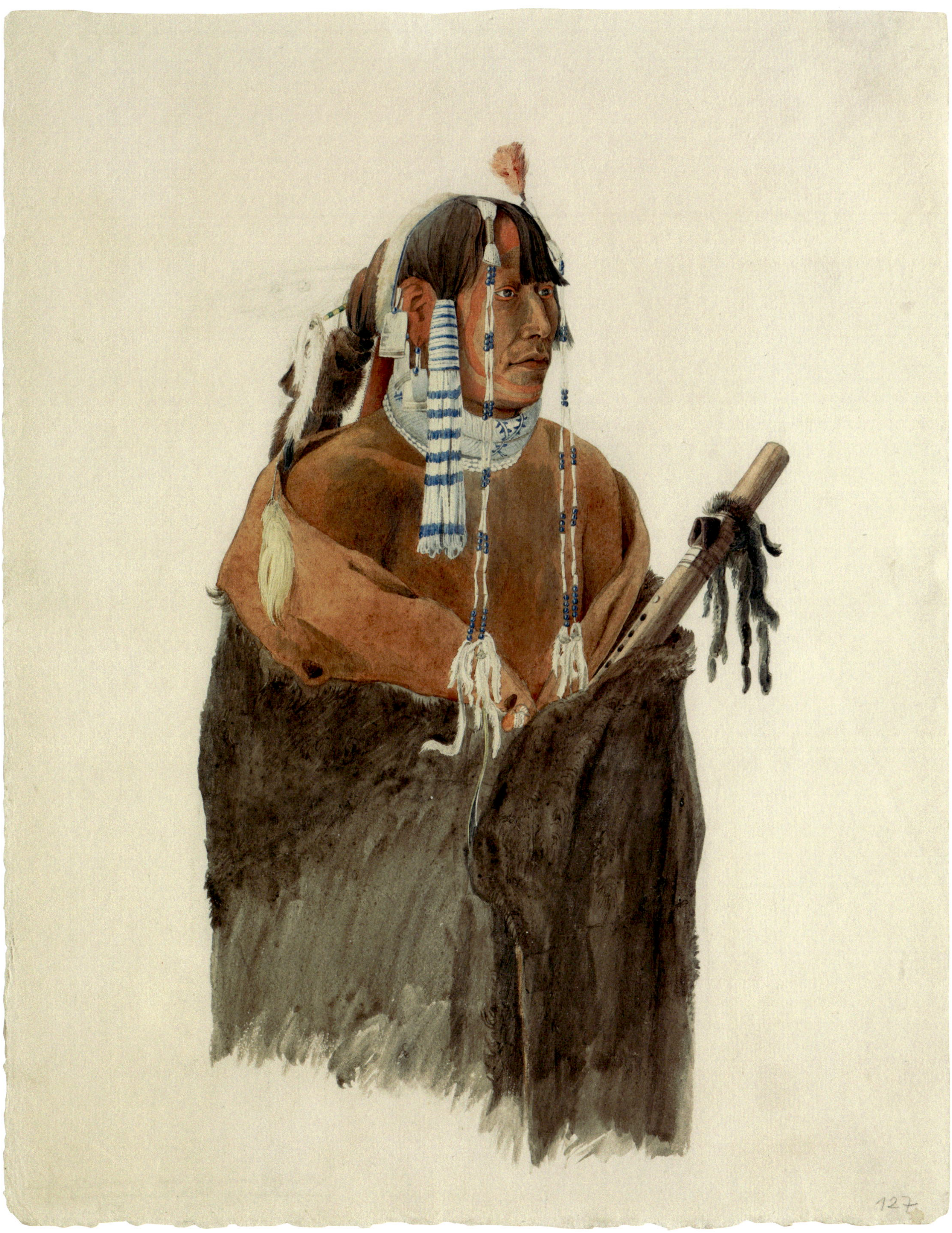

127

17. Upsichtä, Mandan Man

1834

Maximilian described Upsichtä (Great Darkness) as a tall Mandan man with a handsome face who was credited with many war feats, including the killing of three Assiniboine enemies in a single skirmish. Bodmer painted this portrait at Fort Clark in early February 1834. Upsichtä's body was smeared with white clay. Maximilian reported that body and face painting were subjects of personal taste, except in matters pertaining to ritual or to the representation of war deeds. A mirror is bound to the base of Upsichtä's eagle-wing fan. Maximilian remarked on the importance of these items, usually "bought in cardboard cases from the trad-ers," framed in wood (often ornamented with brass nails) by the new owners, hung "from a red ribbon or leather strap," and carried everywhere. As they went about, men would stop occasionally and use the mirror to "comb their hair, and put their clothing in order. . . . Painting their faces is always done in front of this important article of toiletry." (*NAJ* 3:147, 252)

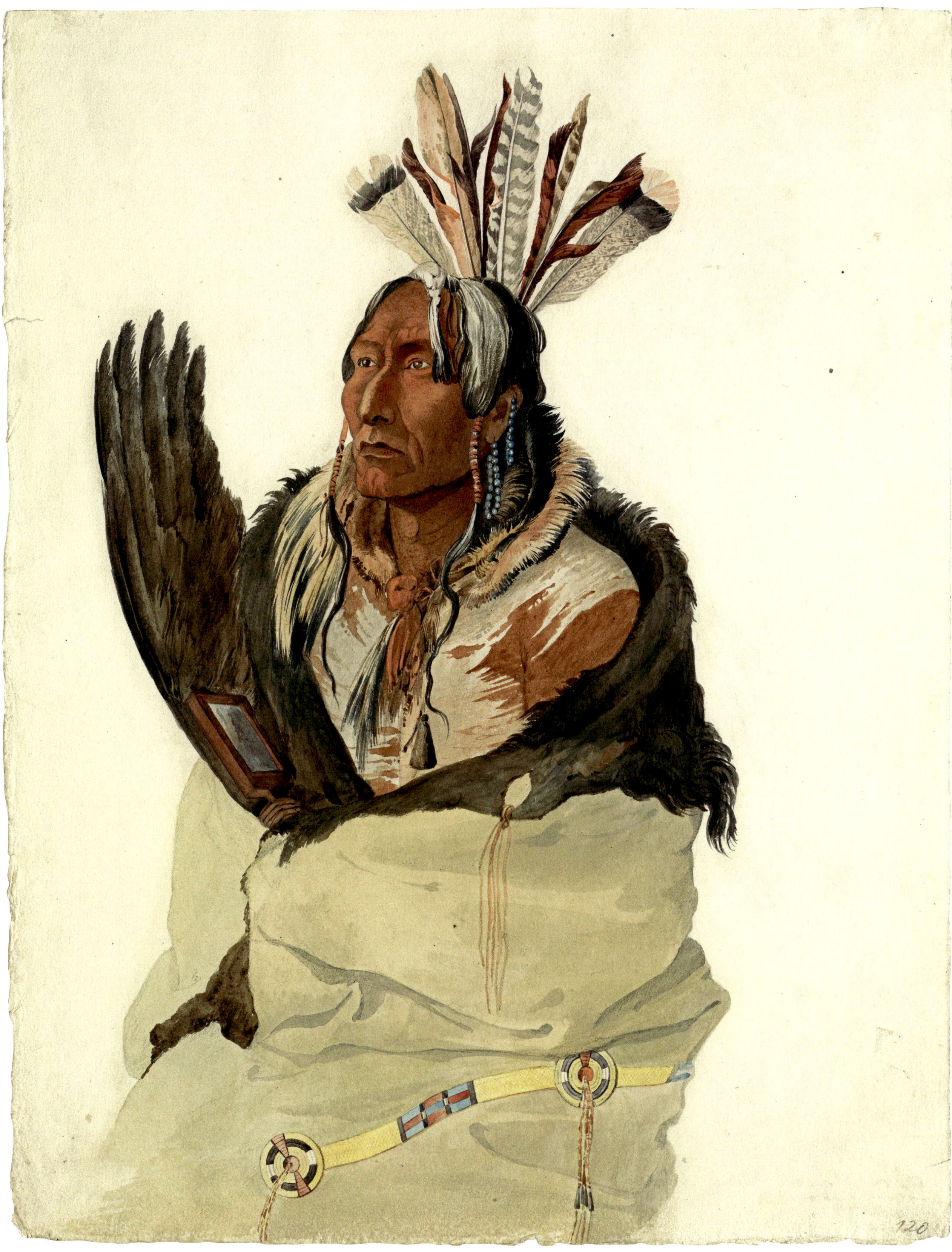

18. Máhchsi-Níhka, Mandan Man
1834

Bodmer composed his portrait of Máhchsi-Níhka (Young War Eagle) at Fort Clark in mid-February 1834. Earlier that month Assiniboines had stolen some horses from the Hidatsas (allies of the Mandans), and Máhchsi-Níhka participated in a retaliatory raid; his blackened face commemorates the fight. He is dressed plainly, as a warrior would for battle. Afterward, someone asked him why he was clothed so poorly for his likeness when everyone else was represented in their best finery. This upset Máhchsi-Níhka, and he angrily confronted Bodmer and Maximilian, who wrote, "All our efforts to make him understand that we wanted to draw him in his simple warriorlike attire were in vain." To appease him, Bodmer made a surreptitious copy of the painting and destroyed it in Máhchsi-Níhka's presence. (*NAJ* 3:256)

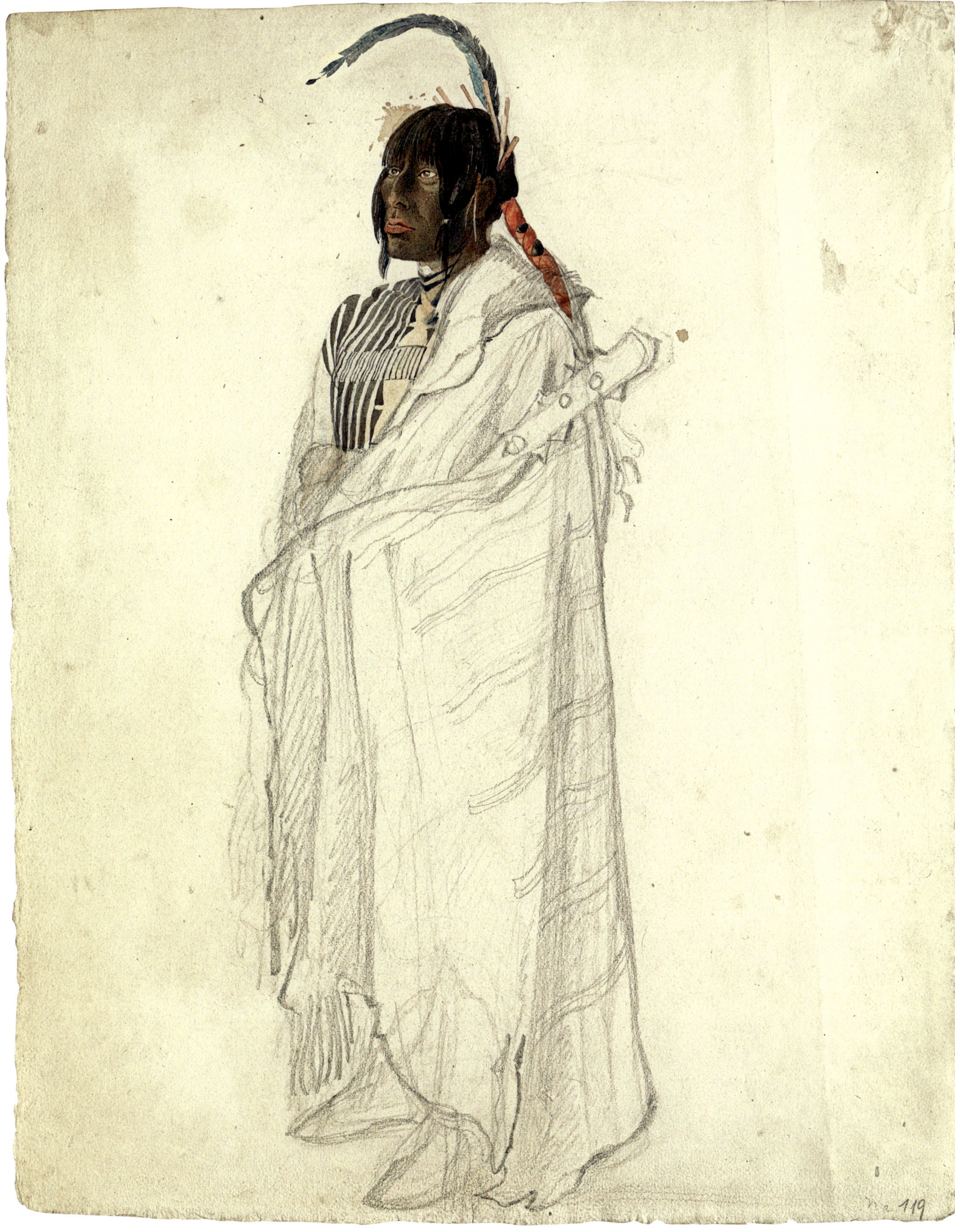

19. Mandan Woman
1834

A German inscription on the reverse of this sketch reads
"Mandan-Frau" [Mandan Woman], but it is believed to
have been written many years after the expedition, and its
veracity cannot be confirmed. In his journal, Maximilian
noted that on April 4, 1834, at Fort Clark, Bodmer drew
"the Arikara wife of the blacksmith" but gave no further
details. Nor does the woman's attire clearly reflect her
tribal affiliation, for she wears a buffalo robe that appears
to be painted in a common Plains style (see pl. 12). Bodmer
depicted very few women in his paintings and sketches.
While Maximilian acknowledged the important roles
of women in tribal society, his interests coincided more
closely with those of male hunters, warriors, and elders
whose society and comradery would have been easier for
male outsiders to access. (*NAJ* 3:279)

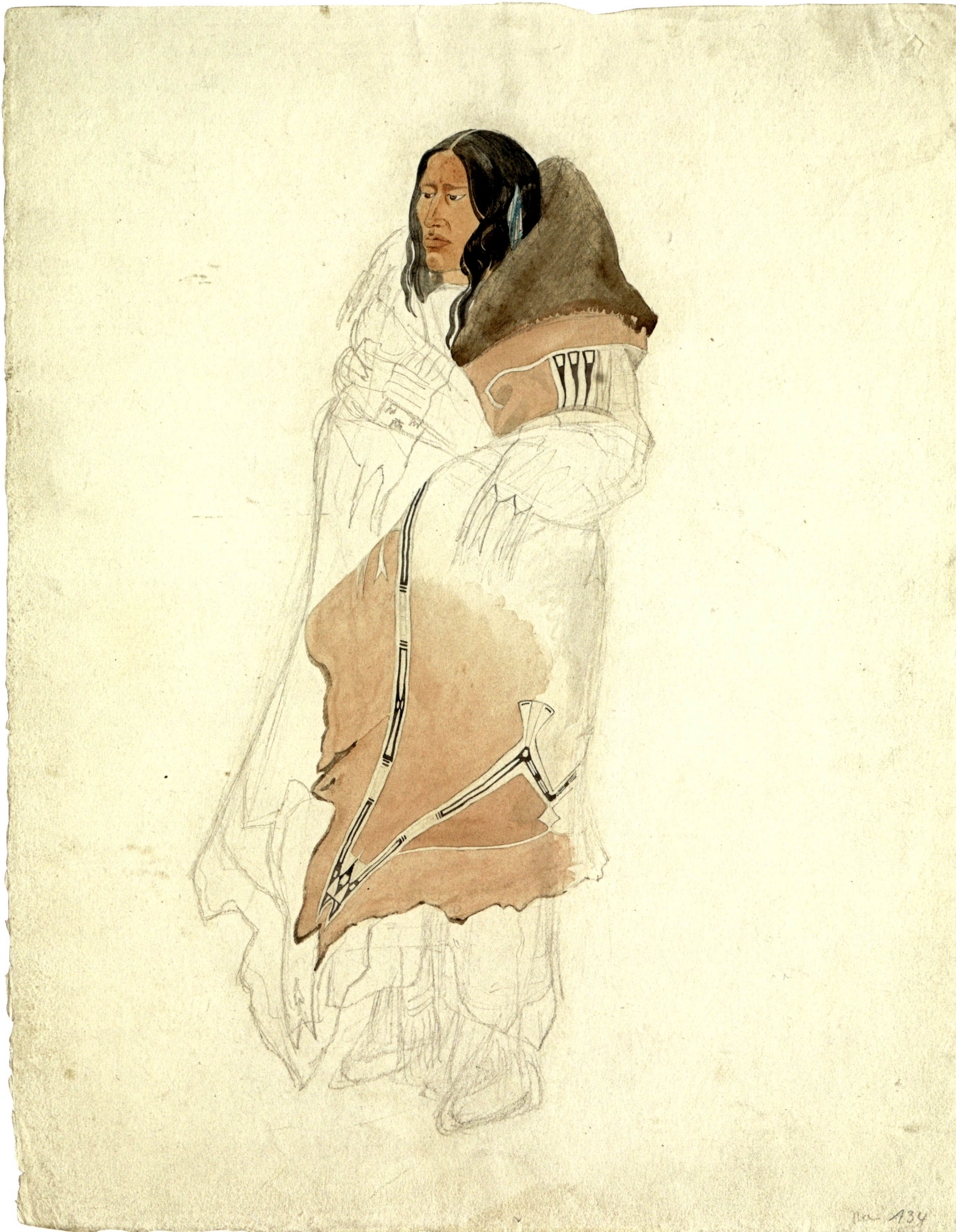

No. 134

20. Síh-Sä,
Mandan Man

1834

Síh-Sä (Red Feather) was raised by James Kipp, the clerk
(administrator) of Fort Clark for the American Fur Company.
Síh-Sä hunted for the fort and took care of the horses. He
spent much time with Maximilian and Bodmer in their
cabin, searched for bird specimens for the prince's collection, and performed other tasks for the visitors. Painted by
Bodmer in March 1834, Síh-Sä is dressed in what he likely
considered his best clothing, including leggings adorned
with wide strips of blue and white beadwork; a necklace
of long, tubular shell or bone beads; and a buffalo robe with
the tanned side brightened by rubbing it with white clay
mixed with water.

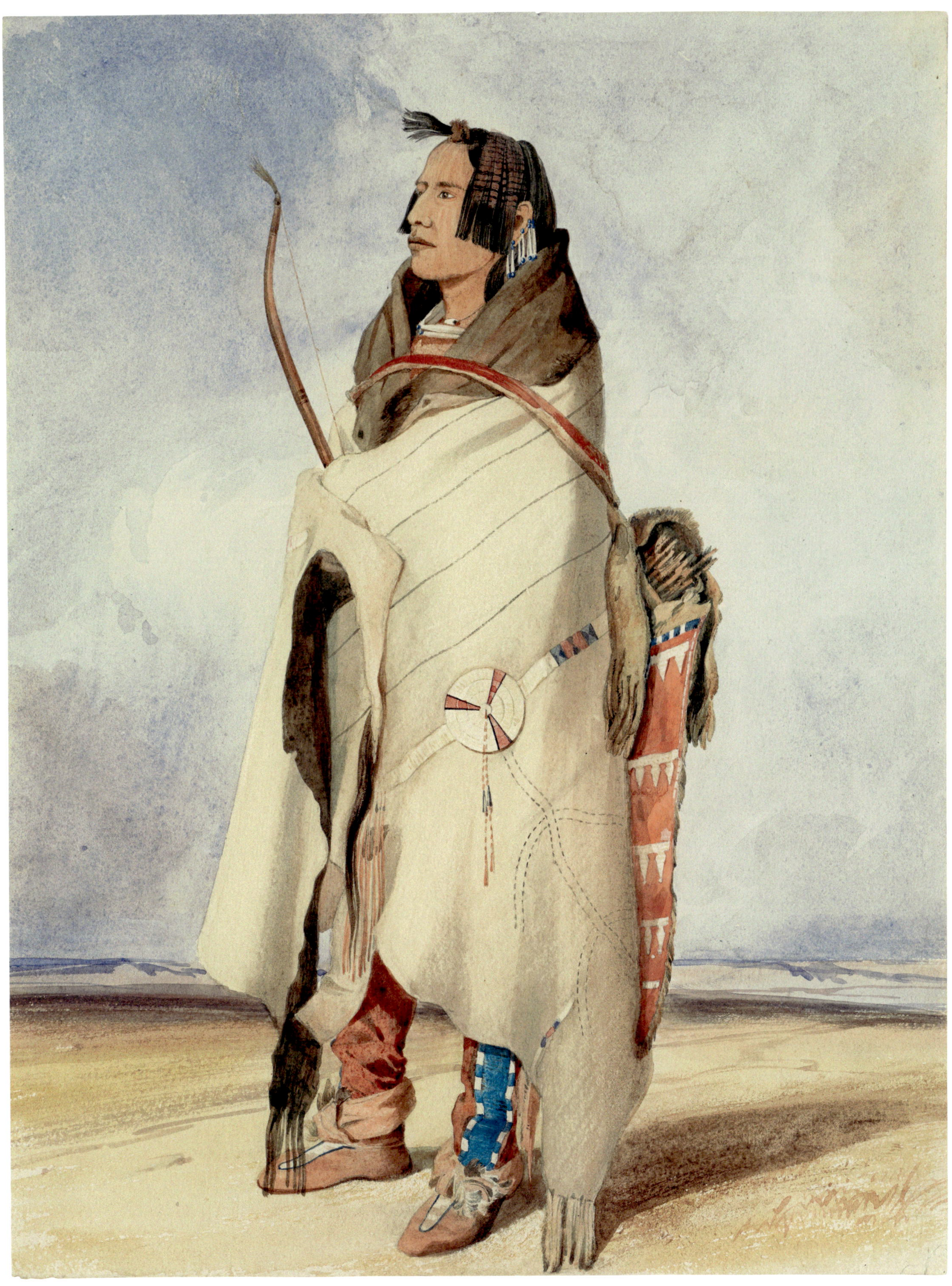

21. Síh-Chidä, Mandan Man

1833

Bodmer's sketches and watercolors fascinated most of the Indigenous people he spent time with. Twenty-five-year-old Síh-Chidä (Yellow Feather) admired Maximilian's artistic skills as well as Bodmer's. He asked the Europeans to draw soldiers for him, to paint a bird on his war shield, and to make a copy of this portrait Bodmer had drawn in December 1833. Here Síh-Chidä wears a buffalo robe decorated with a strip of blue-and-white beadwork as well as an otter-fur tippet "decorated [on the ends] very nicely with red and blue cloth and colored glass beads"; his heel trailers are made of red cloth–lined otter fur. When he posed, Síh-Chidä also asked for paper, pencils, and pigments, and he produced depictions of ceremonial figures, images of Bodmer and Maximilian, and self-portraits, some of which he gave to his hosts (right). (*NAJ* 3:65)

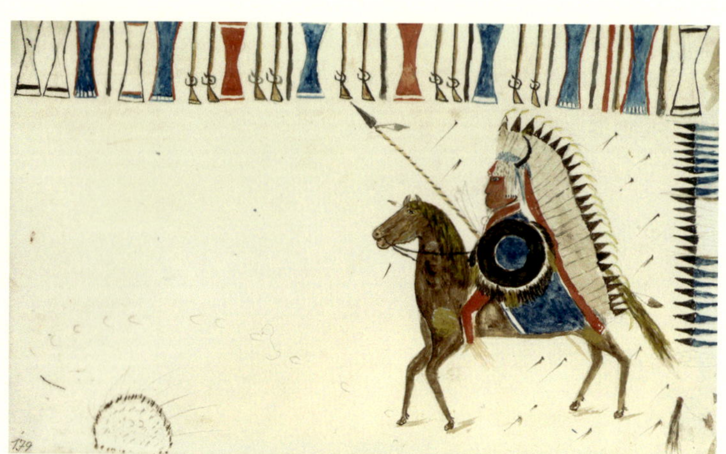

Drawing by Síh-Chidä, Fort Clark, 1833–34, watercolor and graphite on paper. Joslyn Art Museum, Gift of the Enron Art Foundation, 1986.49.319.

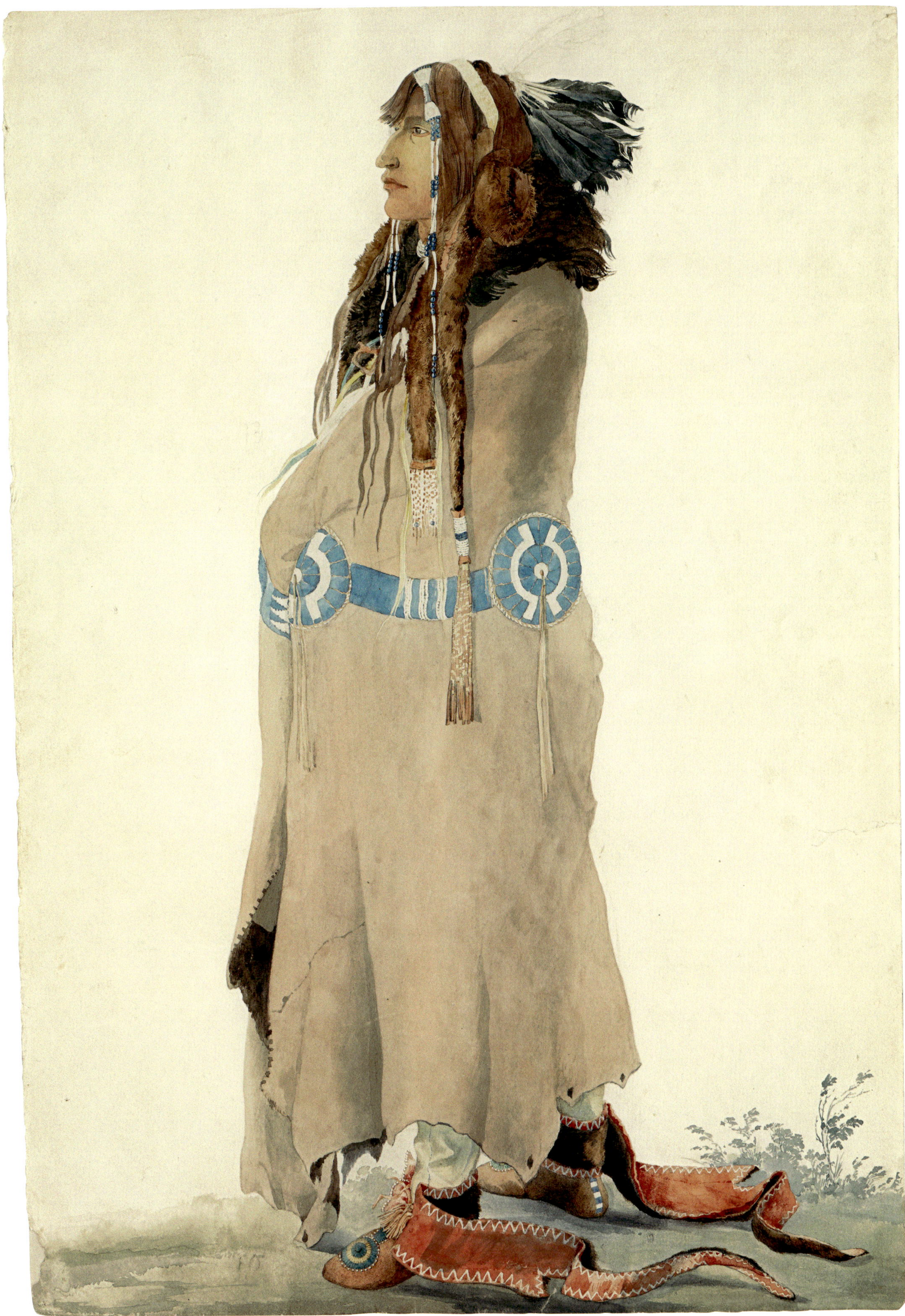

22. Mató-Tópe, Mandan Chief

1834

Mató-Tópe (Four Bears) was a Mandan chief from the village of Mih-Tutta-Hangkusch. Maximilian later wrote that Mató-Tópe "has been so often mentioned in my narrative [because] this eminent man . . . was fully entitled to [such an] appellation, being not only a distinguished warrior, but possessing many fine and noble traits of character." He and Maximilian first met in mid-June 1833 at Fort Clark on the prince's upriver voyage, and they became close friends after Maximilian's party returned to the fort the following November to overwinter. Mató-Tópe was the source for much of what Maximilian learned about the Mandans and their neighbors and allies, the Hidatsas. Mató-Tópe wears a new shirt of bighorn leather, the shoulders trimmed with ermine and panels of colorful quillwork as well as representations of his battle accomplishments, which he likely painted himself. The red spatters on the front presumably recall old war wounds, and a feather headdress such as the one depicted here could only be worn by exceptional men who had earned the right to do so. (*TINA* 453)

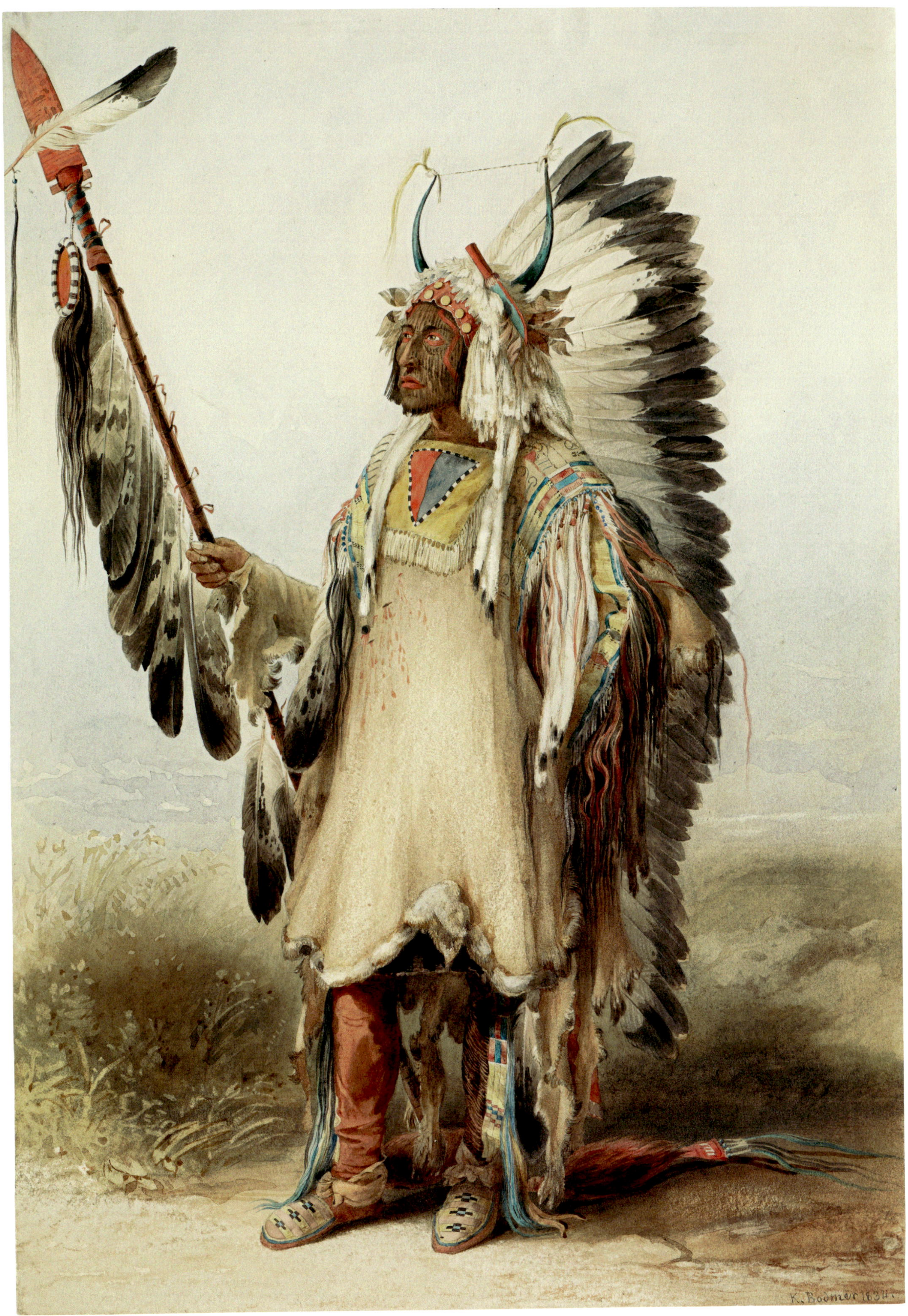

23. Mató-Tópe, Mandan Chief

1834

In this portrait, Mató-Tópe wears numerous emblems of his battle honors. Maximilian's journals add to Bodmer's vivid imagery: "In his hair he had . . . small wooden sticks [representing gunshot wounds]: four yellow, one red, and one blue. . . . On top of each . . . a yellow nail [is] driven in, like a little button. On the back of his head, he wore a large tuft of . . . owl feathers . . . [as well as] eagle feathers stuck radially upright in his hair. . . . One eye was painted yellow, the other red; his forehead and the lower part of his chin [were] red. His body and arms were marked with reddish brown vertical stripes, and his coups [were] indicated by horizontal stripes on his arms. On his chest [was] a yellow hand that indicated he had taken prisoners. . . . Mr. Bodmer portrayed this interesting man . . . [and all] this attire very truly and correctly." Mató-Tópe died in the summer of 1837, a victim of the smallpox epidemic that decimated the Mandan and other communities that year—a calamity still remembered by the Mandan people. As recorded by the trader Francis A. Chardon, Mató-Tópe bitterly admonished whites for bringing the disease to his community.* (*NAJ* 3:240 and NM3)

* Francis A. Chardon, *Chardon's Journals at Fort Clark, 1834–1849*, ed. Heloise A. Able (Pierre: State of South Dakota, Department of History, 1932), 124–25.

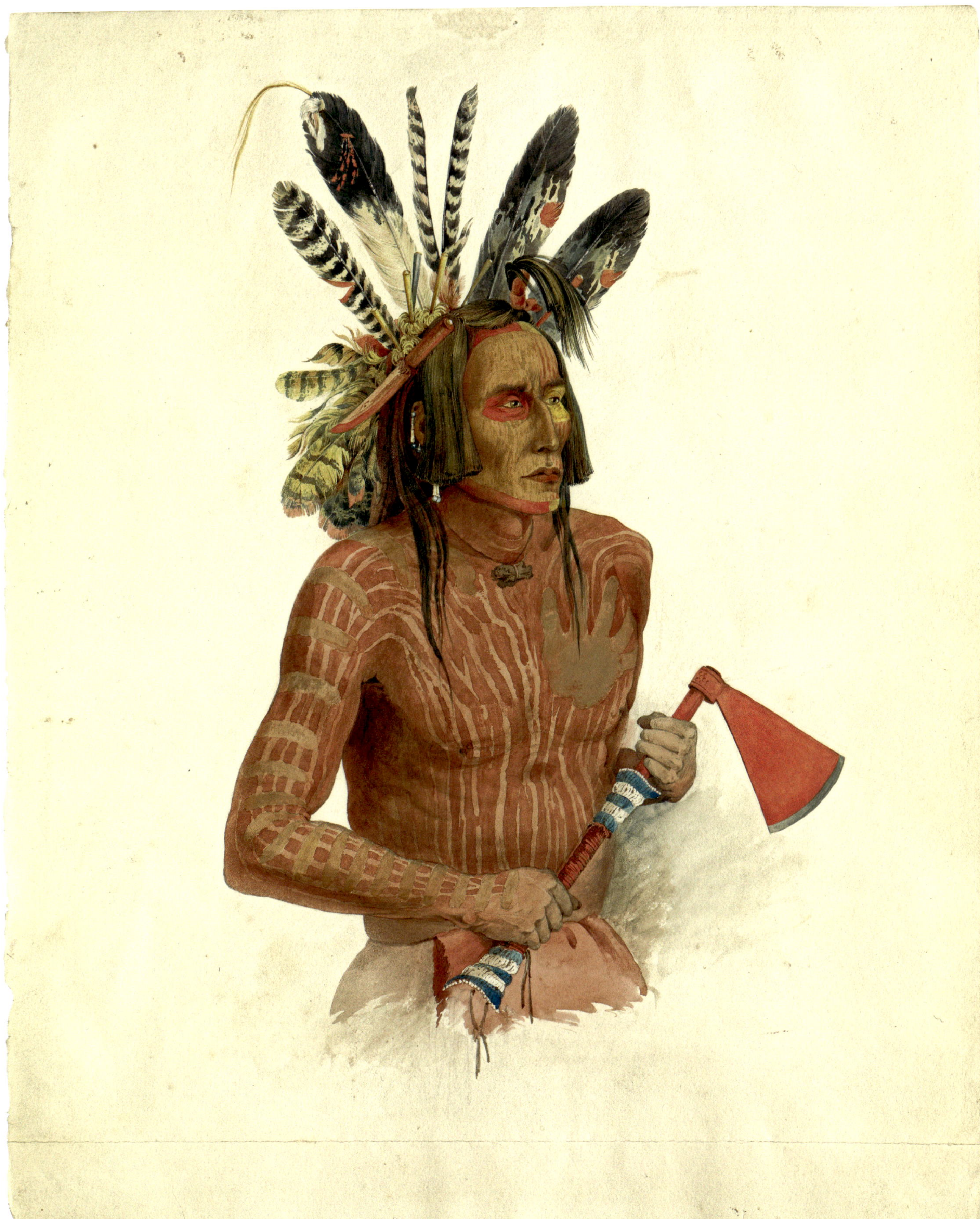

24. Awaschó-dichsas, Hidatsa Man

1834

Maximilian wrote that the name Awaschó-dichsas means Swallow with the White Belly. Awaschó-dichsas posed for Bodmer at Fort Clark on March 4, 1834, his unusual painted robe the focal point of the portrait. Maximilian described the pattern as including "a large circle representing the tracks [and trails] of wolves. At the middle, a round black dot stood for the den, or lair, of the wolves." Perhaps Awaschó-dichsas sought to identify himself with or invoke the hunting powers of the wolf. (*NAJ* 3:267 and nM16)

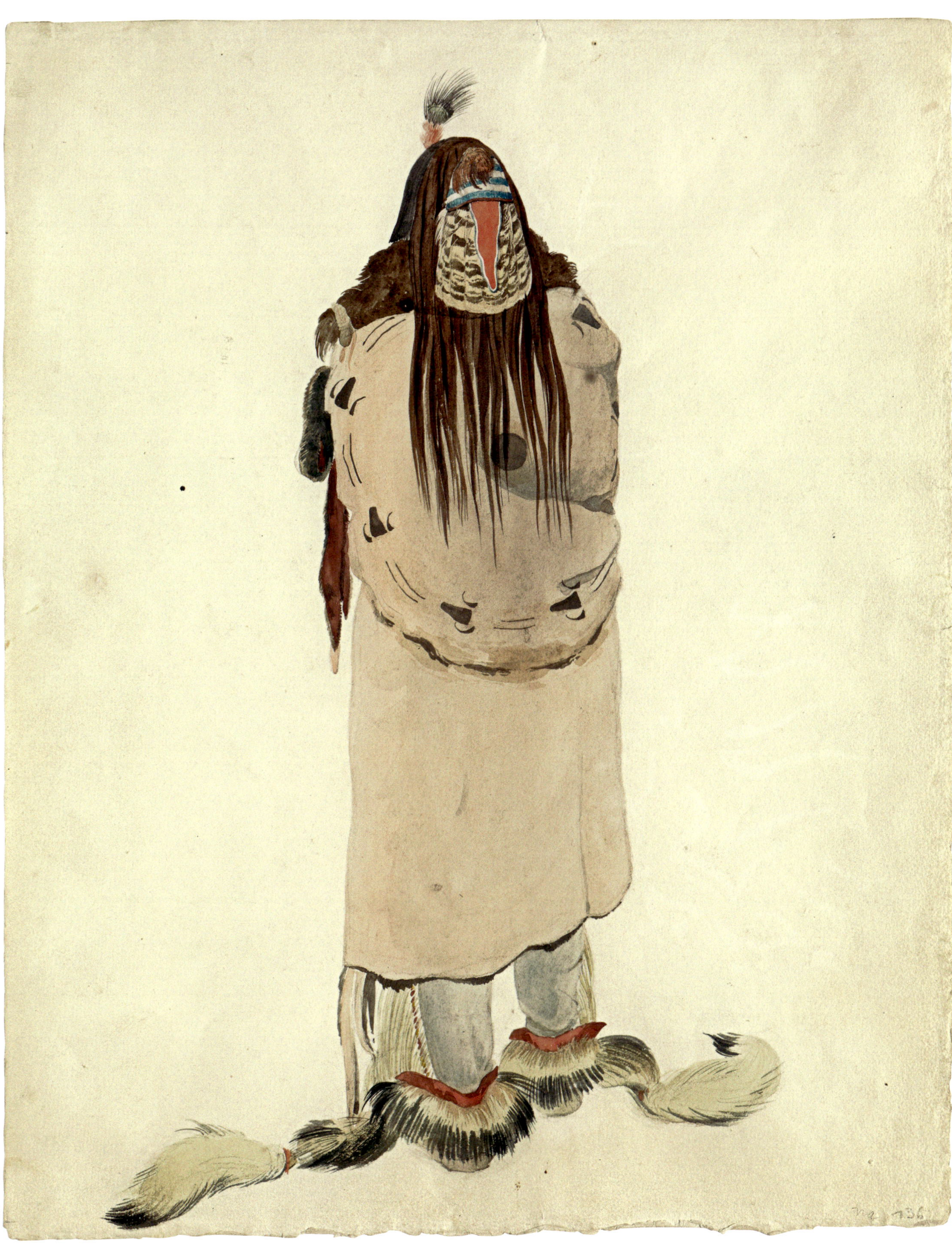

25. Biróhkä, Hidatsa Man

1834

For his portrait—made on March 1, 1834, at Fort Clark—
Biróhkä wore a cap made of white buffalo hide. White
buffalo were rare, and the skin was "an important object
and a great medicine," or vessel of spiritual power. The
Mandans considered the killing of a white buffalo cow "as
important as killing an enemy, and they [purchased such]
hides at high prices," paying "from ten up to fifteen horses."
Biróhkä's beautifully painted robe is a further indication of
his importance. The feathered circle design was popular in
nineteenth-century art of the Plains; Maximilian described
the image as sun-like but noted that it was meant to portray the "feather crown" of the large headdresses worn by
acknowledged war leaders. (*NAJ* 3:54, 149, 183–84)

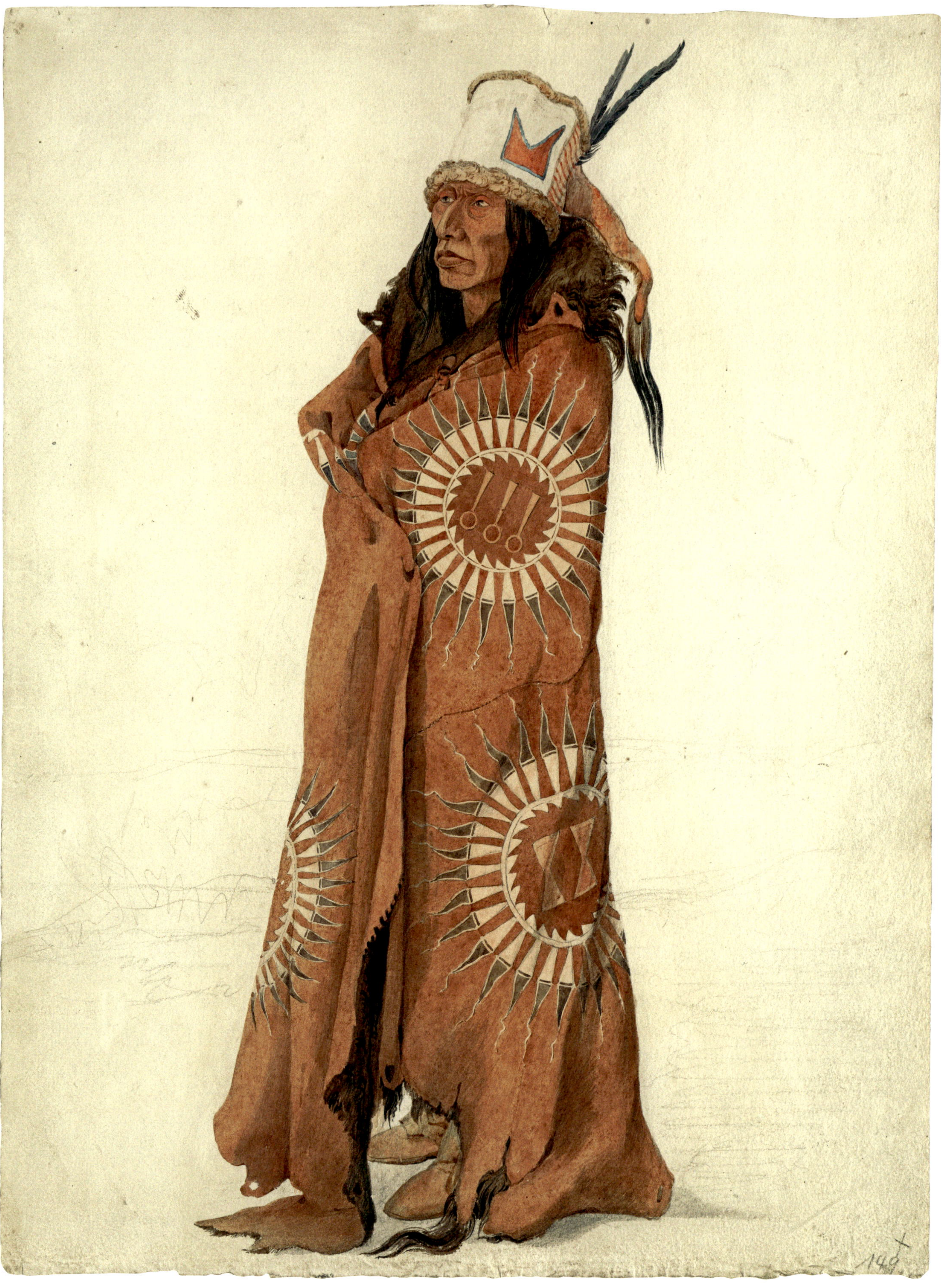

140

26. Addíh-Hiddísch, Hidatsa Chief

1834

Addíh-Hiddísch (Road Maker) was a chief of the village of Awacháhwi, one of three Hidatsa settlements near Fort Clark. He was a respected leader and shared much of what he knew of Hidatsa history with Maximilian. Although he was a frequent visitor that winter, the chief was nevertheless reluctant to have his portrait made, declining to sit for Bodmer until late March 1834. Addíh-Hiddísch's extensive body tattoos are perhaps the most striking aspect of this portrait: "Not only are his chest, arms, and hands tattooed with bluish black horizontal stripes, but his whole legs, too. I had never seen such a heavily tattooed American [Indian]." Done with a needle dipped in a blackish-blue dye made from willow bark and water, Addíh-Hiddísch's tattooed stripes, which likely represent war exploits, are embellished with red paint. His clothing includes items of American or European origin, presumably obtained as gifts or in trade and then personalized: a hat topped with a feather indicating a war feat; a peace medal showcased by the addition of beads and bear-claw pendants; and a metal war axe with a hoop-stretched scalp attached to its handle. (*NAJ* 3:252)

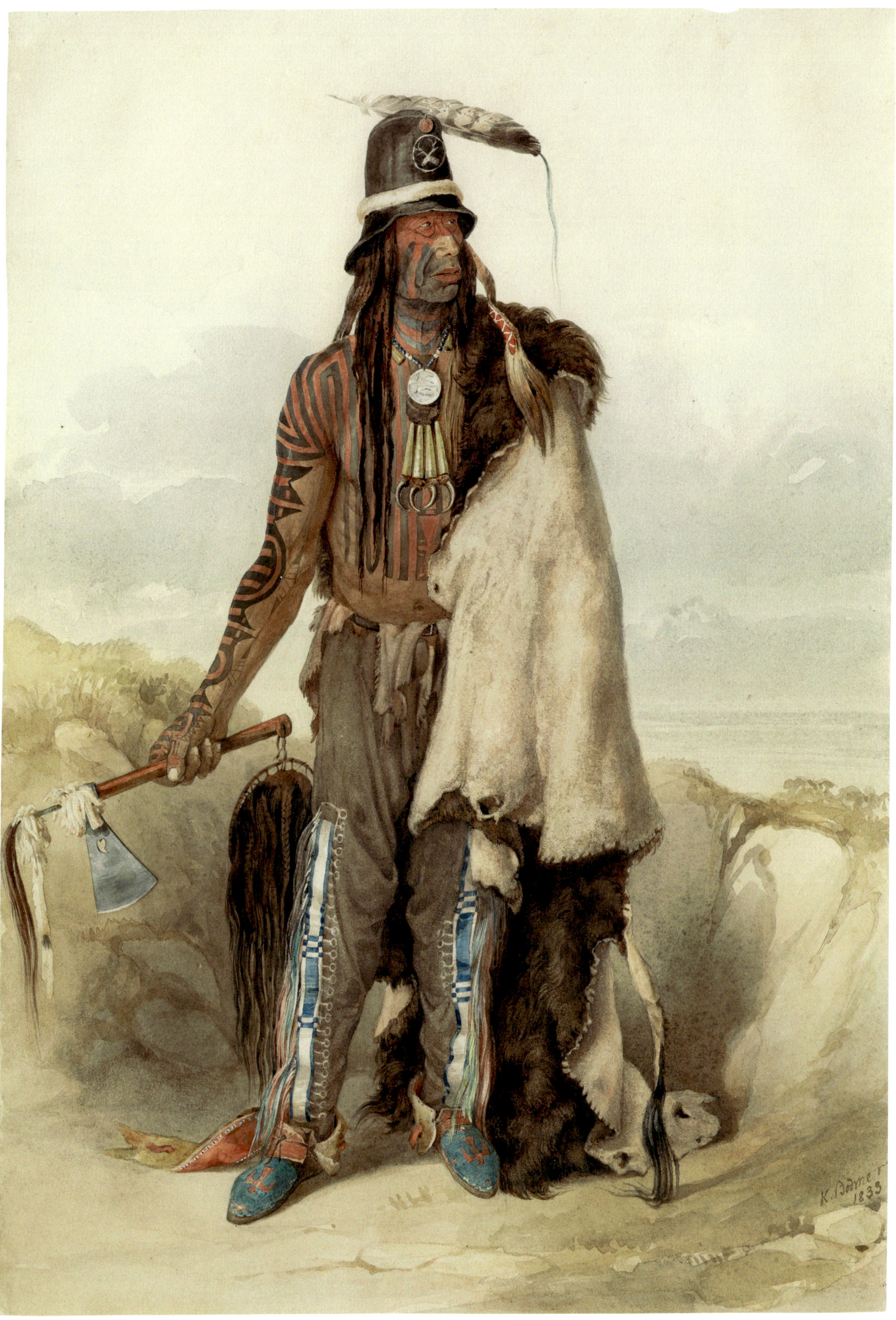

K. Bodmer
1833

27. Ahschüpsa-Masihichsi, Hidatsa Man

1834

This young warrior and a companion visited Maximilian and Bodmer in February 1834 at their Fort Clark cabin, where they admired Bodmer's drawings. Ahschüpsa-Masihichsi posed for a portrait on the twenty-eighth of that month, but returned a few days later, evidently concerned that Bodmer's possession of his likeness might affect the outcome of a war party on which he was about to embark. As a countermeasure, he asked for an image of the artist, and when that request was refused, "he started to work himself and drew Bodmer." Maximilian translated Ahschüpsa-Masihichsi's name as Chief of the Pointed Horn; a modern rendering of it is Young Buffalo Chief. *Ahschüpsa* literally means "sharp horn," referring to a two- to three-year-old buffalo. (*NAJ* 3:256nm11, 266)

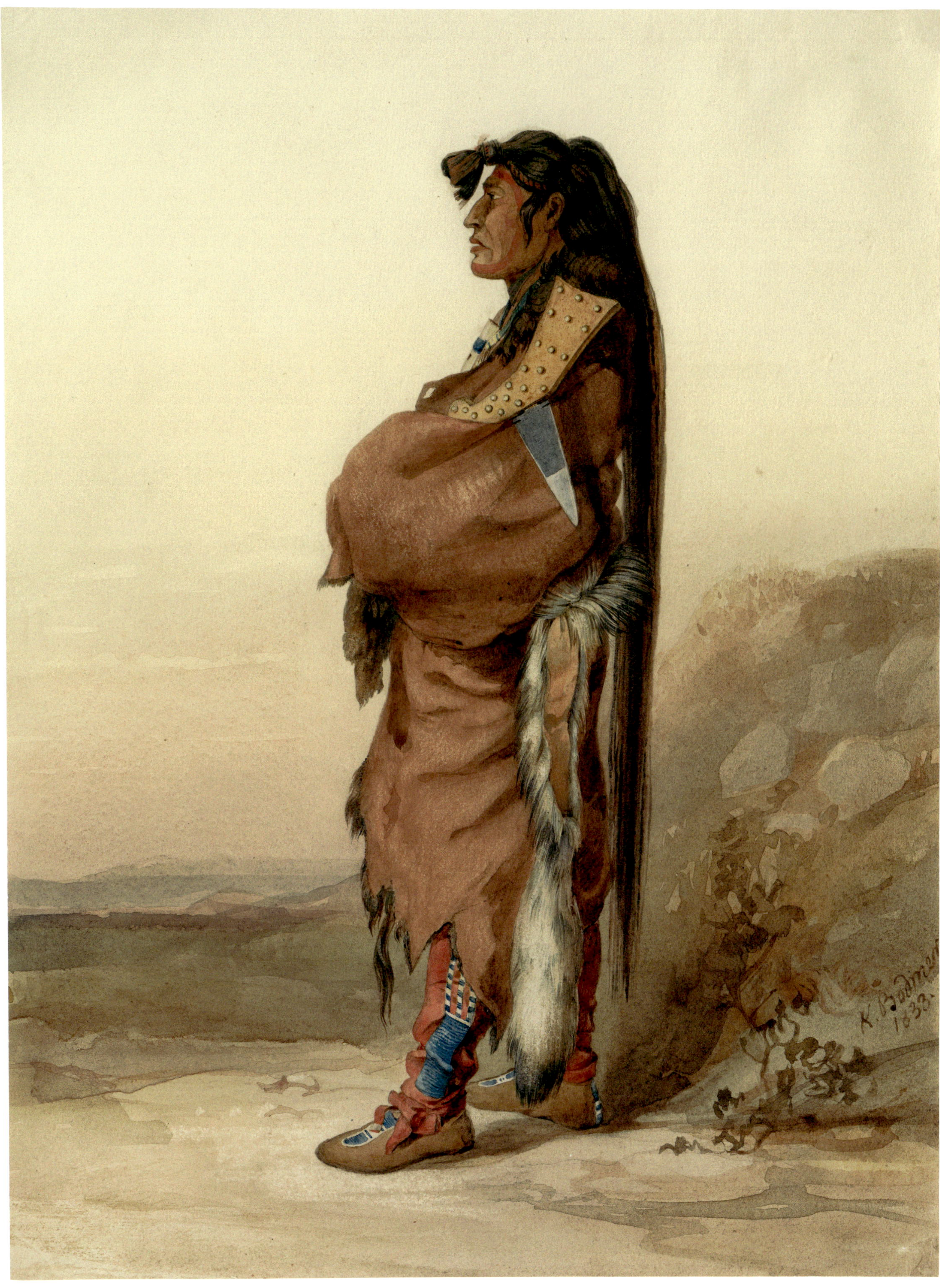

28. Possibly Ahschüpsa-Masihichsi, Hidatsa Man

1834

An inscription on the reverse of this watercolor reads "Ahschüpsa-Masihichsi." However, the handwriting is unattributed, and there is no corroborating text, leaving open the possibility that this is a portrait of a different individual. In a seated pose, this Hidatsa man wears two necklaces, one featuring pendants of dark shell, the other an elaborate blue beaded band suspending a long "war whistle." Maximilian recounted that Mandan whistles were made from the wing bones of birds such as swans, cranes, or wild geese, the species indicating the men's society to which the wearer belonged. When participating in war parties, the men blew whistles as a signal of attack; they were also used prominently in ceremonies. On March 7, 1834, at Fort Clark, Maximilian and Bodmer witnessed more than two dozen warriors of the Mandan Meníss-Óchatä (Dog Society) march into the fort in full society regalia, dancing to a rapid drumbeat and blowing short, repetitive notes on their war whistles. A dancer from the Hidatsa Dog Society, called the Waschúkka-Aechke, is depicted in plate 30. (*NAJ* 3:274)

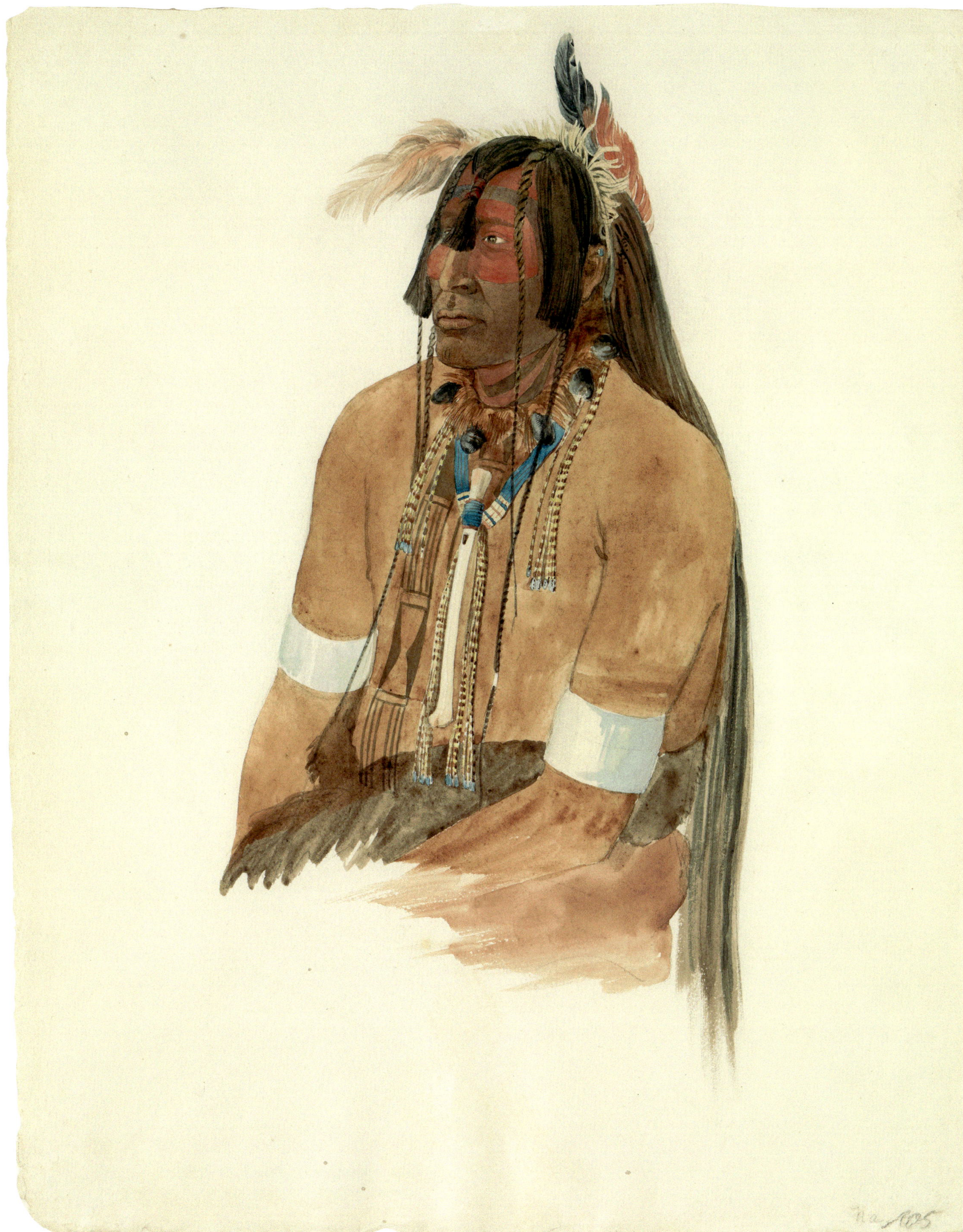

29. Péhriska-Rúhpa, Hidatsa Man

1833

Péhriska-Rúhpa (Two Ravens) was a distinguished warrior
who visited Maximilian and Bodmer's cabin frequently
during their winter at Fort Clark. He often wore beautiful
clothes, which Maximilian admired, noting that Péhriska-
Rúhpa had obtained some of them from the Crows, whose
garments were widely traded on the Plains. Maximilian
remarked specifically on the ribbon of white ermine that
Péhriska-Rúhpa wears transversely across his head; his
bear-claw necklace suspended from a circlet of otter skin;
and his reddish yellow leather shirt with strips of yellow
porcupine quill embroidery running down each arm.
Colorful streamers of ermine, horsehair, and human hair
hang from the sleeves of the shirt. His robe was "especially beautiful, with a . . . colossal sun or, actually, a crown
of feathers [painted] on it." The crown was undoubtedly
meant to represent the large feathered headdress that
could be worn only by warriors who had earned that honor.
In return for posing for two portraits, Péhriska-Rúhpa stipulated that Bodmer "would have to draw his two medicine
birds, the white-headed eagle and the eagle owl, so that he
could keep these figures [and have them] with him when
he perished." (*NAJ* 3:107, 225)

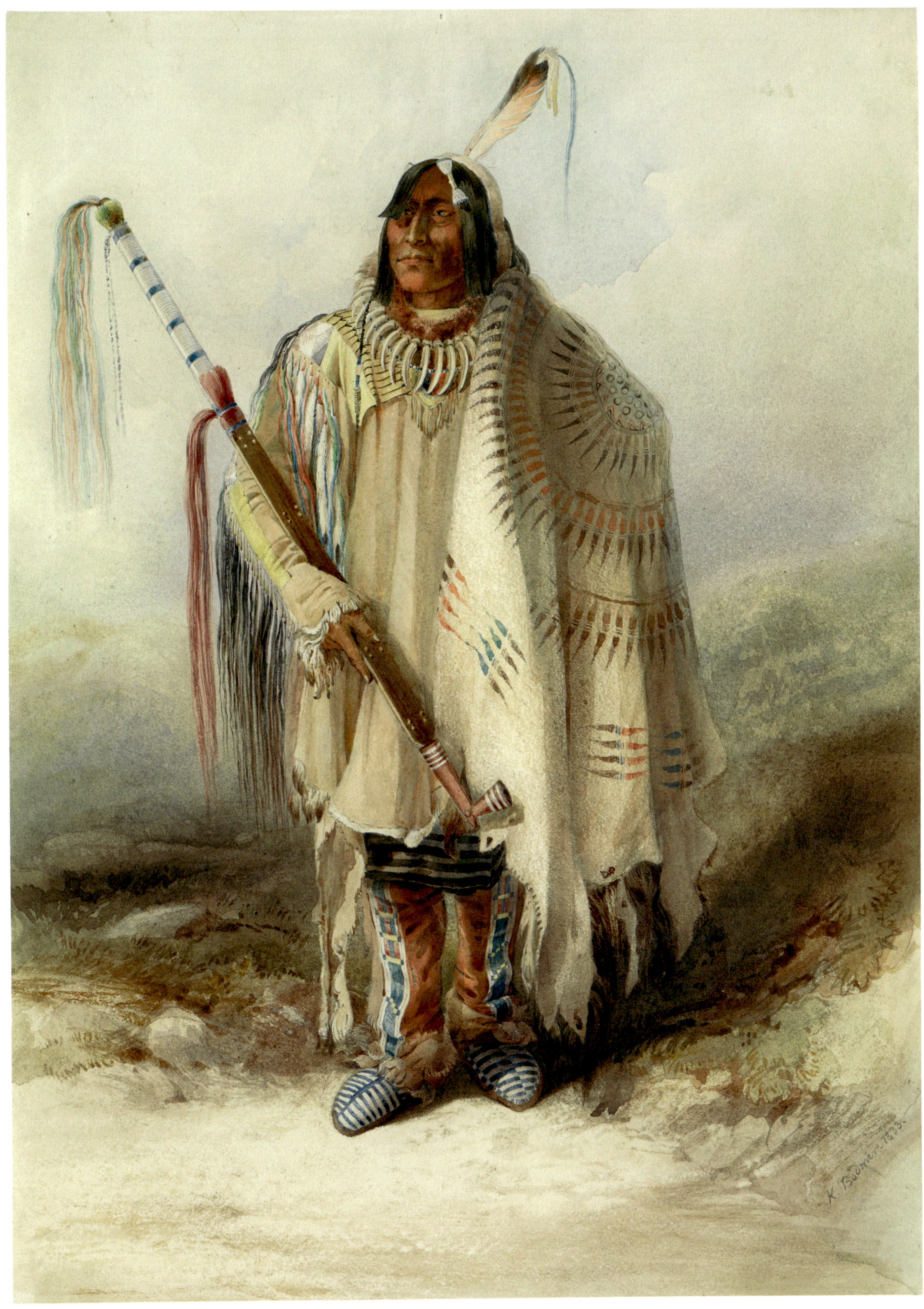

30. Péhriska-Rúhpa, Hidatsa Man

1834

Péhriska-Rúhpa figured prominently in the Waschúkka-Aechke (Dog Society) of his Hidatsa village. He posed for Bodmer in Maximilian's cabin at Fort Clark in full society regalia over a period of several days in mid-March 1834. He "took a long time," wrote Maximilian, dressing for the occasion in a "large black bonnet of magpie tail feathers with a beautiful wild turkey tail in its center. Around his neck he wore a war whistle . . . [and] down his back, two broad strips of cloth." Red cloth is visible around his neck and draped behind his shoulder. The rattle in his right hand, another society emblem, is made of small hooves or dewclaws attached to a slender wooden handle wrapped in ornamental quill- or beadwork. The massive headdress is further embellished with tiny white down feathers attached to the tops of the larger plumes. When Maximilian saw the similarly attired Mandan Meníss-Óchatä (Dog Society) perform on March 7, 1834, he noted admiringly that "when they dance, all these feathers rock up and down." (*NAJ* 3:269, 274)

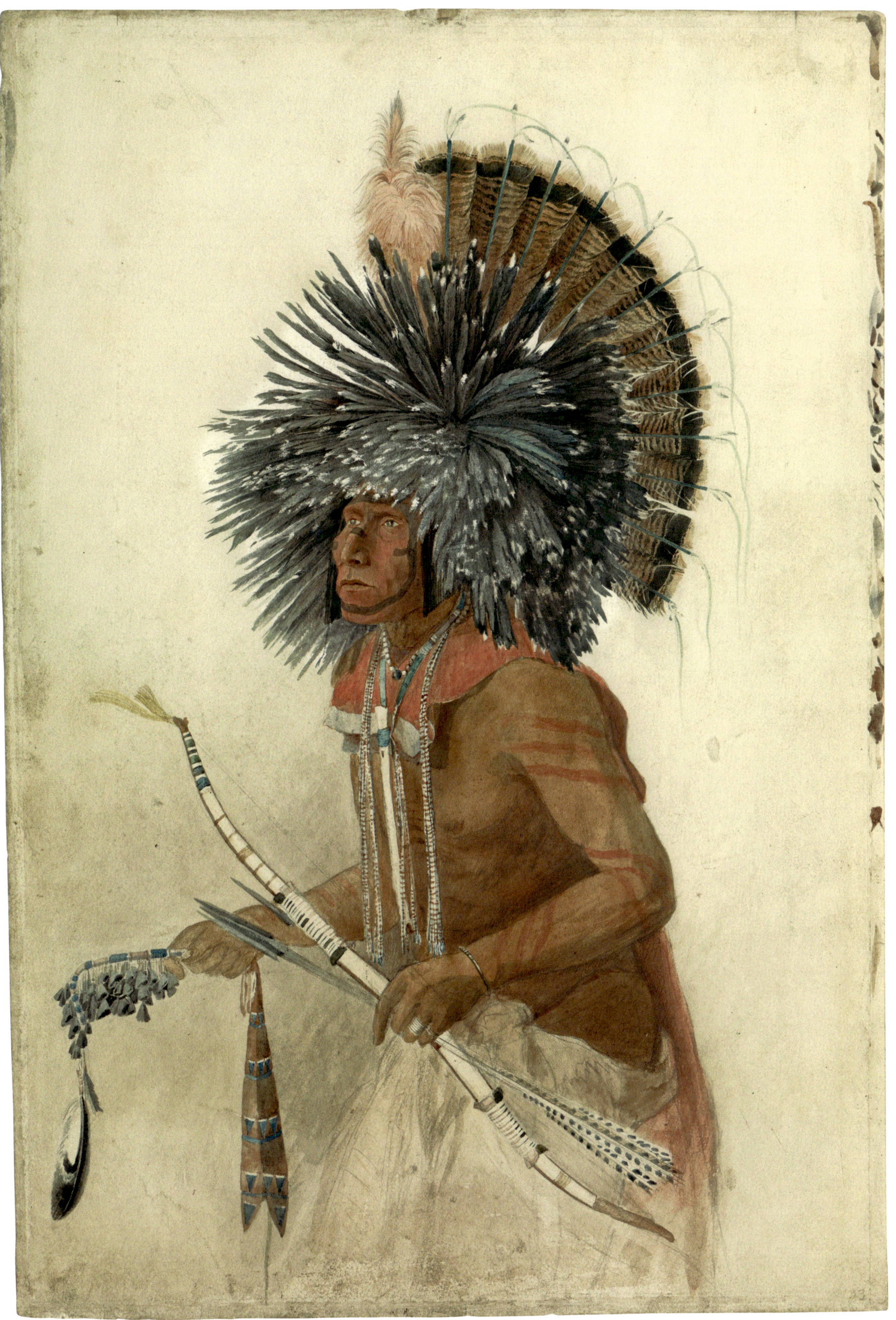

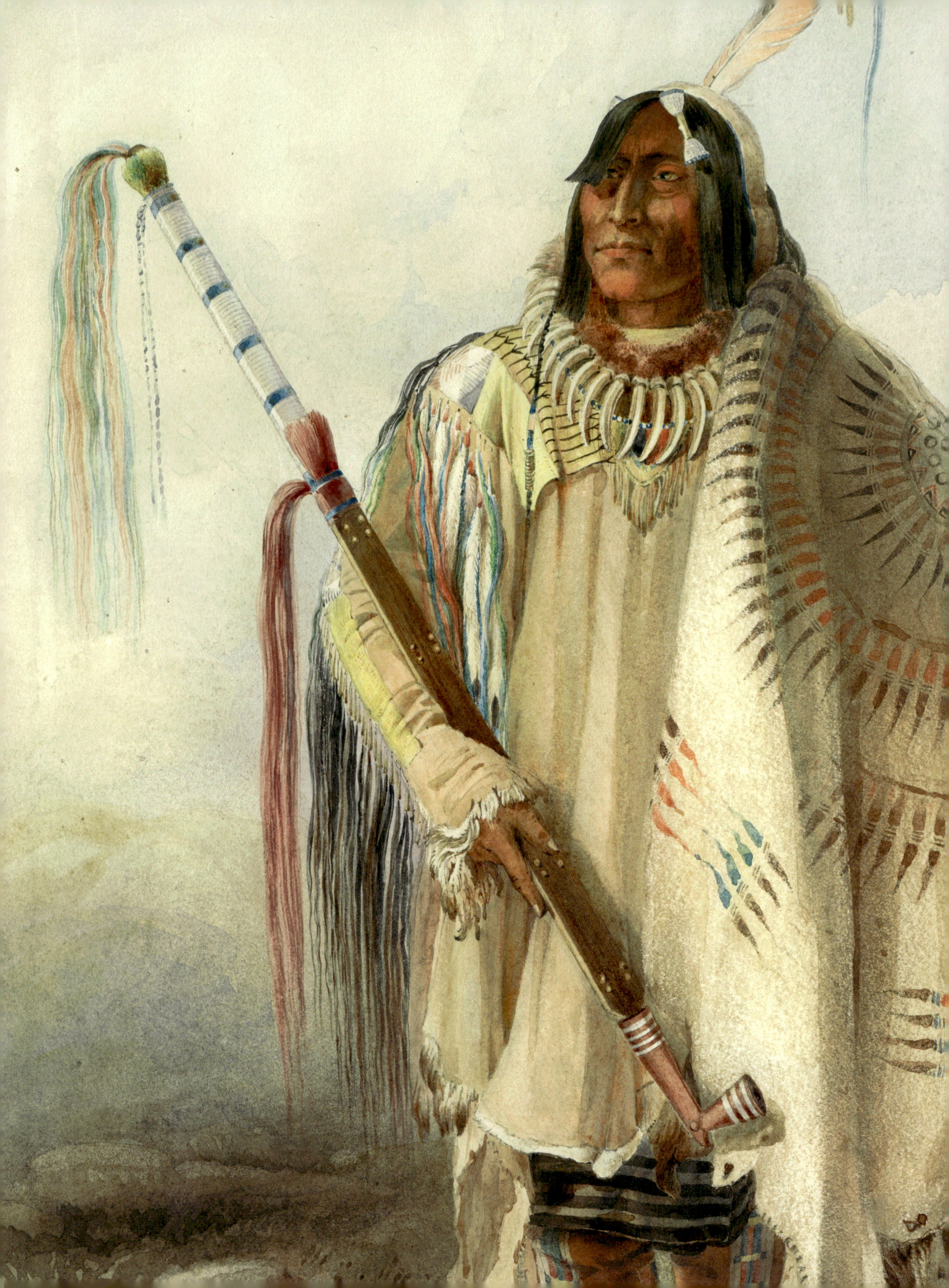

BRINGING THE STORY BACK

AN INTERVIEW WITH GERARD BAKER

PART 2: RELATIONS PAST AND PRESENT

Annika K. Johnson

AFTER DECADES OF LOOKING AT BODMER'S PORTRAITS, Gerard Baker continues to discover new details about Mandan and Hidatsa life. While looking at these images, he explained how a feather was split, a moccasin was stitched, and even how a man groomed his fingernails. His commentary reminds us that in addition to providing valuable documentation of materials and construction techniques, Bodmer's portraits reveal relationships within earth-lodge communities, between cultures, and across time.

ANNIKA JOHNSON: What do you see in Bodmer's full-length portrait of Péhriska-Rúhpa (Two Ravens; pl. 29)?

GERARD BAKER: *This* is a Mandan-Hidatsa man. You can see he is full of pride, nothing can destroy him. He's got powerful medicine, he's got powerful pipe, and he owns the damn world—and you can see it in him. This is my best hero, this guy. I love the way he looks. He's confident, maybe a little bit of worry, but his eyes are confident. And this guy's got blue or light eyes, which I think is just fascinating.[1] He's just strong. Look at his face. If I had to look like anybody in this world, I'd look like this guy.

His bear-claw necklace is from a plains grizzly, which is now extinct, and those things were huge. There have to be over thirty claws on this necklace, which has to do with the ribs of the buffalo. He has plaited porcupine quillwork along his sleeves and down his leggings. How his hair is cut in the front with a braid in the back, he's not in mourning,[2] that's just how he did his style. His pipe was so long it'd take two people to smoke it, otherwise you couldn't light it: You'd put hot coal in the pipe bowl, and put your tobacco on top of that, because they had no matches back in the day. His pipe has dyed horsehair and blue and white beads wrapped around the stem. Péhriska-Rúhpa's moccasins don't match, but I don't think Bodmer would have made that mistake; I don't know why they were made that way. His robe is absolutely beautiful and was only used on certain occasions, I imagine.

Karl Bodmer, *Péhriska-Rúhpa, Hidatsa Man*, 1833 (detail of pl. 29).

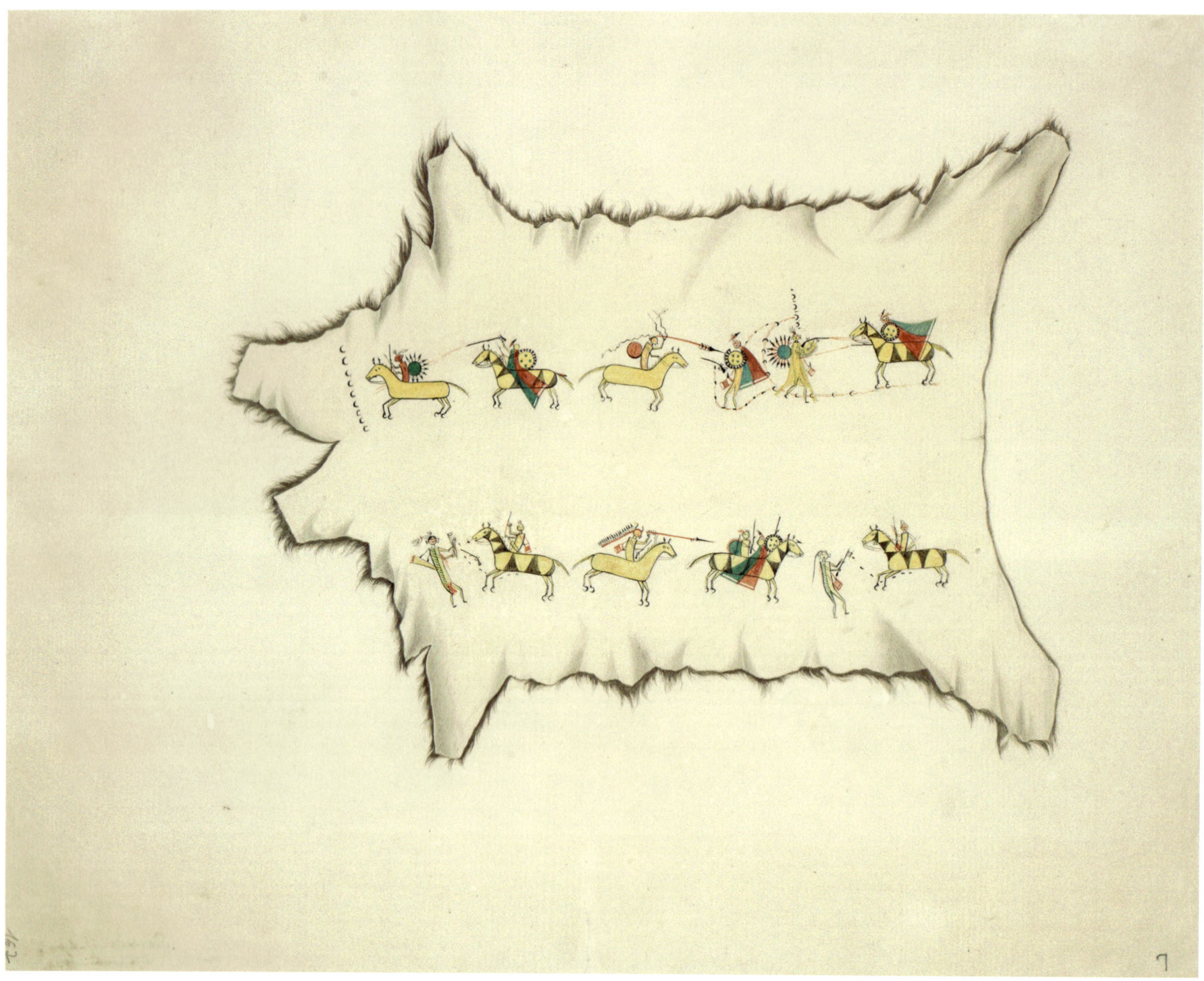

FIGURE 1. Karl Bodmer, *Hidatsa Buffalo Robe*, 1834, watercolor, graphite, and ink on paper. Joslyn Art Museum, Gift of the Enron Art Foundation, 1986.49.307. Maximilian gave Péhriska-Rúhpa a buffalo robe and paints with which to document his experiences on the battlefield, as seen here. Bodmer and Maximilian returned to Europe with the robe.

AJ: Bodmer and Maximilian collected a few extraordinary painted robes during their travels (fig. 1). Why do you think such precious items ended up in Bodmer and Maximilian's hands?

GB: Maybe Péhriska-Rúhpa was good friends with Bodmer; you give really good things to your friends. I think that's why he really liked Bodmer—because Bodmer made an impression of him that would last for eternity. These guys understood that if you take my picture, it's not just a painting. They didn't understand the painting part of it. You were taking *me*, you were putting me on paper, and I'll be there forever. Bodmer told him it's going to be there forever, and he really liked that.

AJ: Do you think Péhriska-Rúhpa had to give approval of his portrait?

GB: Oh, definitely. Bodmer created a rapport with his subjects, whereas George Catlin didn't and got blamed for smallpox. Catlin was good, don't get me wrong, but he was so fast—unlike Bodmer. Catlin painted so many portraits that it became impersonal. He was painting too fast. He wasn't getting a chance to know his subject or what they had or what they meant or what they wore or their background.[3] He was too busy trying to focus on what he was making. Being that fast, he probably made those guys mad. Because he had no time to say, "Oh, it sure is a nice day today."

Back in those days I believe all these white folks that came into our place really did believe that we weren't that intelligent. They were domineering to us. Truly, they treated us like little children, and so we were demeaned that way. I think that was the big difference with Catlin. He was very impersonal to those people because he did so many portraits. He's the one that stole things from them, inside. That's what I've always understood about Catlin.

AJ: You can see the mutual respect between Bodmer and his sitters in a painting like this.

GB: Big time.

AJ: Do you think Bodmer knew he was painting these individual's medicines? Was he painting personal things he shouldn't have?

GB: I don't think Bodmer was there long enough to understand what he could and couldn't do. The people he painted would know what they could show and what they couldn't show. When I look at this I think: What does this guy have on that he didn't tell Bodmer about and Bodmer just painted it anyway?

Bodmer was lucky that he was there in the wintertime, because we had a lot of our ceremonies then, and we could dress this way. Summertime we were doing other things—we were hunting—whereas wintertime we were around the village and doing ceremonies (fig. 2).

On Addíh-Hiddísch (Road Maker; pl. 26), I don't see any medicines hanging off of him other than the simple decoration of the bear claws attached to his peace medal. We know he knew Americans because of his hat—that hat just kills me; he cut the brim off. This guy was a mixture of European and Indian; at the same time, he had his feathers and that means something. Maybe Bodmer missed things that we don't even know about.[4]

AJ: What else do you think is missing in Bodmer's pictures?

GB: To me what's missing is everyday life. It's stuff that we take for granted: it's kids playing, it's us sitting around visiting. The one who really captures some of that is the Hidatsa man Lion Boy, whose ledger drawings from the nineteenth century show a different aspect of Hidatsa life.[5] He shows courtship, and we relied heavily on courtship; we were proud of it. The women were proud of it, too, and were very well known for eloping with men, as a conquest basically. But Bodmer doesn't show that because it was seen as immoral at that time—and still is from a religious standpoint. Everyday cooking is also missing. The implements were good to depict because those were curiosities to cultural outsiders. Maximilian writes about everyday life a little bit, but Bodmer doesn't show it. Another thing that's missing is how we solved disputes in families. We all lived together, and there were ways: You couldn't talk to this person or that person; we had teasing relatives, we had nonteasing relatives. We had people you couldn't even look at. Again, where's that displayed? I've never seen that anyplace, and I'm not sure how they could show that unless you had two people standing back to back and looking the other way. That's what's missing.

AJ: My understanding is that Bodmer and Maximilian did not speak with women that often for several cultural reasons. How do you think the two fit into Mandan and Hidatsa family and gender dynamics?

GB: I think jealousy had a lot to do with that stuff. It was almost a game to take your brother's wife. You have to remember that men had many brothers because of the clan system. You have to think of what they felt at that time. This is going to be terrible to say, but at that time, she was just a woman. Even though she had her own ceremony and her own med-icines, women weren't as important—even though Hidatsas are actually matrilineal, and women are the ones who had the final say. At the same time, we had so many rules and regulations for our women back in those days; men couldn't look at their mother-in-law, they couldn't look at their daughters-in-law. You have to remember it was before Christianity. That was the way of life. We based our life on animals, and we learned from the animals. We learned how to trap eagles from the black bear. We learned how to do certain things from the coyote.

To the Mandan and Hidatsa men, but also to Bodmer, I think a lot of the women weren't important. That's why he didn't put them in there. What he saw from a social standpoint was that the women did the hides, they did the cooking—it was mundane. It was the men's societies that were important because they had all the fancy adornments compared to the women. That's because the men were more likely to get killed on the warpath or hunting or in the environment.

AJ: I understand that a lot of duties and ceremonies that Maximilian recorded in the earth-lodge villages were gendered, including gardening, which is traditional women's work. Can you talk about your gardens and the process you went through to get heirloom seeds?

GB: As I became a historian at Knife River and started researching the villages—looking at Bodmer, looking at Maximilian's stuff, looking at Lewis and Clark—I knew gardening was essential to us because we were the keepers of the corn; that was part of our trade system. So I started wondering what kind of seeds we had left. This family told me that their great-grandmother's stuff was in the Smithsonian and gave me permis-sion to go in her medicine bundle and get a little handful of sunflower seeds, which I still have. I've never planted them because I'm scared to right now. Because I'm a male, I'm not supposed to do a lot of these things with gardening. I can't sing corn songs; I can hardly pray to them because that's not my role. So I had to get permission from the ladies who had the right to plant, who had the right to dig up the soil, and I had to go to them

　　　　FACES FROM THE INTERIOR

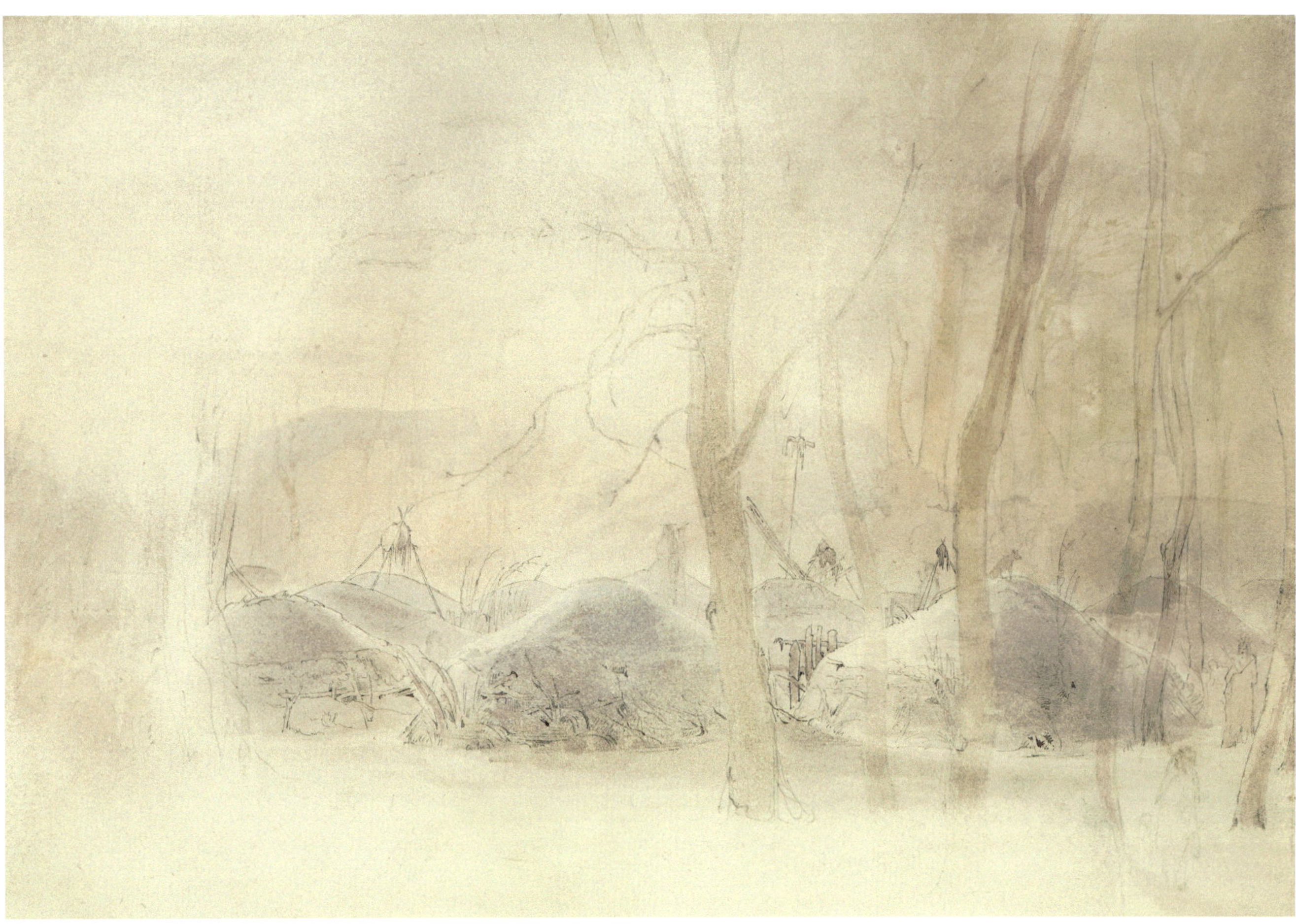

and ask if I could do that at Knife River because I wanted to put a garden there. They gave me the right to dig, to plant, to harvest, to store, and to dry—but they did not give me the right to sing the songs because they've gotta be sung only by the women.

My goal is to get people together, to bring our culture back somehow, and gardening is one of the ways to do it. Historical documents can also bring people together. I found all the [census] rolls of the Hidatsa people at the Smithsonian.[6] So I've got all of the families on big long sheets of paper. My hometown is Mandaree, North Dakota, and my goal is to go there in the summertime and take all these family names and put them on the floor, and then invite people to come in and take them to their family, and record what they've got to say. They would have stories about everybody and could start bringing those back in and share them with the people somehow. We'd start talking about family rather than talking about how bad the politics are. We'd talk legends rather than how we've got no money.

AJ: I'd be interested to see how this census and discussions around families could relate to historical images. Perhaps the people in Bodmer's portraits could be similarly researched?

GB: I've got a lot of goals, and one of them was just that: take all the names from all the people that Bodmer mentions. I did that; I have all the names of different villages and the people in those villages that he listed. My plan was to keep that going with whoever else—Catlin, [anthropologist Robert] Lowie, etc.—that named people in villages. When I first started looking at Bodmer, I was really interested in this. I would try to study the faces in the prints and try to remember who back home looks like that and see if there's any connection. Another thing we could do is look and see where those artifacts are today, medicines and this kind of stuff. But again, a lot of those sacred things I don't have the authority to see.

AJ: We've talked about how there were multiple languages and interpreters at play in the making of these images. How do you think knowledge of Hidatsa, Mandan, or other Indigenous languages can enrich our understanding of these portraits?

GB: The language was already starting to change at that time. We changed the language when we attempted to tell Bodmer through an interpreter what an old man was saying, because at that time we spoke three different dialects within the Hidatsa villages. Just the fact of interpreting and reinterpreting, of hearing the language through their heads, their hearts, and then coming out their arms by writing it down changed the language. You have to pay attention to that.

A personal story that relates to this is about an old man my mom talked about. That guy—his white man's name was Minot Grady—was the last one who spoke the Awadixa dialect. My mom, who couldn't speak a word of English when she was young, said that as a little girl they used to go to community meetings, and he would get up and talk, and nobody could understand him because he spoke the Awadixa dialect.

When I worked at Knife River, I would walk in the hills outside the villages. I would try to talk to the hills, and I would ask them, "How many languages, how many songs have you heard since you've been here?" Of course, they would never answer me—and if they did, I'd faint—but I wish I could hear that. Because song was our language, too. Song is an absolute language in a different category because songs tell a story, songs tell a prayer, songs tell the future, songs tell the past. I used to sing to the hills and see if I could get a reaction. I'd sing my heart out. I'd sing older songs, and then I'd stop and listen. My impression sometimes was that they got mad at me for doing that because I'm singing in a modern way. They're missing the old people, they're missing the old songs, they're missing the old language. Our old language was beautiful because we spoke in a descriptive manner.

So it's been changing since day one—day one being when Lewis and Clark were there, and then Catlin, Bodmer, and later on with Robert Lowie and some of the modern anthropologists. Of course, they changed the language too by their own scientific format. The language is changing all the time. Right now, we're looking really hard for the language Bodmer heard, and the only way we can hear it is through these paintings. The only way we can hear it is through Maximilian's notes. Then we interpret it ourselves and change it. Then, of course, you have the changes when it comes to religion, government, the forced schools. I think of all these factors, and it's kind of overwhelming.

AJ: These images convey so much information about Mandan and Hidatsa people while also misinterpreting and erasing so much knowledge.

GB: Oh, big time. That's why I can tell you these things. We looked at some of these images in detail, and I've looked at them most of my career in detail. And even this time with you, I've found new things. I'm older now, so I've got more experience. I'm not sure if I can see it better, but I can see it differently. If I could sit with these guys and have some way to talk to them—that's why I can't wait to go to the next world and meet these guys.

NOTES

1. Baker explained that blue or light eyes were not uncommon among the Mandan and Hidatsa people, pointing this feature out in many of Bodmer's portraits.
2. In many Plains communities it is customary to cut one's hair after the death of a family member.
3. George Catlin visited Mandan and Hidatsa villages in the late summer of 1832, as recounted in his *Letters and Notes on the Customs, Manners, and Conditions of the North American Indians* (London: George Catlin, 1841) and *O-Kee-Pa: A Religious Ceremony; and Other Customs of the Mandans* (Philadelphia: Lippincott, 1867).
4. Addíh-Hiddísch would have obtained his European-style black hat through trade. He affixed a feather to the hat in the style of Hidatsa head adornment, likely indicating a feat in war.
5. See Mike Cowdrey, "The 'Lion Boy' Ledger of Hidatsa Indian Drawings," in *Important American Indian Art* (New York: Sotheby's, 1997), n.p.
6. Baker refers to an early census taken at the reservation that included each counted person's Indian name, white name, age, status in the family, and status in the tribe.

III

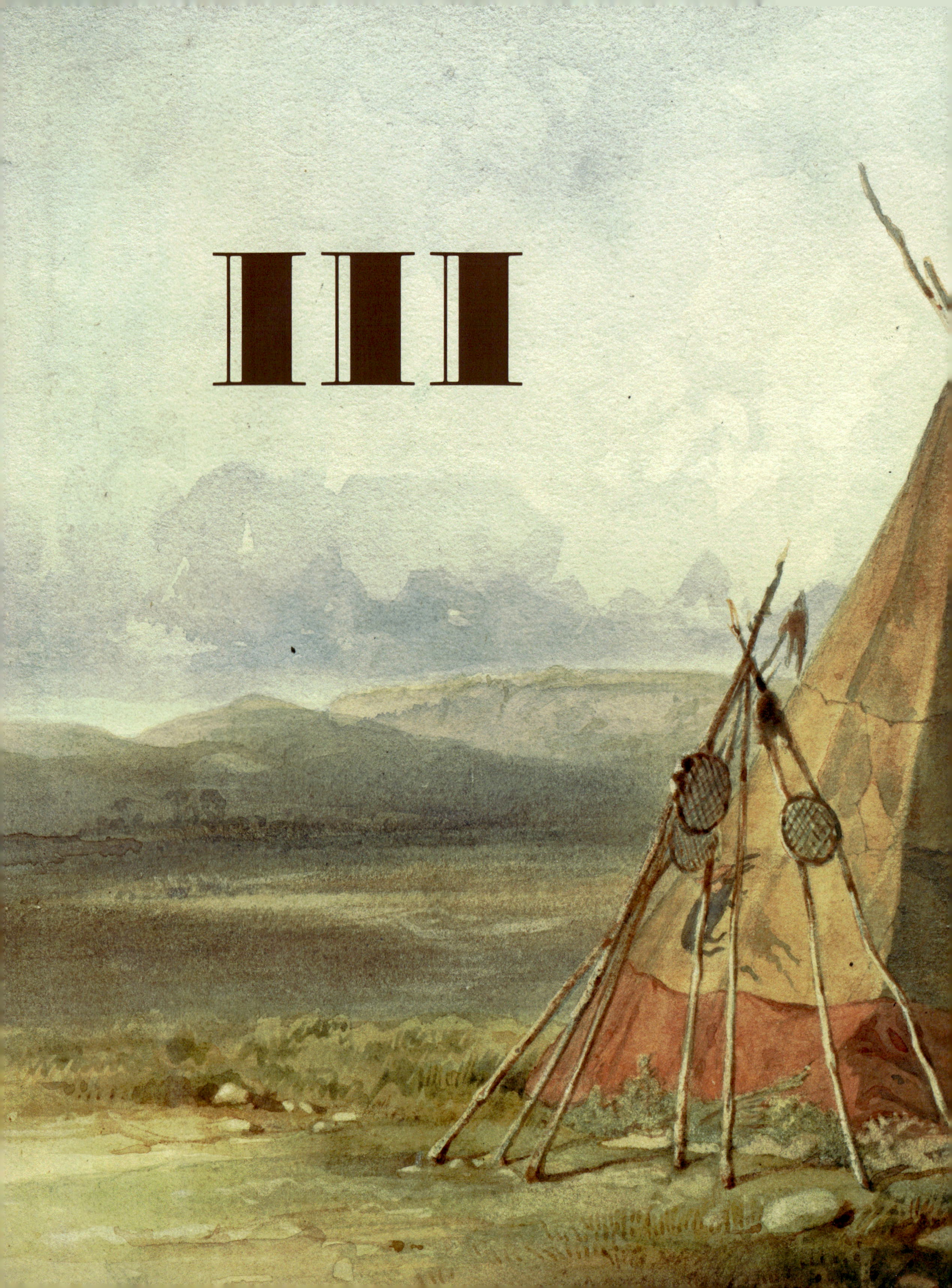

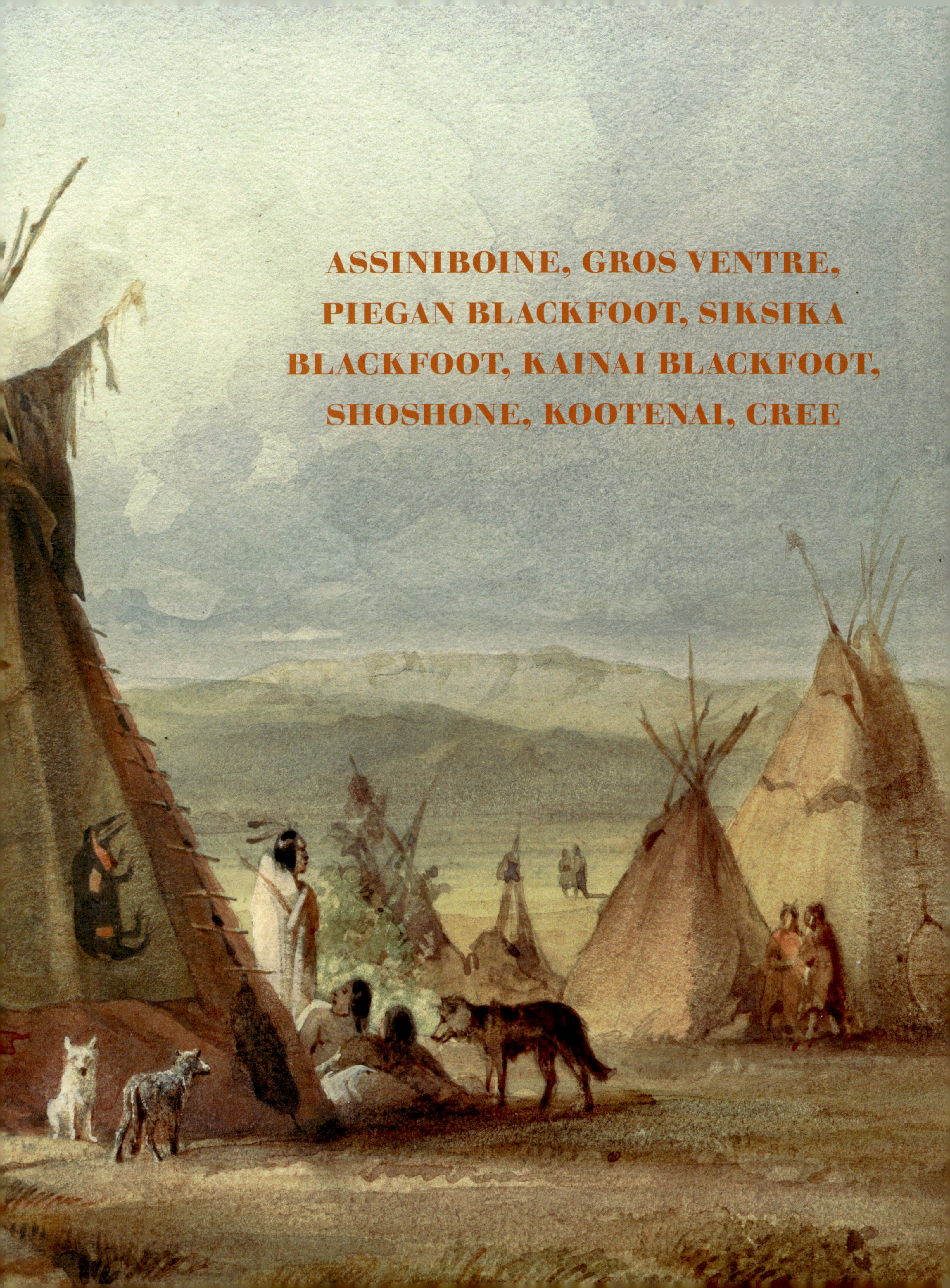
ASSINIBOINE, GROS VENTRE,
PIEGAN BLACKFOOT, SIKSIKA
BLACKFOOT, KAINAI BLACKFOOT,
SHOSHONE, KOOTENAI, CREE

31. Noapeh,
Assiniboine Man

1833

Noapeh was one of many Assiniboine men Maximilian
and Bodmer met during the two weeks they spent at Fort
Union (near the present-day North Dakota–Montana border) in the summer of 1833. Maximilian found Noapeh a
"most interesting" man, wearing "a head ornament with
antelope horns, and between them a crest of black, clipped
feathers. . . . His face was yellowish, his eyelids painted
red. On his chest and in back, his leather jacket or shirt
had large rosettes embroidered with porcupine quills, 8 or
10 inches [in] diameter. . . . The man stood . . . for a long
time for [Bodmer] and was rather patient, even though his
wife, child, and friends often came to call him away." The
prince wrote that Noapeh's name meant Troop of Soldiers,
although a modern English translation would be No Flight.
(*NAJ* 2:237 and n16, 238–39)

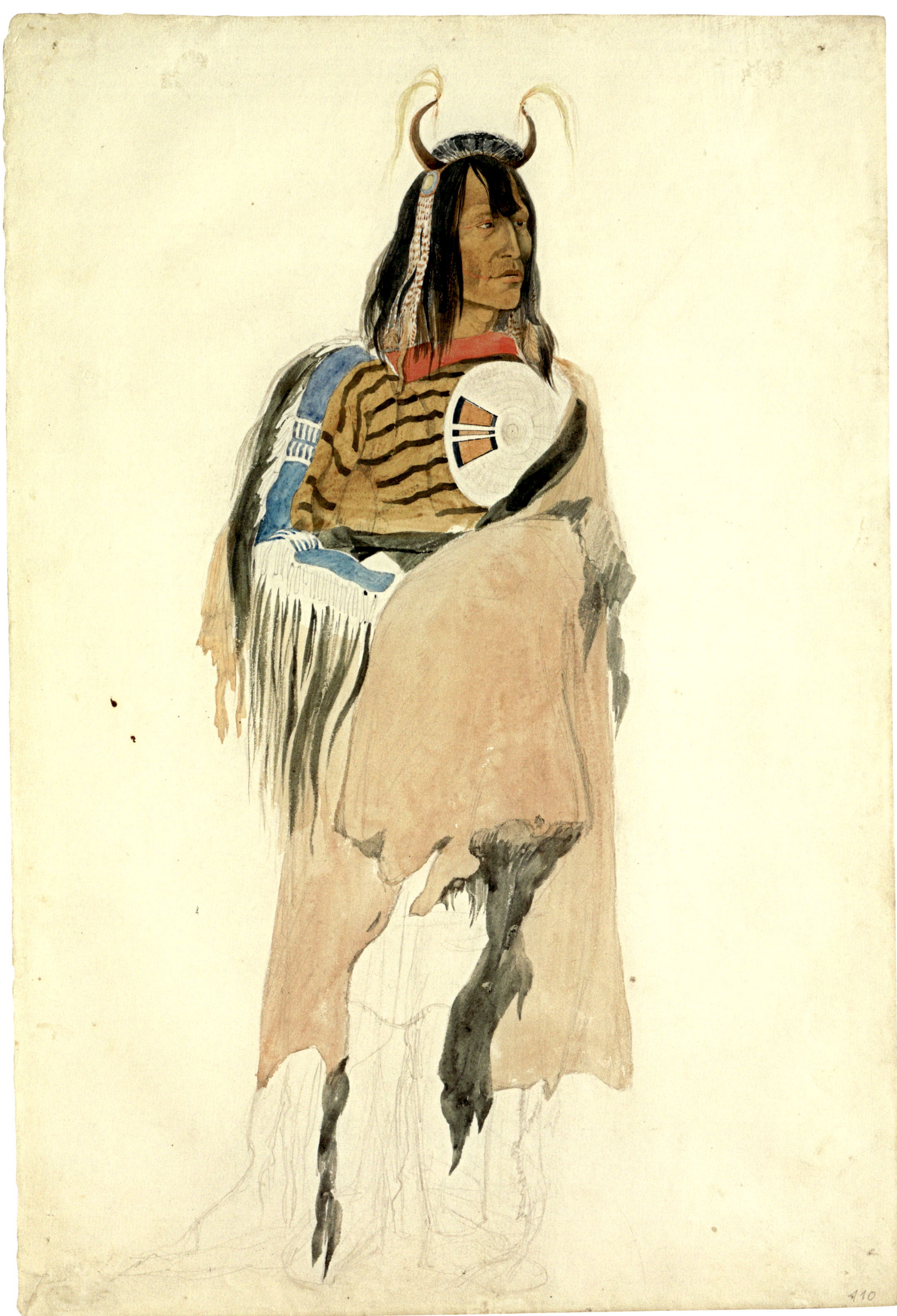

32. Pitätapiú, Assiniboine Man

1833

Pitätapiú was part of a small band of Assiniboines that arrived at Fort Union on June 29, 1833. Maximilian found his appearance remarkable: "His hair hanging down very long and plain, with a clipped tuft in front [that went] down to his mouth. The hair on the side covered his face in such a manner that one saw almost nothing of it. . . . He had fastened a small white shell [to his hair] above each eye. In his hand he carried a bow-lance, longer than a man and draped with long bands made from [tanned] grizzly bear intestines smeared with reddish dye. . . . This slender man, who was still young, carried a round shield . . . covered with whitish leather [painted red and green]. His whip was made of wood and [had] holes drilled into it like a flute." His portrait was painted the following day. (*NAJ* 2:240–41)

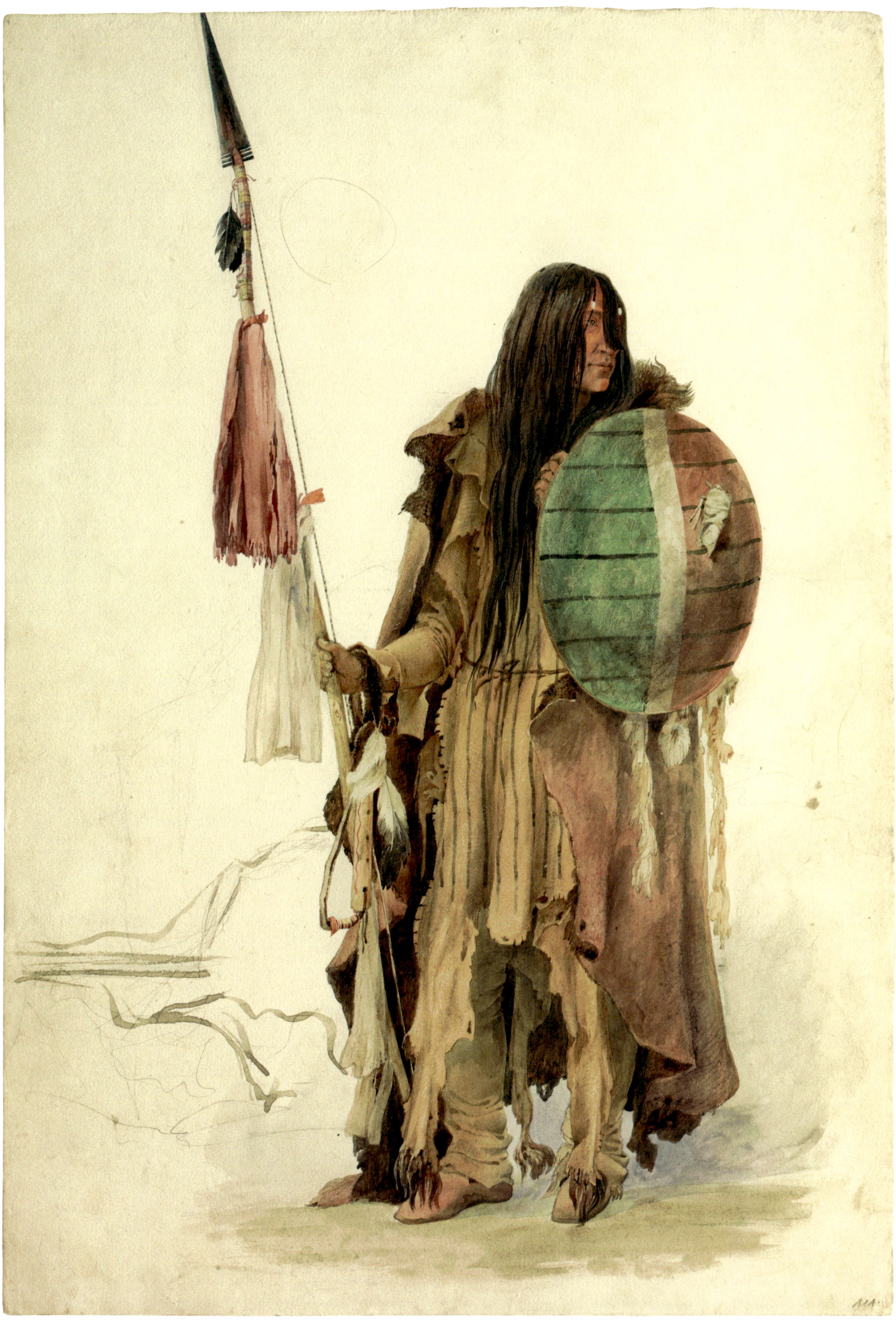

33. Assiniboine Man

1833

We do not know the name of this young man who posed
for Bodmer on June 29, 1833, at Fort Union. All we are
told is that he was "a tall, powerful Assiniboine" who was
"extremely serious until Mr. Bodmer started his music box,
whereupon he began to laugh. . . . His leather shirt was
remarkably clean and attractive [with] very long leather
fringes on the arms, where otherwise [such garments]
often have" locks of horse or human hair. "On the chest the
Assiniboines and Crees wear exceptionally large rosettes,
which one does not see in this manner among the [Sioux]."
(*NAJ* 2:240)

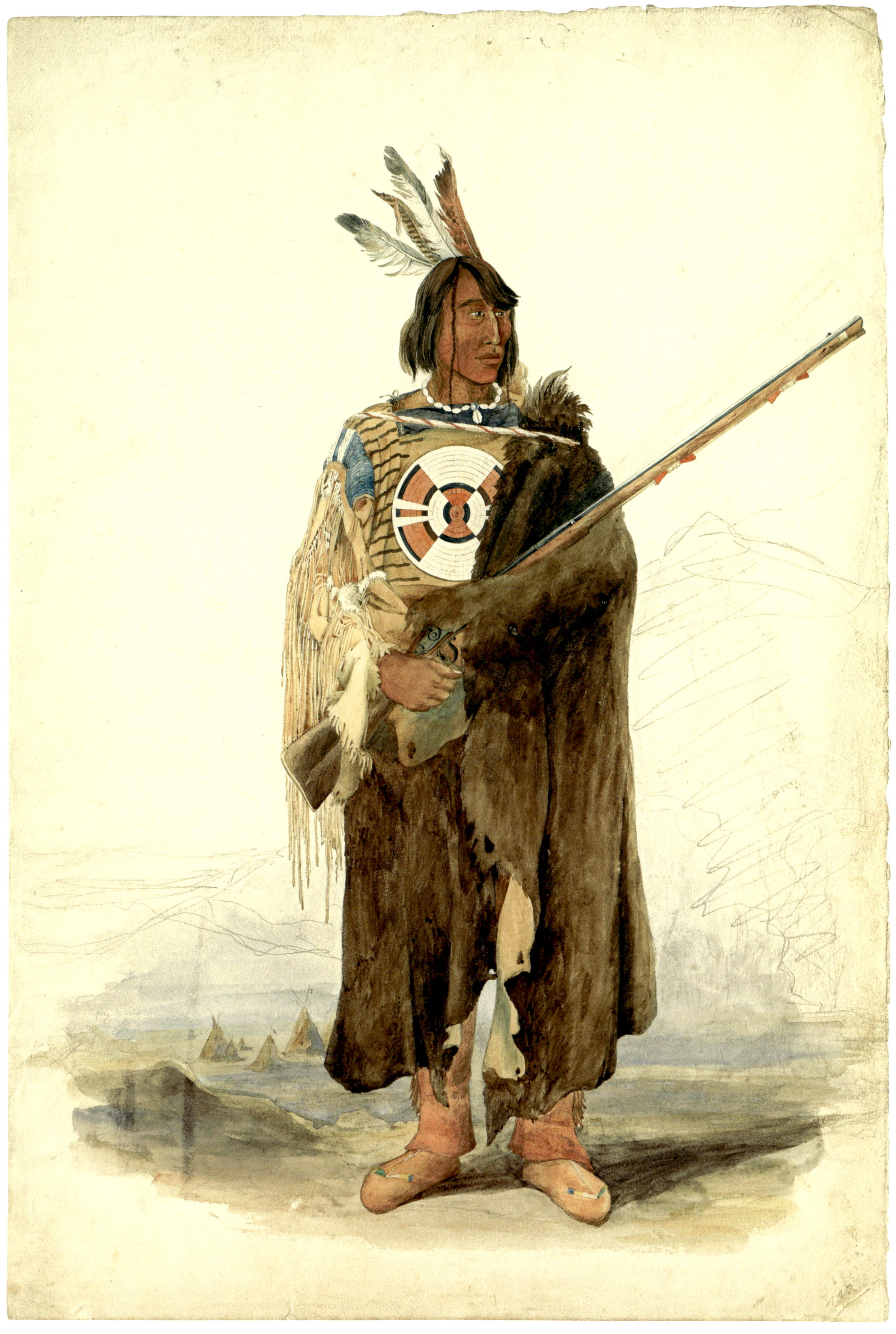

34. Pteh-Skah, Assiniboine Chief

1833

Maximilian and Bodmer met Pteh-Skah (White Buffalo Cow) in October 1833, during their second stay at Fort Union on their return from Fort McKenzie (near the confluence of the Marias and Missouri Rivers in present-day Montana) to Fort Clark (near what is now Bismarck, North Dakota). Pteh-Skah wore a bear-claw necklace and a painted buffalo robe. He asked to be paid for posing, and Bodmer gave him "a neckerchief," among other items. Maximilian later noted that Pteh-Skah's hair was "smeared with clay"; white and red clays were often used as coloring agents by northern Plains tribes. (*NAJ* 3:23; *TINA* 307)

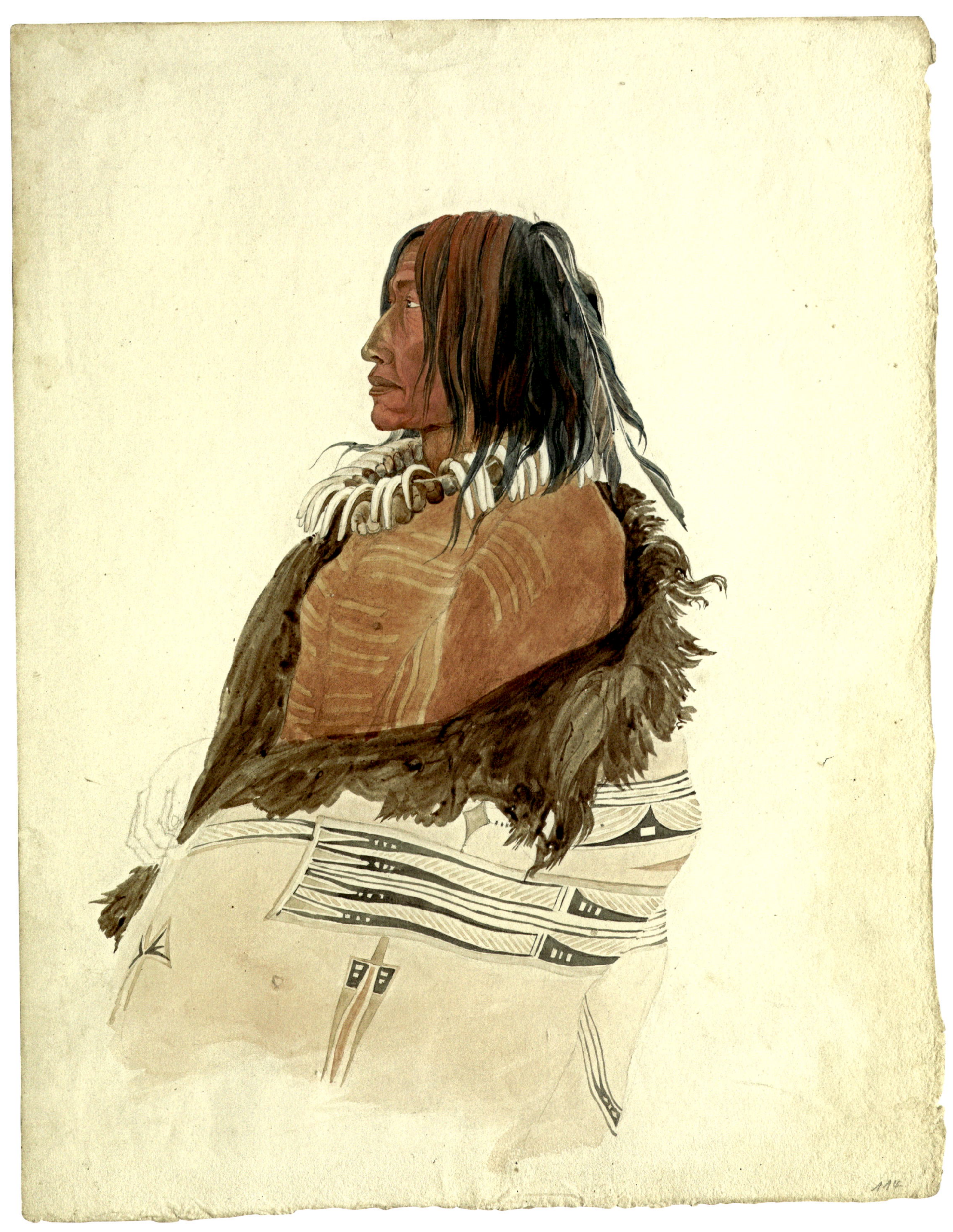

35. Assiniboine and Siksika Blackfoot Girl

1833

This child's portrait was made at Fort Union in October 1833. Maximilian reported that the subject was "the little girl of a Siksika who stays here and always lives with the Assiniboines." Her father had presumably married an Assiniboine and was living with her people; if so, their children would have been considered Assiniboine. Bodmer, likely following the interests of his employer and the cultural protocols of his sitters, depicted few women and even fewer children. (*NAJ* 3:9)

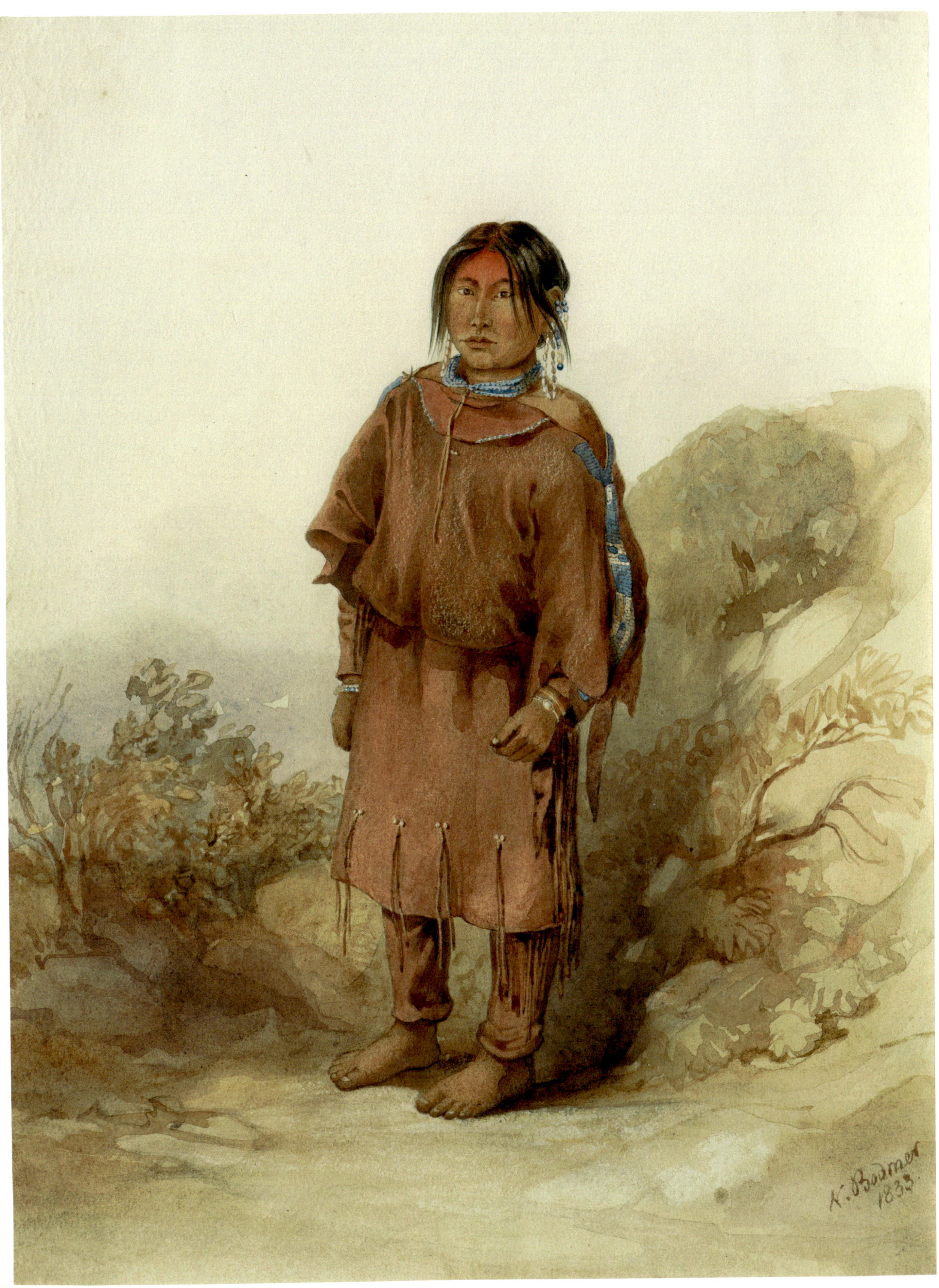

K. Bodmer
1833

36. Niätóhsä, Gros Ventre Chief

1833

Maximilian and Bodmer met Niätóhsä twice, once in
early August 1833 during a tense encounter at a camp
of Gros Ventres (an abbreviation of Gros Ventres des
Prairies) on the voyage upstream to Fort McKenzie,
and again later that month at the fort. Bodmer sketched
Niätóhsä aboard the keelboat *Flora* during their first
meeting. Maximilian noted then that he "had bound his
hair in a knot in front, something only medicine men may
do," and that he "had a substantial bullet wound in his
right arm under the shoulder"—a detail not visible in this
portrait. (*NAJ* 2:333–34)

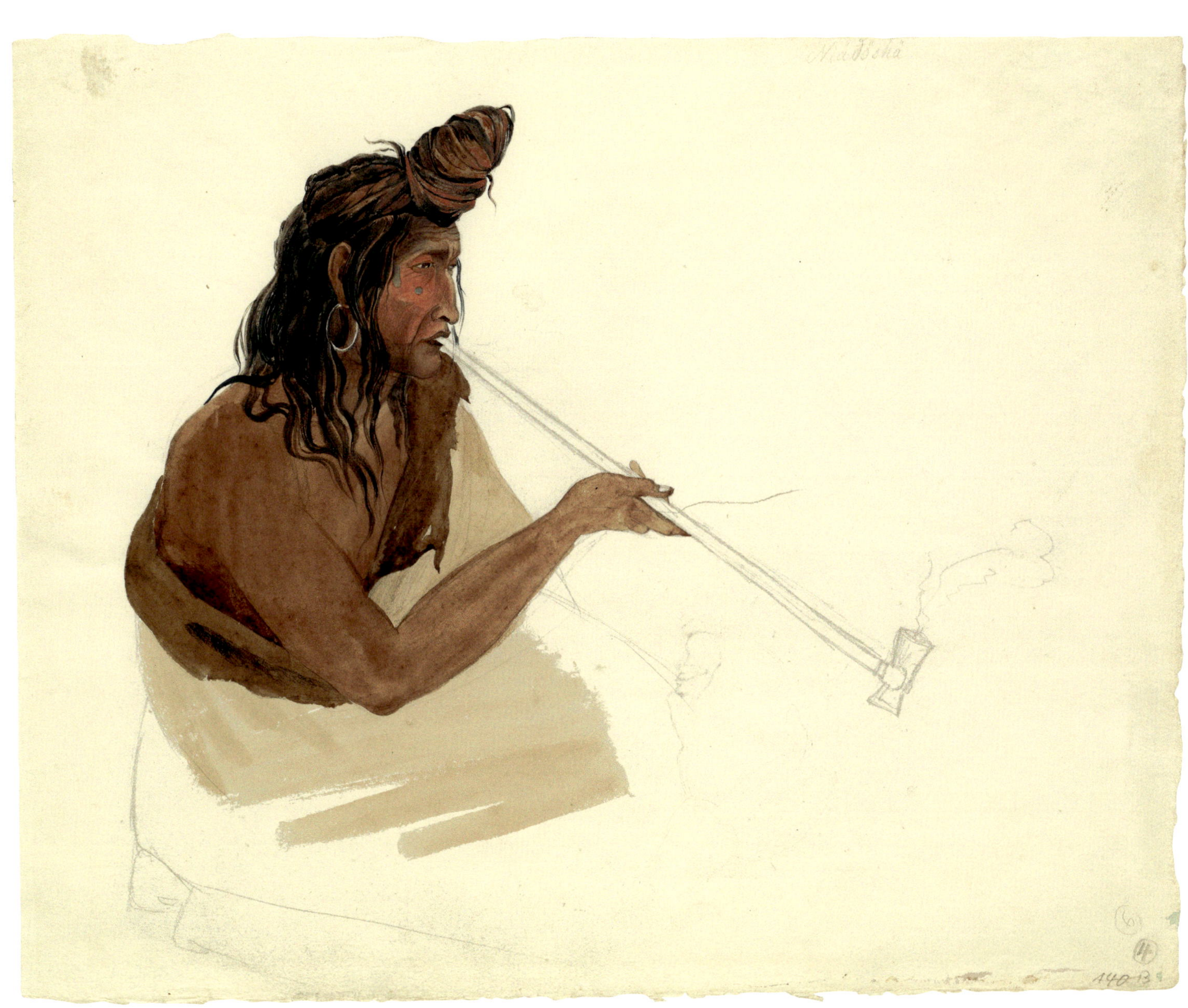

37. Mexkemáuastan, Gros Ventre Chief

1833

As they did with Niätóhsä (pl. 36), Maximilian and Bodmer met this formidable chief twice: first on August 5, 1833, when the *Flora*, with a full cargo of trade goods bound for Fort McKenzie, stopped near a large encampment of Gros Ventres. There was a brief but tense encounter as dozens of men boarded the keelboat, demanding tobacco and other goods, and much relief among the crew when the *Flora* managed to sail safely upriver. Nearly two weeks later, Mexkemáuastan visited Maximilian and Bodmer in their quarters at Fort McKenzie. The prince wrote that "his reddish brown buffalo robe left his right arm and shoulder free; on his back, bow and arrow in their sheaths; in his hand, a short gun with leather cover; leather leggins; his hair tied together in front in a thick, protruding knot. Face [painted] vermilion and blue-violet with mineral color." (*NAJ* 2:370)

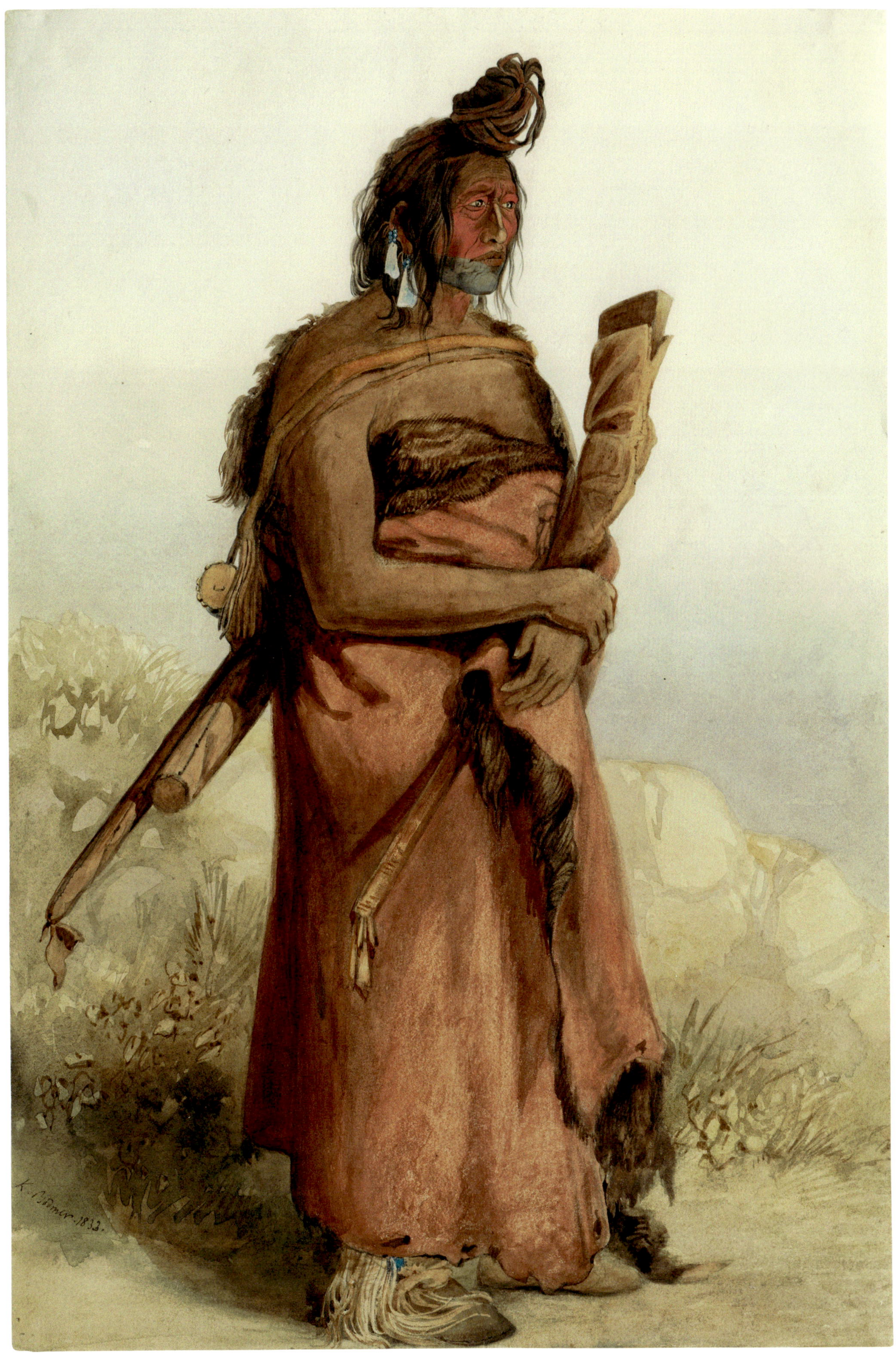

38. Natoie-Poóchsen, Piegan Blackfoot Man

1833

Natoie-Poóchsen was in mourning for a relative when
Maximilian and Bodmer met him at Fort McKenzie on
August 18, 1833. The elderly Piegan man "was seen walking
about with his hair cut off and [his] face and legs smeared
ash-gray [with clay], howling, and sometimes weeping.
Mr. Bodmer took him with this attire into our room, where
he calmly sat down to be sketched. His name . . . means *la
parole de la vie*." Maximilian's French translates as Word
of Life; a modern English interpretation of the name would
be Holy/Powerful Language, suggesting this sitter was a
man of ceremonial or spiritual authority. (*NAJ* 2:376 and
nм26)

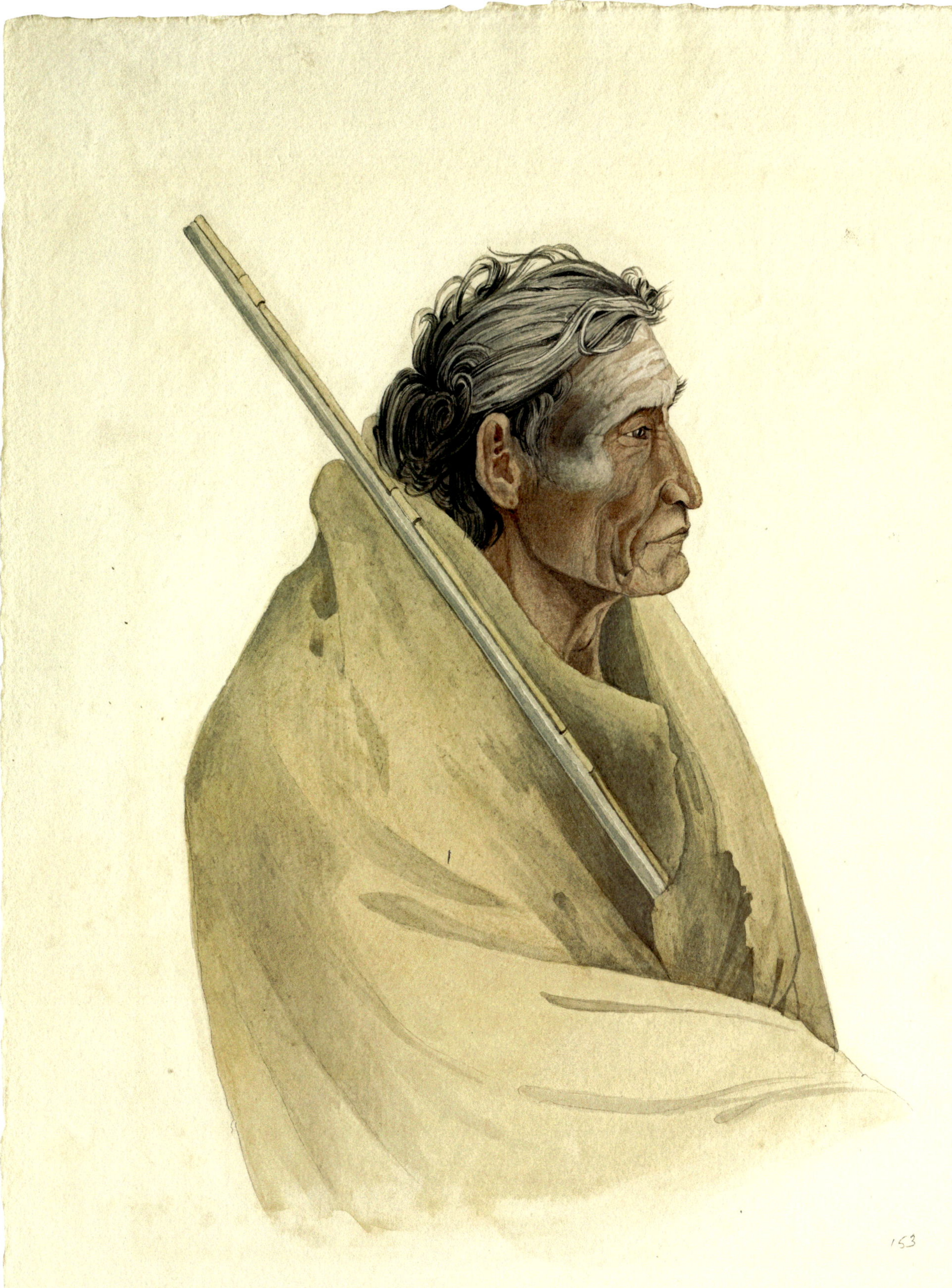

153

NA 153

39. Tátsicki-Stomíck, Piegan Blackfoot Chief

1833

Tátsicki-Stomíck (Middle Bull) was one of the principal chiefs of the Piegan (today recognized as Piegan Blackfeet in the United States), a kindred nation of the Siksika and Kainai referred to collectively as the Blackfoot. On September 2, 1833, when Tátsicki-Stomíck sat for this portrait at Fort McKenzie, Maximilian was disappointed in his everyday clothing, which he called "poor, plain apparel." Tátsicki-Stomíck's face, however, was vividly painted with vermilion and the same bluish pigment as Pioch-Kiäiu (pl. 42). (*NAJ* 2:405)

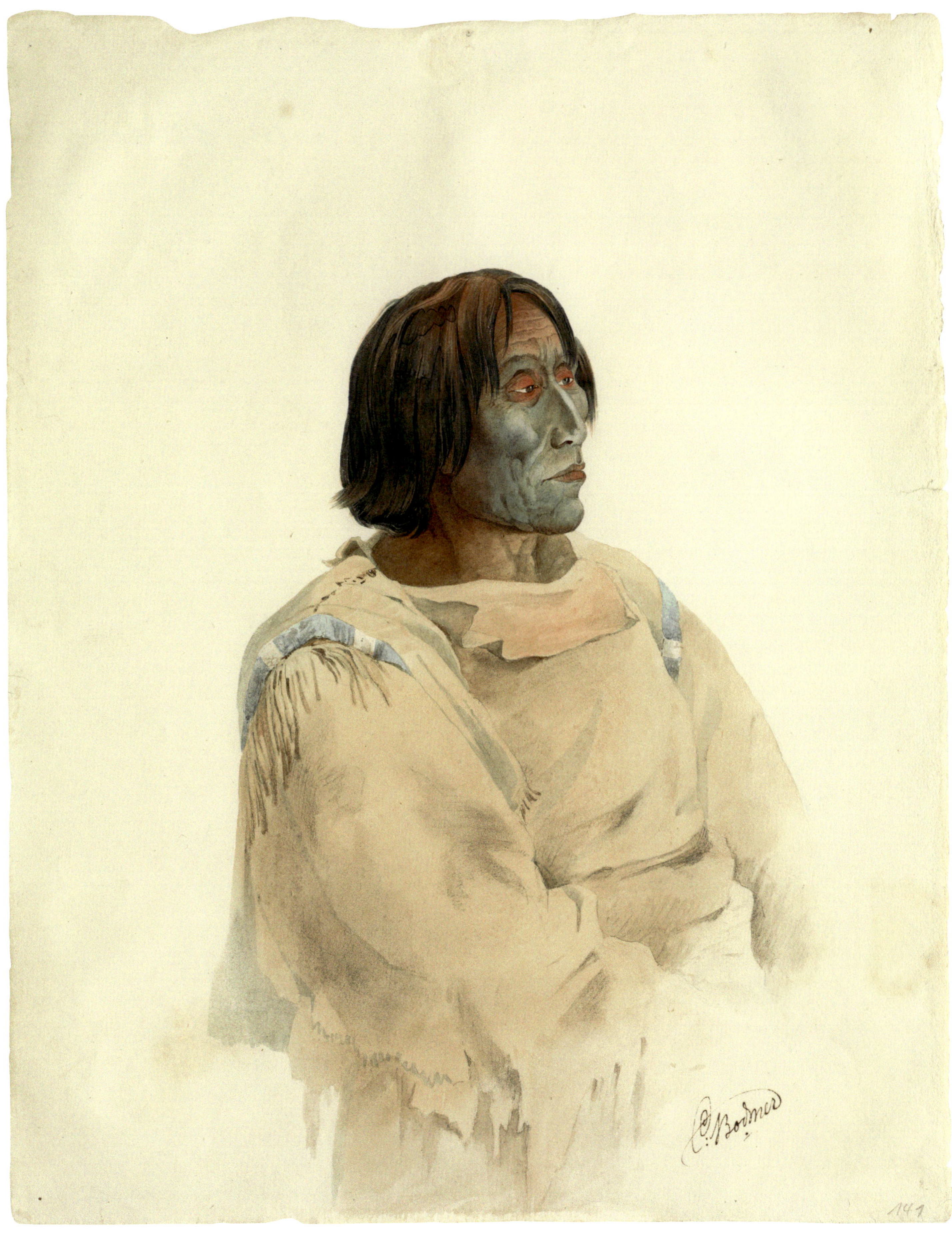

40. Mexkehme-Sukahs, Piegan Blackfoot Chief

1833

Mexkehme-Sukahs was one of several Piegan chiefs Maximilian and Bodmer met during their five-week stay at Fort McKenzie. The fort was established by the American Fur Company in 1832 in an attempt to lure the lucrative Blackfoot trade away from its largest competitor, the Hudson's Bay Company. When the *Flora* arrived at Fort McKenzie on August 9, 1833, a large Blackfoot encampment was outside the walls of the fort, with nearly 800 people gathered to greet the heavily laden keelboat. On August 11, Bodmer drew Mexkehme-Sukahs, who had "painted his face black and red. His leather shirt was lined with rows of shiny [metal] buttons, trimmed on top with otter hide, [and] edged on the shoulders and arms with blue beads. His hair hung disheveled about his head; attached to the crown was a bunch of feathers of birds of prey [along] with white weasel skins, woodpecker heads and beaks, red flaps and cloth strips, and the like." The "weasel skins" include what appears to be an ermine with a blue bead for an eye; there is also one large, pendant bear claw. (*NAJ* 2:365–66)

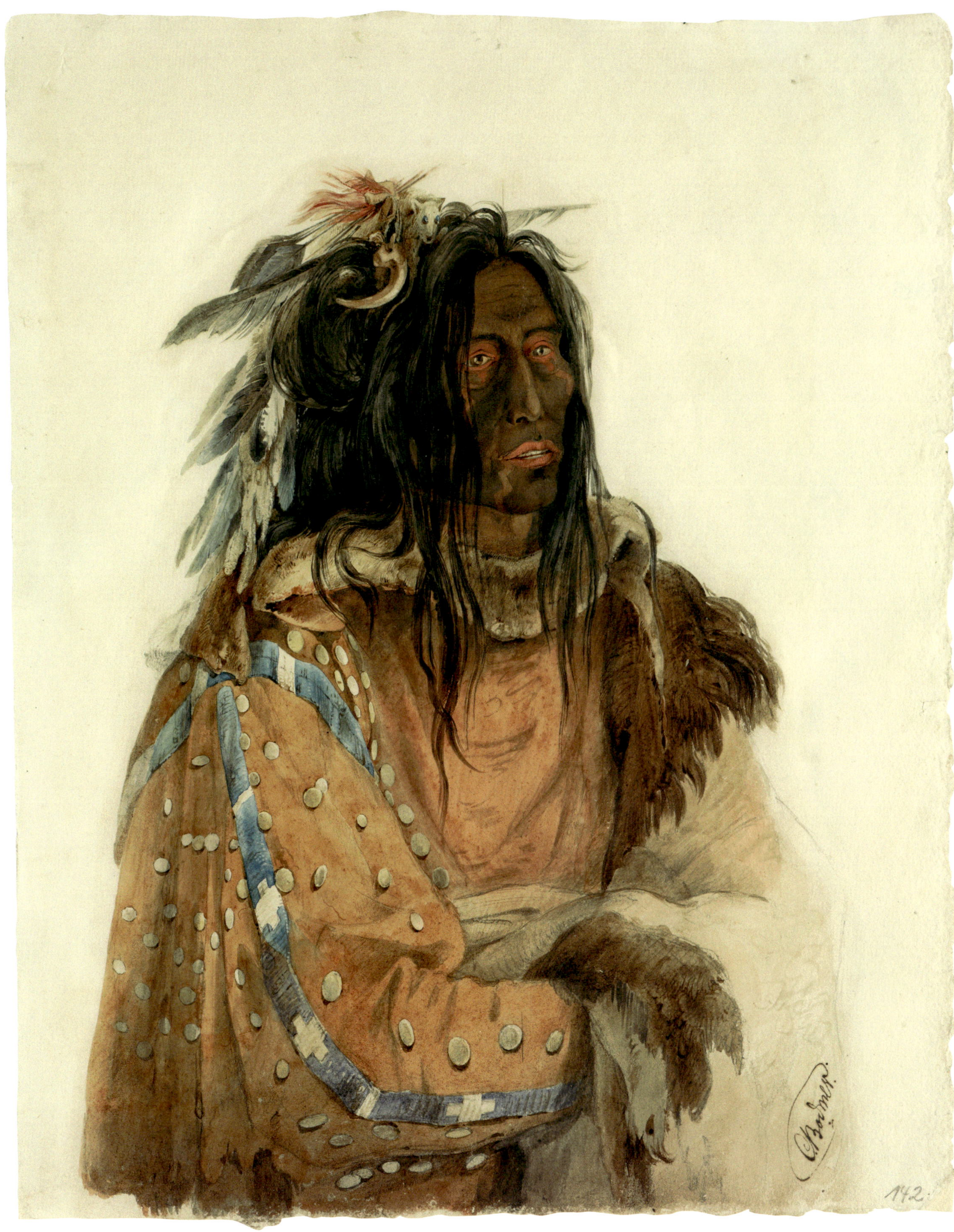

142.

41. Hotokáneheh, Piegan Blackfoot Man

1833

Hotokáneheh often visited Maximilian and Bodmer's quarters at Fort McKenzie, and his likeness was painted over a period of several days in August 1833. He was evidently the keeper of a medicine pipe, which Bodmer rendered in careful detail; Maximilian noted the devout care with which Hotokáneheh unwrapped the pipe before posing. These pipes—associated with war, healing, and the welfare of the people—were kept in special medicine bundles with related ritual objects, and it was a great responsibility to be the owner or steward of one. Hotokáneheh received some ribbons from Bodmer, which he used to decorate the pipe stem, likely intending them as gifts to the pipe, a sign of reverence or respect.

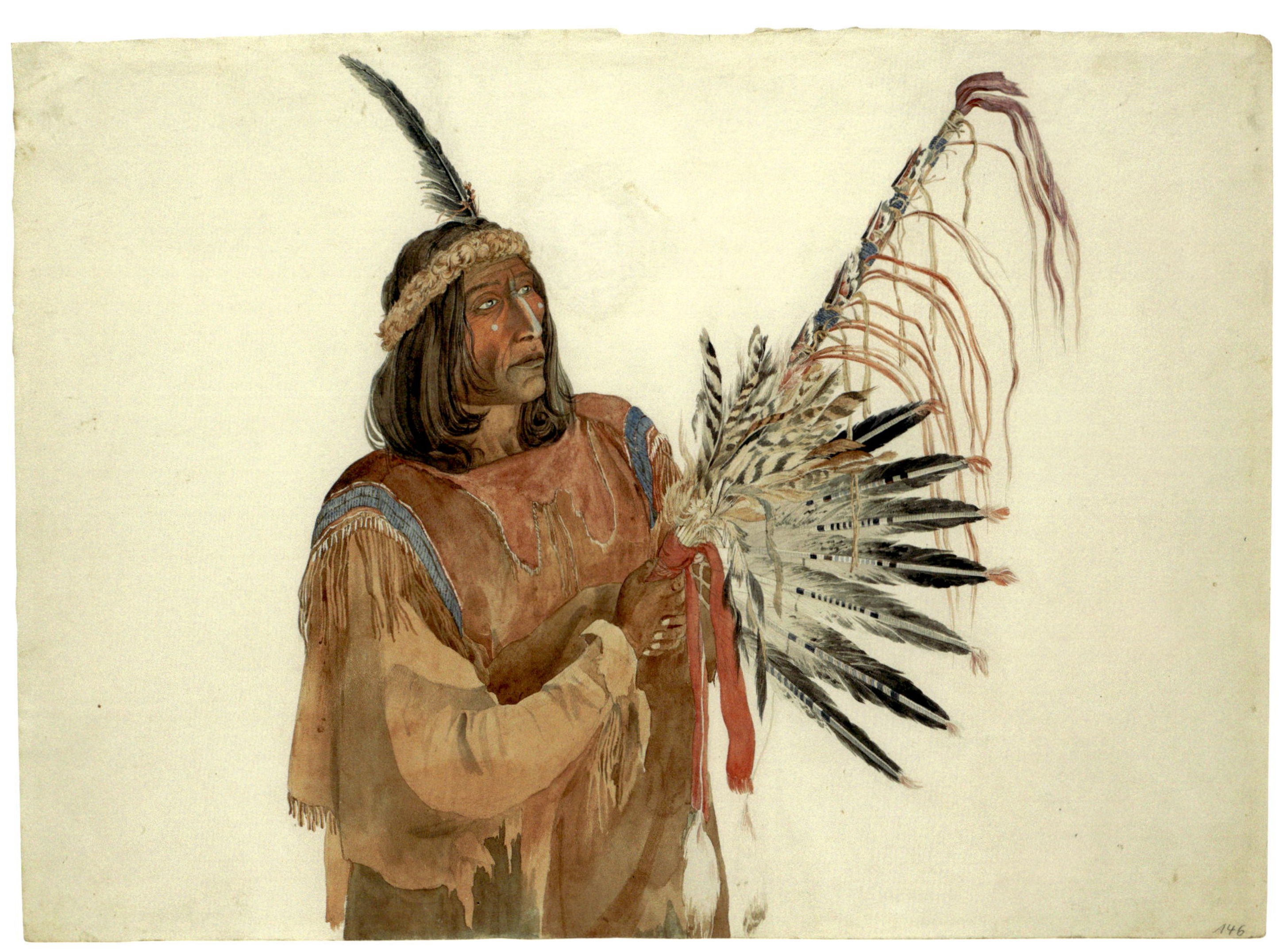

42. Pioch-Kiáïu,
Piegan Blackfoot Man
1833

Bodmer began this portrait of Pioch-Kiáïu (Distant Bear)
at Fort McKenzie on August 2, 1833, completing it the following day. A week later, 600 Assiniboine and Cree warriors attacked the Blackfoot camp outside Fort McKenzie
and killed or injured many people. Pioch-Kiáïu came to
Bodmer afterward to joyously report that "no bullets had
been able to hit him; undoubtedly the reason was that he
had been sketched." Here, Pioch-Kiáïu's hair is smeared
with what appears to be red clay or vermilion and bound
into a knot over his forehead. The blue paint on Pioch-
Kiáïu's face is striking; Maximilian described the pigment
as being made from a bluish metallic ore obtained from
the Rocky Mountains. He had a sample analyzed after
he returned to Europe, and it was found to be "an earthy
peroxide of iron, mixed with clay." (*NAJ* 2:337, 381nm31;
TINA 247)

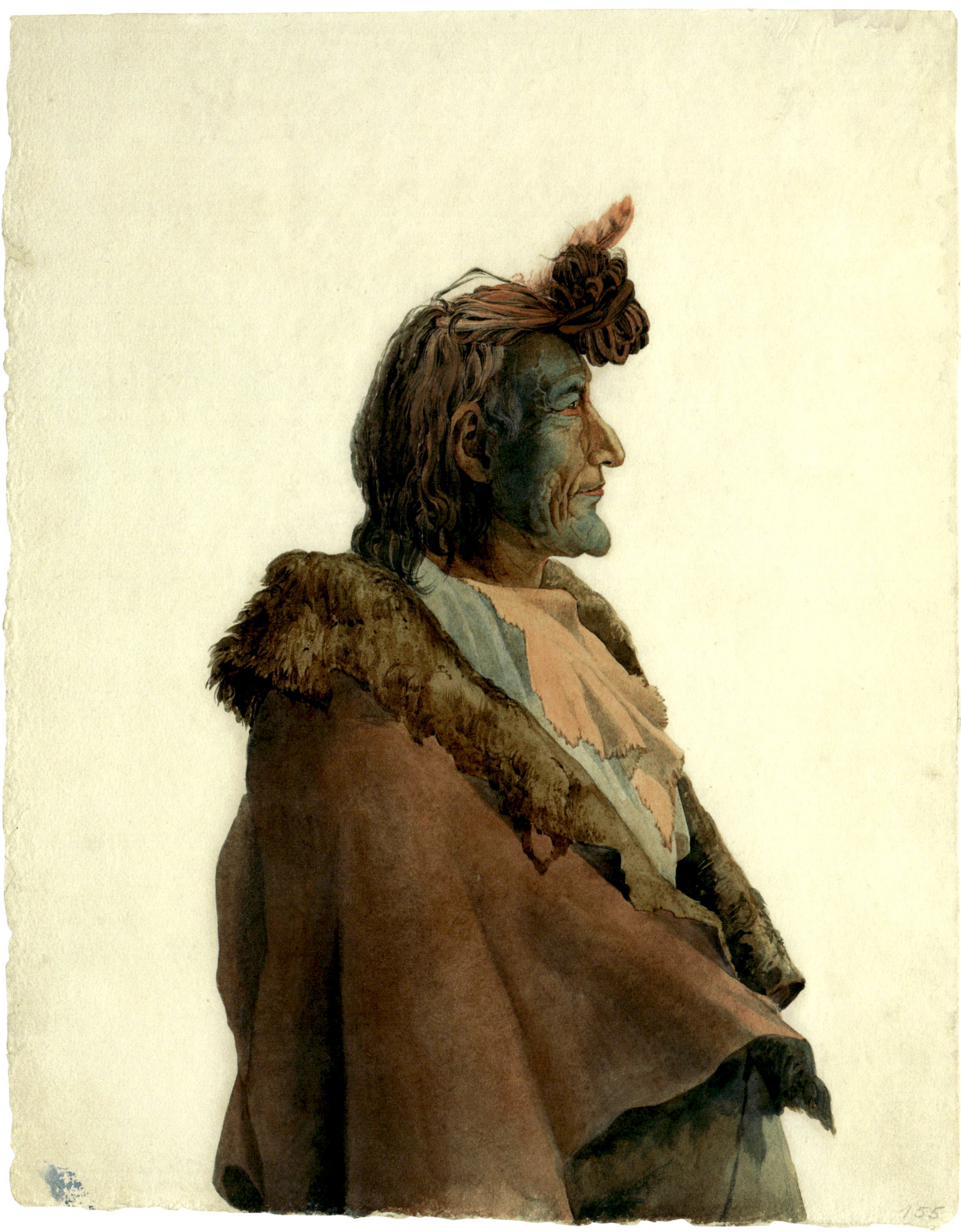

155

43. Piegan Blackfoot or Gros Ventre Man

1833

Inscriptions on an old mat on which this painting was mounted and on a similar rendering owned by the Newberry Library in Chicago suggest that the subject is a Piegan Blackfoot, but the sitter's buffalo robe closely resembles Maximilian's description of a Gros Ventre style of decoration: "Their robes are marked with very attractive parallel stripes of porcupine quills, mostly yellow or yellowish red; little red cloth flaps are sewed on [these] straight downward, one above the other." Robes and other clothing items were frequently exchanged between groups, and styles and techniques were widely borrowed, so the tribal affiliation of this sitter remains uncertain. (*NAJ* 2:443–44)

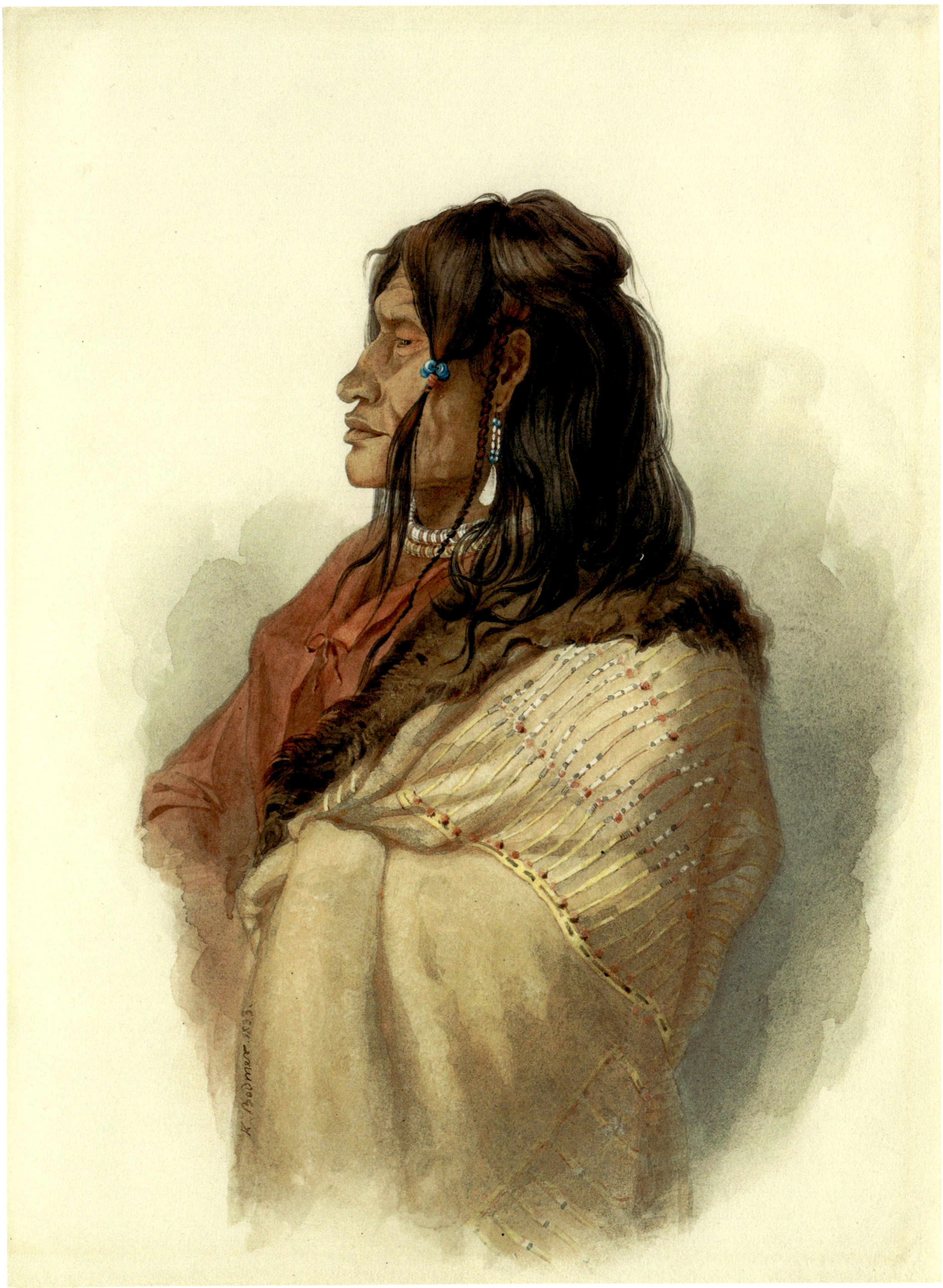
K. Bodmer. 1833.

44. Piegan Blackfoot Man

1833

At Fort McKenzie on August 31, 1833, "Mr. Bodmer
sketched an Indian in a beautifully painted elk hide with
every conceivable heroic deed on it. . . . He was completely
wrapped in the hide and wore his [leather] rifle sheath
wound around his head." Maximilian later observed in his
journal that robes painted with "hieroglyphs" were common among all Indigenous people living along the Missouri
River. These pictographs represented the owner's "deeds
in war: [his] capture of prisoners, weapons, [and] horses;
horse stealing; scalps taken; wounds, and flowing blood."
Many such events have been recorded on this robe: bows
and guns and war axes, presumably taken from enemies;
numerous hoofprints, perhaps representing forays into
enemy territory to steal horses; and many injuries to himself, foes, or comrades—both the figure on the green horse
and his mount appear to have been gravely wounded.
(*NAJ* 2:402, 426)

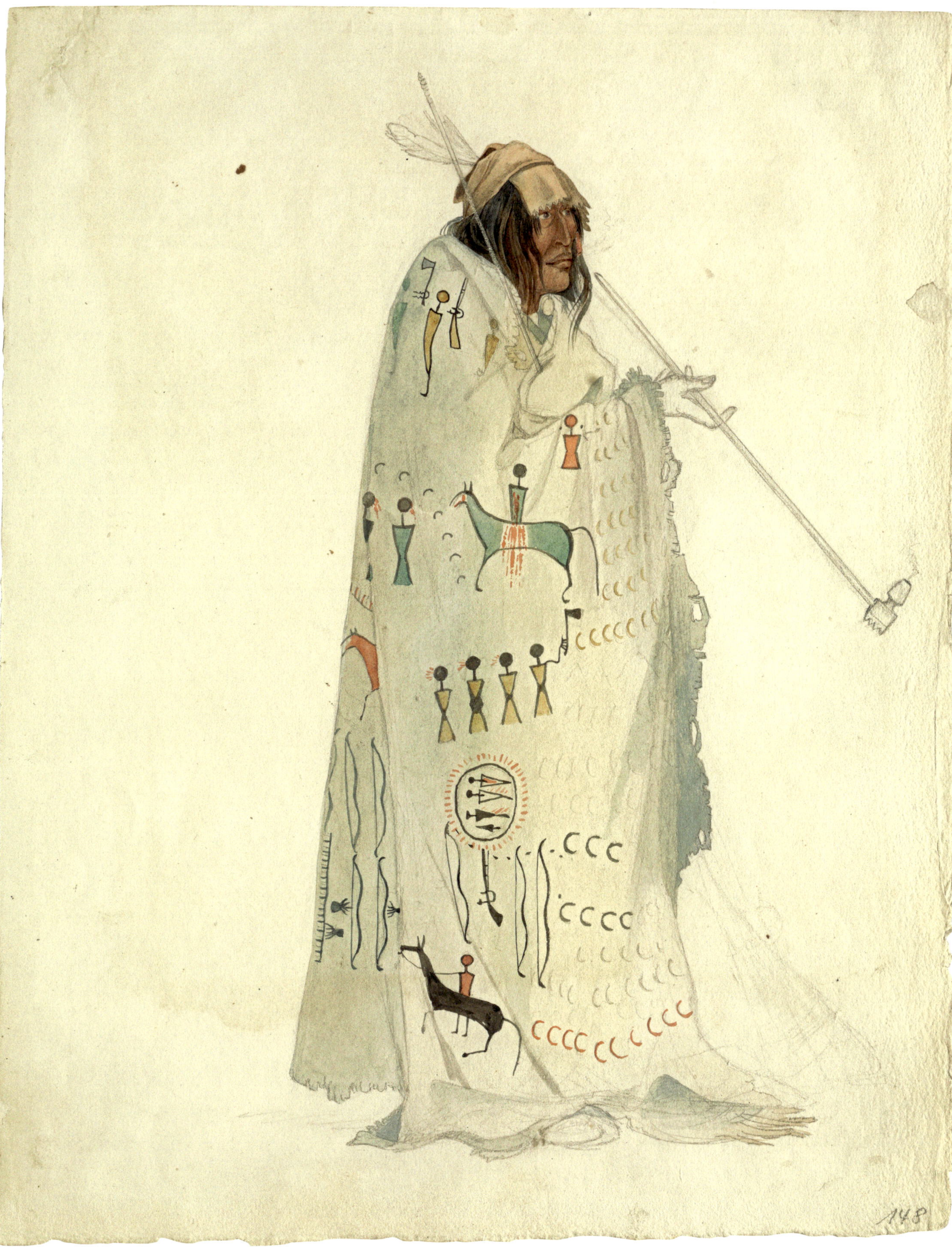

148

45. Kiäsax,
Piegan Blackfoot Man

1833

Maximilian and Bodmer first met Kiäsax in June 1833, when the *Assiniboine* stopped briefly at Fort Clark on its way upriver. This young man was married to a Hidatsa woman and lived at her village near the fort. Kiäsax boarded the steamer intending to travel with the traders into Blackfoot territory to visit his Piegan relatives, but evidently he changed his mind at Fort Union and returned to his wife's home. Later, during the winter of 1833–34, he visited Maximilian and Bodmer at their Fort Clark cabin. In Bodmer's portrait, executed on the *Assiniboine*, Kiäsax carries a flute in the crook of his arm, with a single eagle feather hanging from a string at the end. He is wrapped in what Maximilian called "a Spanish blanket" striped in white, black, and indigo blue; many scholars believe it to be more likely of Navajo origin, but they would agree with Maximilian that the blanket and large metal crucifix are both evidence of trade between the Southwest and the northern Plains. (*NAJ* 2:218)

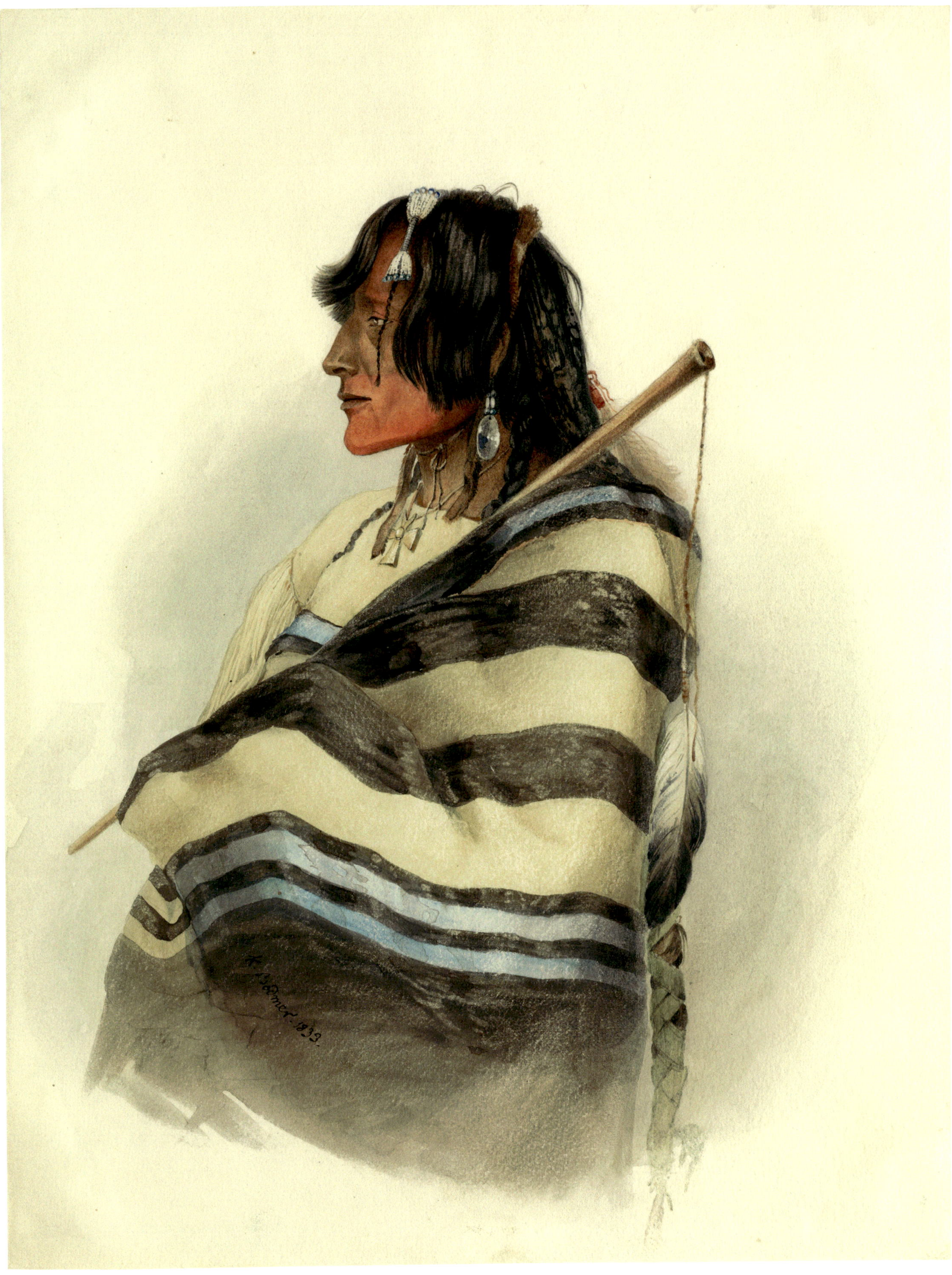

46. Piegan Blackfoot Woman
1833

On August 23, 1833, several Piegan men visited Maximilian's quarters at Fort McKenzie and "were greatly entertained by Mr. Bodmer's portraits. If they found a very good likeness, they recognized it immediately, joyfully called out the name, and clapped their hands." One of the men had brought along his young wife, who Mr. Bodmer drew the next day. Her face is painted with red stripes, and her garments are decorated largely with blue and white beads, including bands of beadwork down the front of the dress and beaded fringe on the shoulders; a beaded belt; beaded moccasins; and beaded bracelets. (*NAJ* 2:386)

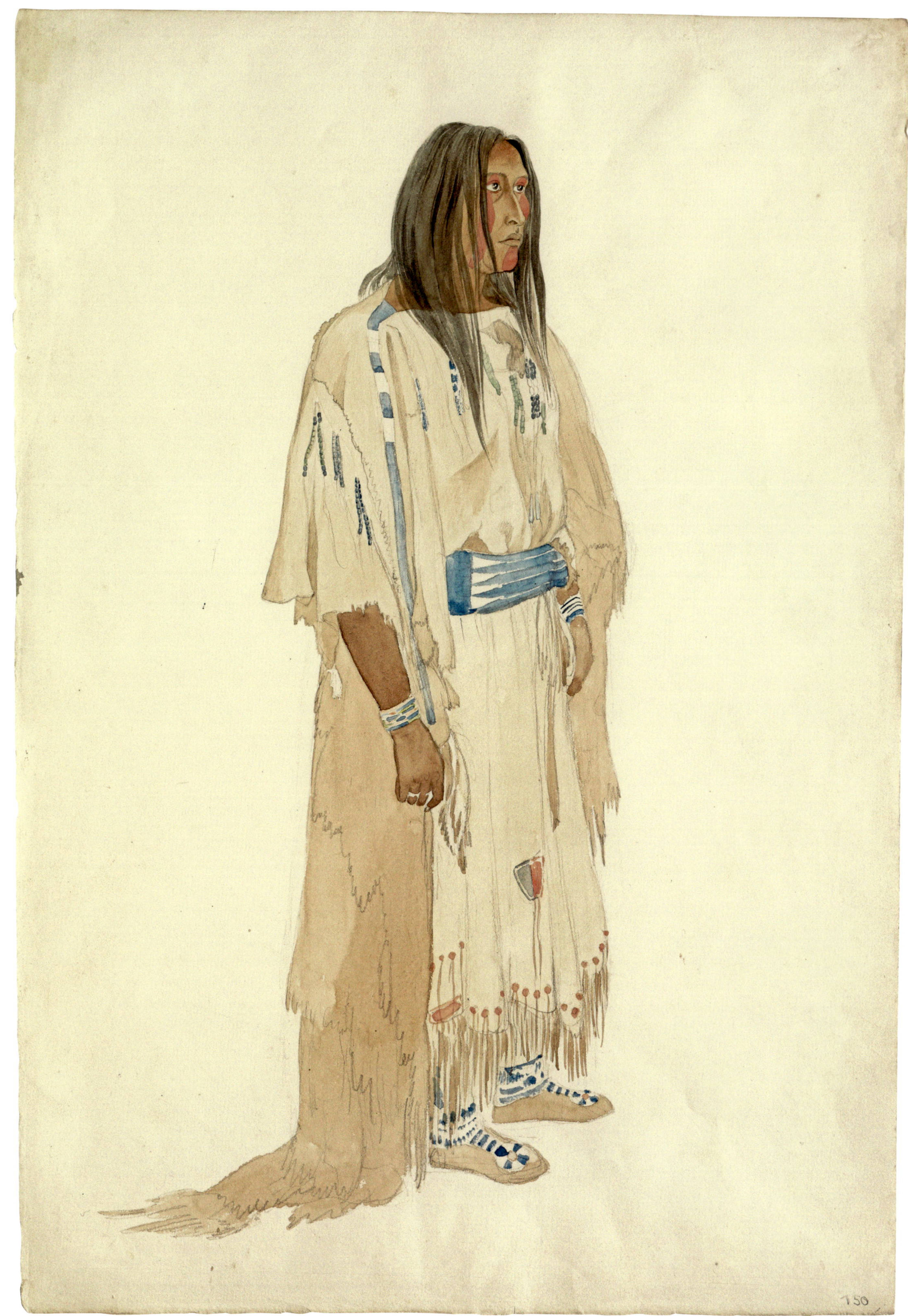

47. Shoshone Woman

1833

In Bodmer's time, the Shoshonean peoples were generally located in and west of the Rocky Mountains. This Shoshone woman was the wife of an American Fur Company employee at Fort McKenzie known as Marceau or Marcereau. She is plainly but attractively dressed, and Bodmer's remarkable attention to detail can be seen in the fringes and the visible stitching on the edge of the cape-like yoke of her hide dress. According to Maximilian, this woman had recently given birth and did not seem well at the time her portrait was painted.

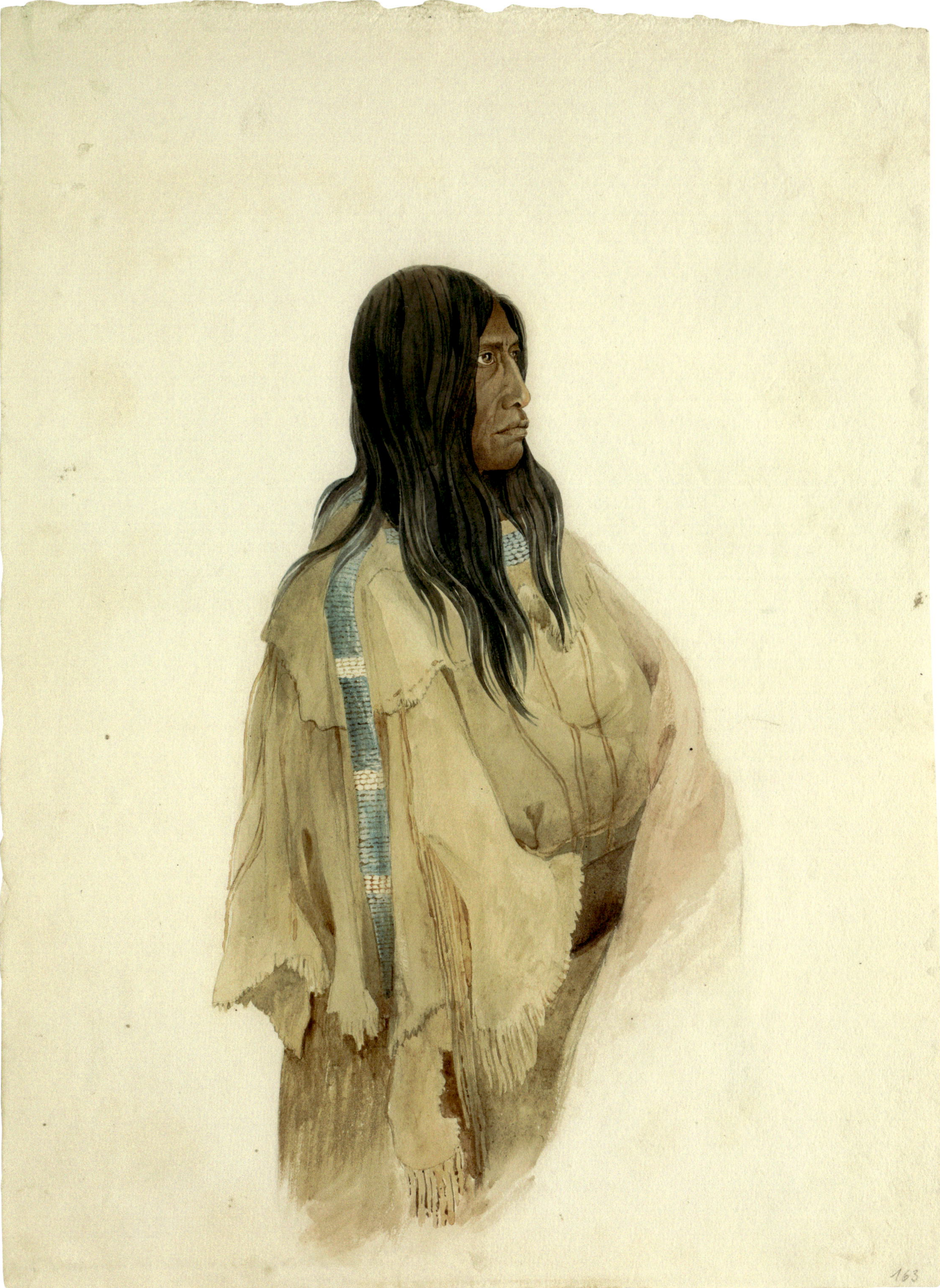

163

48. Makúie-Póka, Piegan Blackfoot Man

1833

Makúie-Póka (Wolf Child) was the son of a Kootenai man (pl. 49) and a Blackfoot mother. Maximilian described him as "a very elegant, finely attired Indian, half Piegan, the tribe to which he also considered himself to belong." His portrait was made at Fort McKenzie over a period of three days. Wrapped in a striped trade blanket, Makúie-Póka's lavish ornamentation includes several metal finger rings; a bear-claw necklace; a choker likely made of braided sweetgrass; hairbows fashioned of beads and dentalium shells; and streamers made of tubular white beads alternating with small round ones of blue and white glass. The long, tubular beads were generally called hair pipes and were manufactured (first of shell, later of bone) on the East Coast for the Indian trade. The hairbows were said by Maximilian to have been a fashion of Mandan or Hidatsa origin, adopted by the Blackfoot and other tribes. (*NAJ* 2:380 and n27)

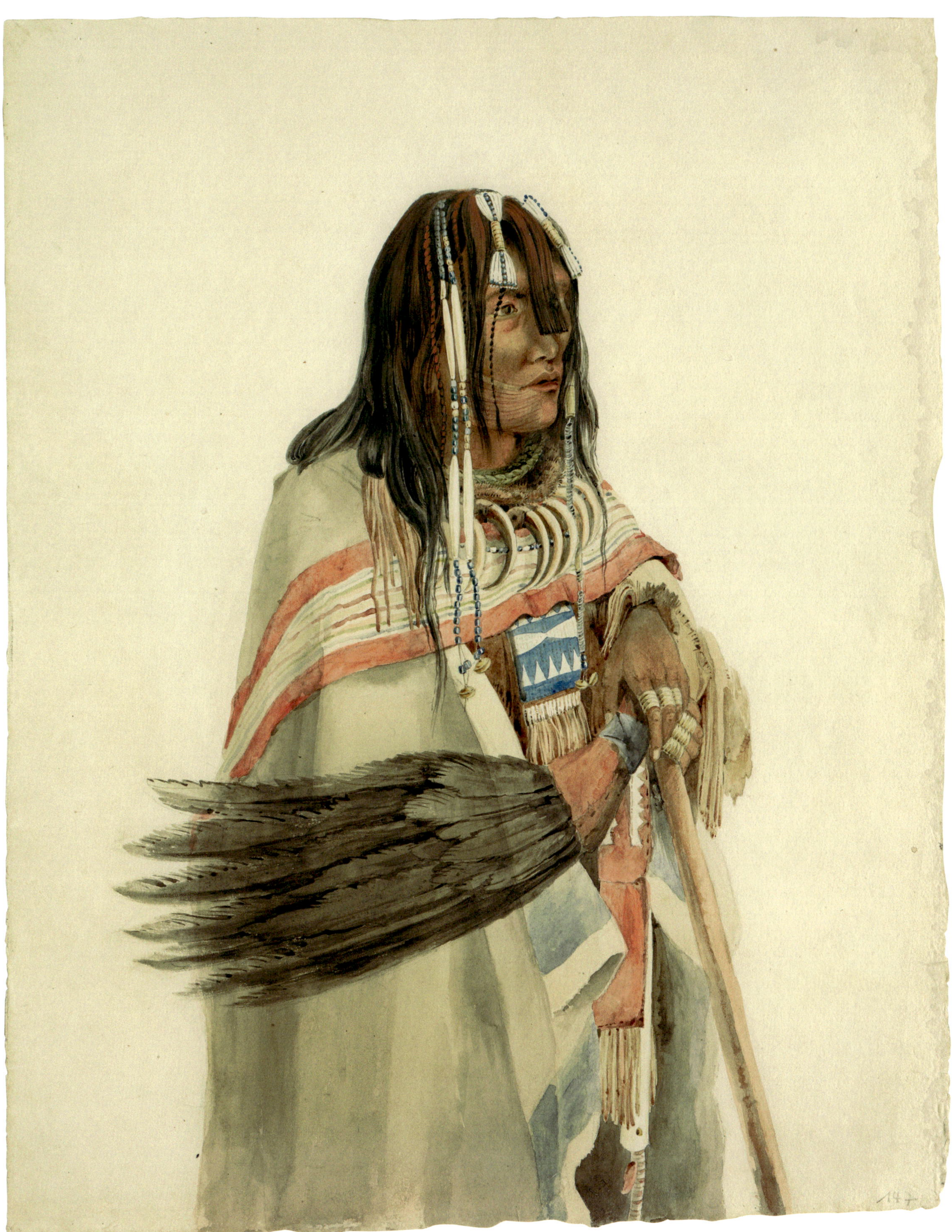

49. Hómach-Ksáchkum, Kootenai Man

1833

Maximilian referred to this man as "the old Kootenai," but his native name—meaning Big/Great Land—is given in Blackfoot, and he had evidently long been a principal Piegan chief. Maximilian later wrote that this "picture . . . and other drawings much amused the [Blackfoot]; they at once recognized them all," praising Bodmer's work. Unlike his son, Makúie-Póka (pl. 48), Hómach-Ksáchkum wears little in the way of ornamentation or trade goods, only a braided sweetgrass necklace and some bits of red and blue cloth on the sleeve of his shirt at the wrist. (*TINA* 272)

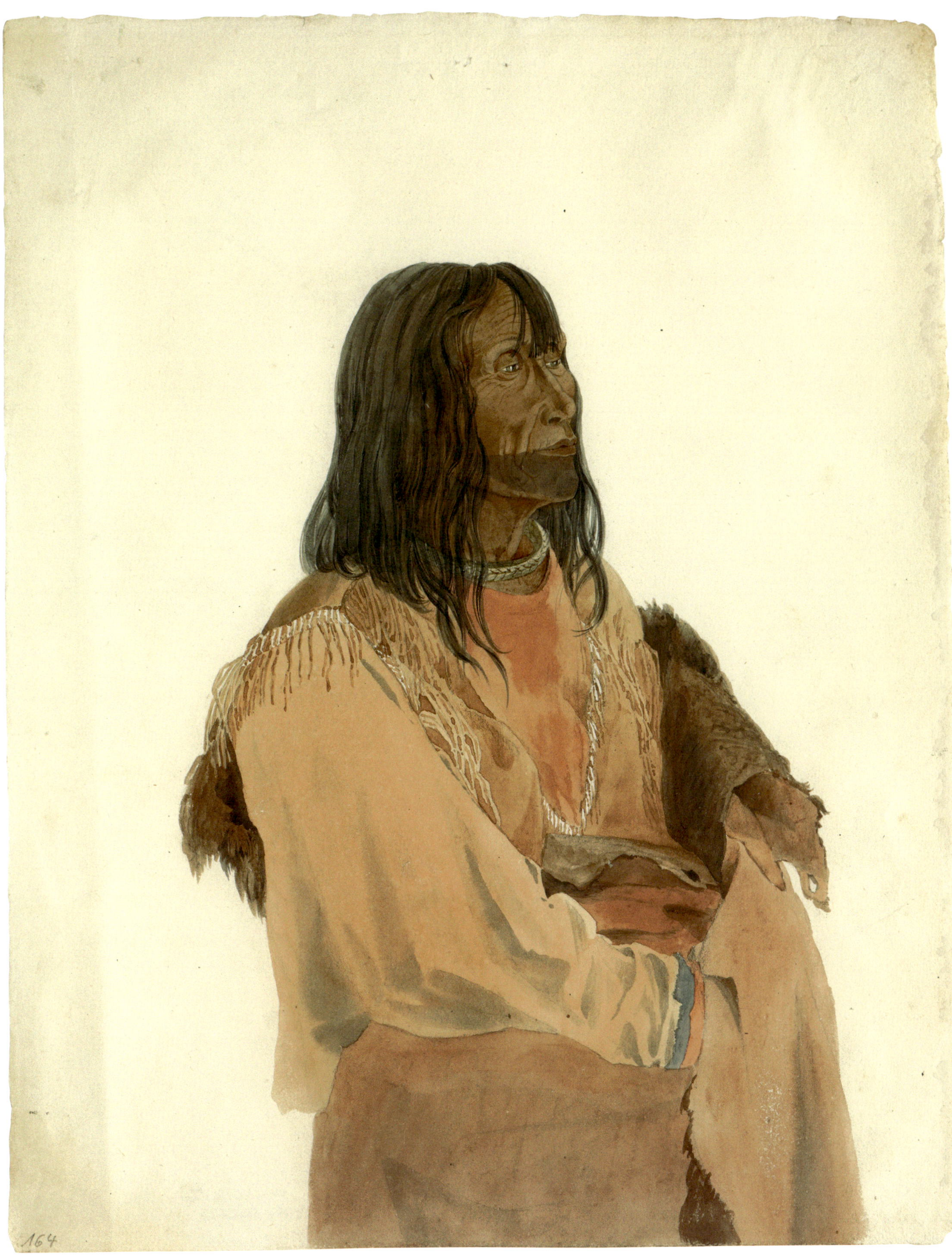

50. Ihkas-kinne, Siksika Blackfoot Chief

1833

Ihkas-kinne (Low Horn) was a Siksika Blackfoot chief
who kept himself and his people somewhat apart from the
numerous Piegans camped around Fort McKenzie. He
had recently been on a raid against the Crows when he
met Maximilian and Bodmer. David Mitchell, in charge
of Fort McKenzie during Maximilian and Bodmer's stay
there in August and September 1833, told Maximilian that
once, when "all the fort's horses" had been stolen—likely
by Kainai or Piegan Blackfoot men—Ihkas-kinne "sought
the [horses] out, and brought them all back except one."
For Bodmer's portrait, he donned "war attire, which on the
naked upper body consists only of several strips of otter
skin stitched together, [on which] he fastened numerous
bits of mother-of-pearl . . . from mussels" or possibly
abalone, which would have been traded from the Pacific
coast. There are also many bright metal buttons and
curved metal bands that might be gorgets. Ihkas-kinne
was reported as having another warrior outfit covered
in pieces of mirror glass. (*NAJ* 2:398 and nM43, 399)

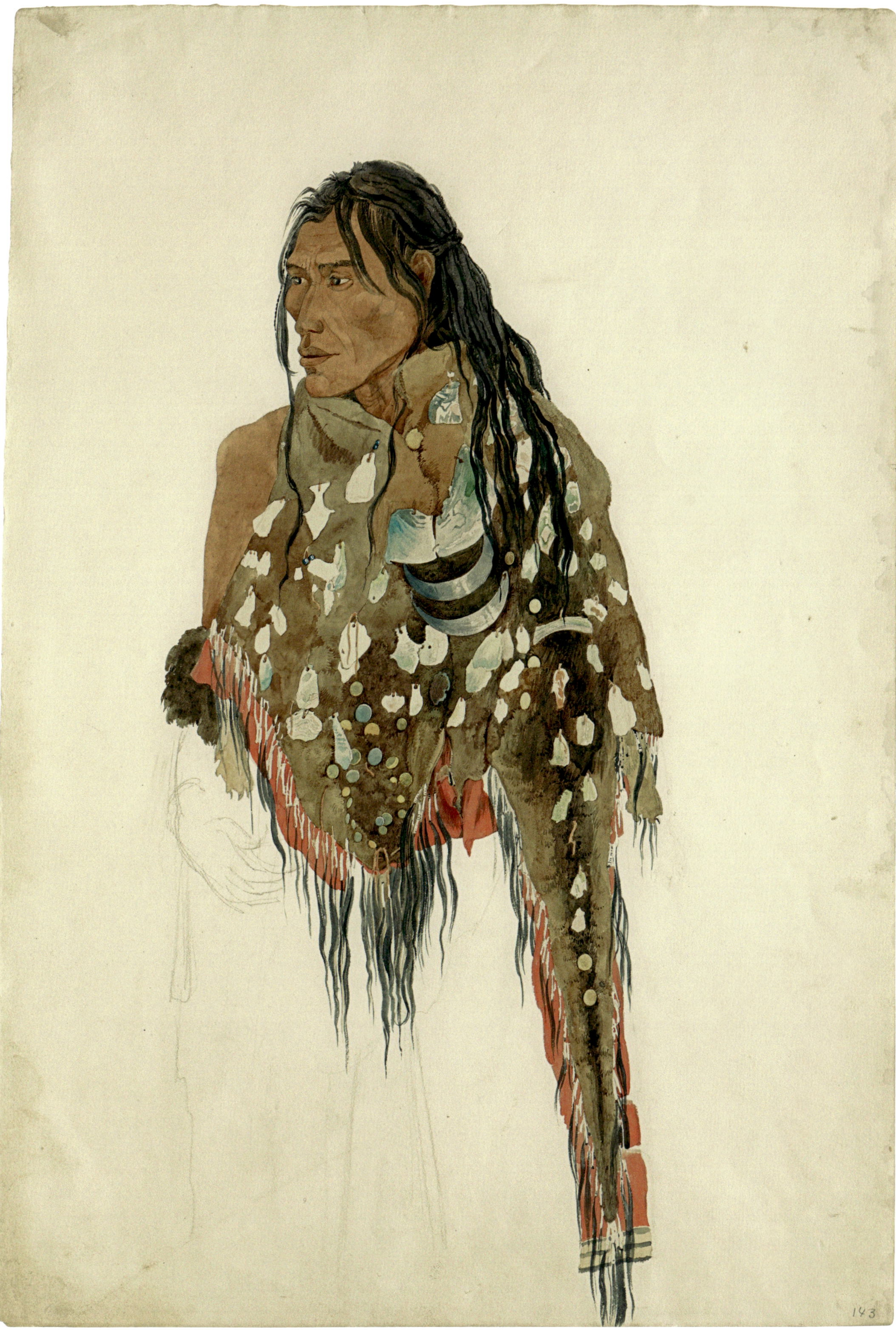

143

51. Stomíck-Sosáck, Kainai Blackfoot Chief

1833

Stomíck-Sosáck was a chief of a small band of Kainai (Blood) Blackfoot Indians camped near Fort McKenzie during Maximilian and Bodmer's stay there in 1833. Maximilian referred to this man in French as La Depouille de Boeuf (Bull's/Ox Hide), but a more accurate translation of his name is Bull's Back Fat, and that is how he is most commonly remembered. Bodmer's portrait, made on September 4, shows him wearing a large peace medal; Maximilian wrote that it bore the image of Jefferson, but in Bodmer's rendering we see the obverse side, depicting the traditional clasped hands and crossed tomahawk and pipe. This watercolor portrait was the basis for an engraved image of Stomíck-Sosáck that illustrated *Reise in das innere Nord-America*. A century later, an anthropologist showed the print to an elderly Blackfoot man, Weasel Tail, who pointed to it and said, "Stomíck-Sosáck." When Weasel Tail was asked how he recognized the subject of the print, having been born considerably later than the portrait was made, he replied, "I knew his son. He looked just like that picture."*

* John C. Ewers, "An Appreciation of Karl Bodmer's Pictures of Indians," in *Views of a Vanishing Frontier*, by Ewers et al. (Omaha: Joslyn Art Museum, 1984), 92.

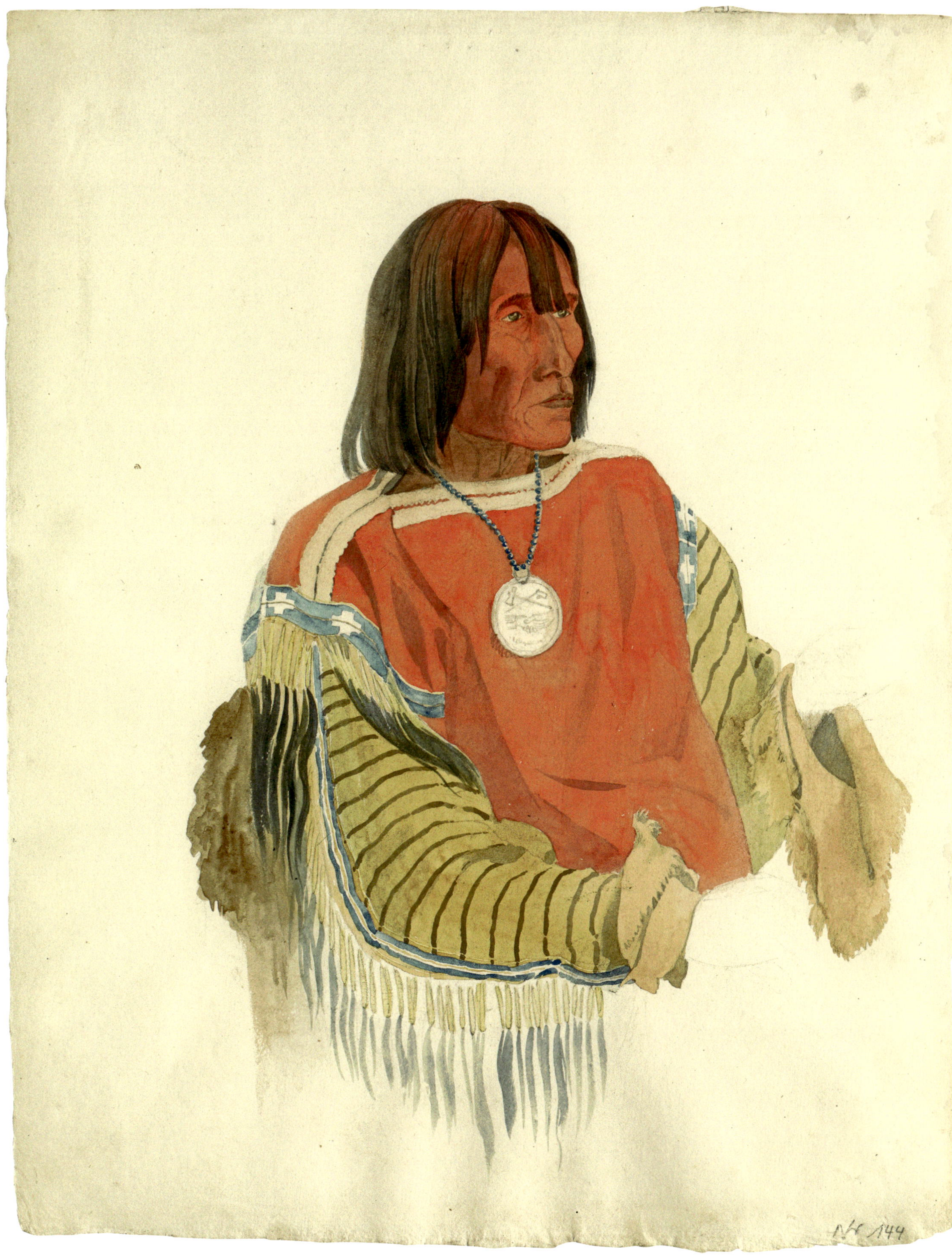
No 144

52. Cree Woman

1833

This woman was the wife of Deschamps, an American Fur Company employee. Her portrait was painted at Fort Union in October 1833, during Maximilian and Bodmer's second stay there, a month-long stop on their journey downriver to Fort Clark, where they intended to spend the winter. Maximilian wrote in his journal only that "she is a pretty woman, tattooed below [and at the sides of] her mouth toward her chin with three bluish black lines." Her most elaborate ornaments are her earrings, consisting of multiple tiers of dentalium shells and blue glass beads. Bodmer carefully rendered a detailed drawing of one ear-ring in the upper right corner of the sheet. (*NAJ* 3:8)

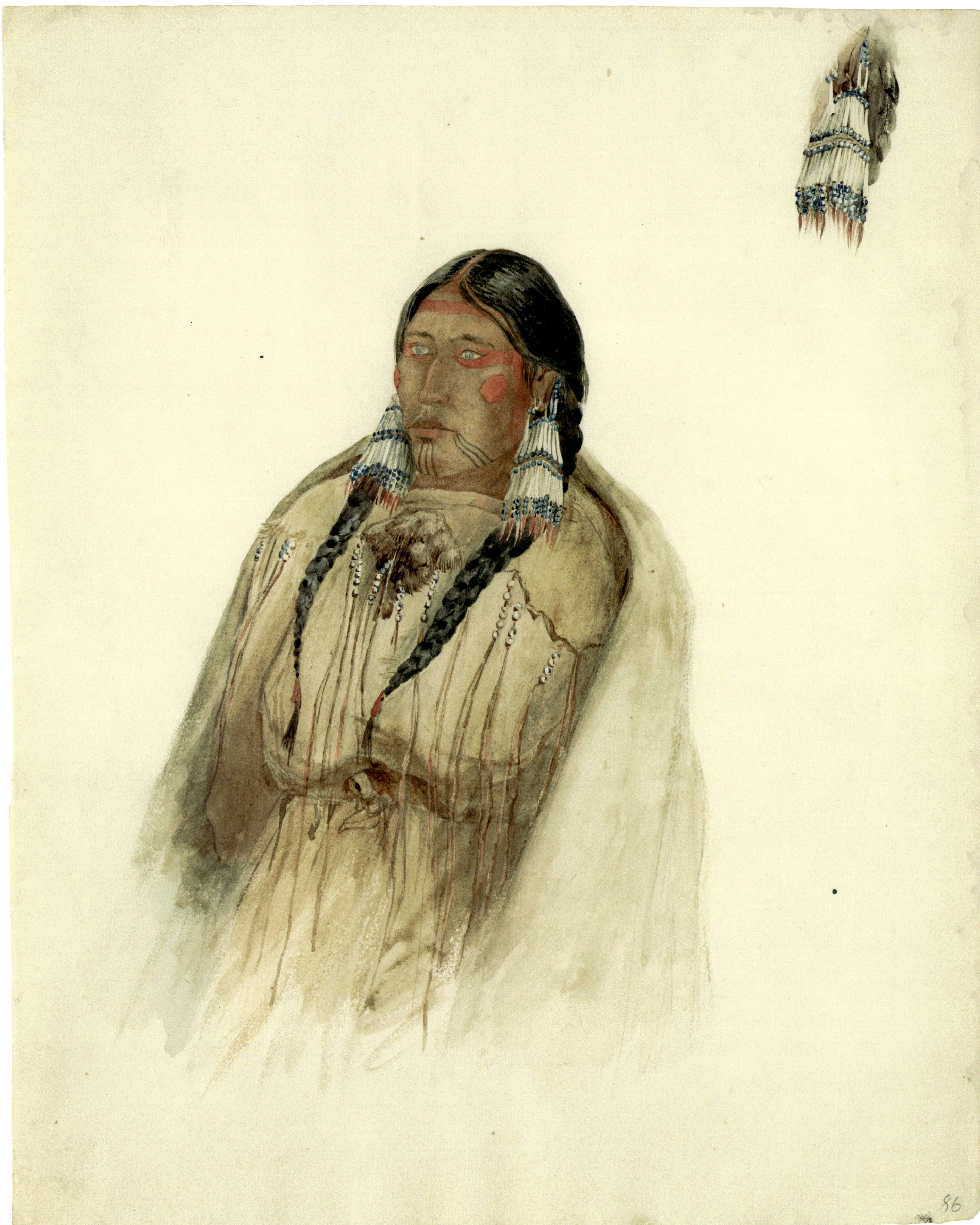

86

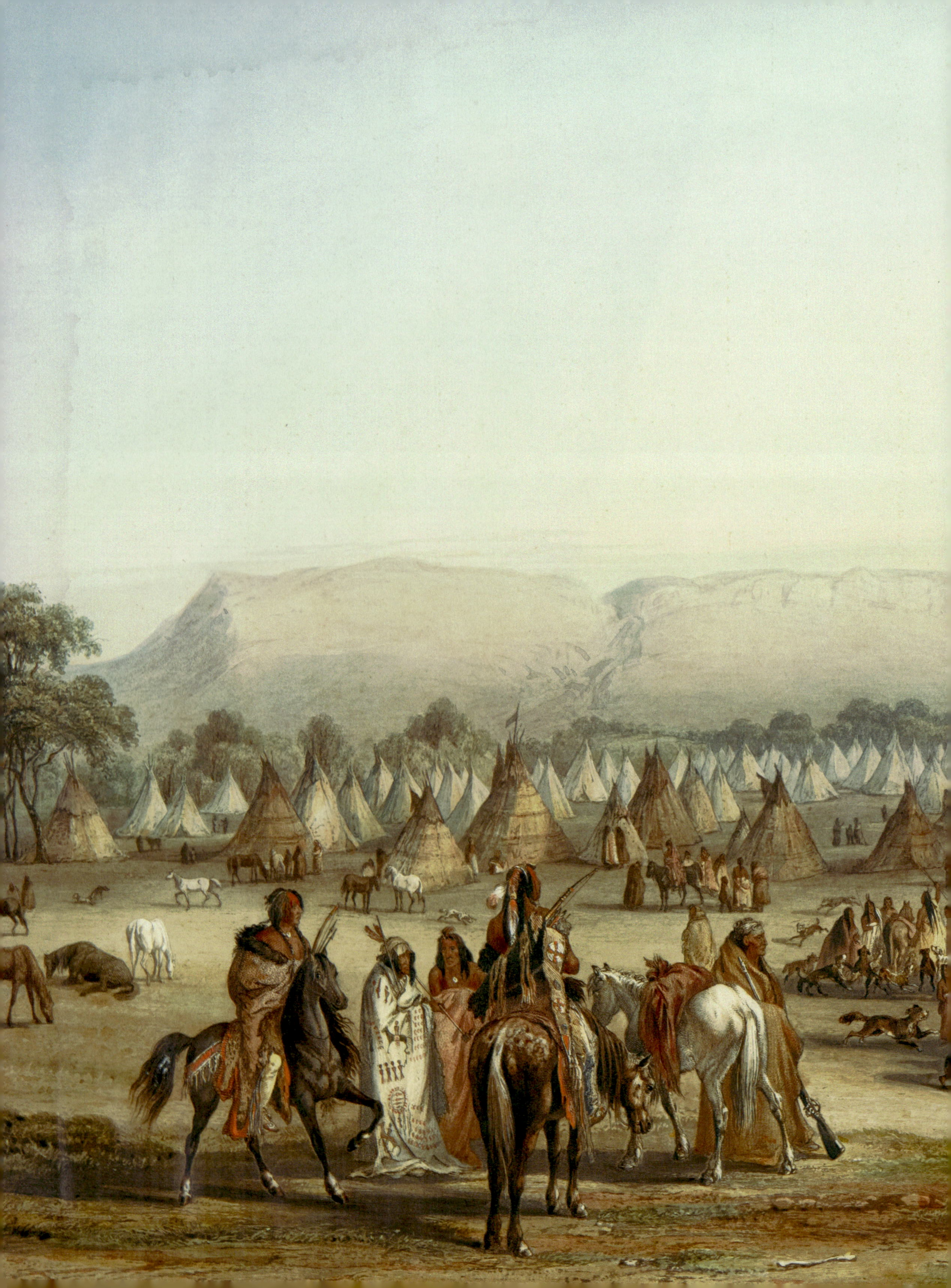

PAINT AND PRINT IN MOTION

KARL BODMER'S *ATLAS*

Kristine K. Ronan

PRINCE MAXIMILIAN OF WIED AND HIS EXPEDITION ART-ist Karl Bodmer returned to Europe in August 1834 after two years of travels across North America and Native territories in the Upper Missouri River basin. In 1836 they began the multiyear process of transforming their varied experiences and written, drawn, and painted documentation into a published travelogue. Narratives of far-flung travels to the Western Hemisphere were extremely popular in Europe in the first decades of the nineteenth century, and Maximilian and Bodmer joined a number of famous European explorers, naturalists, and writers in contributing to this literary trend.[1] These printed works created a publicly available and widely disseminated record of distant peoples, places, and experiences. In Bodmer's case, the planned print edition served as the primary medium for circulating his images, as most of the original watercolors remained in Maximilian's collection for more than a century, until the works were exhibited and toured by the Smithsonian Institution in 1955; they were subsequently acquired by the Northern Natural Gas Company and gifted to Joslyn Art Museum, where they reside today.[2]

A travelogue had not necessarily been Maximilian's original intention. The amateur botanist and ethnographer had published a scientific volume following an earlier expedition to Brazil (1815–17), and he kept extensive scientific records throughout his subsequent two-year sojourn in North America.[3] Yet the completed publication, entitled *Reise in das innere Nord-America in den Jahren 1832 bis 1834* (*Travels in the Interior of North America, 1832–34*), was composed of two letterpress volumes of text whose chapters narrated the course of Maximilian's travels, interspersed with woodcuts and thirty-three illustrative "vignettes" after watercolors by Bodmer.[4] A sumptuous *Atlas*, filled with forty-eight large "tableaux" images, also based on Bodmer's field watercolors, accompanied the two text volumes. The intended audience for such an elaborate multivolume work included government officials and social elites as well

Charles Beyer and Johann Hürlimann, after Karl Bodmer, *Encampment of the Piekann Indians*, n.d. (detail of fig. 6).

as book and print collectors—audiences well outside a narrow scientific readership.

No matter who ultimately purchased his publication, Maximilian clearly expected to convey his North American travels through the medium of print, as he had hired Bodmer, an experienced draftsman for printed pictures, to record the expedition's journey in visual terms. Print production required that complex images be divided into multiple sections that were then engraved separately. Bodmer's anticipation of this process drove his working methods and iconographies in the field. In this way, his North American frontier portraits were conceived and shaped by their future in print.[5]

In the printmaking process, the division of the image into separate sections—or what are termed "separations"—occurred at the level of the *matrix*, the underlying physical material that holds the image prior to printing, such as a stone, a sheet of metal, or a plate of glass. All of Bodmer's tableaux and vignette images were engraved and etched on sheets of metal (fig. 1). Bodmer and various contracted engravers, etchers, and printmakers worked on these matrices; the engraved plates received—and still hold—the products of these agents' labors.[6] Once completed, each plate was inked and run through a press, which reverse imprinted the stored image onto a sheet of paper. This printing process remained captive to the physical properties of the plate, as well as the mechanics and capabilities of print production. Nineteenth-century technical limitations, for instance, meant that one could not print color directly; one could only print tints or add colors by hand.[7]

Contracted by Maximilian to produce fine-art prints for any future publication, Bodmer subjected his works to a long process of physical movement—traveling not only across the frontier, but also by steamer across the Atlantic, by horse to Bodmer's Paris studio, by transfer to engraved plates, and by machine to finished prints. Once completed, prints and plates were shipped among artists, engravers, printers, editors, and publishers, while completed prints and bound books circulated among audiences, book distributors, tradesmen, and salesmen.

Bodmer was always attuned to these various transitions, and his original sketches and portraits do not exist as complete representations within themselves: they are not finished works. Instead, these works continually reference their intended and future printed state. Their uneven completion, visual notations, blank backgrounds, and selected sections of detailed focus reflect their status as ever-moving image-objects. These iconographic patterns emerge across the body of Bodmer's frontier works in acknowledgment of their future as matrices and prints. Knowing that his works were bound for transformation in printers' studios across Europe, Bodmer composed and worked the surfaces of his

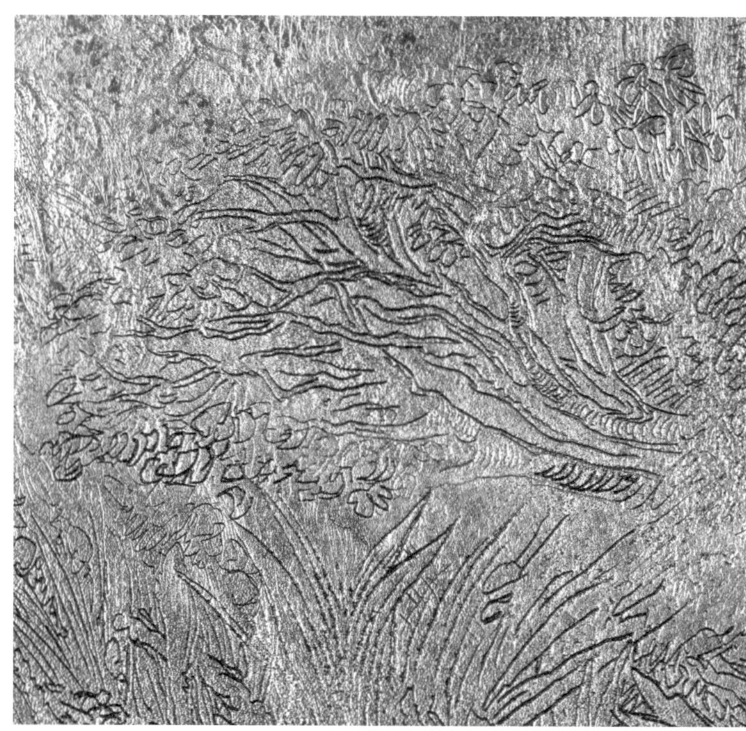

FIGURE 1   Copper and steel printing plate, engraving attributed to Lucas Weber, after Karl Bodmer, Tableau 1, *Forest Scene on the Lehigh (Pennsylvania)*. Joslyn Art Museum, Gift of the Enron Art Foundation, 632.NNG.

compositions accordingly, both on the North American frontier and later in his Paris studio.[8]

THE MAKING OF THE *ATLAS*

Desiring to produce his text in three languages simultaneously, Maximilian contracted three different publishers: one in Koblenz, one in Paris, and one in London. Maximilian supervised the German publisher, which also handled the German edition's subscriptions and sales, while Bodmer, based in Paris by the start of the project in late 1836, oversaw the French and English editions in exchange for a monthly stipend.[9] Bodmer's contract also stipulated that the artist produce all illustrations for the three editions of his publication. These included sixty woodblock illustrations scattered throughout the text, thirty-three quarto-size vignettes placed between text chapters, and the forty-eight imperial folio tableaux that made up the *Atlas*.[10] Bodmer chose a copper- or steel-plate aquatint engraving process for these tableaux and vignettes, a complex and labor-intensive tonal process favored by European landscape artists over the line-based processes of straight engraving. Aquatint plates imitated a painter's washes for broad areas but also utilized numerous intaglio (incising) techniques to enhance or build areas of the design. Aquatints also required a multistage production process, and over the course of the project Bodmer enlisted twenty-nine engravers to produce the eighty-one tableaux and vignette prints for the final volumes.[11]

In addition to the costly and time-consuming printing process, completed prints moved over a vast multinational network, challenging Bodmer's promised completion dates. Prints published with trilingual captions were held by Bodmer's Paris printer, who then shipped them as needed to the three production houses in Paris, Koblenz, and London for compilation into the final volumes. Bodmer eventually proved a rather inept project manager. Maximilian wrote to Hannibal Lloyd, his frustrated British translator, in February 1841 that Bodmer "told us, in spring he would have finished the three last numbers—18–19 and 20," but it was not until November 1842 that the German publisher J. Hölscher received the last of the promised aquatints, and only in May 1844 did Bodmer present a bound *Atlas* to the king of France, Louis Philippe I.[12] The publishing project had taken eight years.

If not a very efficient manager, Bodmer was well-suited for the highly complex processes of print production. Bodmer and his older brother, Rudolf, had learned the genre's mediums of sketching, watercolor, and engraving while traveling with their uncle Johann Jakob Meier, an accomplished *vedutisti*, or maker of *vedute*, small but detailed landscape views usually sold to tourists (fig. 2). Printmaking had long been a family profession, and the brothers followed their forebears when they set themselves up in the Koblenz region of the Rhine in 1828, where Bodmer completed foundational sketches and watercolors while Rudolf produced the finished etchings.[13] Maximilian had stumbled on the pair selling bound travel albums of *vedute* to the region's visitors in January 1832 and soon after hired Bodmer for his North American travel team.

Bodmer's familiarity with prints and printing had likely influenced his hire by Maximilian, who was conscious that his earlier volume concerning

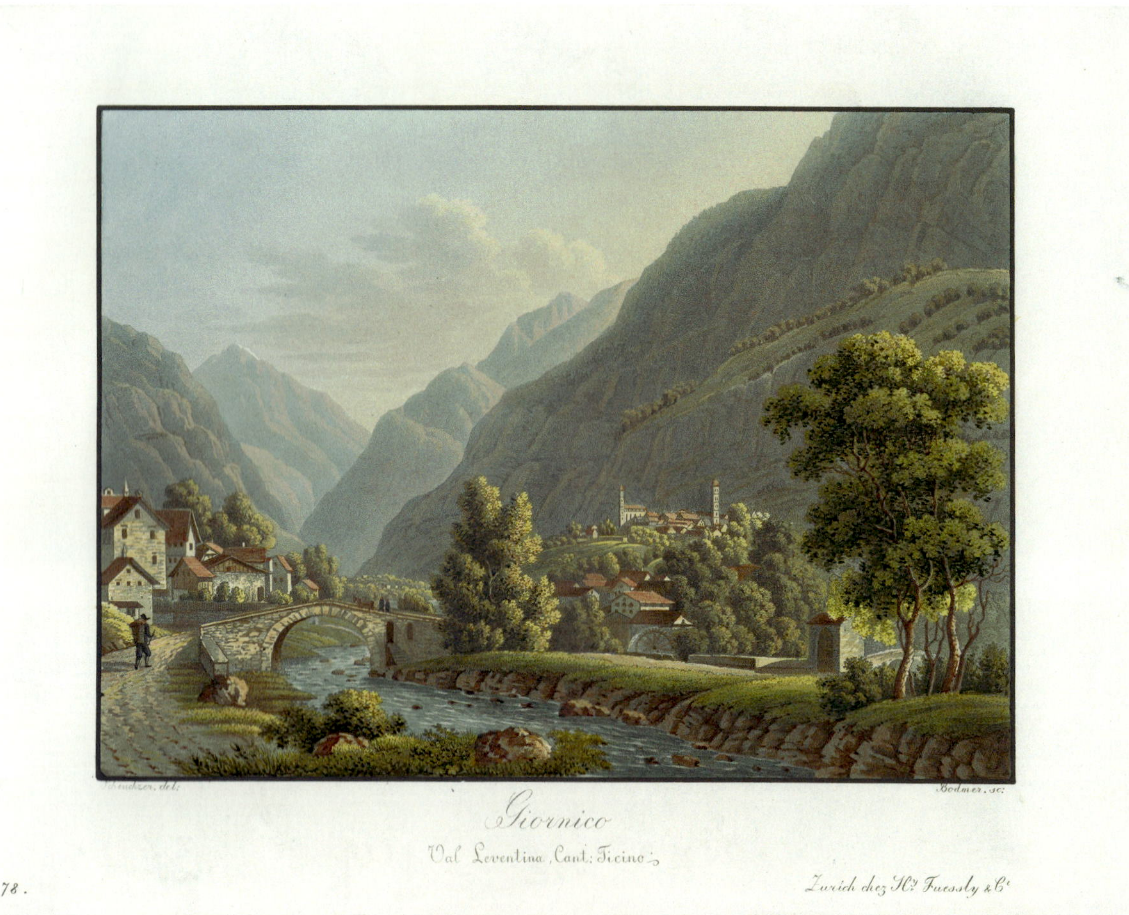

FIGURE 2   Rudolf Bodmer, after Wilhelm Rudolf Scheuchzer, *Giornico, Val Leventina, Cant. Ticino*, colored aquatint from Karl Franz Lusser, *Ansichten der neuen St. Gotthards-Strasse von Fluelen bis Lugano* (Zürich, 1833). Swiss National Library, Gugelmann Collection, GS-GUGE-85-175.

his Brazilian expedition had been criticized as a scientific publication due to his own poor illustration skills.[14] As a *vedutisti*, Bodmer had extensive experience with sketching in variable conditions, copying his own work, and plein-air production, including how to handle issues of cleanliness, weather, and transportation in the outdoors. In addition, Bodmer was well versed in creating compositions that could effectively be broken down into separations once in the printmaker's workshop —steps that were critical during production, as each composition had to be divided into stages that were then engraved or etched separately, often by different professionals who possessed highly specialized skill sets.

This consciousness of future plate separations is evident in the scattered image build-up visible across Bodmer's frontier sketches. Some of these sketches exist in the briefest of graphite outlines. For others, Bodmer employed inks and washes to add details and tones as he pulled out and emphasized particular elements or areas. The degree of finish varies on each sketch, with Bodmer choosing to enhance various outlines, then selecting a few of these for further additions, and so on. Such dispersed attention can be seen in *Taking on Wood in Rainy Weather* (fig. 3), a depiction of a river steamer crew gathering wood during a stop. Bodmer quickly sketched a sloped hillside, felled trees, and figures. He then went back in and further delineated six of the depicted figures. Of

FACES FROM THE INTERIOR

these, five were worked until facial details appeared, and of these, four display fully articulated clothing and pose. Bodmer may have reworked sketches when weather or illness constricted his frontier activities, or he may have pulled out details after his return to Europe in his search for possible plate compositions and usable elements.[15]

These patterns of selective working and scattered details appear in a number of Bodmer's frontier watercolor portraits. In *Mandan Woman* (pl. 19), for instance, Bodmer detailed the woman's facial features and hair in watercolor, but he recorded only scattered areas of the geometrically patterned hide that she is wearing, leaving a majority of the robe's design and the woman's moccasined feet roughly sketched in pencil outline. Completed faces with only partial areas of body paint, tattoo, adornment, or clothing design also appear in portraits of Wakussáse (pl. 2), an Omaha man (pl. 3), Máhchsi-Níhka (Young War Eagle; pl. 18), and Noapeh (Troop of Soldiers; pl. 31). This selective patterning conveys sitters' faces first and foremost, then clothing or pattern details—but only enough to record the sitter's uniqueness. Once versed in Plains material and visual culture, Bodmer grew confident in a system of only partial notation for symmetrical or repeated patterns, such as the large central rosette on the warrior shirt worn by Noapeh, which the artist would fill in later. This system also allowed Bodmer to work quickly, as was sometimes required by men and women who only sat briefly for their portraits.[16] Elements like the robe of the *Mandan Woman* could sometimes subsequently be filled in from the objects Maximilian collected, as he attempted to obtain various articles worn or chosen by sitters.

Even in what may be considered completed portraits, Bodmer made choices as to what to leave out. When Bodmer recorded the likeness of Påsesick-Kaskutäu (Nothing but Gunpowder), an Assiniboine hunter present at Fort Union in October 1833, he meticulously detailed the hunter's hidden face, full winter clothing, and tools of the hunt (fig. 4). The background, however, remained void of any details, save the suggestion of a watery shadow angled from the subject's feet to the paper's borders. This blank setting characterizes all of Bodmer's frontier portraits, and it has left us with no visual details of the converted fort and commercial spaces that Bodmer utilized as his makeshift studios. Påsesick-Kaskutäu's portrait was painted inside the walls of Fort Union, for instance, but nothing in the finished portrait reflects this space.[17] Environments instead entered Bodmer's artistic process once he was back in Europe, when he began to convert his portraits into engraved plates. Thus, a second

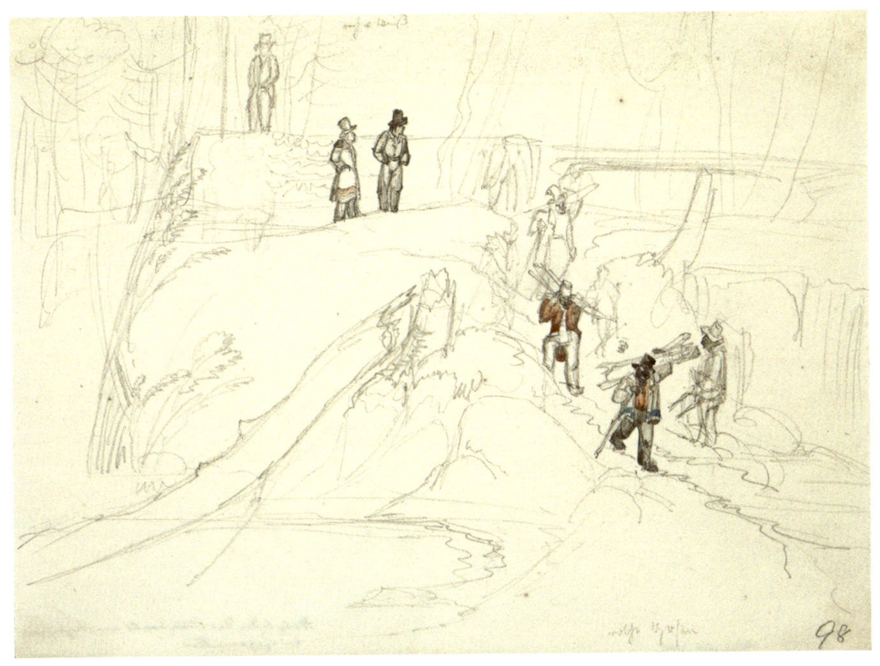

FIGURE 3 Karl Bodmer, *Taking on Wood in Rainy Weather*, 1833, watercolor and graphite on paper. Joslyn Art Museum, Gift of the Enron Art Foundation, 1986.49.108.

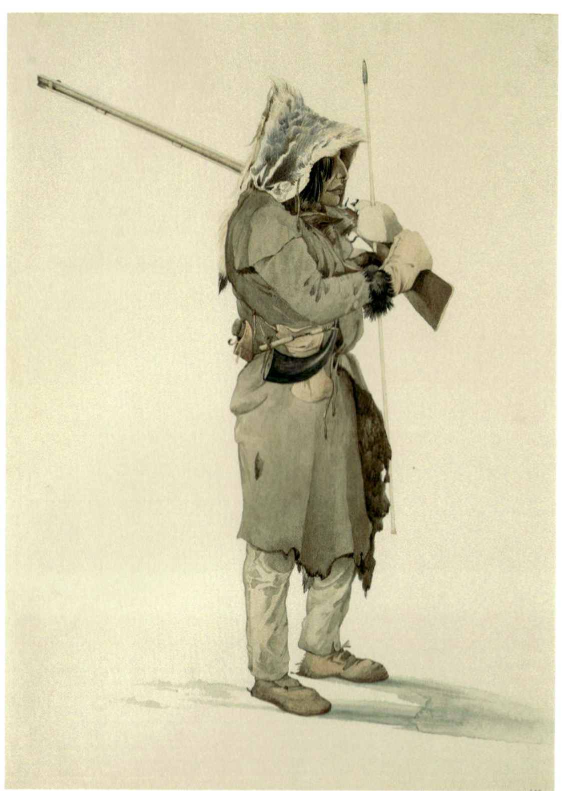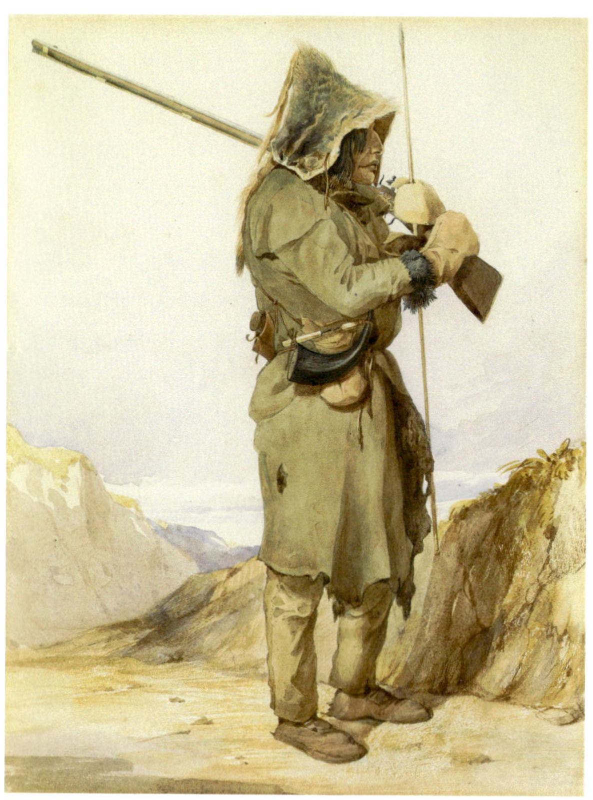

watercolor portrait of Pắsesick-Kaskutäu, likely done in Paris, places the hunter on a sunny but barren mountain pass (fig. 5).

By omitting his sitters' surroundings, Bodmer visually acknowledged the future movement that each image would undergo from the frontier to his Paris studio; from his sketched and painted sheets onto printing plates; and from their origins in fort and steamboat quarters into imagined settings and compositions. Some of these blank-background portraits, like that of Pắsesick-Kaskutäu, would be copied precisely by Bodmer but placed into newly imagined natural settings. Others shifted contexts altogether into highly fanciful scenes of Native life and communities. These more complex scenes involved a variety of sketches and watercolors to produce completed prints. To understand these many layers of image movement as well as Bodmer's working methods for the *Atlas* as a whole, we must read the surviving material remains of Bodmer's drafting and printing process, now scattered across collections in multiple institutions.[18]

IN MOTION: TABLEAU 43

Tableau 43 in the *Atlas*, entitled *Encampment of the Piekann* [Piegan] *Indians* (fig. 6), depicts the temporary settlement of one or more mobile Native bands, or smaller groupings within a larger tribal nation. Among nomadic Plains tribes, which did not maintain permanent village sites, bands regularly moved and camped according to seasonal calendars and food availability. Trading fairs had long been a part of these Native patterns, and in the fur trade of the early nineteenth century, migrations to fort-based trading stations were absorbed into these cyclical routes.

FIGURE 4   Karl Bodmer, *Pắsesick-Kaskutäu, Assiniboine Man*, 1833, watercolor and graphite on paper. Joslyn Art Museum, Gift of the Enron Art Foundation, 1986.49.256.

FIGURE 5   Karl Bodmer, *Pắsesick-Kaskutäu*, 1833, watercolor and graphite on paper. Amon Carter Museum of American Art, 1988.19.

Bodmer's composition shows an encampment on a grassy plain, with a brush-lined river and a distant set of mountains in the background. Dense rows of tipis fill the middle ground, while several distinct figural groups stand scattered across the open grassy plain of the foreground.

The first stage of Bodmer's work was the composition of a full-plate preparatory drawing.[19] This was done in pencil, to permit easy changes, and it marked out the various components of the print. It also identified the elements that Bodmer wanted his hired printmakers to emphasize. The preparatory plate drawing for tableau 43, for instance, shows rich details and shading on the foreground figural groups but leaves the remaining areas in outline only (fig. 7). Detailing visibly decreases as we move deeper into the representational space. The dappled rumps of the foremost horses are ready to move off the page; the mountains are shaped through a single line. The result matches the repeated and selective reworking evident in Bodmer's sketches discussed above, when figural details, shading, and dimensionality were pulled out from the surrounding landscape (see fig. 3).

Selective focal areas worked in this manner also matched the engraving process. Printers typically produced proofs at various stages of plate production to check their plates and give clients a chance to amend or change compositions before more of the intended design was added. This allowed engravers ample time to sand down and reengrave plates as needed. On what appears to be the first proof for tableau 43, pencil marks circle and label several of these figural groupings as "1st," "2nd," and "3rd," which may have served as referents in conversations between Bodmer and the plate's engravers (fig. 8). Bodmer sometimes took advantage of these early proofs to rework his figural groupings, as several surviving proofs from other *Atlas* prints bear pasted-on cutouts of figures in alternative compositions.[20]

This first proof from tableau 43 also suggests that the areas designated as a composition's focal points were printed and perfected first to ensure their continued strength through subsequent stages of printing.[21] The engraving profession itself supported this method of working. Top engravers in the French trade—where Bodmer and Maximilian chose to have the project's plates produced—divided plate engraving into various specialties.[22] Usually an engraver who specialized in figures or portraits initiated the work. Once done, the plate would then pass to the studio of a specialist in landscapes. This engraver then laid in the backgrounds. The early proof of tableau 43 reflects the first half of this process, with only the figural groupings completed; with no hint of spatial grounding, the figures appear to float on the printed page.

Bodmer drew on varied frontier sources when creating these foreground figural groups. On the right edge of the foremost group stands Natoie-Poóchsen (Word of Life), a Piegan Blackfeet elder whose portrait was painted by Bodmer at Fort McKenzie in August 1833 (pl. 38).[23] He is identifiable not only through his profile and pulled-back hair, but also his shouldered gun, whose stock rests on the ground in the print. Natoie-Poóchsen faces the far right of the scene, where two women and their work dogs labor forward, stooped under the weight of their head-perched bundles. This group is based on Numak'aki (Mandan) women that Bodmer

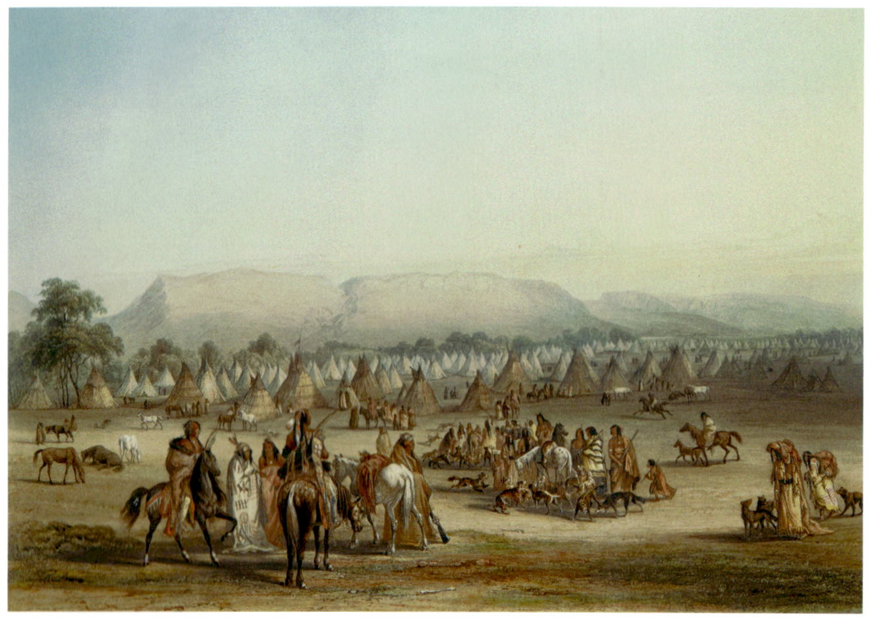

FIGURE 6 Charles Beyer and Johann Hürli-mann, after Karl Bodmer, *Encampment of the Piekann Indians*, 1837–43, hand-colored aquatint. Joslyn Art Museum, Gift of the Enron Art Foundation, 1986.49.517.43.

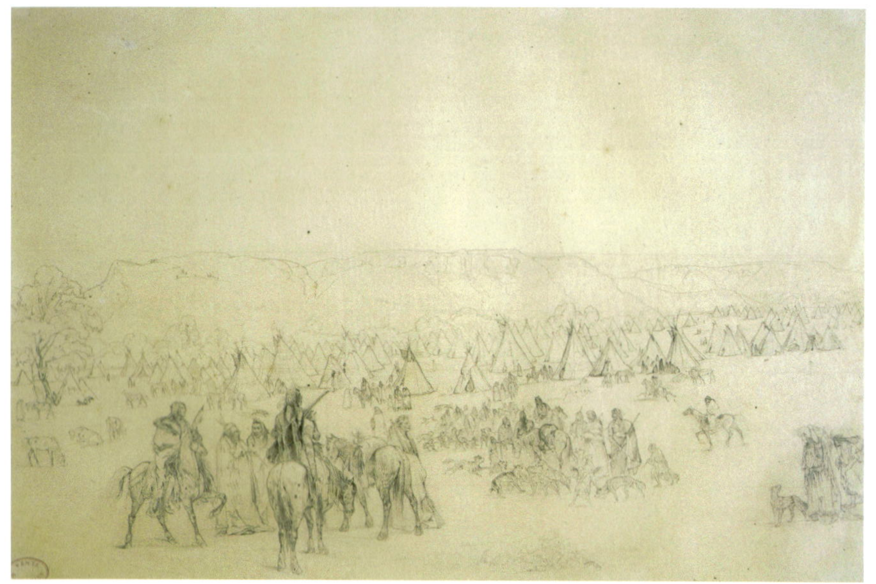

FIGURE 7 Karl Bodmer, *Piegan Blackfeet Camp*, n.d., graphite on paper. Newberry Library, Edward E. Ayer Collection.

FIGURE 8 Unknown artist, after Karl Bodmer, *Encampment of the Piekann Indians*, 1836-43, etching. The Baltimore Museum of Art: The George A. Lucas Collection, purchased with funds from the State of Maryland, Laurence and Stella Bendann Fund, and contributions from individuals, foundations, and corporations throughout the Baltimore community, BMA 1996.48.11461.

had sketched carrying firewood, corn stores, and other supplies between their summer village of Mih-Tutta-Hangkusch (in Numak'aki peoples' language, something closer to Mít uta hako'sh, meaning "east village") and their temporary winter camp near Fort Clark—an American Fur Company post along the Missouri River, 937 miles south of Fort McKenzie—in February 1834.[24] Yet another tribe is represented by a Shoshone woman included in the second figural group, where she stands with a hip-high child and converses with a young warrior whose back is turned to us. This unnamed woman was married to a man called Marceau or Marcereau, an *engagé* (indentured servant) stationed at Fort McKenzie, where Bodmer painted her portrait in early September 1833 (pl. 47).[25]

This small collection of transferred portraits and sketches highlights the fictional aspect of Bodmer's working methods, which sometimes moved portrayed individuals across great distances and distinct communal differences into a single scene. Some portraits appear several times across the project's volumes, adding additional layers to this movement. For instance, the Shoshone woman in tableau 43 also appears in tableau 33, where she is identified as *Woman of the Snake Tribe* (Snake being a name for Shoshone peoples given by outsiders) and placed next to the portrait of another fur-trade wife, a Cree woman from Fort Union who sat for her portrait in early October 1833 (fig. 9; pl. 52).[26] While Bodmer offers us a chance to judge the accuracy of the portrayal in tableau 43 against the portrait in tableau 33, he also confuses us with the woman's placement in a community of Piegan peoples, who would have not only spoken a language dissimilar from her own but worn distinctive dress— a fact that Bodmer chose to ignore in composing the complex scene.[27]

The wide-ranging and repeated movement of earlier frontier-made works into plate compositions relied on Bodmer's skills as a precise copyist. He could quickly duplicate frontier portraits, allowing him to retain his paintings while also giving Native sitters their own copies if requested.[28] In his Paris studio, copying allowed Bodmer to efficiently transfer any number of his works into various plate compositions. He could also duplicate figures from other artists' works and insert them into his own.[29] Such astute copying skills allowed Bodmer to effortlessly reverse his source materials when required by the printing process. Hó-Ta-Mä was a Ponca man with distinctive face paint who sat for his portrait in a hide robe bordered by thick fur (pl. 7).[30] In tableau 43, he sits atop a horse at the far left of the foremost group. In order to show him facing right, Bodmer had to reverse his original portrait for the printing plate, as all printed images were engraved backwards onto the matrix. A surviving pencil-and-wash work suggests that Bodmer reoriented Hó-Ta-Mä to produce a model for the engraver using freehand techniques (fig. 10). Reversed portraits and sketches such as this helped ensure plate accuracy at the smallest of scales and suggest that Bodmer oversaw the involved reversal process himself, rather than leaving these details to his contracted engravers and printers.

While disparate materials came together in single composite scenes, those scenes were themselves divided into multiple stages of composition and creation. After the figural groups were completed for tableau 43 (see fig. 8), a second phase of work added residents scattered among the tipi

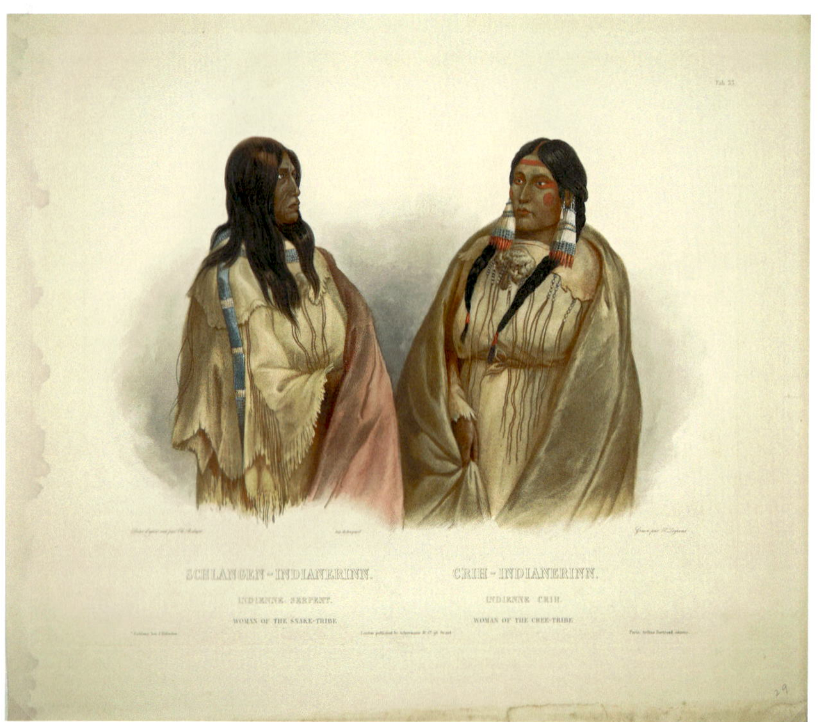

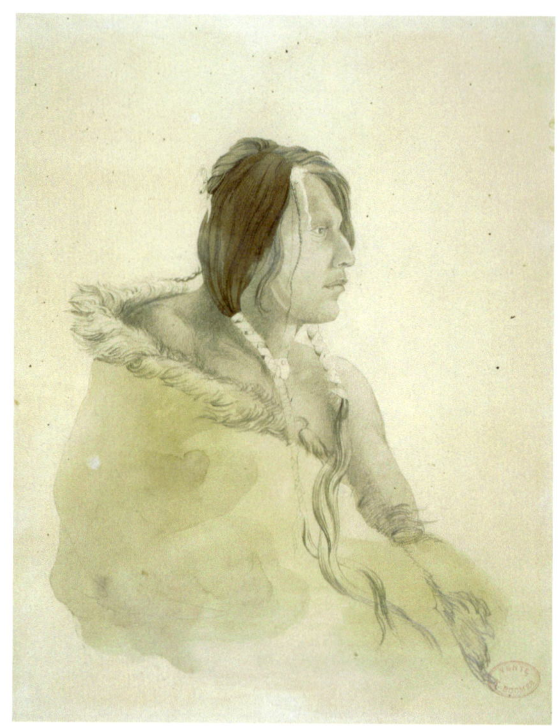

camp. Bodmer's selective detailing is again visible in a related sketch, with stark lines, shaded openings, and designs enhancing the front rows of tipis (fig. 11). Part or all of the sketch may have been done in the field, and the figural groups were significantly altered on the finished plate, but the alignment and number of tipis set out in this sketch were followed precisely in the final design.[31]

This middle ground and the background of tableau 43 were likely done by a second engraver, one who specialized in landscapes.[32] A final surviving proof of tableau 43 likely served as a guide at the close of this second stage, with two thirds of the scene printed and pronounced against a free-hand watercolor landscape (fig. 12). The tones here are predominantly brown, with few of the greens and blues that would dominate the final hand-colored prints (see fig. 6). Bodmer may have taken the opportunity to try out potential palettes with partial proofs such as this in order to explore how the final composition would be affected by various color choices. The final stage of engraving added the mountains and sky tones to the plate, which, when compared to the watercolors, are even dreamier and murkier on this second-stage proof, as aquatinted blues turned the proof's defined mountain edges into distant mists and low-hanging clouds.

Once completed, the *Atlas* traveled along the networks that Maximilian's agents had set up, trackable through a series of letters, agreements, contracts, advertisements, printer prospectuses, subscriber lists, and biographies.[33] By November 1843, for example, Maximilian and Bodmer's completed text volumes and the *Atlas* of the English edition had arrived in New York City, where booksellers Wiley & Putnam at 161 Broadway advertised the availability of a preview copy at its shop, from which customers could place orders.[34]

     FACES FROM THE INTERIOR

FIGURE 9   Paul LeGrand, after Karl Bodmer, *Woman of the Snake-Tribe, Woman of the Cree-Tribe*, 1837–43, hand-colored aquatint. Joslyn Art Museum, Gift of the Enron Art Foundation, 1986.49.433.

FIGURE 10   Karl Bodmer, *Hó-Ta-Mä, Ponca, a Ponca Man*, n.d., graphite and wash. Newberry Library, Edward E. Ayer Collection.

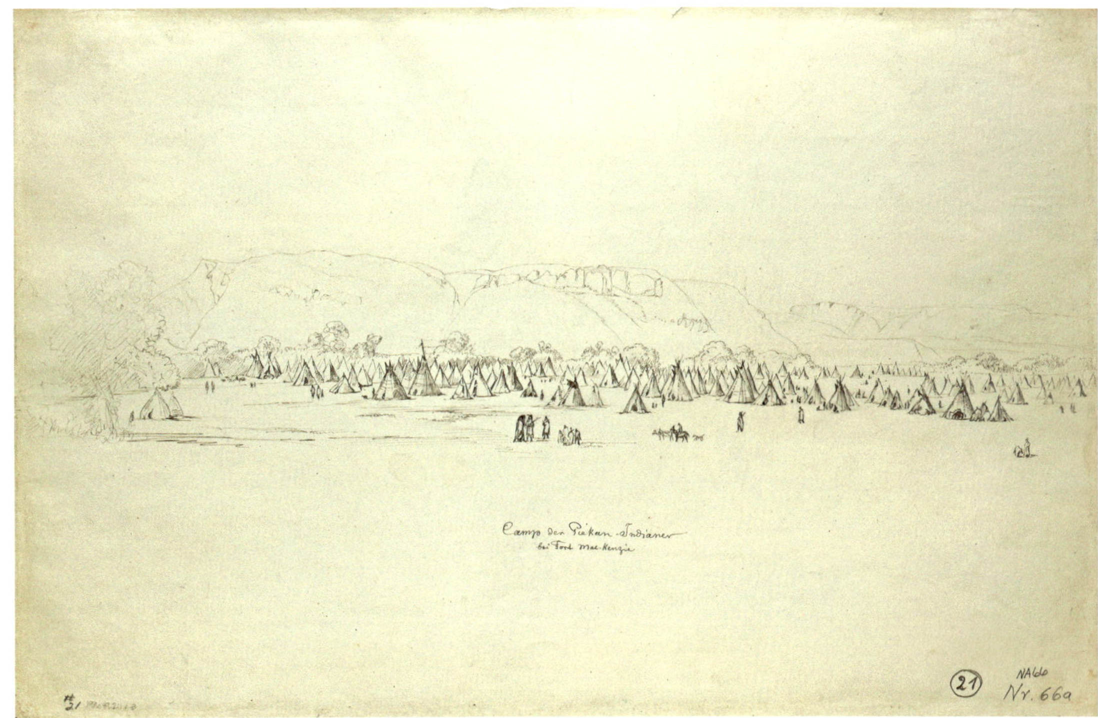

FIGURE 11   Karl Bodmer, *Piegan Blackfeet Camp*, 1833, graphite on paper. Joslyn Art Museum, Gift of the Enron Art Foundation, 1986.49.211.B.

FIGURE 12   Charles Beyer and Johann Hürlimann, after Karl Bodmer, *Encampment of the Piekann Indians*, 1836-43, etching with hand coloring. The Baltimore Museum of Art: The George A. Lucas Collection, purchased with funds from the State of Maryland, Laurence and Stella Bendann Fund, and contributions from individuals, foundations, and corporations throughout the Baltimore community, BMA 1996.48.11462.

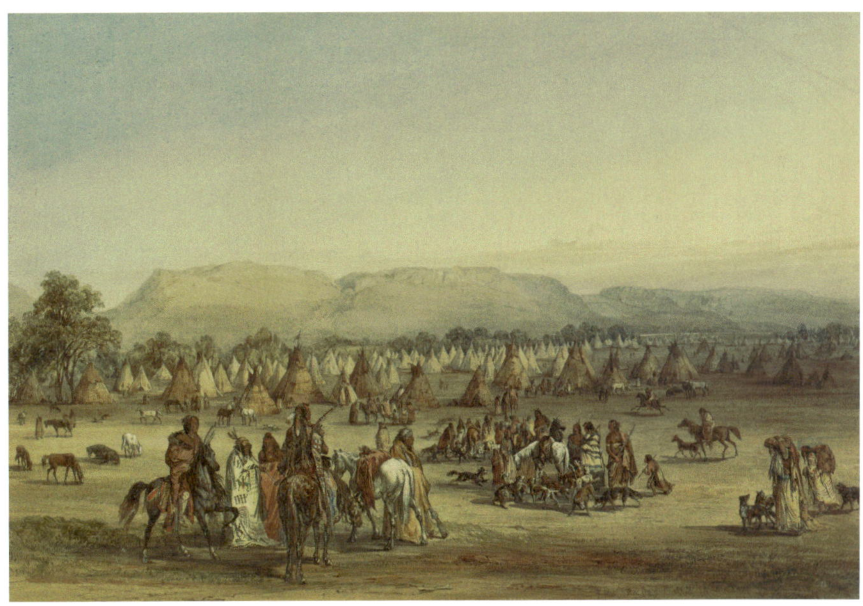

Yet years before the completed volumes reached the market, many of Bodmer's images were adapted into distinct printing processes elsewhere. Thomas McKenney's and James Hall's lavish *History of the Indian Tribes of North America* (1836–44), for instance, included a reengraved version of Bodmer's published tableau 43 (fig. 13).[35] This copy stays true to the original in composition, but it boasts fewer lines and less detailed figures. The color palette has also radically shifted, with some details—such as an all-red dress and bison robe—far removed from the frontier realities of tanned hides.

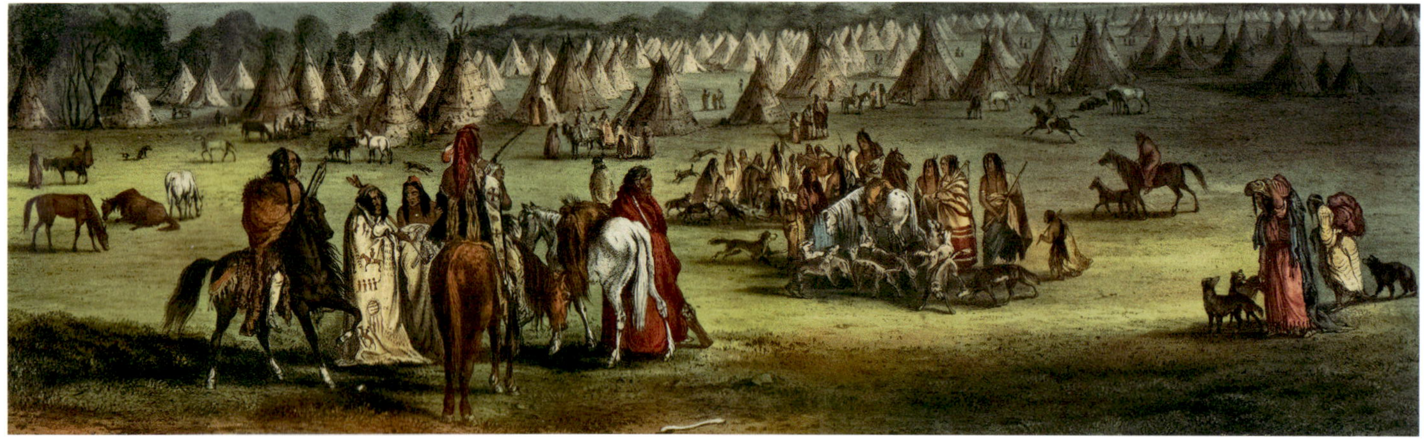

With the publication of *Reise in das innere Nord-America* and its French and English editions in the early 1840s, the dissemination of Bodmer's printed images only increased.[36] Most Bodmer plates were originally issued in print runs of 355, and their wide circulation inspired numerous illustrations in various contexts on both sides of the Atlantic.[37] In 1844, for instance, the Philadelphia-based *Graham's Magazine* ran the first of eighteen images from the *Atlas*, each reengraved by the publication's network of firms. The magazine's print run exceeded 40,000, resulting in a flooding of the American illustrated magazine market with hundreds of thousands of versions of Bodmer's works through 1850. Reengraved copies of Bodmer's images can be found in illustrated editions of the works of George Catlin, the journals of Lewis and Clark, children's readers, and Indian War biographies and publications through the first decades of the twentieth century.

The recirculation of both plates and prints promulgated the historical and cultural distortions of the original compositions, and sometimes more were added—such as the inaccurately colored dress mentioned above—as subsequent engravers were further and further removed from the frontier conditions of the early 1830s and thus could not judge the accuracy of their work themselves. Widely dispersed in ever-increasing numbers, Bodmer's compositions naturalized such distortions; they were viewed as unadulterated windows onto historical Native life on the Plains, a source of "truthful interpretation" for authors and scholars alike.[38] In its continued distribution over the next 180 years, tableau 43 supported an unquestioned tendency to trust Bodmer's images as historical fact.

The accuracy granted to Bodmer's tableaux rested on their underlying source portraits, some of which also moved along complex and ever-enlarging circulation routes. Mató-Tópe (Four Bears), for instance, was a Numak'aki warrior and war chief who sat for two portraits in Bodmer's fort quarters. In both he wears a carved and painted wooden knife, a coup mark that symbolized one of the man's many military victories (pls. 22 and 23).[39] As these portraits circulated and were reproduced, Mató-Tópe became one of the most visible Native leaders of the nineteenth century. Yet he has largely remained anonymous because most of these portraits were detached from their historical contexts and appeared instead

FIGURE 13 Henry Dacre, after Karl Bodmer, *Encampment of the Piekann Indians near Fort McKenzie on the Muscleshell River* (detail), 1844, hand-colored lithograph from Thomas L. McKenney and James Hall, *History of the Indian Tribes of North America* (Philadelphia, 1840–44). Joslyn Art Museum, Museum Purchase with Funds Provided by Walter and Suzanne Scott, 2007.3.3.1.

as unnamed or incorrectly labeled individuals. Today we can recognize Mató-Tópe through the presence of his carved knife.

Bodmer's original frontier portraits, like those of Mató-Tópe, were never complete unto themselves; Bodmer always intended them to move elsewhere, into other compositions and onto various engraved plates. By attending to these many levels of movement and their involved alterations, we can begin to understand how Bodmer's reproduced pictures have acquired multiple sets of meanings through their widespread currency and subsequent contexts—meanings that can have little to nothing to do with their cross-cultural beginnings and originating Native communities on the North American frontier.

NOTES

1. Among these travel texts by Europeans are François-René de Chateaubriand's *Voyage en Amérique* (1827), Michel Chevalier's *Society, Manners, and Politics in the United States* (1839), Charles Dickens's *American Notes for General Circulation* (1842), Alexander von Humboldt's *Vues des Cordillères et monuments des peuples indigènes de l'Amérique* (1810) and *Personal Narrative of Travels to the Equinoctial Regions of the New Continent* (7 vols., 1815–26), Alexis de Tocqueville's *Democracy in America* (1835–40), and Paul Wilhelm's *Erste Reise nach dem nördlichen Amerika in den Jahren 1822 bis 1824* (1835). Americans abroad also participated in the trend: see James Fenimore Cooper's *Notions of the Americans: Picked Up by a Travelling Bachelor* (1828).

2. *Carl Bodmer Paints the Indian Frontier* was an exhibition organized and traveled by the Smithsonian Institution Traveling Exhibition Service between 1953 and 1957.

3. See Maximilian of Wied, *Reise nach Brasilien in den Jahren 1815 bis 1817* (Frankfurt: H. L. Brönner, 1820–21).

4. Details of the publication project can be found in Ron Tyler, "Karl Bodmer and the American West," in *Karl Bodmer's North American Prints*, ed. Brandon K. Ruud (Omaha: Joslyn Art Museum, 2004), 18–23.

5. Elsewhere I give this artistic consciousness and adjusted working method the label of "painting print," a phrase meant to invoke the myriad ways in which printmaking influenced art-making processes. See Kristine K. Ronan, "Painting Print: N. C. Wyeth's Illustrations for *The Last of the Mohicans* (1919)," in *N. C. Wyeth: New Perspectives*, ed. Jessica May and Christine B. Podmaniczky (New Haven, CT: Yale University Press, 2019), 44–57.

6. For an approach to print as labor, see Michael Gaudio, *Engraving the Savage: The New World and Techniques of Civilization* (Minneapolis: University of Minnesota Press, 2008).

7. Chromolithography, for instance, which was developed in the mid-nineteenth century, required each color to be printed from a distinct stone, which was not only time consuming and expensive but also an indirect, layered way to achieve final colors.

8. In this way, Bodmer's images exemplify how "movement *materializes* images," whereby their status "as transported material thing[s] often sneaks into the illusionary register at the level of iconography": Jennifer L. Roberts, *Transporting Visions: The Movement of Images in Early America* (Berkeley: University of California Press, 2014) 163. See also "Objects in Motion: Visual and Material Culture across Colonial North America," ed. Wendy Bellion and Mónica Domínguez Torres, special issue, *Winterthur Portfolio* 45, nos. 2–3 (summer–autumn 2011); François Brunet, "Toward a Transcultural History of American Landscape Images in the Nineteenth Century," in *A Seamless Web: Transatlantic Art in the Nineteenth Century*, ed. Cheryll L. May and Marian Wardle (Newcastle upon Tyne: Cambridge Scholars Publishing, 2014), 3–20; François Brunet, ed., *Circulation* (Chicago: Terra Foundation for American Art, 2017); Gaudio, *Engraving the Savage*; and Monica Blackmun Visonà, "Agent Provocateur? The African Origin and American Life of a Statue from Côte d'Ivoire," *Art Bulletin* 94, no. 1 (Spring 2012): 99–129.

9. Maximilian's contract with Bodmer was signed on November 7, 1836. Bodmer's oversight of the English and French editions was to include their translations,

publication contracts, and production schedules, in addition to sales.

10. Bodmer carved these woodblocks himself, a fact that supports the notion of him as a highly experienced printmaker.

11. For bibliographic details of the printing process, see David C. Hunt, "A Publication History of Karl Bodmer's North American Atlas," in *Karl Bodmer's Studio Art: The Newberry Library Bodmer Collection,* by W. Raymond Wood, Joseph C. Porter, and David C. Hunt (Urbana: University of Illinois Press, 2002), 99–122; Tyler, "Bodmer and the American West"; Brandon K. Ruud, "'A Faithful and Vivid Picture': Karl Bodmer's North American Prints," in *Bodmer's North American Prints,* 47–76; and the individual plate annotations in that volume. For the full list of involved engravers, see Ruud, *Bodmer's North American Prints,* appendix C.

12. Maximilian of Wied to H. E. Lloyd, February 7, 1841, transcription, MS 3215, Edward E. Ayer Manuscript Collection, Newberry Library, Chicago.

13. Details of Bodmer's early training and work are drawn from William J. Orr, "Karl Bodmer: The Artist's Life," in *Karl Bodmer's America* by William H. Goetzmann, David C. Hunt, Marsha V. Gallagher, and William J. Orr (Omaha: Joslyn Art Museum; Lincoln: University of Nebraska Press, 1984), 351. Meier had studied under Henry Fuseli and the landscapist Gabriel Lory.

14. Tyler, "Bodmer and the American West," 8.

15. See, for instance, *The Landing of the Prince Neuwied Expedition* (Baltimore Museum of Art, George A. Lucas Collection, L.33.53.7196), a field sketch that became the basis for tableau 36 and may not have been reworked by Bodmer until preparation for the tableau plate began in Paris.

16. Noapeh (Troop of Soldiers) was one such sitter who posed only briefly, sitting for Bodmer on June 28, 1833. See *The North American Journals of Prince Maximilian of Wied*, ed. Marsha V. Gallagher and Steven S. Witte, trans. William J. Orr, Paul Schach, and Dieter Karch (Norman: University of Oklahoma Press; Omaha: Joslyn Art Museum, Margre H. Durham Center for Western Studies, 2008–12), 2:238 (hereafter *NAJ*).

17. See the October 21, 1833, entry in *NAJ*, 3:21. Likewise, all of Bodmer's portraits associated with the central Missouri region were painted within the Europeans' one-room quarters inside the walls of Fort Clark.

18. This approach invokes recent scholarly interest in such remains as a rich but to date neglected area of print studies. See, for instance, "The Matrix Reloaded" project of Elizabeth Savage at the School of Advanced Study, University of London, which aims to establish archival and cataloguing standards for the tens of thousands of matrices in institutional collections.

19. Bodmer's full-plate composition drawing also survives for tableau 26: Edward E. Ayer Manuscript Collection, Newberry Library, Chicago.

20. See, for instance, Charles Vogel (*inc.* after Karl Bodmer *del.*), *Scalp Dance of the Minatarres* (tableau 27), a proof between first and fourth states with the inked and pasted addition of children by Bodmer: Edward E. Ayer Manuscript Collection, Newberry Library, Chicago.

21. Another early-stage proof that confirms this reading survives for tableau 40: *Troupeau de Bisons*, Baltimore Museum of Art, George A. Lucas Collection, L.33.53.7202 (1996.48.7202).

22. See Stephen Bann, *Parallel Lines: Printmakers, Painters, and Photographers in Nineteenth Century France* (New Haven, CT: Yale University Press, 2001); and specific tableau 43 plate annotations by Marsha V. Gallagher in Ruud, *Bodmer's North American Prints,* 219.

23. See the August 18, 1833, entry in *NAJ*, 2:376.

24. Maximilian recorded this constant traffic of women throughout February; see the February 4, 9, 11, 15, and 16, 1834, entries in *NAJ*, 3:250–51, 253–54, 258, and 260.

25. See the September 6, 1833, entry in *NAJ*, 2:412.

26. See the October 8, 1833, entry in *NAJ*, 3:8. The Cree woman was married to Deschamps, an American Fur Company hunter attached to Fort Union.

27. At least five other figures in these groupings match additional frontier portraits, their sitters also representing a mix of tribal identities. For fuller cross-references, see appendix B in Ruud, *Bodmer's North American Prints.*

28. Péhriska-Rúhpa, for instance, purchased a copy of his first completed portrait on December 25, 1833: *NAJ*, 3:107.

29. See note 20 above. The added child was taken from Theodorus de Bry's engraving *Indian Woman and Young Girl* (1590) and also appears in tableau 18.

30. Hó-Ta-Mä's portrait was painted on May 31, 1833; see the June 1, 1833, entry in *NAJ*, 2:158.

31. When first comparing sketch to finished print, first match the tipis flying a type of pennant, then compare the first rows from there.

32. Work on tableau 43 was split between engravers Charles Beyer and Johann

Hürlimann, but it is unknown who did which portions of the final plate.

33. Hunt, "Publication History," 99–122. Filling out these networked paths is currently the approach of most print studies, which rely heavily on constructing histories around specific works. See, for instance, Georgia B. Barnhill, ed., *With a French Accent: American Lithography to 1860* (Worcester, MA: American Antiquarian Society, 2012); and Marie-Stéphanie Delamaire, "An Art of Translation: American Art and French Prints (1848–1876)," (PhD diss., Columbia University, 2013).

34. The advertisements appear in Tyler, "Bodmer and the American West," 25.

35. Maximilian had sent Bodmer's print to Philadelphia from Europe along with two paintings by Saint Louis artist Peter Rindisbacher; all three works were included in McKenney and Hall's long-running subscription series, the first of its kind produced in the United States. See the July 17, 1832, and March 28, 1833, entries in *NAJ*, 1:72 and 1:384; and Tyler, "Bodmer and the American West," 23–24, 43n72.

   Another early appearance of Bodmer's works was Heinrich Rudolf Schinz's *Naturgeschichte und Abbildungen der Menschen und der Säugethiere nach den neuesten Systemen und vorzüglichsten Originalien* (1834); see Peter Bolz, "Karl Bodmer, Heinrich Rudolf Schinz, und die Veränderung des Indianerbilds in Europa," in *Ein Schweizer Künstler in Amerika* (Zürich: Scheidegger & Spiess, 2009), 66–87; and Tyler, "Bodmer and the American West," 29. Schinz continued to update his included Bodmer plates in the second (1840) and third (1845) editions by reengraving images from the now-published *Atlas* plates.

36. *Reise* was published from 1839 to 1841; the condensed French version, from 1840 to 1843; and the abridged English edition, in 1843. See Hunt, "Publication History," 105.

37. Joslyn Art Museum published a 400-page book to bibliographically document all the variations of the "original" publication; see Ruud, *Bodmer's North American Prints*. Yet even this does not comprise a complete bibliographic inventory, as no two sets of the printed *Atlas* were identical due to print delays and reissues; at least nineteen plates were reissued during the seven-year publication process. For publication numbers, see Hunt, "Publication History," 106; for the publisher's subscription variations, see Tyler, "Bodmer and the American West," 20.

38. John C. Ewers, "An Appreciation of Carl Bodmer's Indian Paintings," in *Carl Bodmer Paints the Indian Frontier: A Traveling Exhibition of Watercolors and Drawings* (Washington, DC: Smithsonian Institution, 1954). See also Ewers's press release for the exhibition, 1953, Smithsonian Institution Archives, Record Unit 290, Box 111. Ewers, deeply invested in nineteenth-century artists' depictions of Native peoples as ethnographic evidence, later protested the transfer of George Catlin's paintings from the National Museum of Natural History to the National Collection of Fine Arts.

39. For historical details on Mató-Tópe and other Fort Clark sitters, see Kristine K. Ronan, "Káma-Kapúska! Making Marks in Indian Country, 1833–34," *19th-Century Art Worldwide* 18, no. 2 (Autumn 2019), https://doi.org/10.29411/ncaw.2019.18.2.23.

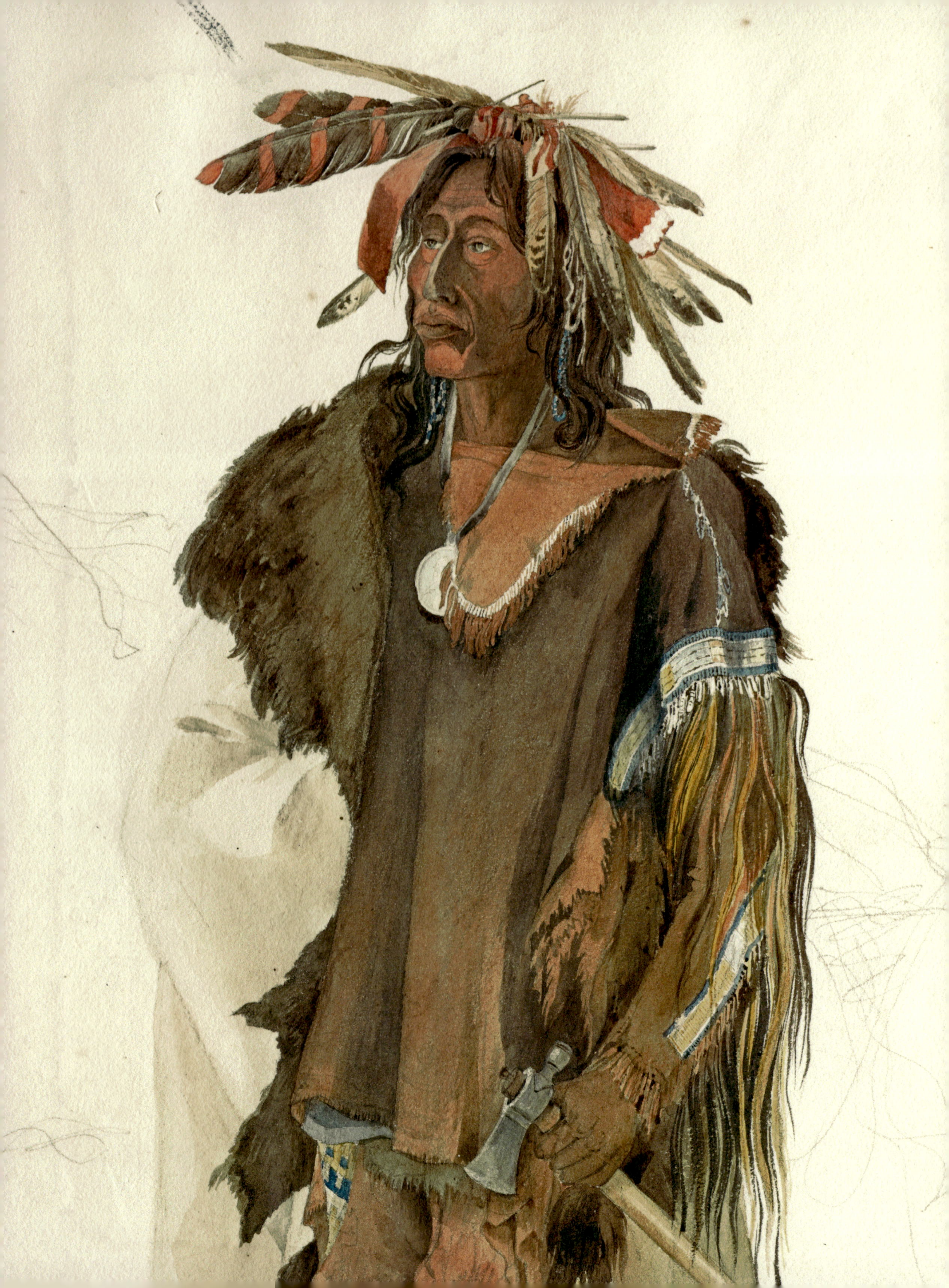

CHECKLIST

All works are collection of Joslyn Art Museum, gift of the Enron Art Foundation. Unless otherwise noted, the medium is watercolor and graphite on paper.

1. *Massica, Sauk Man*, 1833
12 × 8½ inches
1986.49.235

2. *Wakussáse, Meskwaki Man*, 1833
11¹³⁄₁₆ × 8½ inches
1986.49.234

3. *Omaha Man*, 1833
11⅞ × 8½ inches
1986.49.236

4. *Omaha Boy*, 1833
10⅞ × 7⅞ inches
1986.49.372

5. *Schudegácheh, Ponca Chief*, 1833
11⅞ × 8½ inches
Graphite, charcoal, ink, and watercolor on paper
1986.49.241

6. *Passítopa, Ponca Man*, 1833
11⅞ × 8½ inches
1986.49.243

7. *Hó-Ta-Mä, Ponca Man*, 1833
10⅞ × 8¾ inches
1986.49.242

8. *Wahktägeli, Yankton Sioux Chief*, 1833
16⅞ × 11¾ inches
1986.49.245

9. *Tukán-Hätón, Yankton Sioux Chief*, 1833
10¹⁵⁄₁₆ × 8¾ inches
1986.49.259

10. *Psíhdjä-Sáhpa, Yanktonai Sioux Man*, 1834
12⅝ × 10 inches
1986.49.277

11. *Wáh-Menítu, Lakota Sioux Man*, 1833
11 × 8¾ inches
1986.49.247

12. *Chan-Chä-Uiá-Te-Üinn, Lakota Sioux Woman*, 1833
17⅛ × 11⅞ inches
1986.49.246

13. *Pachtüwa-Chtä, Arikara Man*, 1834
17 × 12 inches
1986.49.258

Karl Bodmer, *Wahktägeli, Yankton Sioux Chief*, 1833 (detail of pl. 8).

14. *Leader of the Mandan
Beróck-Óchatä*, 1834
17 × 11¹⁵⁄₁₆ inches
1986.49.264

15. *Máhchsi-Karéhde,
Mandan Man*, 1833–34
17 × 11¹⁵⁄₁₆ inches
1986.49.262

16. *Mándeh-Páhchu,
Mandan Man*, 1834
12½ × 10¹⁄₁₆ inches
1986.49.270

17. *Upsichtä́, Mandan Man*, 1834
12⅝ × 10 inches
1986.49.263

18. *Máhchsi-Níhka,
Mandan Man*, 1834
12½ × 10¹⁄₁₆ inches
1986.49.262

19. *Mandan Woman*, 1834
12⁹⁄₁₆ × 10 inches
1986.49.276

20. *Síh-Sä, Mandan Man*, 1834
12⁵⁄₁₆ × 9½ inches
1986.49.385

21. *Síh-Chidä, Mandan Man,*
1833
17¹⁄₁₆ in. × 12 inches
1986.49.267

22. *Mató-Tópe, Mandan Chief,*
1834
16½ × 11¹¹⁄₁₆ inches
1986.49.383

23. *Mató-Tópe, Mandan Chief,*
1834
13⅞ × 11¼ inches
1986.49.260

24. *Awaschó-dichsas,
Hidatsa Man*, 1834
12½ × 10³⁄₁₆ inches
1986.49.278

25. *Biróhkä, Hidatsa Man*, 1834
12⅝ × 9¹¹⁄₁₆ inches
1986.49.291

26. *Addíh-Hiddísch,
Hidatsa Chief*, 1834
16⁹⁄₁₆ × 11¹¹⁄₁₆ inches
1986.49.388

27. *Ahschüpsa-Masihichsi,
Hidatsa Man*, 1834
12⅛ × 9³⁄₁₆ inches
1986.49.389

28. *Possibly Ahschüpsa-
Masihichsi, Hidatsa Man,*
1834
12½ × 10 inches
1986.49.249

29. *Péhriska-Rúhpa,
Hidatsa Man*, 1833
15⅞ × 11½ inches
1986.49.390

30. *Péhriska-Rúhpa,
Hidatsa Man*, 1834
17⅛ × 11¹⁵⁄₁₆ inches
1986.49.275

31. *Noapeh, Assiniboine Man,*
1833
17¹⁄₁₆ × 11⅞ inches
1986.49.253

32. *Pitätapiú, Assiniboine Man,*
1833
17¹⁄₁₆ × 12 inches
1986.49.254

33. *Assiniboine Man*, 1833
17⅛ × 11¹⁵⁄₁₆ inches
1986.49.255

34. *Pteh-Skah, Assiniboine Chief,*
    1833
    12⁹⁄₁₆ × 10⅛ inches
    1986.49.257

35. *Assiniboine and Siksika*
    Blackfoot Girl, 1833
    10⅝ × 8 inches
    1986.49.378

36. *Niätóhsä, Gros Ventre Chief,*
    1833
    10¹⁄₁₆ × 12⁹⁄₁₆ inches
    1986.49.282.A

37. *Mexkemáuastan,*
    Gros Ventre Chief, 1833
    16⁹⁄₁₆ × 11¼ inches
    1986.49.391

38. *Natoie-Poóchsen,*
    Piegan Blackfoot Man, 1833
    13⅜ × 9⅞ inches
    1986.49.294

39. *Tátsicki-Stomíck,*
    Piegan Blackfoot Chief, 1833
    12⁹⁄₁₆ × 10⅛ inches
    1986.49.283

40. *Mexkehme-Sukahs,*
    Piegan Blackfoot Chief, 1833
    12½ × 10⅛ inches
    1986.49.284

41. *Hotokáneheh,*
    Piegan Blackfoot Man, 1833
    11¹⁵⁄₁₆ × 17¹⁄₁₆ inches
    1986.49.288

42. *Pioch-Kiǎiu,*
    Piegan Blackfoot Man, 1833
    12⁷⁄₁₆ × 10⅛ inches
    1986.49.296

43. *Piegan Blackfoot or*
    Gros Ventre Man, 1833
    11¹⁵⁄₁₆ × 9 inches
    1986.49.394

44. *Piegan Blackfoot Man,* 1833
    12⁹⁄₁₆ × 10 inches
    1986.49.290

45. *Kiäsax,*
    Piegan Blackfoot Man, 1833
    12³⁄₁₆ × 9½ inches
    1986.49.395

46. *Piegan Blackfoot Woman,*
    1833
    17 in. × 12¹⁄₁₆ inches
    1986.49.292

47. *Shoshone Woman,* 1833
    12⁹⁄₁₆ × 9½ inches
    1986.49.305

48. *Makúie-Póka,*
    Piegan Blackfoot Man, 1833
    12⁹⁄₁₆ × 10 inches
    1986.49.289

49. *Hómach-Ksáchkum,*
    Kootenai Man, 1833
    12⅝ × 10¹⁄₁₆ inches
    1986.49.306

50. *Ihkas-kinne,*
    Siksika Blackfoot Chief, 1833
    17 × 12 inches
    1986.49.285

51. *Stomíck-Sosáck,*
    Kainai Blackfoot Chief, 1833
    12½ × 9¹⁵⁄₁₆ inches
    1986.49.286

52. *Cree Woman,* 1833
    11⅞ × 9¾ inches
    1986.49.231

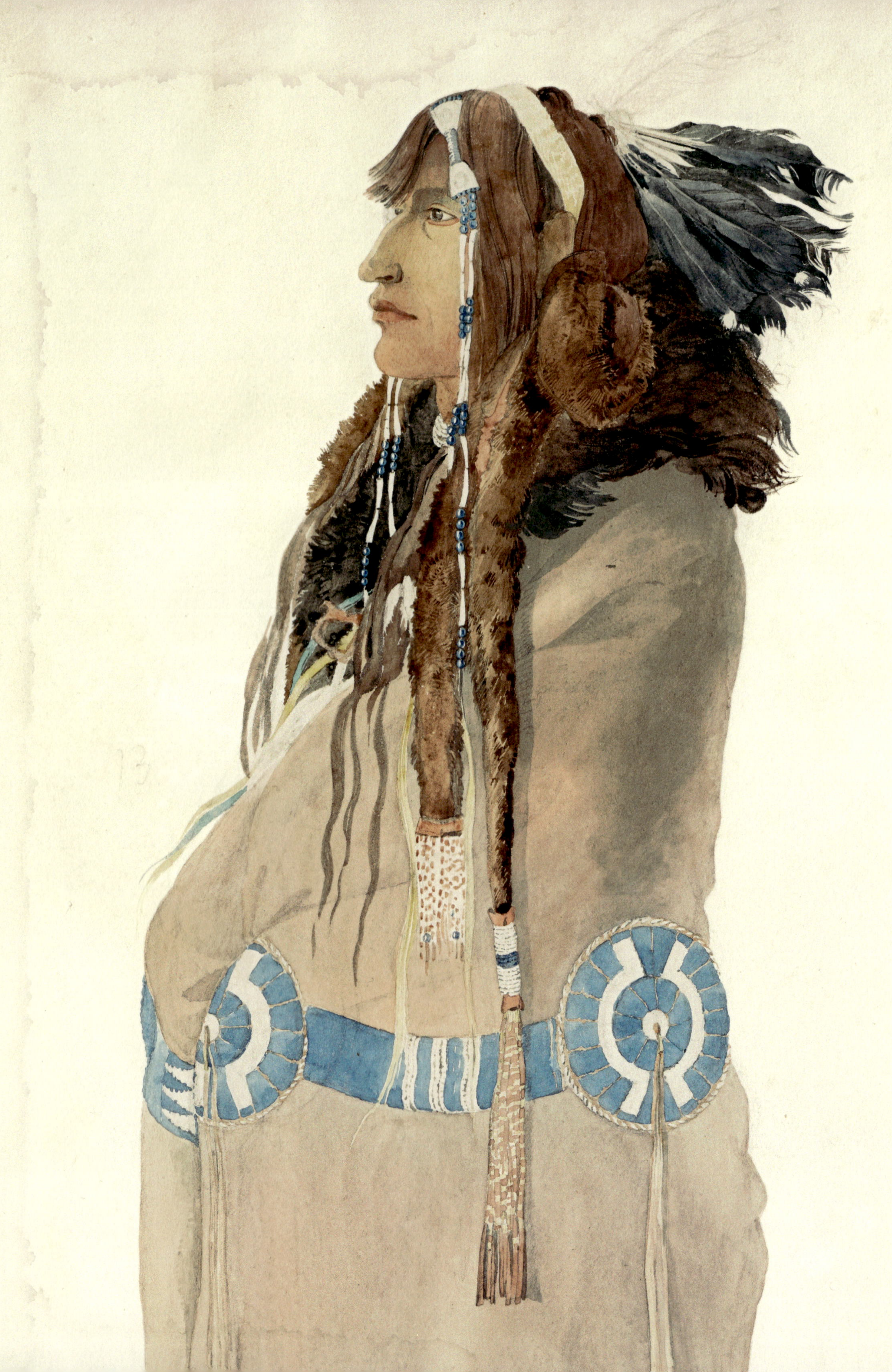

SELECTED BIBLIOGRAPHY

Faces from the Interior draws on the foundational scholarship of previous publications on the Maximilian-Bodmer Collection held in the Margre H. Durham Center for Western Studies, Joslyn Art Museum, as well as the publications of Prince Maximilian of Wied:

Ewers, John C. *Views of a Vanishing Frontier.* Omaha: Joslyn Art Museum, Margre H. Durham Center for Western Studies; Lincoln: University of Nebraska Press, 1984.

Gallagher, Marsha V. *Karl Bodmer's Eastern Views.* Omaha: Joslyn Art Museum, 1996.

Goetzmann, William H., David C. Hunt, Marsha V. Gallagher, and William J. Orr. *Karl Bodmer's America.* Omaha: Joslyn Art Museum; Lincoln: University of Nebraska Press, 1984.

Maximilian of Wied. *The North American Journals of Prince Maximilian of Wied.* Edited by Marsha V. Gallagher and Stephen S. Witte. Translated by William J. Orr, Paul Schach, and Dieter Karch. 3 vols. Norman: University of Oklahoma Press; Omaha: Joslyn Art Museum, Margre H. Durham Center for Western Studies, 2008–12.

———. *Reise in das innere Nord-America in den Jahren 1832 bis 1834.* 2 vols. with picture atlas. Koblenz: J. Hölscher, 1839–41.

———. *Travels in the Interior of North America, 1832–34.* Translated by Hannibal Evans Lloyd. London: Ackermann, 1843.

———. *Travels in North America, 1832–1834: A Concise Edition of the Journals of Prince Maximilian of Wied.* Edited by Marsha V. Gallagher. Norman: University of Oklahoma Press; Omaha: Joslyn Art Museum, 2017.

———. *Voyage dans l'intérieur de l'Amérique du Nord, execute pendant les années 1832, 1833 et 1834.* Paris: A. Bertrand, 1840–43.

Ruud, Brandon K., ed. *Karl Bodmer's North American Prints.* Omaha: Joslyn Art Museum; Lincoln: University of Nebraska Press, 2004.

Karl Bodmer, *Síh-Chidä, Mandan Man*, 1834 (detail of pl. 21).

CONTRIBUTORS

MARSHA V. GALLAGHER is a former curator in Joslyn Art Museum's Margre H. Durham Center for Western Studies. She authored or contributed to several books about Karl Bodmer and Prince Maximilian of Wied, including *Karl Bodmer's America* (1984) and *Karl Bodmer's North American Prints* (2004), and she was an editor of *The North American Journals of Prince Maximilian of Wied* (2008–12).

ANNIKA K. JOHNSON is the Stacy & Bruce Simon Curator of Native American Art at Joslyn Art Museum. She specializes in nineteenth-century Native American art of the Upper Missouri and Mississippi River regions and was awarded her doctorate in art history from the University of Pittsburgh in 2019. Her dissertation, "Agency at the Confluence of Dakota and Euro-American Art, 1835–1912," is a cross-cultural art history of Mni Sota Makhoce, Santee Dakota territory in present-day Minnesota. Community engagement is central to her work as a curator. Her research has been supported by the Smithsonian American Art Museum, the Center for Advanced Study in the Visual Arts, and the Mellon Foundation.

TOBY JUROVICS was chief curator and Richard and Mary Holland Curator of American Western Art at Joslyn Art Museum from 2011 to 2020. Previously, he was a curator of photography at the Smithsonian American Art Museum and the Princeton University Art Museum. A specialist in nineteenth- and twentieth-century photographic surveys of the American West, he has organized exhibitions on Robert Adams, Barbara Bosworth, Emmet Gowin, A. J. Russell, and William Wylie, among many others. He is the author of *Framing the West: The Survey Photographs of Timothy H. O'Sullivan* (2010) and has published essays on the New Topographics, Thomas Joshua Cooper, Steve Fitch, John Gossage, Andrew Moore, and William Sutton. Jurovics is director of the Barry Lopez Foundation for Art & Environment in Santa Fe, NM.

KRISTINE K. RONAN specializes in American and Native American art histories and currently serves as visiting assistant professor in American art at Texas Christian University in Fort Worth. Previously, she was a fellow of the National Endowment for the Humanities (2018–19). She completed her BA in American studies at Yale University and her MA and PhD in the history of art at the University of Michigan. Her work focuses on how images reproduce meanings as they travel, especially at the intersection of material making and image-object mobility within cross-cultural contexts.

SCOTT MANNING STEVENS is a citizen of the Akwesasne Mohawk Nation and director of the Native American Indigenous Studies Program at Syracuse University. There he also teaches courses in the departments of English and art history. He earned his PhD in English from Harvard University. Stevens was formerly director of the D'Arcy McNickle Center for American Indian and Indigenous Studies at the Newberry Library in Chicago. His recent publications include essays on Haudenosaunee art in the modern era and another on the tomahawk and material culture. He is a coauthor of the books *Home Front: Daily Life in the Civil War North* (2013) and *The Art of the American West* (2014). Stevens is also a coeditor of and contributor to the recent collection of essays *Why You Can't Teach United States History without American Indians* (2015) and has contributed a chapter on museums to the recent *Oxford Handbook of American Indian History* (2016).

LISA STRONG is the director of the art and museum studies MA program at Georgetown University and professor of the practice. Prior to her arrival at Georgetown, she served as manager of curatorial affairs at the Corcoran Gallery of Art and assistant professor of American art at James Madison University. She guest-curated an exhibition on Alfred Jacob Miller (1810–1874) for the Amon Carter Museum of American Art and wrote the accompanying book, *Sentimental Journey: The Art of Alfred Jacob Miller* (2009). Strong served as assistant editor of *Corcoran Gallery of Art Catalogue of American Paintings to 1945* and has contributed essays to *Bob Kuhn: Drawing on Instinct* (2012), *Celebrating the American Spirit: Masterworks from the Crystal Bridges Museum of American Art* (2012), *Romancing the West: Alfred Jacob Miller in the Bank of America Collection* (2011), and *Painted Journeys: The Art of John Mix Stanley* (2015).

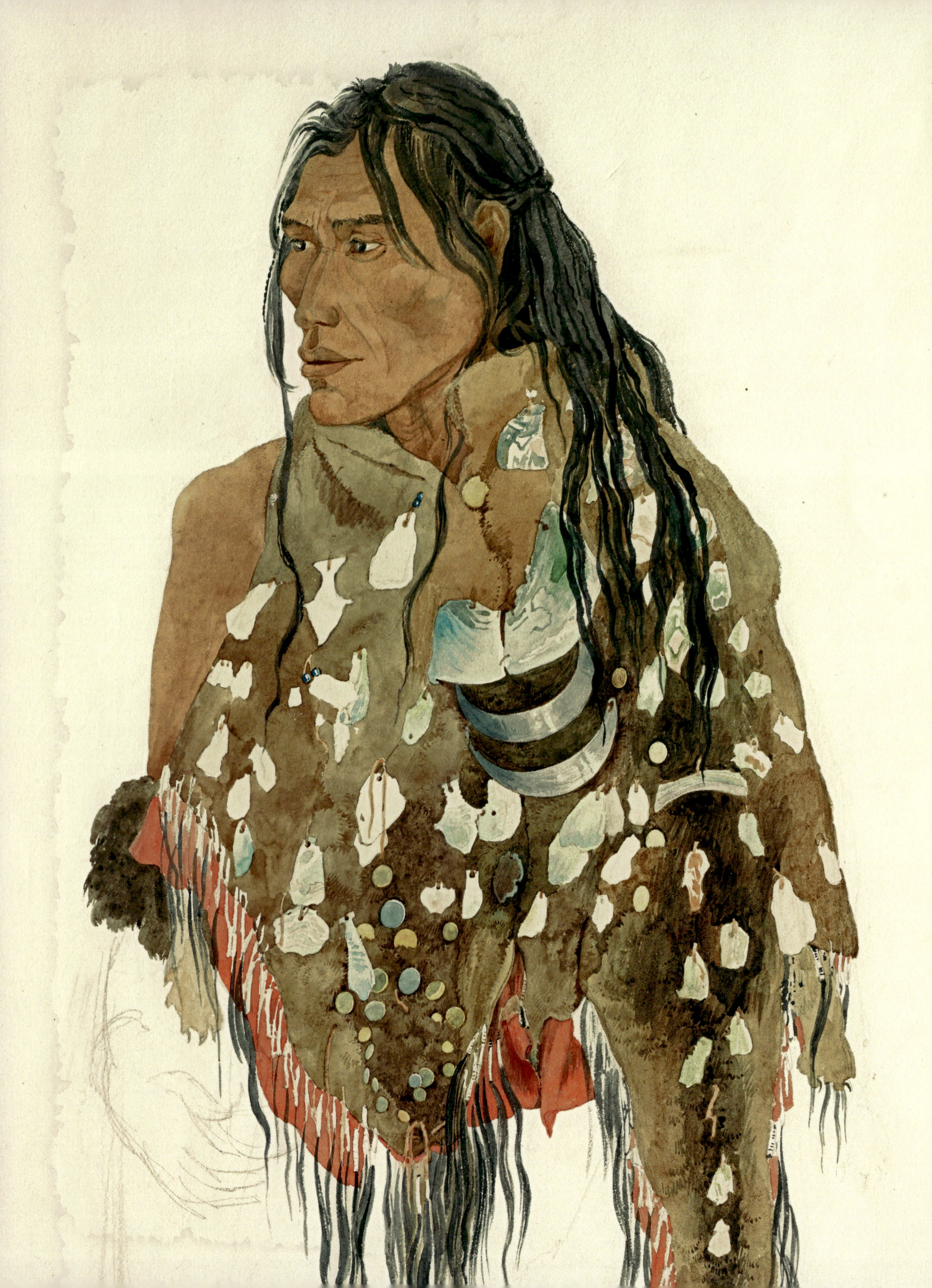

Karl Bodmer, *Ihkas-kinne, Siksika*
Blackfoot Chief, 1833 (detail of pl. 50).

FUNDING WAS PROVIDED BY
Mary and Joe Daugherty

Susan and Michael Lebens
Barbara and Ronald Schaefer

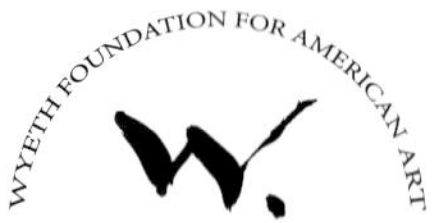

LIBRARY OF CONGRESS
CATALOGING-IN-PUBLICATION DATA
Names: Joslyn Art Museum, author. | Jurovics, Toby, editor. | Becker, Jack F., writer of foreword. | Gallagher, Marsha V. | Johnson, Annika K. | Ronan, Kristine K. | Stevens, Scott Manning. | Strong, Lisa Maria, 1966– | Durham Center for Western Studies.
Title: Faces from the interior : the North American portraits of Karl Bodmer / Toby Jurovics, editor ; with contributions by Jack F. Becker, Marsha V. Gallagher, Annika K. Johnson, Kristine K. Ronan, Scott Manning Stevens, Lisa Strong.
Description: Omaha, Nebraska : Joslyn Art Museum, [2020] | "Margre H. Durham Center for Western Studies." | Includes bibliographical references and index.
Identifiers: LCCN 2020048824 | ISBN 9781735441641 (hardback)
Subjects: LCSH: Bodmer, Karl, 1809-1893—Exhibitions. | Indians of North America—Portraits—Exhibitions. | Portraits—Nebraska—Omaha—Exhibitions. | Joslyn Art Museum—Exhibitions.
Classification: LCC ND2010.B58 A4 2020 | DDC 759.13—dc23
LC record available at https://lccn.loc.gov/2020048824

ISBN 978-1-7354416-4-1

PUBLISHED BY
Joslyn Art Museum, Omaha, Nebraska

DISTRIBUTED BY
University of Washington Press
uwapress.uw.edu

PRODUCED BY
Lucia|Marquand, Seattle
luciamarquand.com

Copyedited by Tom Fredrickson
Designed by Thomas Eykemans
Typeset in Walbaum by Brynn Warriner
Proofread by Bruno George
Indexed by Dave Luljak
Catalogue photography © Bruce M. White, 2019
Color management by iocolor, Seattle
Printed and bound in China by Artron Art Group

Front cover: Karl Bodmer, *Upsichtá, Mandan Man*, 1834 (detail of pl. 17).

Endpapers, front: Karl Bodmer, *First Chain of the Rocky Mountains above Fort McKenzie*, 1833, watercolor and graphite on paper. Joslyn Art Museum, Gift of the Enron Art Foundation, 1986.49.210.

Frontispiece: Karl Bodmer, *Chan-Chä-Uiá-Te-Üinn, Lakota Sioux Woman*, 1833 (detail of pl. 12).

pp. 64–65: Karl Bodmer, *Sioux Camp*, 1833, watercolor and graphite on paper. Joslyn Art Museum, Gift of the Enron Art Foundation, 1986.49.375.

pp. 102–03: Karl Bodmer, *Mih-Tutta-Hang-kusch, Mandan Village*, 1833–34, watercolor, graphite, and ink on paper. Joslyn Art Museum, Gift of the Enron Art Foundation, 1986.49.382.

pp. 148–49: Karl Bodmer, *Assiniboine Camp*, 1833, watercolor and graphite on paper. Joslyn Art Museum, Gift of the Enron Art Foundation, 1986.49.379.

Endpapers, back: Karl Bodmer, *View of the Bear Paw Mountains from Fort McKenzie*, 1833, watercolor and graphite on paper. Joslyn Art Museum, Gift of the Enron Art Foundation, 1986.49.209.

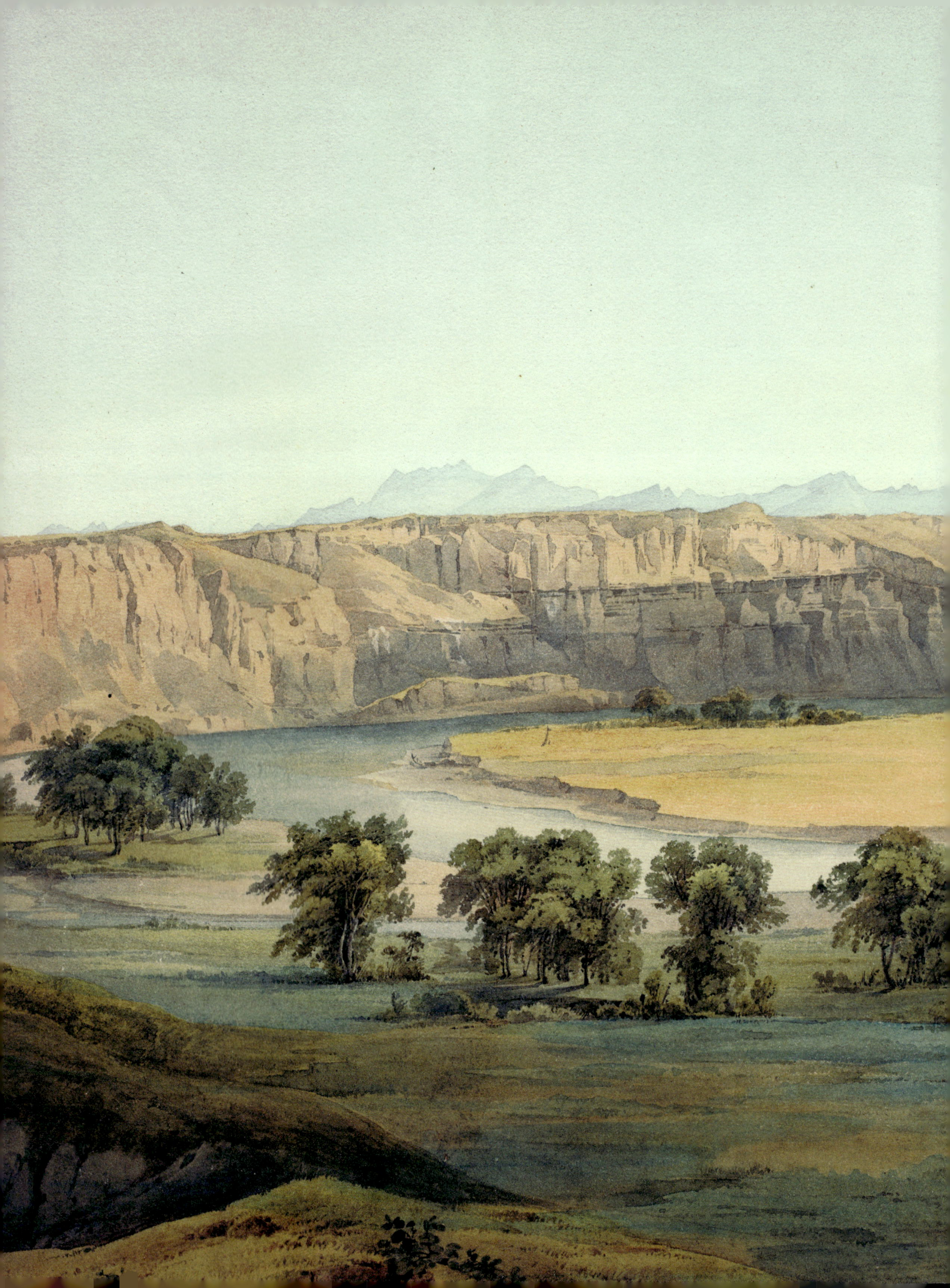